Rule-Based NLP with NLP++

A practical guide to rule-based text analysis with VisualText

David de Hilster
Amnon Meyers

www.bpbonline.com

First Edition 2026

ISBN: 978-93-65891-980

LIMITS OF LIABILITY AND DISCLAIMER OF WARRANTY

Distributors:

BPB PUBLICATIONS
20, Ansari Road, Darya Ganj
New Delhi-110002
Ph: 23254990/23254991

DECCAN AGENCIES
4-3-329, Bank Street,
Hyderabad-500195
Ph: 24756967/24756400

MICRO MEDIA
Shop No. 5, Mahendra Chambers,
150 DN Rd. Next to Capital Cinema,
V.T. (C.S.T.) Station, MUMBAI-400 001
Ph: 22078296/22078297

Published by Manish Jain for BPB Publications, 20 Ansari Road, Darya Ganj, New Delhi-110002 and Printed by him at Repro India Ltd., Rewari.

www.bpbonline.com

Dedicated to

Doris de Hilster

- David de Hilster

The Meyers family

- Amnon Meyers

About the Authors

- **David de Hilster** is an adjunct professor at Northeastern University College of Engineering and co-creator of NLP++ and VisualText. He holds a bachelor's in mathematics and a master's in linguistics from Ohio State University, has four decades of experience in NLP, and is the founder of the Natural Language Understanding Global Initiative.

- **Amnon Meyers** holds a master's in computer science and a master's in organic chemistry from UC Berkeley and a bachelor's in biology from MIT. He spent a decade in aerospace NLP R&D at McDonnell Douglas AI Lab and TRW Space Park, as well as five years at UC Irvine AI Lab, working on DARPA and Navy projects. He is the co-creator of NLP++ and the creator of the conceptual grammar knowledge base system.

Acknowledgements

This work stands on the shoulders of those who supported us in developing NLP++, VisualText, and conceptual grammar, and here we express our deep gratitude.

Our academic work and research in natural language processing was motivated by Professors Richard H. Granger (UC Irvine), Robert Wilensky (UC Berkeley), and Wayne Redenbarger (Ohio State University).

Our research in artificial intelligence was supported by the staff of McDonnell Douglas AI Lab and TRW Space Park AI Lab, spanning more than a decade.

The Meyers family founded Text Analysis International, Inc., whose many staff members enabled the development of the VisualText product suite from 1999 to 2018.

Valued customers, including IBM Global Services UK, Glide Technologies, NASDAQ, Educational Testing Service (ETS), Michael Page International, NewVision Systems, and ShipIndex.org. LexisNexis and the HPCC Systems group enabled the continued development of our technology, spanning a decade.

Most recently, Conceptual Systems LLC is supporting the latest incarnation of the NLP++ architecture.

Much gratitude is owed to our families and loved ones, who have supported us through four decades of NLP academics, research, development, and productization.

Finally, we thank BPB Publications for their faith in a book we believe will revolutionize natural language processing.

Preface

This book introduces a unique programming language, architecture, development environment, and **knowledge base management system** (**KBMS**) for **natural language processing** (**NLP**).

NLP++ is the only general programming language created specifically for NLP applications. The VisualText development environment accelerates the development of text analysis systems. The conceptual grammar KBMS supports hierarchical knowledge and dictionaries that work in tandem with a uniform pipeline architecture.

While many modern NLP systems use statistical and machine learning methods, NLP++ relies on rules, grammars, and knowledge to build accurate "glass-box" analyzers that can justify their processing and are 100% readable and modifiable.

The book teaches all aspects of the language and architecture from the ground up by detailing the development of several sample text analyzers. Also covered is integrating and deploying analyzers. NLP++ syntax, actions, and functions are described, as well as online resources such as code repositories.

A brief overview of the book chapters is mentioned in the following:

Chapter 1: Introduction to NLP++ - This chapter covers the background and history of NLP architectures; introduces the NLP++ programming language and pipeline architecture; provides an overview, advantages, and contrast with other NLP architectures.

Chapter 2: NLP++ Architecture and Language - This chapter covers the multi-pass pipeline architecture and language in detail, including: the sequence file listing the passes, the types of passes, the regions of a pass file, the syntax of the NLP++ code and rule regions, and the structure of the parse tree elaborated by the passes.

Chapter 3: NLP++ Topics - This chapter covers particular aspects of NLP++, including recursion, special files, Unicode handling, and special functions for particular natural languages (e.g., Chinese).

Chapter 4: VisualText - This chapter covers the history of the VisualText integrated development environment, the folder structure of a text analyzer project, the freeware VS Code language extension and its installation, structure, features, and use in building text analyzers. The ample interconnections among text views, parse tree views, knowledge base views, and pass file views enable an unparalleled visual programming methodology that accelerates the development and debugging of text analyzers.

Chapter 5: NLP++ Philosophy and Libraries - This chapter covers the type of thinking that best utilizes NLP++ to emulate human processing of text and details code and knowledge libraries available for use in text analyzers.

Chapter 6: Developing Text Analyzers – This chapter covers the basic processes and tools used in developing text analyzers, including trade-offs and other issues.

Chapter 7: Example Analyzers - This chapter uses existing example analyzers to guide the reader through the text analyzer development process.

Chapter 8: Integrating NLP++ Analyzers – This chapter covers methods for integrating text analyzers into other computer programming environments, such as Python.

Code Bundle and Coloured Images

Please follow the link to download the
Code Bundle and the ***Coloured Images*** of the book:

https://rebrand.ly/fa4896

The code bundle for the book is also hosted on GitHub at
https://github.com/bpbpublications/Rule-Based-NLP-with-NLP-Plus-Plus.
In case there's an update to the code, it will be updated on the existing GitHub repository.

We have code bundles from our rich catalogue of books and videos available at **https://github.com/bpbpublications.** Check them out!

Errata

We take immense pride in our work at BPB Publications and follow best practices to ensure the accuracy of our content to provide an indulging reading experience to our subscribers. Our readers are our mirrors, and we use their inputs to reflect and improve upon human errors, if any, that may have occurred during the publishing processes involved. To let us maintain the quality and help us reach out to any readers who might be having difficulties due to any unforeseen errors, please write to us at: **errata@bpbonline.com**

Your support, suggestions and feedback are highly appreciated by the BPB Publications' Family.

Piracy

If you come across any illegal copies of our works in any form on the internet, we would be grateful if you would provide us with the location address or website name. Please contact us at **business@bpbonline.com** with a link to the material.

If you are interested in becoming an author

If there is a topic that you have expertise in, and you are interested in either writing or contributing to a book, please visit **www.bpbonline.com.** We have worked with thousands of developers and tech professionals, just like you, to help them share their insights with the global tech community. You can make a general application, apply for a specific hot topic that we are recruiting an author for, or submit your own idea.

Reviews

Please leave a review. Once you have read and used this book, why not leave a review on the site that you purchased it from? Potential readers can then see and use your unbiased opinion to make purchase decisions. We at BPB can understand what you think about our products, and our authors can see your feedback on their book. Thank you!

For more information about BPB, please visit **www.bpbonline.com**.

Join our Discord space

Join our Discord workspace for latest updates, offers, tech happenings around the world, new releases, and sessions with the authors:

https://discord.bpbonline.com

Table of Contents

Chapter 1
Introduction to NLP++

Introduction

NLP++ is the only general computer programming language created specifically for **natural language processing** (**NLP**). Its runtime system is written entirely in C++, and NLP++ in many ways resembles the related C programming language. In addition to familiar programming constructs such as functions, statements, variables, and operations, NLP++ integrates a uniform pipeline architecture, the **conceptual grammar** (**CG**) hierarchical **knowledge base** (**KB**) **management system** (**KBMS**), and a parse tree, providing a one-stop shop (or tech stack) for developing complete and accurate text analysis systems. Special NLP++ variables directly address the evolving parse tree and use or update the current KB.

The NLP++ pipeline instance under construction is called a text analyzer. Each analyzer step is called a pass, and the current pipeline is called the analyzer sequence. A pass may consist of a user-defined and human-readable (or *glass-box*) pass file, consisting of code, rewrite rules (or grammar rules), and function definitions. A pass may also consist of a black-box built-in algorithm, typically a simple tokenizer variant that converts the input text to an initial parse tree.

The *VisualText IDE* is critical to the efficient building of text analyzers. The associated runtime environment for VS Code is called the NLP engine (also written as NLP-ENGINE). We will sometimes refer to the original VisualText IDE running on Windows and having an integrated runtime system.

While alternative NLP approaches rely on statistical, neural network, and **machine learning** (**ML**) methods, NLP++ analyzers are rule-based and are primarily built manually. VisualText serves as a force multiplier, enabling rapid prototyping and efficient pathways to scale-up, productization, and maintenance.

Other NLP approaches have used languages such as Prolog, Java, PERL, Pascal, Python, and even C++. None of these provides a comprehensive analyzer development architecture and language, as offered by VisualText and NLP++.

Other NLP pipeline approaches exist, e.g., the GATE system and CoreNLP. Such pipelines are composed of disparate black-boxes or cascading statistical passes, and both pipelines attempt to glue passes together with ad hoc programming code. Accuracy degrades with each successive pass in these approaches.

We will discuss the advantages of NLP++ over statistical methods, namely, the ability to explain and justify the analyzer outputs, as well as support for debugging and enhancing analyzers without limitation.

As a final introductory note, the NLP++ pipeline enables passes to operate synergistically in evolving a single best-first parse tree and conceptual representation of the input text.

Structure

In this chapter, we will discuss the following topics:

- Background
- NLP++ universal programming language
- File extensions
- NLP++ overview
- Early NLP architectures
- Future of NLP++

Objectives

By the end of this chapter, the reader will learn about the NLP++ pipeline architecture and programming language. An introduction to alternative NLP tools and their history will be presented, including a discussion of the differences between NLP++ and earlier systems.

Background

Rule-based NLP supports the processing and understanding of text and natural language via linguistic, logical, and knowledge-based methods and algorithms. Such systems enable computer programs to read and understand text like humans. For example, such systems can be built to justify their output in terms that humans can understand. Explainability promotes trust in rule-based systems, in contrast to statistical systems, which are universally opaque or black-box.

Early rule-based systems

One reason rule-based NLP disappeared from academia and industry has been the lack of a universal computer programming language for text and natural language. In the 1990s, NLP systems were developed using general programming languages like C++ and Java. NLP projects typically spanned years and required many developers. To reduce cost and resources and to simplify development, siloed NLP pipelines were created. Typical silos comprised tokenizers, dictionary lookup, recursive grammars, and semantic processing.

CoreNLP

In the late 1990s and 2000s, these traditional, siloed, rule-based systems incorporated statistical methods, given that comprehensive rule-based systems were difficult to construct manually. Eventually, systems like Stanford CoreNLP[1] were transformed by statistical methods, thereby reducing their accuracy. While these systems claim to be generic tools that can be used out-of-the-box, customizing them to specific NLP tasks is difficult.

A primary concern with Stanford CoreNLP is its reduced accuracy when processing non-canonical or domain-specific text. For example, reports on *Stack Overflow* have noted that even seemingly straightforward cases of coreference resolution can yield counterintuitive results, leading to errors that affect downstream processing[2]. Such inaccuracies make it challenging to rely on the toolkit for critical applications without resorting to post-processing and error correction.

Another significant limitation is the lack of robust out-of-the-box customization. CoreNLP is provided with a fixed set of models and processing pipelines that, while effective for standard language tasks, can be difficult to tailor for specialized applications. Users looking to adapt the system for specific linguistic phenomena or non-traditional text often face hurdles in modifying the underlying configurations and retraining components [3]. This rigidity restricts its applicability when bespoke solutions are needed.

Moreover, the rule-based components of CoreNLP present a steep learning curve. The rules that govern processes such as quote attribution are deeply embedded in the code base, with limited documentation. As a result, users have reported that understanding, modifying, or debugging these rules is challenging and time-consuming[4]. This opaque design not only hampers customization efforts but also complicates integration with broader workflows in which transparency and fine control over linguistic processing are essential.

Natural Language Toolkit

Natural Language Toolkit (**NLTK**) is widely used in educational settings and early-stage research for NLP. However, its accuracy in real-world applications can be problematic. Studies and community discussions have noted that for certain tasks, such as fine-grained linguistic analysis or feature accuracy measurements, NLTK does not always yield reliable results[5]. Accuracy issues become especially evident when processing noisy, informal, or domain-specific text, where modern approaches tend to outperform NLTK's more traditional methods.

In addition to accuracy concerns, NLTK poses challenges in customization. Its design focuses on providing a broad set of tools and resources, but extending the toolkit to specialized applications can be challenging. Several practitioners have observed that reconfiguring the underlying modules or integrating custom models is nontrivial, reducing their suitability for state-of-the-art projects[6].

Despite its historical importance, exemplified by its inclusion in a classic NLP[7] text, NLTK's limitations in both accuracy and ease of customization have become more apparent as the field of NLP has evolved. Users who require higher performance or easier adaptability may need to look toward newer libraries designed for modern NLP challenges. As such, while NLTK remains a valuable resource for learning and prototyping, its shortcomings in practical applications have led many to adopt alternative solutions[8,9,10,11].

NLP++ universal programming language

It was not until the late 1990s and early 2000s that a universal NLP programming language finally appeared. That language, NLP++, allows developers to concentrate on writing text analyzers without having to construct one-off systems of their own.

However, it was not until 2018 that NLP++ was released as open-source freeware, becoming more generally available.

NLP++ is dedicated to building natural language text analyzers. It allows developers to capture and apply linguistic and world knowledge, emulating processes by which humans read and understand text. NLP++ combines bottom-up, island-driven, recursive grammar, and other methods in a multi-pass pipeline architecture that operates on a single parse tree. It works with a hierarchical KBMS, called CG, to dynamically build and use stored knowledge while analyzing text. Applications range from simple syntactic processing to full natural language understanding.

The VisualText IDE exploits NLP++ and CG to rapidly develop text analyzers. Dictionaries, functions, passes, and KBs are readily available to developers, who can quickly build analyzers using such ready-made components. The new VS Code implementation's runtime is called the NLP engine.

File extensions

Given that NLP++ is the only programming language for text and NLP, it now owns some important file extensions, including the `.nlp` file extension, as shown in the following table:

Extension	Description
`.nlp`	NLP++ source code file, original versions used a `.pat` (or *pattern*) file
`.tree`	File containing parse tree data
`.dict`	Human-readable dictionary file
`.kbb`	Human-readable KB file
`.kb`	Internal KB files used by the NLP engine
`.txxt`	An annotated text file that delineates rule matches for a particular pass using three angle brackets <<< or three parentheses (((
`.nlm`	Module file, which contains multiple file types (the letters standing for Natural Language Module file) mod files

***Table 1.1**: File extensions in the NLP engine*

Currently, colorizers for these file types reside in the NLP++ Language Extension for VS Code. Future work includes making colorizers for widely used code editors.

NLP++ overview

NLP++ has been described as the SQL for text and NLP. This is a valid comparison, as SQL is the logical consequence of working with relational databases, while NLP++ is the logical consequence of working with natural language.

Placing data in tables as columns and values, and then creating relations between them, led to SQL. Tokenizing text into trees, matching patterns, and building knowledge led to NLP++. SQL evolved from the need to write programs that manipulate data in database tables. NLP++ evolved from the need to write programs that structure text and find meaning.

Both languages are logical creations for the data they manipulate. Whereas SQL is ubiquitous and runs almost 90% of all databases in the world, NLP++ is not currently well-known. This will change:

- When the world becomes aware that NLP has a universal programming language, much as databases have SQL.
- When rule-based and knowledge-based NLP is recognized as the only way to develop accurate and trustworthy applications.

SQL operates on well-defined tables, whereas NLP++ must deal with the complexities of human language, a much harder task.

Noam Chomsky introduced a classification system for formal grammars, known as the **Chomsky hierarchy**[12]. This hierarchy organizes grammars by their expressive power, which determines what kinds of languages they can generate. It ranges from the most restrictive, regular grammars, to the most expressive, unrestricted grammars. Chomsky initially placed natural human language within the category of context-free grammars, or Type-2, in his hierarchy[13]. This placement reflects the idea that human language can generally be described by rules that allow for recursion and nested structures, characteristics that context-free grammars handle well.

Context-free grammars operate on the principle that a single symbol can replace a sequence of other symbols, regardless of the surrounding context[14]. Such systems are powerful enough to describe sentences with nested clauses, like *the book that the girl whom the teacher praised read was thrilling*. These grammars can be processed by pushdown automata. These theoretical machines that use a stack to manage hierarchical relationships are well-suited to parsing embedded phrases and tracking dependencies between elements such as subjects and verbs across clauses.

Despite this initial classification, Chomsky acknowledged that some aspects of natural language may go beyond the capabilities of context-free grammars. Certain syntactic patterns, such as cross-serial dependencies found in languages like Swiss German[15], or long-distance agreement in complex sentences, suggest that natural language may at times require the expressiveness of context-sensitive grammars, those just above context-free grammars in the hierarchy.

In essence, Chomsky's proposal reflects a nuanced view, while context-free grammars offer a solid foundation for modeling most syntactic patterns in human language, they do not capture every intricacy. Linguists continue to debate whether natural language should be considered truly context-free or if it belongs in a class of mildly context-sensitive systems[16].

NLP++ is an empty language that contains generic structures such as a syntactic tree and hierarchical knowledge, as well as functions and a rule system that manipulate these structures. As such, NLP++ can support any linguistic paradigm. The multi-pass pipeline architecture naturally supports efficient, confidence-first building of language understanding systems, especially when compared to purely grammar rule-based systems.

Just as 80 to 90% of all databases in the world use relational databases and SQL, we anticipate that a majority of language analysis applications will use NLP++. This prediction stems from the fact that true language understanding depends on rules, knowledge, and algorithms, rather than probability-based techniques alone.

NLP++ is 100% transparent (or glass-box), thereby supporting maintenance, debugging, and enhancement, whereas statistical methods (e.g., ML, neural networks, and **large language models** (**LLMs**)) are black-boxes that cannot reliably be understood, fixed, and improved. Statistical systems are especially unsuited for mission-critical applications, such as fully automated medical diagnosis.

Any application that provides reasonably accurate results can be used in mixed-initiative systems, where humans in the loop can validate and correct inaccurate output, while having automation handle the bulk of the workload. This has long been the case in machine translation of languages, where post-editing yields economically viable systems. Even so, accurate and reliable systems that justify their work can best support mixed-initiative as well as fully automated applications.

NLP++ features

NLP++'s overall features are as follows:

- It is the only programming language built specifically for NLP.
- It supports rule-based and KB methods.
- It integrates multiple paradigms in a monolithic pipeline architecture.
- It offers a maintainable, readable, and powerful replacement for REGEX.
- It enables processing unstructured text, which is otherwise a difficult task.

- It is 100% customizable, as opposed to generic, black-box NLP toolkits.
- It serves the NLP Foundation, the Natural Language Understanding Global Initiative community, and the NLP Blockchain and NLP coin (see **https://nluglob.org/**).

Here is a list of a few resources:

1. Resources for NLP++, VisualText, and the NLP engine are available on *GitHub*, *YouTube*, and various websites.
2. The NLP++ VS Code extension can be downloaded at:

   https://marketplace.visualstudio.com/items?itemName=dehilster.nlp&ssr=false#review-details

3. The original implementation of VisualText and NLP++ is documented on the *Text Analysis International* (*TAI*) company website (**http://www.textanalysis.com/**), but TAI shut down in 2018.
4. An old but useful help documentation repository is available at:

   https://www.textanalysis.com/help/help.htm

Highly integrated

Practical NLP systems must encompass a variety of methods to support lexical, syntactic, semantic, discourse, and pragmatic processing for a real-world task. Two primary ways of achieving this are:

- To develop the individual components and integrate them later.
- To develop the overall system in an integrated fashion.

Here we focus on the second method. Further, we describe an architecture in which an arbitrary number of processing passes may be elaborated, where each pass invokes its own processing algorithm and uses its own data. For example, one pass may use a pattern-based matching algorithm and an associated set of rules to recognize location constructs in a text.

Each pass can be viewed as a **Yet Another Compiler-Compiler** (**YACC**) or Bison grammar with its attendant code actions.

The passes of the multi-pass architecture are constrained to share a single parse tree. Each pass receives the cumulative parse tree, elaborates it further, and then hands it to a subsequent pass. While the constraint to a single parse tree appears to limit the handling of ambiguity, we touch on various methods that address ambiguity within the architecture.

In addition to managing a unique parse tree, the passes may also update and access an integrated KB, as well as general programmatic data structures. VisualText uses a hierarchical KBMS for mapping knowledge in a more natural fashion than a relational database.

A unifying programming language is a key component of the architecture, enabling NLP developers to manage the passes, parse tree, associated knowledge, and programming constructs.

The following are some advantages of the architecture:

- **Integration**: A spectrum of strategies and levels of granularity can interact within a single framework.
- **Modularity, extensibility, maintainability**: Passes can be elaborated such that each performs a simple and modular task.
- **Flexibility**: Passes may be added to the framework in any order, so that work that was initially glossed over or forgotten may be added in at a later point.
- **Feedback, deferral**: Rather than making uninformed decisions upfront, passes can be implemented to gather data and try things out, to increase confidence in subsequent processing decisions.
- **Context**: By splitting the NLP system into multiple passes, each pass may be constrained to operate on particular contexts. For example, a parsing pass might work only within noun phrases or within the header zones of a text being analyzed.
- **Automation**: Passes within the architecture can dynamically create and execute new passes, e.g., based on patterns learned from a corpus.

The architecture can be readily embedded within a programming language and implemented within a graphical development environment, affording substantial efficiencies for language engineering. Analyzers and sequences of passes can be configured for reuse as templates or as libraries.

While the architecture accommodates various application types, such as information extraction, full-scale parsing, language generation, and translation, we shall assume that the primary application under discussion is analysis, such as information extraction.

We refer to the NLP++ programming language[17] and its implementation in the commercial VisualText IDE as exemplars of this methodology.

We discuss applications built using the multi-pass methodology, including the TAIParse general analyzer (now called **parse-en-us**) and *Resume Analyzer* developed with NLP++.

Early NLP architectures

TexUS[18] constitutes an early version of a multi-pass, multi-strategy NLP architecture. TexUS lacked a unifying programming language but enabled passes to be matched with rule sets and declaratively maintained the NLP system definition, knowledge, rules, and even parse trees within a unitary KBMS. With a scant two-person-month customization effort using a nine-month-old IDE, our analyzer achieved an impressive result at *MUC-3*[19].

A treatment of NLP architectures and IDEs appears in a TAI review[20].

Architectures based mainly on a single paradigm, such as cascaded finite state transducers, e.g., INTEX[21] and FASTUS[22], or pattern-based processing, e.g., DEFT[23], are known as **hybrid architectures**, e.g., GATE[24] and PAKTUS[25].

History

VisualText and NLP++ were created by TAI, which operated from late 1998 to 2018. *De Hilster* led VisualText development, while *Meyers* focused on implementing the NLP++ language and runtime. Meyers' compiler writing background (APL compiler, PLAIN compiler, and YACC grammar systems) strongly influenced the implementation of NLP++ as a pipeline of passes consisting of rewrite rules and associated actions. De Hilster and Meyers worked closely to develop a highly integrated *one-stop shop* for building accurate, product-grade NLP applications. Currently, *Conceptual Systems LLC (California)* holds the VisualText and NLP++ properties.

Future of NLP++

The authors believe that NLP++ will eventually be taught in mainstream computer science classes. The main reason for this is that every programmer must at some time deal with unstructured data, and until now, REGEX has been the only rule-based system available. Once NLP++ is ubiquitously known, it will enable many new kinds of text applications.

Once a programmer learns NLP++, they will not go back to REGEX. There are some things that are just too hard for REGEX, but easy for NLP++. Unstructured text that has been too difficult or expensive to process can be effectively handled with VisualText and NLP++.

Great digital migration

As several people have recently observed, NLP++ is the SQL for text and natural language. There is now a universal computer programming language for natural language. We can start to create governed repositories of comprehensive dictionaries, KBs, and NLP algorithms that can be constantly updated for use by all.

Eventually, rule and KB NLP systems will be integrated into a variety of critical systems.

Conclusion

We have introduced the NLP++ architecture and programming language, as well as the tightly integrated VisualText IDE. We have discussed the history of preceding systems and alternative NLP approaches.

In the next chapter, we detail the NLP++ architecture and the NLP++ programming language.

True or false

1. NLP++ includes statistical and machine learning algorithms.
2. NLP++ passes may be written using several programming languages.
3. The original VisualText IDE ran on Windows.
4. The accuracy of non-NLP++ pipelines typically degrades when more passes are added.
5. The CoreNLP and NLTK systems may be difficult for users to customize.
6. All passes in an NLP++ pipeline may be read and edited.
7. NLP++ supports many paradigms, such as bottom-up analysis.
8. The .nlp file extension is reserved for use in NLP++.
9. Alternate pipelines typically integrate components that are developed separately.
10. TAI developed the first versions of NLP++ and VisualText.

Answers

1. False
2. False
3. True
4. True
5. True
6. False
7. True
8. True
9. True
10. True

Multiple choice questions

1. **The NLP++ architecture does not include which of the following:**
   a. Pipeline of pass files
   b. Knowledge base
   c. Database
   d. Parse tree
2. **Which of the following are statistical methods:**
   a. Machine learning
   b. Knowledge-based
   c. Expert system
   d. Neural network
   e. Rule-based
   f. Grammar-based
   g. Object-oriented
   h. Large language model
3. **The NLP++ programming language does not address:**
   a. Pipeline passes
   b. Knowledge base
   c. Dictionary
   d. Parse tree
   e. Matched rule

Answers

1. c
2. a, d, h
3. a

Short answer questions

1. Explain what rule-based NLP is and how it supports the processing and understanding of text.
2. Describe one reason why rule-based NLP disappeared from academia and industry in the 1990s.
3. List two primary concerns with Stanford CoreNLP as mentioned in the text.
4. Explain why NLTK is widely used in educational settings and early-stage research for natural language processing.
5. What is NLP++ and when did it become open-source?
6. Describe the role of VisualText in the development of text analyzers.
7. Describe each of the NLP++ file types:
    a. .nlp
    b. .tree
    c. .dict
    d. .kbb
    e. .txxt
8. Compare NLP++ to SQL in terms of their logical progression and usage.
9. Explain the Chomsky hierarchy and its relevance to natural language processing.
10. Discuss why NLP++ is considered efficient compared to purely grammar rule-based systems.

References

1. **Stanford CoreNLP: https://stanfordnlp.github.io/CoreNLP.**
2. **AZpublic: Stanford CoreNLP wrong coreference resolution: https://stackoverflow.com/questions/30362691/stanford-corenlp-wrong-coreference-resolution.**
3. **MaraudingLily: How to resolve coreferences for a specific Noun phrase in Stanford CoreNLP: https://stackoverflow.com/questions/29466351/how-to-resolve-coreferences-for-a-specific-noun-phrase-in-stanford-corenlp. 2015.**

4. CoreNLP's quote attribution is barely usable/has very low accuracy: https://github.com/stanfordnlp/CoreNLP/issues/1090.
5. nltk measure the accuracy of the new features: https://datascience.stackexchange.com/questions/58291/nltk-measure-the-accuracy-of-the-new-features. 2020.
6. AI Jokers. Examining NLTK's Natural Language Toolkit: Restrictions and Difficulties: https://aijokers.com/ai-review/examining-nltks-natural-language-toolkit-restrictions-and-difficulties. 2020. [access from https://aijokers.com/ai-review]
7. Steven Bird, Ewan Klein, and Edward Loper, Natural Language Processing with Python – Analyzing Text with the Natural Language Toolkit: https://www.nltk.org/book.
8. Edward Loper and Steven Bird, NLTK: The Natural Language Toolkit (Department of Computer and Information Science, University of Pennsylvania, July 2002).
9. Steven Bird and Edward Loper, NLTK: The Natural Language Toolkit, in Proceedings of the ACL Interactive Poster and Demonstration Sessions (Association for Computational Linguistics, July 2004), 214–217: https://aclanthology.org/P04-3031.
10. Community Contributors. NLTK measure the accuracy of the new features: https://datascience.stackexchange.com/questions/58291/nltk-measure-the-accuracy-of-the-new-features. 2020.
11. Noam Chomsky, Three Models for the Description of Language, IRE Transactions on Information Theory 2, no. 3 (1956): 113-124.
12. Noam Chomsky, Syntactic Structures (The Hague: Mouton, 1957).
13. John E. Hopcroft and Jeffrey D. Ullman, Introduction to Automata Theory, Languages, and Computation (Reading, MA: Addison-Wesley, 1979).
14. Stuart M. Shieber, Evidence Against the Context-Freeness of Natural Language, Linguistics and Philosophy 8, no. 3 (1985): 333–343.
15. Aravind K. Joshi, Tree Adjoining Grammars: How Much Context-Sensitivity Is Required to Provide Reasonable Structural Descriptions? in Natural Language Parsing, ed. David R. Dowty, Lauri Karttunen, and Arnold M. Zwicky (Cambridge: Cambridge University Press, 1985), 206–250.
16. Amnon Meyers, Multi-pass Multi-strategy NLP (Text Analysis International, Inc., 2003): https://www.textanalysis.com/tai-multi2003.pdf.
17. Amnon Meyers and David de Hilster, Description of the TexUS System as Used for MUC-4 (McDonnell Douglas Electronic Systems Company, June 1992), presented at the Fourth Message Understanding Conference (MUC-4), McLean, Virginia, https://aclanthology.org/M92-1029.

18. **David de Hilster and Amnon Meyers, Description of the INLET System Used for MUC-3 (McDonnell Douglas Electronic Systems Company, May 1991), presented at the Third Message Understanding Conference (MUC-3), San Diego, California, https://aclanthology.org/M91-1027.**
19. **Text Analysis International, Inc. Integrated Development Environments for Natural Language Processing. Sunnyvale, CA, October 2001: https://www.textanalysis.com/TAI-IDE-WP.pdf.**
20. **Michel Silberztein, INTEX: An FST Toolbox, Theoretical Computer Science 231, no. 1 (January 2000): 33–46, https://www.sciencedirect.com/science/article/pii/S0304397599000158.**
21. **Jerry R. Hobbs, Douglas Appelt, John Bear, David Israel, Megumi Kameyalna, and Mabry Tyson, FASTUS: A System for Extracting Information from Text, in Human Language Technology: Proceedings of a Workshop Held at Plainsboro, New Jersey, March 21–24, 1993 (HLT, March 1993): https://aclanthology.org/H93-1026.**
22. **William Noah and Rollin V. Weeks, TRW: Description of the DEFT System as Used for MUC-5, in Fifth Message Understanding Conference (MUC-5): Proceedings of a Conference Held in Baltimore, Maryland, August 25–27, 1993 (MUC, August 1993): https://aclanthology.org/M93-1020.**
23. **Hamish Cunningham, Yorick Wilks, and Robert J. Gaizauskas, GATE—a General Architecture for Text Engineering, in COLING 1996 Volume 2: The 16th International Conference on Computational Linguistics (COLING), 1996: https://aclanthology.org/C96-2187/.**
24. **Bruce Loatman, PRC Inc: Description of the PAKTUS System Used for MUC-3, in Third Message Understanding Conference (MUC-3): Proceedings of a Conference Held in San Diego, California, May 21–23, 1991 (MUC), 1991: https://aclanthology.org/M91-1029.**

CHAPTER 2
NLP++ Architecture and Language

Introduction

NLP++ is a computer programming language that breaks down text into tokens, builds the tokens into syntactic trees using rules and functions, and builds semantic knowledge into **conceptual grammar** (**CG**) **knowledge bases** (**KBs**). The language includes functions, rewrite rules, operators, and variables specific to its internal representations of text and knowledge. NLP++ uses general C/C++ like programming language constructs, as well as integrally addressing rule matching and the associated KB. See also *Multi-Pass Multi-Strategy NLP* (**https://www.textanalysis.com/tai-multi2003.pdf**).

Structure

In this chapter, we will discuss the following topics:

- Multi-pass pancake pipeline
- Regions of a pass file
- Code syntax

Objectives

By the end of this chapter, the reader will learn about the NLP++ multi-pass pipeline architecture, the regions of a pass file, and the syntax of the NLP++ code and rewrite rules.

Multi-pass pancake pipeline

One NLP++ user described the NLP++ pipeline as a stack of pancakes. The idea is that if something more is needed somewhere in the pipeline, one just adds another pancake to the stack. Refer to the following figure:

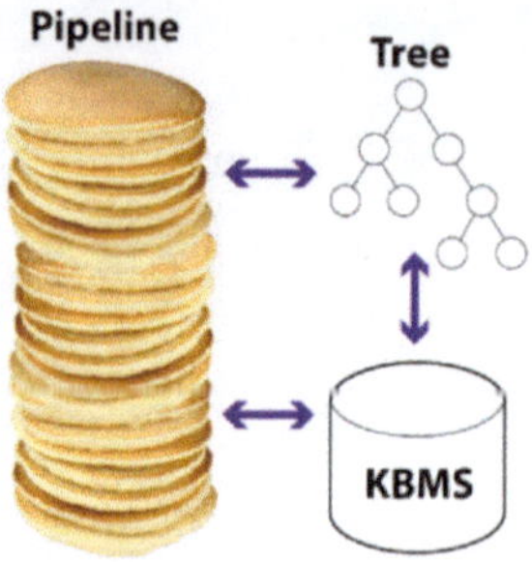

Figure 2.1: Multi-pass pipeline as a uniform, flexible stack of pancakes

Given that every pass in the pipeline can access the parse tree and KB, this allows for precise systems that are easy to build, fix, and enhance.

The analyzer sequence file (**`analyzer.seq`**) specifies the ordering of passes and the parsing algorithm to apply to the rules of each pass (as described in the following section).

NLP++ runtime and IDE architecture

Details of the current NLP++ runtime system (or NLP) are largely beyond the scope of the present book. The same holds for the original Windows VisualText version.

In the NLP engine implementation, NLP++ analyzers and KBs are executed in an interpreted fashion. Compilation can, in principle, be accomplished using the older VisualText **integrated development environment** (**IDE**), but various changes would first need to be made in both cases.

Special actions for the **Rule File Analyzer** (**RFA**) for the NLP++ language definition and **Rule File Analyzer B** (**RFB**) (for NLP++ analyzer code) are not detailed herein, as they are relevant only to the VisualText system architect. Their action names typically begin with the prefixes **`rfa-`** or **`rfb-`**. Documentation of these analyzers, which read the NLP++ language definition itself, as well as the user-coded NLP++ analyzer code, may appear in separate documentation for the runtime system.

Passes

The **`analyzer.seq`** pass file drives every NLP++ text analyzer. It is located in the **`spec`** folder in every analyzer folder.

Role of analyzer.seq

In NLP++, an analyzer is not one big program but a pipeline or sequence of passes, thus naming the file extension **`.seq`**. Each line in the **`analyzer.seq`** sequence file names a pass, which consists of a file of NLP++ rules, code, functions, and comments, with the exception of the very first pass, which is always a tokenizer. The file lists the ordering of passes to execute when processing input text.

Tokenizers and user passes

There are two types of passes: system passes and user passes. Currently, the only system passes available to developers are tokenizers, and a tokenizer pass must occur first in the sequence file (**analyzer.seq**, which specifies the sequence of passes in the pipeline). Developers can choose from one of the tokenizers, as listed in the following table. All other passes are human-readable (either user-created or copied from available libraries and analyzers). Specialized analyzers such as the RFA may include additional system passes.

Tokenizer	Description
token	Default tokenizer. Separates text into alphabetic/numeric tokens and special characters, including emojis.
dicttok	Same as token pass, but includes KB dictionary lookup for alphabetic tokens.
dicttokz	Same as **dicttok**, but omits white space in the initial parse tree. Places whitespace information in non-whitespace tokens.
chartok	Separates the text into individual characters.
cmltok	Specialized tokenizer for OCRed text.

Table 2.1: Tokenizer types

Note: By default, grammar rule examples in this book assume that the parse tree has all whitespace removed (e.g., with the dicttokz tokenizer). Otherwise, whitespace tokens such as _xWHITE and _xBLANK must separate phrase elements of a rule, as needed.

Whitespace-free parse trees

A parse tree without whitespace tokens is compact and lends itself to short and readable rewrite rules, thereby yielding a faster text analyzer. The **dicttokz** tokenizer creates an initial parse tree that omits whitespace tokens. Instead, several attributes record whitespace information for use by the analyzer (see the following table).

As most prose words are preceded by whitespace, the absence of a **no-whitespace** (**NOSP**) attribute implicitly records whitespace separating words. Current tokenizers do not count the number of space characters, only their absence or presence.

A nuance in these parse trees is that the first token of a new line may have no preceding whitespace, but is usually not conjoined with the last token of the preceding line. The developer must account for such cases (whether or not the parse tree includes whitespace).

Attribute	Type	Description
NL	Num	Count newlines preceding the current node
TABS	Num	Count preceding tabs
NOSP	1 or 0 (bool)	1 if no preceding spaces, else 0
SP	1 or 0 (bool)	1 if preceding spaces, else 0

***Table 2.2:** Attributes in whitespace-free parse tree*

To format lines and paragraphs in whitespace-free parse trees, the **LINES_nosp** pass is available. An implementation of this pass is shown in the following code. Note that it marks the root node with paragraphs (**PARS**), a total count of paragraphs, and paragraph (**PAR**), which says that the current line starts a new paragraph (i.e., the first node on the line is preceded by two newlines). This may be incomplete, as a single newline might separate paragraphs in some input texts (the SP attribute is not shown in the following version):

```
@PATH _ROOT
@PRE

<2,2> varz("NL");
<3,3> var("NL")
@POST
  if (N("NL",1) > 1) {
  ++X("PARS"); # Count potential paragraphs.
    ++S("PAR");
  }
  singler(1,2);
@RULES
_LINE [unsealed] <-
  _xANY
  _xWILD [star fail=(_dummy)]
  _xANY [opt lookahead]
  @@
```

Anatomy of analyzer.seq

The analyzer sequence file specifies the sequence of passes to execute when an NLP++ analyzer is invoked. It is a human-readable text file that can be edited directly. The safest is to specify the analyzer sequence using the VisualText IDE. The name of the file is **analyzer.seq**, and it is located in the **spec** folder along with the NLP++ pass files that make up the analyzer. Here is what a typical **analyzer.seq** file looks like:

```
1    dicttokz     nil    # Gen:   Convert input to token list
2    folder       initStuff # Folder name
3    nlp          init    # initialize KB
4    nlp          KBFuncs    # KB Library functions
5    nlp          funcs    # User defined functions
6    end          initStuff # end of initStuff folder
7    nlp          LinesDictTokZ     # Break text into lines
8    rec          numbered    # Categorize the numbers
9    …
10   /nlp         output    # Output the result to appropriate output
```

When the engine runs, it loads its pass files and executes each pass as specified in the sequence file. A line in the **analyzer.seq** file, representing a pass, looks like one of:

```
tokenizer-variant  <tab>  nil           <tab> # comment-text
algorithm-type       <tab>  pass-name    <tab> # comment-text
special-type       <tab>   argument      <tab> # comment-text
```

The first element of each line is the type of pass, the second is an argument, and the third is a comment. The first line is always a tokenization pass (detailed later). Currently, nil is the only second argument. Initial tokenizers are simple and hardwired.

Most subsequent lines are user passes, with **algorithm-type** NLP (representing standard pattern matching) and rec (representing recursive pattern matching). The second argument in both cases is the pass file name, omitting the file extension **.nlp**.

A group of passes may be collected in a folder, starting with a line marked folder and ending with a line marked end. The second argument in this case is the folder name. Nested folders are not supported, currently.

With the NLP algorithm, pattern matching traverses the parse tree only once. With recursion, pattern matching traverses the parse tree until no more matches are found. As with all recursive algorithms, the developer must guard against infinite loops.

Finally, if a user deactivates a pass using VisualText, a backslash is placed at the start of the sequence file line (for example, see *line 10* in *Anatomy of analyzer.seq* section).

Note: Original VisualText includes a GRAM tab and RUG automated rule generation capability, with associated stub regions in the analyzer sequence file.

The following figure shows a pop-up of the analyzer sequence editing Window by clicking on the first pass:

Figure 2.2: Pop-up of analyzer sequence editing Window by clicking on first pass (dicttokz tokenizer)

Above, double-clicking the tokenize pass (no matter the type of the tokenizer) opens the **analyzer.seq** file. Suppose something goes wrong in the **analyzer.seq** file, then it can be edited by hand. However, for the most part, this file is completely left alone.

Inside a pass file

Each pass file is organized into regions (or zones), using @ directives, as follows:

- **@DECL** single optional region for user-defined functions.
- **@CODE** single region contains NLP++ code to execute before pattern matching.
- **@PATH** or **@NODES** line specifies the parse tree context where rules apply (only one such line is allowed per pass file). Only unsealed nodes work in the **@NODES** list.

The following set of regions for rule matching can repeat in a pass file, ordered as follows:

- **@PRE** region uses a special syntax for conditions to accept a rule match.
- **@CHECK** region uses NLP++ code for conditions to accept a rule match.
- **@POST** region executes NLP++ code after a successful rule match in the following **@RULES** region Special NLP++ actions enable reductions of matched phrases.
- **@RULES** regions contain pattern matching rules.

The following is deprecated:

- **@RECURSE** region is a named region containing repeating rule regions, as above. It is invoked by the recurse phrase element modifier.

The pass file structure can be modularized as desired. For example, some passes might contain only user-defined functions. Note that forward declaration of functions is supported in NLP++ (that is, functions may be defined in passes later than their use).

One may use the term rule pass for a pass containing only rewrite rules, code pass for one containing only code, and functions pass for one containing only functions. However, in a real or production-grade analyzer, a code region almost always accompanies a rule region. At a minimum, a code region may print the pass name to a debugging or verbose output file. Typically, a pass also checks whether it should exit due to an earlier failure, task completion, or other condition. When a function is built exclusively for a particular pass, a modular approach places the function definition in that pass, and so on. The term pass file is unimpeachable. The following sections describe the regions of a pass file in greater detail.

Chaining, feeding, and debugging

As each pass modifies the same parse tree (and shared KB), the ordering is critical. A pass that creates nodes or attributes feeds later passes; one that deletes or masks information can bleed them. The VisualText IDE highlights each pass's matches and lets you reorder, inactivate, or place passes in folders to fine-tune flow and debug step-by-step.

Together, the analyzer sequence and the NLP++ language give you total control over multi-pass, rule-driven text analysis from raw tokens to deep semantic structures.

Regions

Table 2.3 lays out the regions of an NLP++ file and their ordering, representing a complete pass of an analyzer. Each pass file operates on the parse tree as built up by all the preceding passes operating sequentially. As discussed, the analyzer sequence file lays out the ordering of the passes within the pipeline, with one pass and its attributes per line.

Functions may optionally be defined first, in a single **@DECL** region. Functions may be used prior to their definition (*lookahead functions*), and passes containing only functions are often implemented for modularity and readability.

A single NLP++ code region (**@CODE**) optionally follows, prior to rule matching in the current pass. For example, code conditions may determine if the pass is to be skipped, and global variables may be set and updated.

A pass containing rules should specify the parse tree context in which rules match. Either one **@PATH** or one **@NODES** line is used, never both.

> Note: **A common error is to omit a context line or to specify an incorrect context. When no rules match in a pass, this is often the culprit.**

Multiple rule matching regions typically occur within a pass file, separated by the **@RULES** specifier. Each **@RULES** region may be preceded by **@PRE** and **@CHECK** regions, which set conditions for matching to take place.

Once a rule match is accepted, code in the preceding **@POST** region executes. An empty **@POST** region automatically generates an implicit **single()** reduce action. A nonempty **@POST** region without reduce actions does not automatically create a suggested node. Multiple **group()** actions may reduce all or parts of the matched right-hand side phrase, optionally followed by a final reduce action such as **single()**. Alternatively, a rule match may simply gather information, place information on parse tree nodes, highlight the matched text, etc. **_xNIL** serves as the noop suggested element of a rule, when reduce actions are absent.

Note the following:

- All regions may optionally end with a double at-sign version. For example, a **@CODE** region may end with **@@CODE**. Rewrite rules must end with **@@**.
- This is because **@MULTI** traverses a subtree in indeterminate ways; the singlet [s] attribute could cause an infinite loop. Therefore, use it with care.
- A cycle of **@PRE**, **@CHECK**, **@POST**, and **@RULES** regions ends and a new one begins when any of these same markers is encountered after a rewrite rule.

Refer to the following table:

Region	Type	Description
@DECL	Declarative area for functions.	User-defined NLP++ functions.
@CODE	Specifies a region where NLP++ code is executed outside of a **@RULES** region.	NLP++ code executes before any rule matching.
CONTEXT (or **SELECT**)	One line, either **@PATH**, **@NODES**, or **@MULTI** (below), specifying parse tree locations for rule matching.	**@PATH** is a single path. **@NODES** and **@MULTI** are lists of disjoint parse tree nodes.

Region	Type	Description
`@PATH`	Path of parse tree nodes down from the root.	The last node in the path is the context for rule matching.
`@NODES`	List of parse tree nodes.	Each node in the list is a separate context for rule matching. Warning: **Only unsealed nodes are valid contexts here.**
`@MULTI`	List of parse tree nodes, each a root of its subtree.	All nodes in the subtree are context nodes. Note: **Does not check the unsealed flag, nor the singlet and base attributes.**
`@PRE`	Specifies a region of preprocessing for a rule or rules.	Precedes the `@CHECK` region.
`@CHECK`	Specifies conditions on nodes before accepting a rule match.	Precedes the `@POST` region.
`@POST`	Specifies a region of post-processing when a rule match is accepted.	Precedes the `@RULES` region.
`@RULES`	Specifies a region for rewrite rules.	Each rule ends with `@@`.

Table 2.3: Regions in the pass file

@DECL regions

A `@DECL` region may optionally appear as the first, or only, region of a pass file. This is where NLP++ functions are defined by the analyzer developer. No separate function declarations are used in NLP++, and functions may be defined in passes following their use (lookahead functions, forward reference).

As NLP++ is a loosely typed language, no particular return type is specified in a function definition. It is up to the developer to ensure that a function returns values consistent with its use. In every case, zero (0) can be used as an empty return value.

A function may also return an array of multiple values and value types.

Note: **NLP++ does not currently support an array of arrays.**

Recursive functions work as expected. As with rules in recursive passes, the developer must guard against infinite loops in recursive functions.

Function definitions

NLP++ functions have syntax similar to C/C++ functions, except that the function definition also serves as its declaration. Function definitions are in the following form:

```
FunctionName ( L vars serve as arguments)  { function body }
```

Function names can only be alphabetic characters, no numbers, and no punctuation.

While all variable types may appear within a function, it is safest to primarily use additional local or **L()** variables to promote modularity. Global or **G()** variables are best accessed rather than modified locally. **X()**, **N()**, and **S()** variables require knowing exactly what contexts and what rule matches the function is currently operating inside of, and so can lead to errors when rules or contexts are modified. Use with caution and document well in the pertinent locations, to keep rules and their associated functions in sync.

Functions can optionally return a value. The return value can be any type, including string, numeric, parse tree node, concept, or even an array of mixed types. (As noted, nested arrays are not implemented.) The following is an example of a function definition and function call:

```
@DECL

myfunction(L("var"))     # Define your function.
{
    "output.txt" << "Entering myfunction." << "\n";
    G("tmp") = L("var");   # Assign value to global var. (Not good practice)
    L("tmp") = L("var");   # Assign value to local var.
    return L("tmp") * 2;   # Return a value.
}

@CODE
"output.txt" << myfunction(3) << "\n";    # Call your function.
@@CODE
```

@CODE regions

The **@CODE** region executes NLP++ code in the current pass, prior to any rule matching.

An important use is to allow conditional execution of the current pass file. In this way, multiple types of analysis sequences may reside within one analyzer. The **exitpass()** function exits a pass prior to any rule matching.

As there is currently no region for executing code after rule matching is done, any such code must be placed in the **@CODE** region of a succeeding pass.

@PATH, @NODES, or @MULTI context line

The **@PATH**, **@NODES**, and **@MULTI** lines specify the parse tree locations, or context, where rule matching occurs in the current pass. With these, the developer controls and constrains where and when rule matching occurs. Note that passes may be designated as recursive, but these context lines likewise limit where recursion occurs. **@PATH**, **@NODES**, and (to a lesser extent) **@ MULTI** enable optimized parsing of text.

A pass file may contain only one context line. If absent, the rule matching context is undefined and may default to the **_ROOT** node of the parse tree.

Hint: **If no rules match, check for a missing or incorrectly specified context line.**

The **@PATH** list of nodes specifies a single pass, while the **@NODES** and **@MULTI** lists specify disjoint nodes that serve as context, wherever they occur in the parse tree.

The **@MULTI** context line is rarely used, as it loosely constrains the rule matching context.

@PATH

The **@PATH** line specifies a single parse tree path (or context) in which to match the rules that follow. The path always starts with the **_ROOT** node and works its way down to the last named node, which serves as the immediate parent for rule matching. In the following example, the **_datetime** rule matches only within sentences under paragraphs under the parse tree root:

```
1  @PATH _ROOT _paragraph _sentence    # <====== Context line
2  #       (1)    (2)         (3)
3  @RULES
4  _datetime <-
5       _date
6       _time
7       @@
```

The context variable **X(num)** (explained later in this book) uses numbers starting with **1** for **_ROOT**, **2** for its child, and so on (as shown in *line* 2 above). Without a number, **X()** refers to the last node in the context (**named _sentence**, in the above example). As the **@NODES** line may specify various nodes at various depths and paths, **X()** and **X(var)** without a number, referring to the last (or parent) context node, are standard.

@NODES

@NODES specifies a list of parse tree nodes (i.e., contexts) where rewrite rules in the **@RULES** regions will match. In the following example, the pass traverses all **_sentence** and **_title** nodes in the parse tree, trying to match the **_pp** rule that follows (one can imagine that this finds prepositional phrases within sentence and title nodes. Note that the absent **@POST** region automatically executes a **single()** reduce action when a match is found).

Warning: **@NODES selector operates only on unsealed nodes, enabling hiding parts of the parse tree, for efficiency. This is another reason why rules may not magically match.**

```
@NODES _sentence _title   # ▯ Context line of unsealed nodes

@RULES
_pp <-
    _prep
    _np
    @@
```

@MULTI

@MULTI specifies a list of parse tree nodes, each serving as a subtree where rule matching may occur. That is, every node of a selected subtree serves as a rule-matching context. **@MULTI** traverses a subtree from bottom to top, so that a rule match higher in the tree does not affect the traversal lower down in the tree.

As noted, **@MULTI** may override the singlet and base mechanism because it traverses every node. It may also be computationally expensive and result in infinite loops. Hence, it should be used sparingly and carefully.

@RULES region

The **@RULES** regions are the workhorse of many NLP++ analyzers, collectively holding all the grammar rules (i.e., rewrite rules) that match patterns within the parse tree. Typically, matched nodes are grouped (or reduced) under a newly created suggested node, and that node (as well as the matched node phrase) may receive updated attributes and values. More complex manipulations of the matched nodes (such as reducing them individually) may be coded using the **group()** action within the **@POST** region.

As noted, the **@RULES** region may be preceded by **@PRE** and **@CHECK** regions that set additional conditions for matching a rule, beyond merely matching a set of parse tree nodes. Typically, a **@POST** region also precedes the **@RULES** region, specifying actions to perform once a rule has matched. An empty or absent **@POST** region automatically invokes a default **single()** reduce action.

Actions on the matched nodes may also be specified within the phrase elements themselves, as described in the following section.

@RULES

A rule region is bounded by the **@RULES** marker and the next region marker (**@RULES**, **@CODE**, etc.) or the end of the file.

The following are rule and KB notes:

- As detailed later, a rewrite rule (or simply rule) consists of a phrase of elements and a suggested element. Each phrase element matches zero or more parse tree nodes (or **pnodes**), and the suggested element specifies the construction of a new parse tree node upon accepting a rule match. The term rule element (or element, or elt for short) applies to both a phrase element and a suggested element.
- NLP++ also addresses components of the KB, whose backbone is a hierarchy of concepts. Each concept may store private data in a single KB phrase consisting of a list of KB nodes. KB nodes are not attached to the hierarchy, but only to their owning concept. Otherwise, a KB node structure is identical to a KB concept. It is easy to confuse parse tree nodes vs. KB nodes, as well as rule phrases vs. KB phrases. (KB phrases and KB nodes are de-emphasized in the current NLP engine version of VisualText.) See also KB phrases and nodes.

The following are action or function notes:

- NLP++ distinguishes functions and actions. Functions are fully general and are analogous to C/C++ functions. Actions, on the other hand, are predefined functions specifically written for rule-matching contexts and the like. Some may not take NLP++ general NLP++ expressions as arguments. For example, **singler(num1,num2)** is a type of rule reduction action that requires **num1** and **num2** to be literal numbers, e.g., **singler(1,2)**. The more general call **singler(L("num1"), L("num2"))** fails. In this case, **1** and **2** refer to specific phrase elements of a specific rule, so generalization is disallowed by design.
- Some actions have been updated to full-fledged functions, and future NLP++ versions may generalize some additional actions. For example, **pncopyvars()** has various forms, only one of which is a full-fledged function, and the rest are actions that implicitly copy variables to the suggested node of a rule match.

Pass file tokens

Here are the tokens allowed in a **@RULES** region, as listed in the following table:

Token	Description
#	Comment text till the end of the line is ignored.
AAA or NNN	Literal tokens are completely alphabetic or completely numeric.
_AAA	Nonliteral tokens must begin with an underscore. All the remaining letters must be alphabetical (may expand to underscore, num, dash someday).
"XXX"	Strings get double quoted. Everything within a string is taken literally (except backslashed characters).
\{character}	Backslash any non-alphanumeric {character} you want taken literally.
\\	Literal backslash character.
\	At the end of the line, escapes end of line to nothing (unimplemented).
\X	where X=abnrftv special escapes in C/C++.
@AAA	Reserved start-of-region markers in the pass file (e.g., @RULES).
@@AAA	Reserved end-of-region markers in the pass file (e.g., @@RULES).
<-	Rule arrow.
@@	Rule terminator.

Table 2.4: Token syntax in @RULES region

Large structures

Default rule matching is case-insensitive; the rule writer can add restrictive actions, like **uppercase()**, as needed. Unconstrained wildcards cannot be the start, end, or trigger element of a phrase. Optional elements also cannot be rule trigger elements.

The following table lists the syntax of large structures in the **@RULES** region:

Large structure	Description
[AAA=XXX AAA=(XXX XXX) AAA]	Pairs. Square brackets enclose the key=value pairs for a rule element (phrase element or suggested element). A sample rule with pairs: _np <- _xWILD [one match=(a b) ren="noun"] @@
AAA(XXX,XXX....)	Action, @CHECK, and @POST action language.
<NUM,NUM> AAA(XXX,XXX...)	Pre-action, <NUM,NUM> is a range of rule elements that must execute the action during rule matching.

Table 2.5: Syntax of large structures in @RULES region

Rule region

When you place multiple rules in the same **@RULES** region, they share the same **@PRE**, **@CHECK**, and **@POST** regions. When feasible, this makes pass files more readable. The following pass file example shows where the various regions are to be placed relative to each other:

```
# Conditions and post-actions for the group of rules below go here
@RULES
_pp <- _prep _np @@
_np <- _adj _noun @@

# Conditions and post-actions for the group of rules below go here
@RULES
_s <- _np _vp _np @@
_s <- _np _vp @@
```

All rules under a **@RULES** region share the same **@PRE**, **@CHECK**, and **@POST** code.

Rule components

A rewrite rule within the **@RULES** region consists of the following components, where **elt** is short for element:

suggested-elt <- elt1 elt2 ... eltN @@

The list of elements is matched against a phrase of contiguous parse tree nodes, and the suggested element specifies the creation of a new node, if any. Optionally, rules may match without creating a new node, indicated by the suggested element **_xNIL**. Code in the governing **@POST** region controls the updates to the parse tree upon a successful rule match.

The rewrite rule components are listed in the following table:

Component	Description
suggested-elt	Names and otherwise specify the creation of a new parse tree node, under which the matching nodes are placed. Typically, a rule creates a nonliteral node (denoted by an underscore, as in **_np**, but creating a new literal node (i.e., alphabetic token) is also allowed.
<-	The rewrite arrow symbol, which also appears in traditional linguistic rewrite rules. Declares that parse tree nodes matching the right-hand elements may be edited and placed under the new node created for the suggested element.
elt1 elt2 ... eltN	List of elements to be matched against a phrase of nodes in the parse tree.
@@	End marker for a single rule.

Table 2.6: Rewrite rule components

Phrase element modifiers

Each rule element, including the suggested element, may include a list of element modifiers. The element modifiers are placed after the element name, in a comma-separated list, and bounded by square brackets. Some element modifiers have synonyms. The modifier trigger, for example, can be written as **`[trigger]`**, **`[trig]`**, or **`[t]`**. Some modifiers can take a numeric value, e.g., **`[min=5 max=10]`**, or a list of values, e.g., **`[match=(the an a)]`**. Note that key-value lists do not use commas as separators. The following template lays out the structure of a rule, comprising a suggested element and one or more phrase elements:

```
@RULES
_suggestedElt <-
    phraseElt [eltModifier1 eltModifier2 ...] . . .
    @@
```

The next three tables list the phrase element modifiers available in an NLP++ rewrite rule. The following table lists modifiers that specify the number of nodes that can be matched:

Phrase element modifier	Type	Description
`max`	NUM	Specify the maximum number of nodes to match. `max=0` or `max` absent matches an indefinitely large number of nodes. E.g., `_htmltag <- \< _xWILD [min=1 max=100] \> @@`
`min`	NUM	Specify the minimum number of nodes to match. 0 means the current element is optional. E.g., `_np <- the [min=0 max=1] boys @@`
`one`	NONE	Match exactly one node. (Short for `min=1 max=1`). `_det <- _xWILD [one match=(the an a)] @@`
`opt`, `option`, `optional`, `o`	NONE	Match a minimum of 0 and a maximum of 1 node. (Short for `min=0 max=1`). E.g., `_vgroup <- _modal [opt] _have [opt] _be [opt] _verb @@`
`plus`	NONE	Indefinite repetition. Match 1 or more nodes. (Short for `min=1 max=0`).
`star`	NONE	Indefinite repetition. Match 0 or more nodes. (Short for `min=0 max=0`). Note that unconstrained `_xWILD` defaults to star.

Table 2.7: *Number of nodes to match for an element*

The following table lists modifiers that specify how nodes can be matched:

Phrase element modifier	Type	Description
`deaccent, deacc, da`	`NONE`	Match alphabetic, ignoring any accent marks on characters. E.g., `_adj <- flambe [deaccent] @@`
`excepts, except`	`LIST`	For `xWILD` only. Matching an item on the except list negates the effect of a match on the match or fail list. Must be accompanied by a single match or a fail list. `_xWILD [s match=(_sent) except=(_question)]`
`fails, fail`	`LIST`	For `_xWILD` only. Fail to match if the node matches anything on the list. E.g., `_par <- _xWILD [fail=(_endofpar _par) min=1 max=0] @@`
`matches, match`	`LIST`	For `_xWILD` only. Match if the element is in a match list. Used as a restricted wildcard and succeeds only if one of the list names matches a node. E.g., `_james <- _xWILD [match=(jim jimmy james) singlet min=1 max=1] @@`
`singlet, s`	`NONE`	Search a node's descendants to match the current element. Stop looking down when a node has more than one child, or has the base attribute set. E.g., `_abbr <- _unk \. [s] @@` see base suggested element modifier.
`tree`	`NONE`	Search the node's entire subtree for a match (Overuse of this may degrade analyzer performance).
`trigger, trig, t`	`NONE`	Match the current element first. E.g., `_np <- _det _quan _adj _noun [t] @@` matches `_noun` first.

Table 2.8: Element constraints and modes of matching

The following table lists modifiers that perform actions on matched nodes, once the entire rule match has been accepted:

Phrase element modifier	Type	Description
`group, gp`	`NAME`	Gather nodes that match the current element under a single node with `NAME` as its name. Analogous to the `@@POST` action `group()`.
`layers, layer, attrs, attr`	`LIST`	A list of mini-reductions on a phrase element that matches a single node.

Phrase element modifier	Type	Description
`lookahead, look`	`NONE`	Mark the leftmost lookahead element. Subsequent rule matches continue at the first lookahead node. Warning: **Actions must not reduce the lookahead node and those to its right.** (Otherwise, the current pass may error and exit abruptly.)
`recurse, nest, passes, pass`	`LIST`	Invoke a recursive rule region (in the current pass) on nodes that matched the current element [deprecated]. E.g., `_tag \$ <- _xWILD [nest=(tagrules)] @@`. (See `@RECURSE` region.)
`rename, ren`	`NAME`	Rename every node that matches the current element to `NAME`. E.g., `_locfield <- _location \: _xWILD [ren=_locname] _xEND @@`

Table 2.9: Element actions after matching

Suggested element modifiers

Modifiers for the suggested element are listed in *Table 2.8*. As with phrase elements, the suggested element modifiers are enclosed in square brackets and separated by whitespace (not commas), as in the following code template:

```
@RULES
_suggestedElt [eltMod1 eltMod2=(a b) ...] <-
    phraseElt ...
    @@
```

The following table suggests element modifiers available in NLP++:

Suggested element modifier	Type	Description
`base`	`NONE`	The new suggested node becomes the bottom-most node to search when looking down a singlet chain for a match (see singlet element modifier above).
`unsealed`	`NONE`	The new suggested node becomes available to the `@NODES` context specifier.

layers layer attrs attr	LIST	Also, a phrase element modifier. After a normal reduction, perform additional reductions, naming new nodes as in the list. This enables layering attributes in the parse tree. For e.g., `_noun [layer=( _np _pp)] | _possibleNoun @@` creates a `_noun`, then `_np`, then `_pp` node, each a parent of the previous.

Table 2.10: Suggested element modifiers in rewrite rule

Some phrase elements and suggested elements have modifiers that take a value or list of values, implemented as a name-value pair, i.e:

```
rule element [modifier=value(s) ...]
```

For example:

```
_noun [rename=_np]
November [num=11 abbrev="NOV"]
_xWILD [s plus match=(_xALPHA _xNUM) except[(_header)]
```

The following table lists the types of values allowed for rule element modifiers:

Modifier type	Description
NAME	Takes one value like `rename="_np"`
NUM	Takes one value, e.g., `max=3`
LIST	Takes a list of values like `match=(a an the)`
NONE	These types do not take values

Table 2.11: Types of values for rule element modifiers

Rule element types

Each rule element, including the suggested element, consists of a literal or a nonliteral. Suggested elements specify the naming of a new node, while phrase elements specify the nodes to be matched in the parse tree. A rule element can be either of:

- **Literal**: A token node, or real text token.
- **Nonliteral**: An alphabetic node name beginning with the underscore character `_`.

A literal is usually a terminal node (or leaf node) in the parse tree. It represents an alphabetic word, a number, a control character, and a punctuation character.

Note: NLP++ allows literal names on nonleaf (or nonterminal) nodes in the parse tree, but this is not recommended, in general. Such nodes do not behave identically to true literal leaf nodes.

A nonliteral is usually a nonterminal node (also called an **internal node**). It represents a node that dominates other nodes, i.e., is their parent or ancestor. Here, too, it is possible for a nonliteral node to be a leaf, but this should also be minimized (e.g., excising children of a nonliteral change it to a leaf node). The initial underscore character _ of a name is the NLP++ convention marking nonliteral nodes.

Every node other than the root node of the parse tree (called `_ROOT`) is also a child or descendant node (descendent is also a correct spelling).

Special rule elements

NLP++ has a set of predefined phrase elements that make rule matching more powerful. These special phrase elements match various types of nodes and parse tree boundaries.

Special phrase elements are described in the following table. The only special suggested element is `_xNIL`, which denotes a dummy suggested element:

Rule element	Description
`_xNIL`	No suggested element. The only special suggested element. The `@POST` region must be nonempty, else a suggested node named `_xNIL` is created. In the `@POST` region, the `group()` action serves to reduce matched nodes. `_xNIL` may be used when the rule examines and manipulates matched nodes in a specialized fashion.
`_xWILD`	Match anything, the workhorse phrase element. Lone `_xWILD` is an unrestricted wildcard. `modifier=value` pairs can restrict what is matched. **Note: With match, fail, and except lists, `_xWILD` becomes a powerful wildcard matching element.** See the *Note* following this table.
`_xANY`	Match any single node. **Warning: A rule written with `_xANY [max=0]` will not work.** `_xANY` is not implemented as a wildcard. `_xWILD` is usually preferable.
`_xALPHA`	Match an alphabetic token, including extended ANSI chars. The deaccent element modifier can handle accented chars as well.
`_xCTRL`	Match control and non-alphabetic extended ANSI characters.
`_xNUM`	Match a numeric token.
`_xEMOJI`	Match an emoji token.

Rule element	Description
_xPUNCT	Match a punctuation token.
_xWHITE	Match a whitespace token, including newline.
_xBLANK	Match a whitespace token, excluding newline. Equivalent to **_xWILD [match=(t)]**.
_xCAP	Match an alphabet with an uppercase first letter.
_xCAPLET	Match an alphabet consisting of a single capitalized letter.
_xLET	Match an alphabet consisting of a single letter.
_xEOF	Match the end of the file.
_xSTART	Match if at the start of the current parse tree phrase.
_xEND	Match if at the end of the current parse tree phrase.

Table 2.12: Special rule elements

Note: NLP++ uses C/C++ like syntax for special characters like newline and tab. Newlines are \n, and tabs are \t. Punctuation characters are similarly escaped with a backslash.

Behavior of _xWILD special rule element

We describe the behavior of the special element **_xWILD**. Given the parse tree phrase:

```
the three bears
```

The following rule matches the above literal nodes (assuming NOSP in the tree):

```
_np <- the _xWILD bears @@
```

However, the following version will not match:

```
_np <- the _xWILD [match=(_xALPHA)] bears @@
```

In this case, greedy matching causes the wildcard to gobble up the **bears** node, so that the **bears** element fails to find that node. The following version fixes the problem:

```
_np <- the _xWILD [match=(_xALPHA) except=(bears)] bears @@
```

This example is trivial, but it illustrates a general way of using **match**, **fail**, and **except** lists in wildcard matching. In summary, a lone **_xWILD** matches till the next rule element. An **_xWILD** with restrictions may need to explicitly include the next element as a terminator.

Unrestricted wildcards at the start and end of a rule phrase are flagged as disallowed. The more limited **_xANY** may be used in this case.

The standard way to match lists of tokens is via **_xWILD**. For example:

```
_xWILD [plus match=(_xWHITE)]
```

It is safer and easier to modify than:

```
_xWHITE [plus]
```

@POST

The **@POST** region code executes only after an accepted rule match within the immediately following **@RULES** region, and after any phrase element actions in the matched rule.

Warning: **This is because @POST actions may modify the parse tree by adding, removing, and moving nodes; the ordering of actions must be such that the numbering scheme for rule elements and nodes remains in sync after each action.**

For example:

```
excise(2,2); excise(4,4);
```

Deletes node 2 first and then node 5, if it still exists, not node 4. This could crash the analyzer. The correct ordering is:

```
excise(4,4); excise(2,2);
```

Note: **The phrase numbering updates after each parse tree manipulation.**

The **@POST** region actions are divided into four groups:

- Node actions
- Reduce actions
- Print actions
- Variable actions

Warning about @POST region

An empty or absent **@POST** region automatically causes execution of an implicit **single()** reduce action, once a rule is successfully matched. This groups all the matched nodes under a new suggested node, as named by the left-hand side of the matched rewrite rule (even if that name is **_xNIL**).

A nonempty **@POST** region only executes the code within that region, with no automatic reduction. For example, if the **noop()** action is the only reduce action present, then the matched nodes are not grouped. To mimic the empty **@POST** region, include the **single()** reduce action.

When a rule's phrase includes the lookahead element modifier, the associated **@POST** region must not reduce the lookahead node or those that follow it. For example, an empty or absent **@POST** region executes a **single()** reduce implicitly, causing the current pass to abort.

A correct use of the lookahead modifier follows:

```
@POST
  singler(1,3);
@RULES
  _np <- the three bears _vg [lookahead] @@
```

Here, matched nodes for **the three bears** are reduced to a noun phrase (**_np**) when the next node matches **_vg**, a verb group. The matching algorithm then continues at the matched **_vg** node, as it is the designated lookahead node. Absent the lookahead modifier, matching would continue at the node following the **_vg** node, if any.

Reduce actions

The most common reduction actions are single, singler, and group. The term reduces, or reduction, refers to the process of simplifying or shortening a phrase or clause while maintaining its grammatical integrity. Putting it simply: reducing one or more nodes to a single node.

The workhorse reduces action in the **@POST** region to a **single()**. It is a single-tier reduction that places the matched parse tree nodes under the newly built suggested node. For example, in the following code, when a determiner and a noun are matched, the matched text is printed to the file **debug.txt**, and the matched nodes are then placed under the new **_nlp** node:

```
@POST
"debug.txt" << "Matched phrase: " << phrasetext() << "\n";
single();

@RULES
_np <- _det _noun @@
```

As discussed elsewhere, a missing or empty **@POST** region results in an automatic, implicit **single()** reduction, and if the **@POST** region contains code but no reduce action, then no reduction is performed. In the following example, a **_np** suggested node is not created, because the **@POST** region is both not empty and lacks a reduce action:

```
@POST
"debug.txt" << phrasetext() << "\n";

@RULES
_np <- _det _noun @@     # (Replace _np with _xNIL)
```

NLP++ enables writing rules with left and right boundaries (or context) for the phrase we are interested in. In the following example, **_det** (or determiner) is a reliable start for a noun phrase, while a verb can delimit the noun phrase's end boundary. The **singler()** action places the first three matched nodes under a new suggested node named **_np**. Note that the lookahead modifier assures that the verb will be considered next by the rule-matching algorithm (see earlier warning about misuse of lookahead modifier in *Table 2.9*):

```
@POST
"debug.txt" << phrasetext() << "\n";
singler(1,3);

@RULES
_np <- _det _noun _noun _verb [lookahead] @@
```

Splicing

The opposite of a reduce action is a splice action, which dissolves (i.e., excises) the matched top-level nodes and restores their children to the top-level of the matched phrase.

When analyzing text, a common first step is to group the parse tree into lines. This enables finding line-oriented formats, such as headers, field-value pairs, and structures such as sections and paragraphs. Once these have been found, the analyzer splices or removes line nodes from regions identified as prose. These parts of the parse tree can then be reorganized with paragraph and sentence nodes.

The formatting analyzer discussed later illustrates this analysis methodology.

The various post actions are tabulated in the following table:

Post action	Description
noop()	Perform no **@POST** reduce action. This is a convenience to disable the default **single()** reduce action.
single()	Single-tier reduce. Reduce the entire set of nodes that matched a rule phrase.
singler (num1,num2)	Single-tier reduce of a range of matched rule elements. E.g., if finding a period to be end-of-sentence, reduce the period to **_eos**, not the whole matched sentence.
singlex (num1,num2)	Single-tier reduce of a range of matched rule elements. All nodes not in the range are excised. E.g., match an HTML tag, reduce the name, and zap the rest of the tag.
singlezap()	Single-tier reduce. Excise all the nodes in the matched phrase.
merge()	Single-tier reduce that dissolves the top-level nodes in the matched phrase.

Post action	Description
`merger (num1,num2)`	Single-tier reduce that dissolves the top-level nodes in the matched range.
`listadd listnum, itemnum [,keep]`	Add a new node to a list node's children. If the item occurs after the list (**`listnum < itemnum`**), it is added as the last child. If the item occurs before the list, it is added as the first child. The optional keep **`arg`** can be true or false. If true, it retains the intervening nodes (if any) in the list. If false, it excises the intervening nodes. Absent keeps defaults to true.
`excise (num1,num2)`	Excise the nodes matching the range of elements from the parse tree. For multiple excise actions, operations must be ordered such that the excise with the highest **`num1`** is listed first, etc. As noted in the earlier **`@POST`** section.
`splice (num1,num2)`	Dissolve the top-level nodes of the given range.
`group (num1,num2,labelstr)`	Reduce the range of rule elements (**`num1,num2`**) and name the group node **`labelstr`**. Unlike other reduce actions, the **`group`** function can be repeated (See earlier *@POST* section about changing parse tree numbering). Note that a group can take **`L()`** variables as arguments, and so on.
`setlookahead(num)`	Set the node that the rule matcher will continue with, after the current rule match is done. **`num`** node is the lookahead.

Table 2.13: Post actions for a matched rewrite rule

Node actions

We discuss sealed and unsealed suggested element modifiers, as well as the base and singlet mechanisms for matching embedded nodes of the parse tree.

Sealed and unsealed

In a normal rule reduction, the suggested node is sealed as an optimization. This makes it inaccessible to the **`@NODES`** context selection mechanism, which looks for listed nodes throughout the parse tree, then uses the phrases below them for rule matching. Marking a node unsealed makes it visible for rule matching.

The **`@NODES`** selector starts at the root of the parse tree, then looks only within a path of unsealed nodes for node names matching the **`@NODES`** list. The path from the **`_ROOT`** node then serves as context for rule matching. Unlike **`@NODES`**, the **`@PATH`** selector and its list specify a complete parse tree context, and so does not depend on nodes being unsealed.

The example following rule roughs out is a set of nodes ending in a period, creating a **_sentence** node. The unsealed modifier makes such a **_sentence** node accessible to further rule matching via the **@NODES** selector (assuming its ancestors are also unsealed):

```
@RULES
_sentence [unsealed] <- _xWILD [plus] \.  @@
```

The **@NODES** selector is flexible in that, e.g., **_sentence** nodes may be processed wherever they occur. However, this comes at a cost in speed, as the whole parse tree is searched for such nodes. **@PATH**, in contrast, optimally specifies an exact context, but at a cost of flexibility.

Say that in a subsequent pass (shown in the following code), we want to count **_np** nodes within **_sentence** nodes. The **@NODES _np** specifier looks only for **_np** nodes within ancestors that are unsealed. If the sentence rule above omits the unsealed modifier, then noun phrases within those sentences are not traversed:

```
@NODES _np

@POST
 ++X("nouns");
@RULES
_xNIL <- _noun @@
```

Singlet and base

The base suggested element modifier specifies that the reduce node will be the bottom-most node in a singlet chain. That is, subsequent rules using the singlet (or **[s]**) element modifier will look down the chain of descendant nodes, but not below a node labeled with the base attribute. Singlet says, *look down a chain of single nodes, while base says, stop looking further down.*

A singlet and base provide a mechanism for layering multiple attributes, such as syntactic and semantic ambiguities, directly into the parse tree.

The following example shows the use of the base modifier. The rule reduces a node **labeled _noun** to an **_np** and places the base attribute on the **_np** node:

```
@RULES
_np [base] <- _noun @@
```

A subsequent rule searching for **_noun [s]**, as shown in the following code, will not find it in **_np** nodes created as above. Even though the s (or singlet) modifier says to look below a node for **_noun**, it will not look below the **_np** node labeled with the base modifier:

```
@RULES
_np <- _adj _noun [s] @@
```

Note: Among the functions below, `pncopyvars()` has four variants. The variant `pncopyvars(pnode1,pnode2)`, which copies variables from one parse tree node to another, is a fully general NLP++ function that may appear in `@CODE` regions as well as rule matching regions. All other variants implicitly copy variables to the suggested node resulting from a successfully matched rewrite rule.

The following table specifies **`@POST`** actions that modify parse tree nodes matched by the current rule:

Post action	Description
`pncopyvars(pnode1,pnode2)`	Copy variables from **`pnode1`** to **`pnode2`** [NLP++ function].
`pncopyvars (pnode)`	Copy variables from the **`pnode`** to the suggested node.
`pncopyvars (num)`	Copy variables from the **`num`** phrase node to the suggested node.
`pncopyvars (0)`	Copy variables from the last phrase node to the suggested node.
`pncopyvars()`	Same as **`pncopyvars (0)`**.
`setbase (num, bool)`	Set the base attribute of the **`num`** node to true or false.
`setunsealed (num, bool)`	Set the unsealed attribute of the **`num`** node to true or false.
`xrename (name [, num])`	Rename the **`num`** context node to **`name`**. If num is absent or 0, rename the last context node.

Table 2.14: Parse tree node actions in @POST region

Print actions

The following table specifies **`@POST`** actions that print to a file or to standard output [many are deprecated]:

Print action	Description
`print (str)`	Print the literal string **`str`** to standard output.
`printr (num1, num2)`	Print the text for the rule element range from **`num1`** to **`num2`** to standard output.
`prchild (file, num, name)`	Look for the named node immediately under the **`num`** phrase node. If found, print its text to a file.
`prtree (file, num, name)`	Look for the first named node in the subtree under the **`num`** phrase node. If found, print its text to a file.
`prxtree (file, prestr, num, name, poststr)`	Like **`prtree`**, but prints a string before and after the found subtree node. E.g., **`prxtree ("out.txt", "date: ", 3, "_date", "\n")`** prints out a line like **`"date: 3/9/99"`** if a **`_date`** node is found within the matched subtree of element **`3`**.
`prlit (file, str)`	Print the literal string **`str`** to the file.

Print action	Description
`fprintnvar (file, var, num)`	To file, print the value of variable **var** in the **num** element's node.
`fprintxvar (file, var, num)`	To file, print the value of variable **var** in the **num** context node.
`fprintgvar (file, var)`	To file, print the value of the global variable **var**.
`gdump (file)`	Dump global vars and values to a file.
`xdump (file, num)`	Dump vars and values in the **num** context node to the file.
`ndump (file, num)`	Dump vars and values in the **num** element's node to the file.
`sdump (file)`	Dump vars and values in the suggested node to the file.
`prrange (file, num1, num2)`	Print the text in the range of rule elements (**num1**, **num2**) to a file.
`pranchor (file, num1, num2)`	[Deprecated] print a web URL to a file. Treat the rule phrase range (**num1**, **num2**) as a URL. Use the global variable named base to resolve and print complete relative URLs. A prior pass must find the base HTML tag and set the base appropriately. Not using the file's URL, so not handling cases where **<base>** itself is a relative URL.

Table 2.15: Print actions in the @POST region

Variable actions

The following table lists variable actions, which are a legacy implementation. Standard NLP++ code accesses and modifies variables of all types:

Variable action	Description
`addstrs`	Add a string to the multi-string global variable **var**. Fetch the string from the nodes matching the rule element **num**. **var** should have been declared using the **@CODE** action **varstrs()** [removed]. Use NLP++ array syntax instead.

Table 2.16: Legacy variable actions

@PRE

The **@PRE** region uses a specialized syntax to set preconditions for accepting a rule match.

@PRE action syntax

The actions used in the **@PRE** region have a mandatory range. Their form is:

```
@PRE

<num,num> pre_action_name(args....)
```

The **@PRE** action applies to each rule element in the **<num, num>** range individually.

@PRE actions operate only on tokens or leaf nodes of the parse tree, at present. So, if the current node covers more than a single leaf node, the **@PRE** action automatically fails. Another thing to be careful of is that **@PRE** actions disregard the base attribute of a node. That is, even if the current node or a subnode has the base attribute set, the **@PRE** action will look under it for the leaf node.

The following table lists the actions available in the **@PRE** region:

PRE action	Description
uppercase()	Succeed if the leaf token is all uppercase.
lowercase()	Succeed if the leaf token is all lowercase.
cap()	Succeed if the leaf token has a capitalized first letter.
length (num)	Succeed if the leaf token has a length exactly equal to **num**.
lengthr (num1,num2)	Succeed if leaf token length is in the range of lengths (**num1,num2**), inclusive.
numrange (num1,num2)	Succeed if the leaf token is a number in the given range.
unknown()	[Obsolete] Succeed if the leaf token is an unknown word. Meaningful only if a prior pass has marked alphabetic words using a dictionary.
regexp (str)	Succeed if the regular expression **str** is matched. **str** may include characters, with **?** meaning a single char, ***** meaning 0 or more chars.
regexpi (str)	Like **regexp**, but case insensitive.
var (str)	Succeed if the matched node has a variable called **str** with a nonzero value.
vareq (str,str_or_num)	Succeed if the matched node has a variable called **str** whose value equals a string or numeric value in **str_or_num**.
varne (str,str_or_num)	Succeed if the matched node has a variable called **str** whose value does not equal a string or numeric value in **str_or_num**.
varz (str)	Succeed if the matched node has a variable called **str** with a zero value (or lacks the variable altogether).
debug()	Succeed unconditionally. Used to place a C++ breakpoint at a particular rule.

Table 2.17: Actions in @PRE region

@PRE example

The following is an example rule that uses **@PRE** actions, taken from the date-time analyzer. A previous pass marked the numeric nodes as possible date numbers, i.e., as day, month, and year. The current pass uses the **@PRE** conditions on nodes in the rule in order to make sure that the numbers are in the correct range.

A sample text matched by the rule in the following is:

Monday, 25 August 2025

```
###############################################
# Fri, 12 Dec 2014
###############################################

@PRE
<1,1> var("day");
<3,3> var("day");
<4,4> var("month");
<5,5> var("year");

@POST
S("weekday") = N("day",1);
S("day") = num(N("$text",3));
S("month") = N("month",4);
S("year") = num(N("$text",5));
single();

@RULES
_date <-
    _xALPHA   ### (1)
    \, [opt] ### (2)
    _xNUM     ### (3)
    _xALPHA   ### (4)
    _xNUM     ### (5)
    @@
```

@CHECK actions

`@CHECK` actions operate after the rule's right-hand-side phrase has matched and all `@PRE` conditions have been satisfied. `@CHECK` actions help set conditions for the final acceptance or rejection of the rule match.

Two special NLP++ actions operate in the `@CHECK` region. When a rule match is to be rejected, the function `fail()` is called. To accept the match, call the `succeed()` function. Both actions immediately exit the `@CHECK` region.

While the set of `@PRE` conditions is built-in, the `@CHECK` region uses general NLP++ code to set additional conditions on the rule match.

The `@POST` region, if any, is executed after a `succeed()` call, after the `@CHECK` region code completes without encountering a `succeed()` or `fail()`, and after an empty `@CHECK` region. As noted, an empty POST region implicitly executes the `single()` reduce action.

Both `succeed()` and `fail()` may occur inside a user function written to operate in the `CHECK` region. Such hidden or non-modular use should be minimized and should be well-documented with comments in the affected passes, rules, and user functions.

The following table lists the actions in the `@CHECK` region:

Check action	Return type	Description
`fail()`	`NONE`	Reject and immediately exit the rule match.
`succeed()`	`NONE`	Accept rule match and immediately go to the POST region, if present. [Empty or absent `@POST` region executes implicit `single()` reduce action.]
`or(num1,num2)`	`NONE`	[Obsolete][broken]

***Table 2.18**: Actions in @CHECK region*

Code syntax

We will discuss NLP++ language syntax and topics in the following subsections.

Functions

User functions are introduced in the section *Function definitions*, within the discussion of `@DECL` regions. The following sections discuss many built-in functions available in *Appendix B, NLP++. NLP++ Actions and Functions* provides tables of built-in actions and functions, as well as documenting files of useful utility functions available to the NLP++ developer.

The original VisualText IDE version enables developers to code C/C++ functions and then call them from NLP++ code, thereby extending the language. This capability is not yet available in the current NLP engine implementation.

Built-in functions

NLP++ has built-in functions for the following areas, all of which are subheadings within *Appendix B, NLP++*:

- Rule region actions
- KB functions
- String functions
- Special functions
- Spelling functions
- Math functions

Variables

NLP++ variables differ from those of other programming languages because NLP++ variables must additionally address the components of the KB, parse tree, rewrite rules, and the context in which rules execute. A single capital letter denotes the location or domain where variables are managed, while the variable name is enclosed within double quotes and parentheses. For example, **`G("verbose")`** is a global variable named **`verbose`**. Any valid NLP++ string can be used to name a variable. The NLP++ runtime uses hashed string tables to handle variable names efficiently.

The following are the lists that should be noted:

- As NLP++ variables may place (or access) named attributes on parse tree nodes and KB concepts, we often use the words variable and attribute interchangeably.
- We often conflate a rule phrase element with the parse tree node that it matches. We might refer to the nth rule phrase element as the nth node, and vice versa.
- The name pass file variable is preferred to the old term parse tree node variable.
- A common programming error confuses parse tree nodes with KB concepts.
- As the letters **`G`**, **`L`**, **`X`**, **`S`**, and **`N`** denote locations or domains, a future version of NLP++ could introduce a **`C`** locator for KB concepts. As well, P could represent parse tree nodes outside the purview of a matched rewrite rule (these could serve as local variables in all regions).
- For textual clarity, we often use **`G()`**, **`L()`**, **`X()`**, **`S()`**, **`N()`**. Also, **`X(num)`** and **`N(num)`** are valid NLP++ code references to context nodes and matched phrase nodes, respectively.

Pass file variable types in NLP++ apply to specific domains. They comprise two broad classes:

- **General variables (G, L)**:
  - `G` designates global variables.
  - `L` designates local variables.
- **Rule region variables (X, S, N) operate when a rule's phrase has matched**:
  - `X` designates variables on a context node.
  - `S` designates variables on a suggested node.
  - `N` designates variables on a matched phrase node.

The **X**, **S**, and **N** variables are activated only when a rule phrase has matched nodes in the parse tree. In view of this, we now name them collectively as rule region variables, rule match variables, or simply rule variables. This is because each manages variables on a parse tree node; they have been called parse tree node variables, or simply node variables. However, **G** and **L** variables may also take node values, so these latter names are inaccurate.

A matched rule phrase may still be rejected by **@PRE** and **@CHECK** region conditions. Even when a rule match succeeds, a new suggested node is not always created. In these cases, the **S** variable, which places attributes and values on the suggested node, serves as temporary storage. In particular, it enables the **@CHECK** and **@POST** regions to share information. **L** local variables, on the other hand, are not visible across these two regions.

The following table describes the variable types:

Variable type	Value	Description
`G(varstr)`	Any	Global variable, in all code areas. Variable name is arbitrary **varstr**.
`L(varstr)`	Any	Local variable, in all code areas. Used as a function argument. **@CHECK** and **@POST** locals are blind to each other. See **S()** var.
		Context node variable; points to the **num** node in **@PATH** line.
`X(varstr,num)`	Any	Unsafe for use with **@NODES** line.
`X(varstr)`	Any	Context node variable; points to the current node in **@NODES**.
`X(num)`	Node	Context node variable; points to the last node of **@PATH** line.
`X()`	Node	The **num** context node in the **@PATH** line.
		The current context node in **@NODES** line.

Variable type	Value	Description
S(varstr)	Any	Variable on the suggested rule node. Used in **@CHECK** and **@POST**. If the rule match is accepted and reduced, the suggested node is placed in the parse tree; else, it is deleted. **S()** vars serve as temporary vars for a rule, e.g., if there is no reduce action.
N(varstr,num)	Any	Phrase node variable, points to the node matching **num** phrase elements.
N(varstr)	Any	Phrase node variable, points to the node matching the last phrase element.
N(num)	Node	Node matching **num** phrase element.
N()	Node	Node matching the last phrase element.

Table 2.19: NLP++ variable types

General variables

The global and local variable types described in the following are general variables, as in other programming languages:

- **G variables**: Global variables can be used in NLP++ functions, **@CODE** regions, and in **@CHECK** and **@POST** regions of rules. Some global typically refer to key areas in the CG KB (i.e., the top-level concepts of the KB hierarchy). For example, inserting a new analyzer **@CODE** pass in the NLP engine generates the following code, which makes or fetches a concept called **kb** directly under the root of the hierarchy:

```
@CODE

G("kb") = getconcept(findroot(),"kb");
SaveKB("mykb.kbb",G("kb"),2);

@@CODE
```

The following are typical global variables, taken from the initialization pass of the English parser:

```
G(„verbose“) = 1; # Flag verbose output.
G("error") = 1;     # Flag error output.
G("hilite") = 1;    # Flag highlighting passes.
```

- **L variable**: Local variables are the second type of general variable. Local variables are denoted by the letter `L` and appear in various locations: in the `@DECL` region as function parameters, and as temporary variables in `@CODE`, `@CHECK`, and `@POST` regions. Refer to the following code:

```
@DECL

myfunction(L("var"))      # Define your function.
{
    "output.txt" << "Entering myfunction." << "\n";
    G("tmp") = L("var"); # Assign value to global variable.
    L("tmp") = L("var");  # Assign value to local variable.
    return L("tmp") * 2;  # Return a value.
}

@CODE
L("starting value") = 3;
L("new value") = myfunction(L("starting value"));# Call function.
@@CODE
```

Rule region variables

Rule region variables, or rule variables for short, address particular nodes involved when a rule's phrase has matched. The variable types **N**, **S**, and **X** refer to phrase nodes, suggested nodes, and context nodes, respectively. They are explained in more detail in the following:

- **N variable**: The `N`, or phrase node variable, can appear within the `@CHECK` and `@POST` regions of a rule (as well as in a function body, with care). Forms:

```
1. N(varname,num)          # Variable on node matching numth phrase
   element.
2. N(varname) or N(varname,0)    # Variable on node matching last phrase
   element.
3. N(num)                  # Node matching numth phrase element.
4. N()           # Node matching last phrase element.
```

It accesses and updates variables in the node matching the `num` phrase element of a rule.

Warning: **`N` variable expects a phrase element matching only a single node.**

The following rule example matches three nodes: a determiner, an adjective, and a noun. If they all match a portion of the parse tree, the rule succeeds, creates the suggested node named **_np** as the parent of the matched nodes, and executes the code in the **@POST** area. The code statements move information from the matched nodes to the suggested node. In this case, the special variable **$text** fetches the buffer text from each node, which is then copied to a variable on the suggest node. For example, the suggested node gets a noun phrase head variable called **head** whose value is fetched by a special variable **$text** from phrase node number **3** (the **_noun**). See the table of special variables for a description of **$text** and related variants.

Note: In the following rule, each element is on a separate line with a comment displaying its position. The VisualText IDE automatically formats rules this way for convenience.

```
@POST
S("attribute") = N("$text",2);
S("head") = N("$text",3);
single();

@RULES
_np <-
    _det            ### (1)
    _adj            ### (2)
    _noun [plus] ### (3)
    @@
```

Matching multiple nodes, the **_noun** in the above rule phrase may match any number of nodes. The following code example handles multiple nodes matching a single phrase element. Such code can be placed in the **@CHECK** and **@POST** regions:

```
L("first") = eltnode(3);          # First node matching elt 3.
L("last")  = lasteltnode(3);     # Last  node matching elt 3.

# Loop through nodes matching elt 3.
L("n")       = L("first");          # Setup an iterator.
L("end")    = pnnext(L("last")); # One past the matched nodes, else 0.
while (L("n") != L("end"))         # Loop through matched nodes.
  {
  "output.txt"<< "node text="    # Print each node's text to a file.
               << pnvar(L("n"),"$text") << "\n";
```

```
    L("n") = pnnext(L("n"));         # Move to next parse tree node.
    }
```

- **S variable**: The **S** rule variable refers to the suggested node created when a rule match is accepted. In the following example, the rule creates a suggested node (named **_np**) representing a noun phrase, and the code in *line* 2 adds the **_noun** node's text to the suggested node, in an attribute named **"root"**. The suggested element **_np** appears on *line 6*:

```
1     @POST
2   S("root") = N("$text",2); # attr "root" = node text matching elt 2.
3   single();
4
5   @RULES
6   _np <-
7      _det [opt] ### (1)
8      _noun      ### (2)
9      @@
```

Upon analyzing the sentence *John kicked the ball,* the parse tree printout below shows the **root** attribute in *lines 1 to 6*. The first line shows the **root** attribute containing the text from *line 3*, and *line 6* shows the **root** attribute **ball** from *line 10*:

```
1   _np [0,3,0,3,3,16,node,fired,blt, ("root" "John")]
2     _noun [0,3,0,3,2,26,node,fired]
3        John [0,3,0,3,0,0,alpha, ("NOSP" 1) ("cap" 1) ("noun" 1)
                                                    ("pos num" 1)]
4   _verb [5,10,5,10,2,26,node]
5     kicked [5,10,5,10,0,0,alpha, ("SP" 1) ("verb" 1)   ("pos num" 1)]
6   _np [12,19,12,19,3,16,node,fired,blt, ("root" "ball")]
7     _det [12,14,12,14,2,26,node,fired]
8        the [12,14,12,14,0,0,alpha, ("SP" 1)("determiner" 1)
                                                    ("pos num" 1)]
9     _noun [16,19,16,19,2,26,node,fired]
10       ball [16,19,16,19,0,0,alpha, ("SP" 1) ("noun" 1) ("pos num" 1)]
```

- **X variable**: Every NLP++ rule matches within a parse tree context defined by either the **@PATH** list or **@NODES** list. The **X** context variable addresses any of the ancestor nodes of the current parse tree path (specified by the **@PATH** list). In the case of **@NODES**, the bare

X() variable addresses the immediate parent node in which rules are being matched (i.e., one of the named nodes in the **@NODES** list).

Note: Omitting the context and getting zero rule matches is a common programmer error.

In the following code on *line 1*, the path comprises four ancestor nodes. In *line 4*, we see that the **X** variable refers to ancestor 3, a context node named **_sentence**. As no POST action performs a reduce, this rule merely copies the year information to the current **_sentence** node. **_xNIL** indicates that no rewrite rule reduce should be present (else the suggested element left of the arrow should name a suggested node to create):

```
1   @PATH  _ROOT  _paragraph  _sentence  _datetime
2   #         1          2          3           4
3   @POST

4    X("year",3) = N("year",1);
5   @RULES
6      _xNIL <- _datetime    ### 1
7      @@
```

This is because the **@NODES** selector searches the entire parse tree for named nodes on its list; the location and depth in the parse tree may vary, and so the parse tree path and exact context should not be hardwired into the rule matching regions. For example:

```
@NODES _np _vg
```

Searches for noun phrases (**_np**) and verb groups (**_vg**) wherever they occur in the parse tree. So, with the **@NODE** selector, we should use the forms **X()** and **X(varname)**, with no numeric argument. These refer only to the context parent node (**_np** or **_vg**), or its attribute **varname**, respectively. If ancestor context is needed, it could be added as attributes when creating each **_np** and **_vg**, in this example. If the entire context path is known unambiguously, one could use the **X** form with a number argument, but this is not recommended in general. It is natural to use **@PATH** in such a case.

Warning: A common programming error is to use X(varname,num) with @NODES, with the mistaken idea that, in the above example, 1 refers to _np, and 2 refers to _vg. X(1) is always the parse tree root, X(2) is its child in the current parse tree path context, and so on.

The sample rule in the following is matched directly under a **_LINE** or a **_TEXTZONE** context node. The **_np** node created in *line 10* receives an attribute called **root** from phrase element **2** in the rule (i.e., the **$text** value from the **_noun** on *line 12*). *Line 5* indicates on the context node that a match was **"found"** (where **1** may represent Boolean true). *Line 6* shows a C/C++ style way to increment or bump the value of the attribute **noun** on the context node. *Line 7* has the **single()** reduce action, saying that the suggested **_np** node is to be created, grouping the matched right-hand side nodes under it. Note that the **single()** call should be the final structure-altering code in the **@POST** region, as it substantially alters the parse tree.

```
@NODES _LINE _TEXTZONE

@POST
S("root") = N("$text",2);
X("found") = 1;
++X("noun");
single();

@RULES
_np <-
    _det [opt]    ### (1)
    _noun         ### (2)
    @@
```

The following code shows the state of the parse tree after matching the above rule (with the same text input as earlier). In *line 2*, the **_LINE** context node has the **"found"** attribute set to **1**. Also, the **"noun"** attribute is set to **2**, reflecting that both **"John"** and **"ball"** were matched as **_noun** nodes in the **_np** rule. Lastly, two **_np** nodes were created via the **single()** reduce action, in *line 3* and *line 8*.

```
1   _ROOT [0,19,0,19,0,0,node,un, ("TOT LINES" 1) ("TOT TABS" 0) ("TOT LOWERS" 3) ("TOT CAPS" 1) ("TOT UPPERS" 0) ("TOT NUMS" 0)]
2   _LINE [0,19,0,19,2,14,node, ("det" "the") ("found" 1)  ("noun" 2)]
3     _np [0,3,0,3,4,18,node,fired,blt, ("root" "John")]
4       _noun [0,3,0,3,3,26,node,fired]
5           John [0,3,0,3,0,0,alpha, ("NOSP" 1) ("cap" 1) ("noun" 1)]
6     _verb [5,10,5,10,3,26,node]
7         kicked [5,10,5,10,0,0,alpha, ("SP" 1) ("verb" 1)]
8     _np [12,19,12,19,4,18,node,fired,blt, ("root" "ball")]
9       _det [12,14,12,14,3,26,node,fired]
10          the [12,14,12,14,0,0,alpha, ("SP" 1) ("determiner" 1)]
11      _noun [16,19,16,19,3,26,node,fired]
12          ball [16,19,16,19,0,0,alpha, ("SP" 1) ("noun" 1)]
```

Special variable names

To get useful information from the parse tree and other sources when analyzing a text, special variable names are provided. They all start with a dollar sign (**$**) and are predefined built-in variables. This is because **S()** nodes are not added to the parse tree till a rule match is accepted; constructs like **S("$text")** are not used. Functions like **phrasetext()** can fetch the full text of a matched rule's text.

Notes on special variables

Special variable names must be quoted. E.g., **N("$text", 2)**.

You should not assign to or create your own dollar-sign variables. NLP++ reserves these.

Types of special variables

Here we describe the types and uses of special variables, which enable accessing internal information about the parse tree and KB from the NLP++ runtime environment.

Note: We use variable and attribute interchangeably throughout this book. However, we prefer variables for parse tree nodes and attributes for KB concepts.

The special variables are organized in six groups.

General-purpose special variables use the **G()** variable type:

- Runtime variables
- File variables
- Parser variables

Node-specific special variables use **N()** and **X()** for:

- Text variables
- Letter-case variables
- Test variables

Special runtime variables in the following table provide information about the type of input (folder vs. file) and whether we are processing the first or last file of a batch. These are new in the NLP engine implementation of VisualText, which we abbreviate as N-E.

Special variable	Type	Description
$isdirrun	G	Return 1 if analyzing a folder, else 0. (N-E 1.26.0)
$isfirstfile	G	Return 1 if at the first file of a batch, else 0. (N-E 1.24.0)
$islastfile	G	Return 1 if at the last file of a batch, else 0. (N-E 1.24.0)

Table 2.20: Special runtime variables

Special file variables provide information about the current input file. Note that analyzer input may also come via a buffer or a stream. In the following table, assume the Windows input file is, e.g., `G("$input")`, with value:

`"D:\dev\analyzers\Resume\input\Dev1\rez.txt"`

Special variable	Type	Description
`$anaspath`	G	Parent folder for the analyzer projects (N-E 2.1.0)
`$apppath`	G	Analyzer's base folder: `D:\dev\analyzers\Resume`
`$kbpath`	G	Base folder path + `\kb\user` folder: `D:\dev\analyzers\Resume\kb\user` (N-E 1.27.0)
`$inputpath`	G	Input path: `D:\dev\analyzers\Resume\input\Dev1`
`$inputparent`	G	Last folder in input file path: `Dev1`, given input file `D:\apps\Resume\input\Dev1\rez.txt` (N-E 1.26.0)
`$input`	G	Input file: `D:\dev\analyzers\Resume\input\Dev1\rez.txt`
`$inputname`	G	Input file name: `rez.txt`
`$inputhead`	G	Input file head: `rez`
`$inputtail`	G	Input file extension: `txt`

Table 2.21: Special file variables

Special parser attributes in the following table provide information about the current parse of a text:

Special variable	Type	Description
`$passnum`	G	Number of the current pass being executed.
`$rulenum`	G	Number of the current rule within the current pass file.

Table 2.22: Special parser variables

The treatment of text is to process a text; it is first placed in a static buffer. That is, the text in the buffer cannot be modified, so that the original text and its offsets can always be referenced. The buffer holds the raw text. At the same time, the analyzer may modify the input text, which affects only the parse tree, not the buffer. Each leaf node holds its own snippet of text, and we refer to the total modified text as the tree text. If a nonleaf node's text is modified, it now holds its own version of the text, and text below it is ignored.

The special attribute named text. In traversing the parse tree to build a text, when the special attribute named text appears on a node, one does not traverse below it. Programmers should modify a node's text attribute only as needed to override the entire text of its subtree.

Examples that fetch the input text:

- **pnvar(pnroot(), "$text")** fetches the entire tree text.
- **pnvar(pnroot(), "$raw")** fetches the entire raw text.
- **inputrange(X("$ostart",1),X("$oend",1))** fetches the raw text, assuming **X(1)** is the root node.

The following are a few things to note:

- **findroot()** fetches the root concept of the hierarchical KB, while **pnroot()** fetches the root node of the parse tree. It is easy to confuse these when programming.
- Each platform (Windows, Linux, Mac) treats the end of line specially, with a varying number of characters. This must be accounted for when computing offsets, e.g., for highlighting snippets of text.
- The cleanup in *Table 2.23* refers to removing leading and trailing whitespace, converting whitespace separation and newlines to single space characters, and the like. This supports cleaner and more readable output of text snippets.

Special text variables provide information about the state of the parse tree.

Special variable	Type	Description
$raw	**N, X**	Raw text of node, not cleaned up
$text	**N, X**	Raw text of node, cleaned up
$treeraw	**N, X**	Parse tree text of node, not cleaned up
$treetext	**N, X**	Parse tree text of node, cleaned up
$xmltext	**N, X**	Same as **$raw**, but convert HTML/XML chars. E.g., **"<" => "<"**
$length	**N, X**	Length of node's **$treeraw** text
$ostart	**N, X**	Start text offset of node in **$raw** text
$oend	**N, X**	End text offset of node in **$raw** text

Table 2.23: Special text variables

Warning: They return zero if a referenced node covers multiple words. Using these variables for the X() context nodes is not useful, in general.

Special letter-case variables in the following table provide information about the uppercase and lowercase text of nodes representing single words:

Special variable	Type	Description
$lowercase	**N, X**	Return 1 if the underlying single token is all lowercase, else 0. Not identical to **lowercase() @PRE** action.
$allcaps	**N, X**	Return 1 if the underlying single token is all-caps, else 0.
$uppercase	**N, X**	Same as **$allcaps**, differs from **$cap**. Not identical to **uppercase() @PRE** action.
$cap	**N, X**	Return 1 if the underlying single token is capitalized, else 0. Not identical to the **cap() @PRE** action.
$mixcap	**N, X**	Return 1 if the underlying single token is mixed-case, else 0.

Table 2.24: Special letter-case variables

Special test variables in the following table check the status and context of parse tree nodes:

Special variable	Type	Description
$start	**N, X**	Return 1 if the referenced node starts its phrase, else 0.
$end	**N, X**	Return 1 if the referenced node ends its phrase, else 0.
$exists	**N**	Return 1 if the referenced node exists, else 0. Checks if at least one node has matched an optional phrase element of a rule.
$unknown	**N, X**	[Obsolete] Return 1 if the token underlying node is an unknown word. Must be preceded by calling the **lookup() @CODE** action. Not identical to the **unknown() @PRE** action.

Table 2.25: Special test variables

The special variables **$uppercase**, **$lowercase**, and **$cap** differ from the analogous **@PRE** actions in that they all traverse down to the leafiest node they can find. The corresponding **@PRE** actions only chain down if the **[s]** or singlet flag is present in the associated phrase element(s). Also, the **$-variables** are not stopped by a base attribute in a node.

Special node references

N, **X**, and **S** variables can, in addition to referring to a node's variables, refer to the node itself. Thus, **N(2)** refers to the first node that matches element **2** of a rule's phrase. **N()** or **N(0)** refers to the last rule element's (first or only) node. Similarly, **X(2)** refers to the second context node in the **@PATH** dominating the current rule. **S()** refers to the suggested concept.

Variable types

NLP++ is a loosely typed language. The same variable can be assigned an integer in one statement and a string in the next, as in the following code example. Type is determined by usage -- there are no type declarations for variables.

```
G("tmp") = 123;
G("tmp") = "abc";
```

Variables can take multiple values, in which case they are called arrays or lists. Each value in an array can be of an arbitrary data type. Array numbering starts at zero (0), i.e., zero-based.

The following statements setup an array with two values:

```
G("tmp")[0] = 123;
G("tmp")[1] = "abc";
```

One can traverse an array by incrementing an iterator variable. For example:

```
L("ii") = 0;
L("val1") = G("tmp")[L("ii")];
L("val2") = G("tmp")[++L("ii")];
```

Data types

NLP++ data types for variables are shown in *Table 2.24*. Numeric overflow and underflow are not flagged. For example, the maximum **`int`** is 9,007,199,254,740,992 (i.e., 2^53 power) and must be checked by the developer as needed.

The following are the lists to note:

- Regarding the Boolean type, NLP++ functions in general use 1 (or nonzero) to represent true, and 0 to represent false. However, some legacy actions use the quoted values true and false as arguments. These include **`setbase()`** and **`setunsealed()`**.
- The following table focuses on KB data types named attribute, value, phrase, and node, which are all associated with KB concepts. The parse tree versions of these are discussed elsewhere at length:

Data type	Abbreviation	Characteristics
String	**`str`**	Sequence of characters, e.g., **`G("name") = "w3c";`**
Integer	**`int`**	52-bit integers, e.g., **`G("num") = 32776;`**
Float	**`float`**	52-bit floating point numbers, e.g., **`G("flt") = 123.456;`**

Data type	Abbreviation	Characteristics
Boolean	`bool`	1 or 0 (Boolean implemented as a numeric nonzero for true and the numeric 0 for false).
Ostream	`ostream`	Output stream `G(filename) << expr`; prints by referring to the `ostream` value of `G(filename)`. See the open file NLP++ function.
Concept	`con`	Concepts are the main objects in the KB. They have string names and optionally one or more attributes, e.g., `G("myConcept") = makeconcept(G("root"),"My Name");`
Attribute	`attr`	Attributes are associated with concepts and KB nodes. They have string names and optionally have one or more values, e.g., `G("myAttribute") = addattr(G("myConcept"),"is");` **Note: Distinct from parse tree node var/attr.**
Value	`val`	Values are the values of KB attributes. They can be strings, numeric, or concepts: e.g., `addconval(G("myConcept"), "is", "John Smith");` **Note: Distinct from the value of a parse tree node's var/attr.**
Phrase	`phr`	A phrase is a sequence of nodes owned by a single concept, not attached to the hierarchy. E.g., create the first node of a phrase: `G("USPhrase") = makephrase(G("US"),"United");` add the last node of the phrase: `addcnode(G("US"), "States");` **Note: Distinct from rewrite rule phrase.**
Node	`node`	KB node belonging to a concept's phrase. Serves as a proxy or instance of a concept. **Note: Distinct from a parse tree node.**
Array	`array`	The values of an array, or multi-valued variable, can be any simple values. **Note: Nested `ARRAY` types are not currently supported.**
Pnode	`pnode`	Parse tree node. Unrelated to a KB node. Formal nomenclature for a parse tree node.

Table 2.26: NLP++ variable data types

Conditional statements

Conditional statements in NLP++ are much like those in C/C++. They include **`if`**, **`else if`**, and **`else`**, which are bounded by curly braces.

The following code is from the function **CopyConAttrs** in the **KBFuncs.nlp** library pass file:

```
if (L("type") == 1) {
    addnumval(L("to"),L("name"),getnumval(L("vals")));
} else if (L("type") == 2) {
    addconval(L("to"),L("name"),getconval(L("vals")));
} else if (L("type") == 3) {
    addnumval(L("to"),L("name"),getfltval(L("vals")));
} else {
    addstrval(L("to"),L("name"),getstrval(L("vals")));
}
```

Loops

Currently, NLP++ includes only the **while** loop construct. Loops are mainly used to iterate through parse tree nodes, KB concepts, attributes, attribute values, arrays, and lists.

The VisualText user interface brings up the autocomplete options in the following figure, when you type **while**:

Figure 2.3: *VisualText Autocomplete for while loop*

The four while loops use an iterator function specific to each type of list object. The following is an example of four types of loops, each with its iterator function (**next**, **pnnext**, **nextattr**, and **nextval**):

```
while (L("con")) {  # KB CONCEPT LIST
    # do something with the concept
    L("con") = next(L("con"));
}
while (L("node")) { # PARSE TREE NODE LIST
    # do something with the node
    L("node") = pnnext(L("node"));
}
while (L("attr")) { # CONCEPT ATTRIBUTE LIST
```

```
        # do something with the concept attribute
        L("attr") = nextattr(L("attr"));
    }
    while (L("val")) { # CONCEPT ATTRIBUTE-VALUE LIST
        # do something with the concept value
        L("val") = nextval(L("val"));
    }
```

Note: **Unfortunately, NLP++ does not currently have analogous parse tree node versions of iterators for attributes and values. These must be copied to arrays and then traversed, as in the next section (Array and list loops). The functions `pnvar`, `pnvarnames`, and `varinlist` do fetch arrays from a parse tree node, as one way to access parse tree attributes and values.**

Array and list loops

The following are the lists that should be noted:

- NLP++ lists and arrays are identical linked list data structures, and nested arrays are not currently implemented. Any discussion of one data structure applies to the other.
- Apart from the special iterators discussed above, NLP++ currently has no explicit iterators for lists of attributes and values in parse tree nodes and in the various variable types (**G**, **L**, **X**, **S**, **N**). Instead, traversal relies on array indexing, which is not optimized, as arrays are implemented as linked lists.

Note that **arraylength** never returns zero (because a variable with 0 value may be an array with 0 as its zero value). The following is an example of iterating through an array:

```
L("len") = arraylength(L("arr"));  # Length always 1 or more.
L("ii") = 0;                       # Zero-based iterator.
while (L("ii") < L("len")) {       # Loop through array ...
  # Do something with nth array element.
  "output.txt" << L("arr")[L("ii")] << "\n";
  ++L("ii");                       # Iterate to next array element.
}
```

Concept loops

When working with the KB, it is common to loop through concepts.

To record sentences in the KB, an analyzer may use the function **MakeCountCon** to construct a series of concepts of the same type, in this case, sentences. In order to keep sentences in sequence, the function **MakeCountCon** (found in the **KBFunc** utility functions pass) automatically creates concepts with numbered suffixes. The following rule creates sentence concepts under an article concept representing the current input text (see *line 2*):

```
1   @POST
2   S("con") = MakeCountCon(G("article"),"sentence");
3   addstrval(S("con"),"text",N("$text",1));
4   single();
5
6   @RULES
7   _sentence <-
8       _xWILD [fail=(_endSent _BLANKLINE)]          ### (1)
9       _xWILD [one match=(_endSent _BLANKLINE)]     ### (2)
10      @@
```

The following code shows the article concept as the NLP entity extraction analyzer progresses (Refer to *Chapter 7, Example Analyzers, NLP entity extraction* section):

```
article
  sentence001: text="Nathalia Ribas…", "person_count"=3
    person001: con=["concept" "people" "Nathalia Ribas"]
    person002: con=["concept" "people" "Eduardo Costa"]
    person003: con=["concept" "people" "David de Hilster"]
  sentence002: text="Nathalia is finishing… ", "person_count"=1
    person001: con=["concept" "caps" "Nathalia Ribas"]
  sentence003: text="Their project improves AI's…"
  sentence004: text="De Hilster is… Initiative", "person_count"=1
    person001: con=["concept" "people" "De Hilster"]
```

Concepts with numeric suffixes also serve as IDs for the **KBFuncs** function **JsonKB**, which converts any KB to an equivalent JSON structure. Here is the article concept in the KB transformed to a JSON object using **JsonKBL**:

```
{
  "article": {
    "sentence": [
      {
        "id": "001",
        "text": "Nathalia Ribas and Eduardo Costa, ...",
        "person_count": "3",
        "person": [
```

```
        {
          "id": "001",
          "con": "concept people Nathalia Ribas"
        },
        {
          "id": "002",
          "con": "concept people Eduardo Costa"
        },
        {
          "id": "003",
          "con": "concept people David de Hilster"
        }
      ]
    },
    {
      "id": "002",
      "text": "Nathalia is finishing her bachelor's …",
      "person_count": "1",
      "person": [
        {
          "id": "001",
          "con": "concept caps Nathalia Ribas"
        }
      ]
    },
    {
      "id": "003",
      "text": "Their project improves AI's …"
    },
    {
      "id": "004",
      "text": "De Hilster is also the founder of the …",
      "person_count": "1",
      "person": [
        {
          "id": "001",
```

```
                "con": "concept people De Hilster"
            }
        ]
    }
  ]
 }
}
```

Parse tree node loops

Looping through parse trees is useful for accessing information gleaned by an analyzer. For instance, the formatted text example analyzer (Refer to *Chapter 7, Example Analyzers, Formatted text analysis* section) traverses the entire tree in the final output pass file. The following example shows functions useful in parse tree node loops. Imagine that the final tree consists of paragraphs with sentences underneath. Note that the parse tree is traversed in order to build concepts in the KB.

```
1   L("para") = pndown(pnroot());      # Paragraphs are under root.
2
3   while (L("para")) {                # Iterate through paragraphs.
4       L("sent") = pndown(L("para")); # Sentence is under paragraph.
5
6       while (L("sent")) {            # Iterate through sentences.
7           L("con") = MakeCountCon(G("sentences"),"sentence");
8           addstrval(L("con"),"text",pnvar(L("sent"),"$text"));
9           L("sent") = pnnext(L("sent"));
10      }
11
12      L("para") = pnnext(L("para"));
13  }
```

In *line 1,* **pndown** retrieves the first child of **pnroot**, the root of the parse tree. The root's children represent paragraphs, in this case. The first **while** loops through the paragraphs (*line 3*). A second **while** loops through the children of each paragraph, sentences in this case.

For each sentence, the code on *line 7* constructs a concept like **sentence001**, **sentence002**, etc., by calling the **KBFuncs** function **MakeCountCon**. On *line 8,* **addstrval** adds a **text** attribute to the sentence concept, whose value is the text of the sentence node.

Note that on *line 8,* the **pnvar** function uses the special variable (or attribute, if you like) **$text** to fetch the text of the sentence node.

Concept attribute loops

To loop through a concept's list of attributes, use the **findattrs** and **nextattr** functions:

```
G("attrList") = findattrs(G("fruit"));

while(G("attrList")) {
    getsval(G("attrList")) << "\n";
    G("attrList") = nextattr(G("attrList"));
}
```

Concept attribute value loops

To loop through values of a concept's attribute, use the **attrvals** and **nextval** functions:

```
G("valList") = attrvals(G("attrList"));

while(G("valList")) {
    L("name") = attrname(G("valList"));
    G("valList") = nextval(G("valList"));
}
```

Recurse region

The following are a few points to be noted:

- Recurse region is a deprecated NLP++ construct, because the context it operates on is more visible and accessible when placed in its own passes. For example, if one roughs out the boundaries of a noun phrase in a top-down approach, more than one pass may create such noun phrases, and more than one pass may then operate within those noun phrases.
- Another drawback is that the context node of a recurse region is not readily available. The **X** variable continues to refer to the **@PATH** or **@NODES** line of the current pass file, and the current parse tree node context needs to be recorded in some way. The rule using a recurse element could setup a **G** or **X** attribute and value to record the matched node as context.
- A recurse region cannot contain a code region or a select line (**@PATH** or **@NODES**). A select line would be meaningless, since the recurse region operates on a phrase specified by the rule element that invokes it.

The recurse region allows the developer to embed multiple passes within a single pass file. Each recurse region acts like an independent pass. However, such a pass can only be invoked from elements of a matched rule. The phrase that the recurse pass operates on is the set of nodes that match an invoking rule element. Here is an example taken from the RFA, which parses the pass files themselves:

```
# Start of recurse region. A name is required.
@RECURSE actionpass

# Start of one rule region within the recurse region.
@RULES
# The pass converts literals (e.g., "single") to actions in context.
_ACTION <- _LIT @@

# End of recurse region. (@@RULES marker is optional).
@@RECURSE
# ....
# A main rule region.
@RULES
    _POSTS [base] <- _soPOST
    _xWILD [matches=(_LIT _ACTION) recurse=(actionpass)]
    _eoPOST [opt] @@ # Simplified rule for @POST actions region.
```

In the above example, when the RFA sees a plain word like **`single`** in a file, it does not know whether to reduce it to an **`_ACTION`** or not. However, within the markers **`@POST`** and **`@@POST`**, the literal should be treated as an action. This allows the parentheses in pass file actions to be optional when the action takes no arguments. For example, **`single()`** and **`single`** are equivalent.

Note: Nowadays, we do not recommend such a loose syntax for function or action calls.

In general, **`@RECURSE`** mini-passes enable a mechanism for roughing out a text and then applying the correct assignments when the context has been determined unambiguously.

Other uses include traversing matched nodes in order to perform cleanups, data gathering, deletions, and so on.

Strings

Strings in NLP++ are designated by double quotes. They are concatenated by using the **+** plus sign operator. To guarantee that a value is a string, use the str function to try to convert it to a string. If the str call fails, NLP++ fails with an error message.

Numbers

Numbers in NLP++ can be integers or floating-point numbers. The size of numbers can be very large, given that NLP++ internals use double-sized C++ variables. This allows for integer numbers up to 9 quintillion (9,007,199,254,740,992) or 2^53.

This is important in today's news articles that often use the word trillion. The following code is part of the dictionary library file for English number words:

```
...
seventy s=number numeric=70
eighty s=number numeric=80
ninety s=number numeric=90
hundred s=number numeric=100
thousand s=number numeric=1000
million s=number numeric=1000000
billion s=number numeric=1000000000
trillion s=number numeric=1000000000000
```

Numbers have the usual operators in NLP++, including **+**, **-**, **/**, and *****. Several math functions are available, as follows:

Math function	Type	Description
abs (num)	**INT**	Returns the absolute value of the passed-in number.
random (from-number, to-number)	**FLOAT**	Returns a number between the two numbers.
mod (number)	**INT**	Returns the modulus of the number.
log10 (num)	**FLOAT**	Returns the **log10** of a number.

Table 2.27: Built-in math functions

The NLP++ **num** function can convert a string like *020* to the number *20*. This is useful for converting number-like strings into actual numbers, as also performed by some tokenizer passes. Note that matched **_xNUM** tokens do not automatically create a numeric attribute, and so their matching text must be explicitly converted to numbers. The following code is an example that uses attributes added by a tokenizer (e.g., **"day"**, **"month"**, **"year"**):

```
@PRE /
<1,1> var("day");
<3,3> var("day");
<4,4> var("month");
<5,5> var("year");
```

```

@POST
S("weekday") = N("day",1);
S("day") = num(N("$text",3));
S("month") = N("month",4);
S("year") = num(N("$text",5));
single();

@RULES
_date <-
    _xALPHA     ### (1)
     [opt]      ### (2)
    _xNUM       ### (3)
    _xALPHA     ### (4)
    _xNUM       ### (5)
    @@
```

Arrays and lists

NLP++ arrays and lists are identical and interchangeable data structures. Nested arrays are not supported. See the section about *Array and list loops*.

Analyzers may store data in the KB, reducing the need to build and store information elsewhere. The KB can also be saved, providing a permanent repository for knowledge. Conversely, some analyzers minimize using the KB in order to seamlessly refresh the runtime environment when processing multiple text inputs.

A nice feature of NLP++ functions is that they can return multiple values via an array. The following example builds an array from scratch and then traverses it. Note that array indexing is zero-based:

```
# Build array.
L("arr")[0] = "red”; # Zero-based.
L("arr")[1] = "orange";
L("len") = arraylength(L("arr")); # Fetch array length.
"array.txt" << "length=" << L("len") << "\n";

L("ii") = 0; # Iterator.
while (L("ii") < L("len”)) {     # While array index is valid...
```

```
    L("val") = L("arr")[L("ii")]; # Fetch indexed array value.
    # Do something with array element.
    "array.txt" << "val" << L("ii") << "=" << L("val") << "\n";
    L("ii")++;                    # Increment array index.
}

# Copy entire array.
L("arr2") = L("arr");    # Assigning an array CREATES A COPY.
L("arr2")[0] = "violet"; # Change value to validate it was copied.

# print both arrays:
"array.txt" << "array=" << L("arr") << "\n";
"array.txt" << "array2=" << L("arr2") << "\n";
```

A trick to initialize an array is an assignment like:

```
L("array")[9] = 0;
```

The array indexes from `0` to `9` will all have the value `0`, as NLP++ initially sets values to zero.

Note: **Make sure this is the case before relying on this in your code.**

Operators

Most NLP++ operators are modeled on the C/C++ programming language. The main addition is the confidence operator, `%`. This enables convenient accumulation of evidence in terms of percentage confidence. The following table shows an operator precedence table, with the highest precedence at the top:

Operator	Description	Associativity
`++ --`	Post increment, decrement	Left to right
`++ --`	Pre increment, decrement	Right to left
`!`	Logical NOT (unary) !0 = 1, !1=0 (no NLP++ boolean type)	Right to left
`+ -`	Unary plus, minus	Right to left
`% * / %%`	Remainder, multiplication, division, and special confidence operator	Left to right
`+ -`	Addition, subtraction	Left to right
`< > <= == != >=`	Relational operators	Left to right

Operator	Description	Associativity
`&& ||`	Logical AND, OR	Left to right
`=`	Assignment	Right to left (multiple assignment works)
`*= /= += -= %%=`	Shorthand assignment (unimplemented)	Right to left
`<<`	Output operator	Left to right

Table 2.28: NLP++ operators

Output operator

The **<<** output operator is modeled on the C++ operator. Only the following form is supported, currently:

```
filename << expression << expression .... ;
```

For example:

```
"output.txt" << "Hello, NLP++!" << "\n";
```

The following are a few points to be noted:

- The file named by filename should have been created by a prior **fileout(filename)** code action. If that has not been done, then the output operator will create the global variable **G(filename)** with the output stream as its value. The default output mode for the file is append, which cannot be modified by the user at present. Also, the default output folder is the **log** folder for the current input file -- also not under user control at present.
- The **openfile()** and **closefile()** functions offer a second way to setup file streams, enabling a full file path to be specified.

Confidence operator

Say you have 80% confidence that a parse tree node is a name. You could write this into a global variable as:

```
G("name confidence") = 80;
```

Now, you want to account for a new piece of corroborating evidence. Say the standalone confidence of that evidence is 70%. You could combine both estimates as:

```
G("name confidence") = G("name confidence") %% 70;
```

This yields a new percent confidence between 80% and 100%.

The **%%** operator guarantees that adding or subtracting confidence always stays within the range of 0 to +100, providing an intuitive way to gather evidence and compare confidences using a single scale of measurement. A future NLP++ update may use a range of -100 to +100, which would allow 100% confidence against something.

Conclusion

This chapter described the NLP++ pipeline architecture and programming language in detail. In addition to the constructs of C++ like languages, NLP++ integrally addresses the pass files of the pipeline, the grammar rules and parse trees under construction, and the KB structures accessed and built during the analysis of a text.

NLP++ variable types, functions, and actions must encompass the many contexts required for a comprehensive NLP architecture.

In the next chapter, special NLP++ topics are explored, including recursion, KBs, and dictionaries, as well as the handling of Unicode, emojis, and the special needs of languages such as Chinese.

True or false

1. NLP++ is the only programming language specifically designed for text and NLP.
2. NLP++ is tied to a specific type of natural language processing.
3. The name and code syntax of NLP++ is inspired by C++.
4. The pancake model inspired the creation of the analyzer sequence.
5. Each analyzer pass can be seen as a YACC or Bison grammar with its code actions.
6. The pipeline architecture of NLP++ is considered to be flexible.
7. Tokenization is not a required pass in an NLP++ analyzer.
8. The analyzer.seq file can be edited by hand or is automatically edited by VisualText.
9. A @PATH and @NODES context can occur in the same NLP file.
10. A @DECL region cannot be in the same file as a @CODE or @RULES region.
11. In a @RULES region, more than one rule can share a @POST region.
12. The attributes for a rule element are called rule element modifiers.
13. There are less than 12 element modifiers in NLP++.
14. The name "group" denotes an element modifier and an action in the @POST region.
15. A rule reduction can be made by using single, singler, singlex, or group.
16. The "splice" action is a type of reduction.

17. The @PRE region is executed after matching all the phrase elements.
18. NLP++ has a REGEX-like function available in the @PRE region.
19. In the @PRE region, var checks to see if a node has a particular attribute.
20. There are 6 types of variables in NLP++.
21. All special variable names are quoted and start with a $.
22. The largest integer allowed in NLP++ is 9,007,199,254,740,992.
23. There are 10 data types in NLP++.
24. Boolean is a valid data type in NLP++.
25. Conditions in NLP++ include if, else if, and else.
26. There are for loops in NLP++.
27. A recursive pass is invoked up to 10 times and then it is aborted.
28. Using succeed and fail in a recursive pass is one way to control recursion.
29. .kb and .kbb files can be edited safely by hand.
30. The dictionary is stored in the KB under concept/sys/dict.
31. The repository dehilster-analyzers under the VisualText GitHub repository contains examples of NLP++ dictionaries and KBs.

Answers

1. True	2. False	3. True
4. False	5. True	6. True
7. False	8. True	9. False
10. False	11. True	12. True
13. False	14. True	15. True
16. False	17. False	18. True
19. True	20. False	21. True
22. True	23. False	24. False
25. True	26. False	27. False
28. True	29. False	30. True
31. True		

Multiple choice questions

1. **Which of the following are NOT advantages of NLP++:**
   a. It includes neural networks and machine learning algorithms
   b. It supports rule-based and knowledge-based methods
   c. It is the only programming language built specifically for NLP
   d. It must include rules as part of all analyzers
   e. Integrates multiple paradigms in a monolithic pipeline architecture
2. **Which of the following are not part of the pancake analogy for the NLP++ pipeline:**
   a. Convenience to insert new logic where needed.
   b. After tokenizing, the rigid requirements for placement of passes.
   c. The modularity of any pass in the analyzer sequence.
3. **Which of the following are not advantages of the NLP++ architecture**:
   a. Integration
   b. Modularity, extensibility, maintainability
   c. Flexibility
   d. Use of statistical methods
   e. Feedback, deferral
4. **Choose all the valid NLP++ tokenizer passes:**
   a. chartok
   b. cmltok
   c. dicttok
   d. dicttokz
   e. token
5. **Which of these is not a type in the analyzer.seq file:**
   a. folder
   b. tmp
   c. nlp
   d. end
   e. rec
6. **Choose all regions that are not part of a pass file:**
   a. @PRE
   b. @RECURSE
   c. @NODE
   d. @PATH
   e. @RULE

7. **Which rule modifiers are not part of NLP++:**
   a. o
   b. equals
   c. expects
   d. s
   e. nest
8. **Which are not valid special rule elements:**
   a. _xNIL
   b. _xCAPLET
   c. _xEOF
   d. _xANY
   e. _xPLUS
9. **Which are not reduced actions:**
   a. setlookahead
   b. singlem
   c. singler
   d. singlex
   e. singlezap
   f. merge
10. **Which of these are part of the rule region:**
   a. @NODES
   b. @PRE
   c. @DECL
   d. @CHECK
   e. @CODE
   f. @POST
11. **Which of these functions is not limited to the @CHECK region:**
   a. exitpass
   b. fail
   c. succeed
12. **Which one of these is not a special variable:**
   a. $length
   b. $end
   c. $treeraw
   d. $ostart
   e. $islastfolder
13. **The global special variable $islastfile:**
   a. Returns true if the current file is the last in a folder
   b. Tests to see if a pass file name is the last in the folder
   c. Is used when the NLP engine is at the last file of a batch of folders and files
   d. Returns the last file name in a given folder

14. **Which data type is not part of NLP++:**

    a. Integer b. String

    c. Boolean d. Float

15. **Which group of functions is not found in NLP++:**

    a. Math functions b. Graphic functions

    c. Spelling functions d. String functions

16. **Which types of next are there when using while loops in NLP++:**

    a. Concept b. Phrase

    c. Node d. Attribute

17. **Which is not an iterator function in NLP++:**

    a. pnnext b. arraynext

    c. nextattr d. next

18. **Recursive passes are:**

    a. Executed up to 10 times before they are aborted

    b. Not detectable ahead of time by the NLP engine

    c. Executed repeatedly on specified contexts until no rules match

    d. Are not allowed in NLP++

19. **Which of these file types is not specific to NLP++:**

    a. .kb files b. .kbb files

    c. .dict files d. .txt files

20. **Which tokenizers work with the KB and dictionary files:**

    a. token b. dicttok

    c. chartok d. dicttokz

Answers

1. a d	2. b	3. d
4. a b c d e	5. b	6. c e
7. b c	8. e	9. b
10. b d f	11. a	12. e
13. b	14. c	15. b

16. a c d	17. b	18. c
19. d	20. b d	

Short answer questions

1. Describe NLP++ and its unique qualities.
2. Describe what one NLP++ user called the pancake model.
3. Explain what is meant by feedback and deferral in the NLP++ architecture.
4. Describe the analyzer.seq file and its use.
5. Describe the difference between the @PATH and @NODES regions.
6. Explain how a @RULES region can have more than one rule.
7. Explain the special rule elements that deal with capitalization.
8. Define the terms reduce or reduction in the NLP++ rule system.
9. Explain the unsealed attribute for the suggested rule element.
10. Explain the singlet and base attributes for phrase elements.
11. List the order of execution of these regions: @RULES, @POST, @PRE, @CHECK
12. In general, the @CHECK region is used for what purpose?
13. List the five types of variables in NLP++ and their purpose.
14. Describe the $treetext, $treeraw, and $raw special variables.
15. Describe how one can process a folder of files using the NLP engine and display the final KB when the last folder is processed.
16. Explain how one can loop through the attributes and values of a concept using nested while loops.
17. Create an example text that would benefit from a recursive pass.
18. Describe ways to break out of an analyzer that hangs (in an infinite loop).
19. Explain how NLP++ can be used to create a dictionary and KB files.

CHAPTER 3
NLP++ Topics

Introduction

Recursive grammars constitute a critical tool for text analysis. NLP++ allows for any number of recursive passes in order to strictly control and constrain the recursive algorithm.

Dictionary, **knowledge base** (**KB**), and mod files provide the information needed for accurate and complete text analysis.

The enhanced Unicode handling of NLP++ supports processing languages such as Chinese and special character sets such as emojis.

Structure

In this chapter, we will be covering the following topics:

- Recursion
- Special files
- Unicode handling
- Special language functions

Objectives

By the end of this chapter, the reader will learn about NLP++ recursive passes, required information files (i.e., dictionaries and KB files), and handling of world-wide character sets such as Chinese, via Unicode.

Recursion

Recursion is a well-known concept in computer science, in which a function can call itself. In fact, any computer programming language that has functions can create recursive functions. This is true for NLP++.

However, there is another type of recursion in NLP++: the recursive pass. The rules in such a pass are called repeatedly until no rule fires, resulting in a recursive grammar. In fact, a single rule can be constructed so as to match a nested text format repeatedly. A rule can create a new parse tree node that is then matched by another rule in the same pass, repeatedly. A text with nested headers is one example that can benefit from recursion. Natural languages naturally include recursive constructs, such as nested clauses within a single sentence. A bit of extra care is needed when coding in recursive passes. Refer to the *Writing rules in the recursive pass* section.

Marking a recursive pass

To make a pass recursive, simply right-click on that pass and choose **Recursive**, as shown in the following figure:

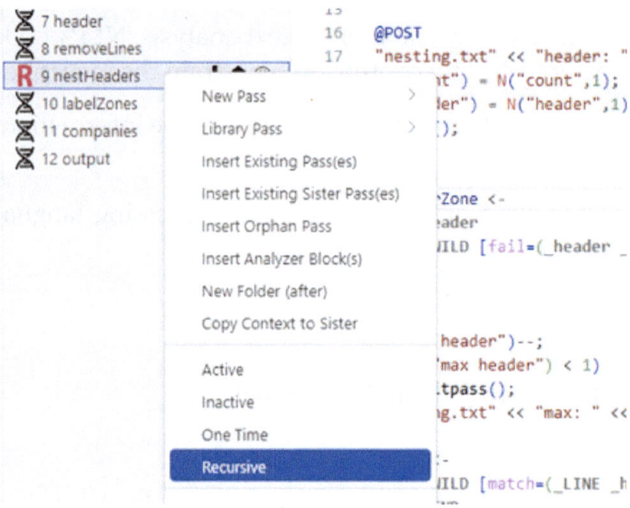

***Figure 3.1:** Making a pass recursive*

When you do this, the DNA icon changes to a red capital letter **R**.

Parsing recursive text

We reference *Tutorial 3* on the VisualText NLP++ YouTube channel to learn about recursion in NLP++ (see **https://youtu.be/UoaPSf5kL94**).

Markdown text

Our sample text is a markdown file that includes nested headers. Our NLP++ analyzer converts those to nested tree structures in the parse tree. The following is the text:

```
# John G. Doe

johngdoe@fakeitall.com

```

```
## Overview
I am a computer programmer.
## Experience
### Company Not
- Blogger, 2019 to 2020
- Manager, 2020 to present
### Fakery Inc.
- Janitor, 2016 to 2018
- Programmer, 2018 to 2019
```

In markdown files, headers are designated by pound signs (**#**), and the number of pound signs signifies the header's nesting level. One pound sign is header 1, two is header 2, etc.

The text has three levels of headers. Ideally, a single rule would handle any nesting level.

Analyzer sequence

The following table lists the analyzer sequence for the *Tutorial 3* parser:

Number	Pass	Description
1	`tokenize`	Convert input to token list
2	`init`	Initialize the KB
3	`KBFuncs`	Load library of KB functions
4	`Lines`	Process input lines
5	`RemoveWhiteSpace`	Remove whitespace from input
6	`RemoveBlankLines`	Remove blank lines from input
7	`header`	Process markdown headers
8	`removeLines`	Remove the line parse nodes that are no longer needed
9	`nestHeaders`	Process header recursively
10	`labelZones`	Label text zones
11	`companies`	Identify company names
12	`output`	Generate output

***Table 3.1:** Tutorial 3 analyzer sequence*

Next, we examine some important passes in this analyzer.

Header pass

The **header** pass contains one rule that handles all levels of headers, as shown in the following:

```
1  ##############################################
2  # FILE: header
3  # SUBJ: comment
4  # AUTH: David de Hilster
5  # CREATED:  2022-08-29 11:30:3
6  # MODIFIED: 2025-09-09 AM.
7  ##############################################
8
9  @NODES _LINE
10
11 @POST
12 X("header") = 1;
13 S("header") = N("$text",2);
14 S("count")  = strlength(N("$text",1));
15 if (S("count") > G("max header")) {
16   G("max header") = S("count");
17 }
18
19 "header.txt" << L("header") << " " << str(S("count")) << "\n";
20 single();
21
22 @RULES
23 _header <-
24    _xWILD [min=1 match=(\#)  gp=_HASH]  ### (1)
25    _xWILD [plus fail=(_xEND) gp=_TEXT]  ### (2)
26    @@
```

The context line (*line* 9 above) finds every line node (**_LINE**) in the parse tree.

The rule starting on *line* 23 has two phrase elements. If the rule fires (or succeeds), it puts the matched nodes under a new node named **_header**. Phrase element 1 (*line* 24) matches one or more pound sign (**#**) nodes and groups these under a new node named **_HASH**. Phrase element 2 (*line* 25) matches everything after the pound signs to the end of the line, grouping these under a new node named **_TEXT**.

Note: That `min=1` and plus both mean 1 or more.

Once a header is matched, the **`@POST`** actions do several things:

- Mark the **`_LINE`** context node (from *line 9*) as a header (*line 12*).
- Save the header text onto the **`_header`** parse node (*line 13*).
- Save the level of the header by counting the pound signs (*line 14*).
- If the header level is the highest so far, update the global variable *max header* (*line 15* and *line 16*). This will be important for our recursive pass.

> **Note: An NLP++ variable starts with a value of 0 if unset.**

Again, it is important that the header pass can match any level of header. The only other way is to make a rule for every header level, requiring that we know the maximum nesting of headers in advance. Such a header pass might look like:

```
@RULES
_header1 <= \# xWILD [plus fail=(_xEND)] @@
_header2 <= \# \# xWILD [plus fail=(_xEND)] @@
_header3 <= \# \# \# xWILD [plus fail=(_xEND)] @@
_header4 <= \# \# \# \# xWILD [plus fail=(_xEND)] @@
...
```

Subsequent to this pass, the analyzer would need a separate pass for each header level, ordered from the highest to the lowest, which would be tedious and inefficient.

Nested headers pass

To take advantage of the recursive pass in NLP++, we must do two things. First, we match the highest-level headers and work our way down. Then we terminate the recursion.

Examine the two rules of the **`nestHeaders`** analyzer pass in the following:

```
@NODES _ROOT

@CHECK
if (N("count",1) == G("max header"))
       succeed();
fail();

@POST
```

```
"nesting.txt" << "header: " << N("count",1)  << " "
                               << N("header",1) << "\n";
S("count")  = N("count", 1);
S("header") = N("header",1);
single();

@RULES
_headerZone <-
      _header                                               ### (1)
      _xWILD [plus fail=(_headerZone _header _xEND)]        ### (2)
      @@

@POST
G(“max header”)--;
if (G("max header") < 1)
      exitpass();
"nesting.txt" << "max: " << G("max header") << "\n";
@RULES
_xNIL <-
      _xWILD [plus match=(_LINE _headerZone)]         ### (1)
      _xEND                                           ### (2)
      @@
############################################################################
```

Recursive algorithm

Recursion works in a surprising way. When a rule match succeeds, rule matching restarts at the beginning of the current context (**_ROOT** of the parse tree, in the above pass). Recursion stops, and the pass exits when traversing the entire context fails to match any rule.

It is because this is a recursive pass; it is usual for the rules to work from the deepest nesting (or bottom) up to the shallowest (or top). In this case, we match the highest-numbered headers first, down to the lowest level.

The first rule matches two elements:

- A **_header** node
- Anything up to the next header or end of the context (**_xEND**)

To match only the current header level, this rule uses a **@CHECK** action (*line* 2 to *line* 5). If the rule succeeds, we record the level (*line* 8) and header text (*line* 9), then reduce to a **_headerZone** (*line 10* and *line* 12). Then we continue matching at the start of the current context.

The first rule recursively matches all the headers at the current nesting level. When none remain, the second rule matches the last part of the context (**_xEND**), which is either a **_LINE** or a **_headerZone**. It then decrements the header level. If zero, then all levels have been handled, and the pass is exited (*lines 18 and 19*). Otherwise, because this rule succeeded, recursion continues at the next lower nesting level, starting again at the beginning of the context.

The recursive pass operations are tracked by outputting to the debug file **nesting.txt**:

```
header: 3 Company Not
header: 3 Fakery Inc.
max: 2
header: 2 Overview
header: 2 Experience
max: 1
header: 1 John G. Doe
```

The tree resulting from pass 9 looks like:

***Figure 3.2**: Tree resulting from recursive pass 9*

Note: Tutorial 3 assumes that headers are followed by at least one _LINE node. A challenging exercise is to modify the nestHeaders recursive pass to handle empty headers, i.e., those followed only by a _header, _headerZone, or end of the context region (_xEND).

Writing rules in recursive passes

In recursive passes, the developer must take extra care in order to guard against infinite grammar loops. For example, matching the simple rule in the following causes an infinite loop:

```
@POST
  single();
@RULES
  _np <- _noun [s] @@
```

The culprit here is the **[s]** or singlet element modifier. The first time the rule matches, it creates an **_np** node. It then matches a second time (and beyond), because **[s]** tells the pattern matcher to look down the singlet chain under the new **_np** node, where it again finds and matches the **_noun** node underneath. The successful match layers a second **_np** node as parent of the first **_np** node, and so on, indefinitely. Some ways to forestall such loops are:

- Use the base suggested element modifier. Change the above example to:

```
@POST
  single();
@RULES
  _np [base] <- _noun [s] @@   # SENTINEL
```

  Here, the recursive pattern matcher does not search under the **_np** node the second time around, because **_np** is now the base, or bottom, of a singlet chain. It tells the pattern matcher: *stop here, do not try to match below me.*

- Check a flag on the suggested node. In the following rule, a **@PRE** action finds the **loop_guard** variable on the **_np** node, causing the match to fail the second time around (and so on). In this way, the rule only reduces **_noun** once, as intended.

```
@PRE
<1,1> varz("loop_guard"); # SENTINEL.
@POST
  ++S("loop_guard");         # SENTINEL.
  single();
@RULES
  _np <- _noun [s] @@
```

- Match and reduce multi-element phrases, as these terminate the singlet chain search (which stops when a branch, or node with multiple children, is found). Note that at least two of the phrase elements must be matched. In all cases, we recommend using code comments to warn that this is the sentinel, or guard, against an infinite loop.

- Minimize the use of `[s]` in recursive passes, when feasible.

Breaking out of infinite loops

The NLP engine tries its best to detect recursion and stop the process flow, but occasionally, the analyzer gets into an infinite loop, and the user must break out of it.

If the NLP engine detects what it thinks is an infinite loop, it prints out an error message in the Logging window:

`Possible infinite loop.`

To abort an infinite loop, the user can try the **Cancel** button in the **Analyzer: Running...** pop-up in the bottom right of the VisualText window. Clicking on the **Cancel** button attempts to stop the **`nlp.exe`** process from running. This could take a few seconds to stop. Refer to the following figure:

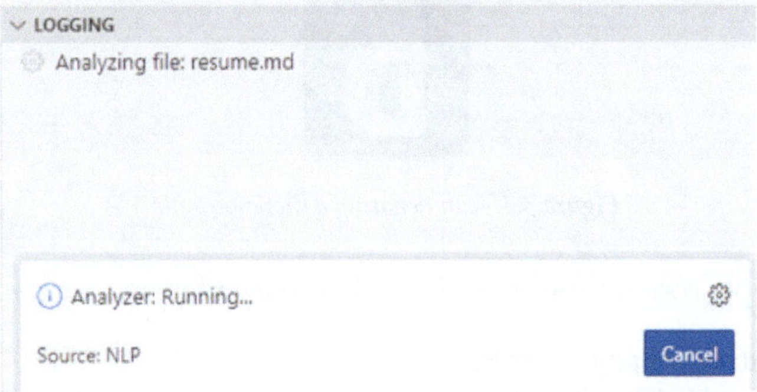

Figure 3.3: *Clicking on cancel in VisualText attempts to kill the nlp.exe process*

If clicking the **Cancel** button does not work, open a system list of the running processes and kill the active **`nlp.exe`** process. The method differs in Windows, Linux, and macOS.

Special files

Recent additions to NLP++ include the .dict files, a line-oriented format for lexical dictionaries, and the .kbb files, which use indentation to represent descending layers of the knowledge hierarchy. With a text editor (or a special-purpose analyzer), one can create both .dict dictionaries and .kbb knowledge bases for NLP++ analyzers.

Dictionary and KB files in the **`kb/user`** folder of an analyzer (created and seen in the KB view of VisualText) are loaded into the KB if the analyzer uses any tokenizer that starts with dict, including:

- **`dicttok`**
- **`dicttokz`**

If these tokenizers are not used, the analyzer does not load the dictionary or KB files.

Dictionaries

Dictionaries in NLP++ are located in the *sys* part of the KB hierarchy, under the concept *dict*. In the first VisualText IDE, dictionaries were loaded and saved using **.kb** command files. In 2022, *David de Hilster* created a more human-readable version of dictionaries, distinguished by the **.dict** file extension.

Dictionary files

Dictionaries files (**.dict**) allow developers to easily add words, phrases, and attributes for use in NLP++ analyzers. VisualText represents them with a book icon:

Figure 3.4: Icon denoting a dictionary file

The following is sample content for an NLP++ dictionary file:

```
1   # Contents: dictionary sample
2   are root=be pos=verb
3   of s=prep
4   # This is another comment
5   prime number full="math term"
6   natural language processing l=nlp
```

Each dictionary entry occupies one line. The entry starts at the first character and ends if an attribute-value pair is encountered, or at the end of the line. An attribute-value pair has the form **attr=value** (Extra whitespace separators may not be handled). An entry is not limited to alphabetic characters.

The following table lists a description of each of the lines in the above file:

Line	Dictionary line	Description
1	**Content**: dictionary sample	The first line should be a descriptive comment.
2	**are root=be pos=verb**	This is a typical one-word dictionary entry for the word **are**, with attributes and values. **pos** is a special attribute (see following table).

Line	Dictionary line	Description
3	**of s=prep**	The special s or suggested attribute creates a suggested node (**_prep**) and puts the entry text node(s) under it. Node name = "_" + attr value.
4	This is another comment	Comments are located anywhere in the file.
5	Prime number **full="math term"**	Attribute values can contain spaces, special characters, and numbers, within double quotes. Builds **_phrase** node automatically for a multi-word entry.
6	Natural language processing **l=nlp**	This uses the special **l** or literal attribute that creates a literal node (i.e., with no underscore). This basically creates a literal word and places the entry underneath.

Table 3.2: Sample dictionary items with descriptions

Let us apply the above dictionary file to the following text.

```
are of prime number natural language processing
```

The resulting parse tree is in *Table 3.3*. Running the sample dictionary file in *Table 3.2* on the text line above yields the parse tree nodes in the following table. The word *are* gets the attributes in *line 2* above. Actually, the special **pos** attribute adds **verb=1** and increments **pos num**, as seen in the following table. The word *of* is placed below **_prep** due to the special suggested (or **s**) attribute (*line 3*). The multi-word dictionary line *prime number* automatically gets a **_phrase** node built for it (*line 5*). The new "nlp" nonleaf word node is built automatically by the special literal attribute (*line 6*).

Node	Attributes
are	[0,2,0,2,0,0,alpha, ("NOSP" 1) ("lower" 1) ("root" "be") ("verb" 1) ("pos num" 1)]
_prep	[4,5,4,5,0,0,node, ("SP" 1) ("NL" 1) ("lower" 1)]
of	[4,5,4,5,0,0,alpha, ("SP" 1) ("NL" 1) ("lower" 1)]
_phrase	[7,18,7,18,0,0,node, ("SP" 1) ("NL" 1) ("lower" 1) ("full" "math term")]
prime	[7,11,7,11,0,0,alpha, ("SP" 1) ("NL" 1) ("lower" 1)]
number	[13,18,13,18,0,0,alpha, ("SP" 1) ("lower" 1)]
nlp	[20,46,20,46,0,0,node, ("SP" 1) ("NL" 1) ("lower" 1)]
natural	[20,26,20,26,0,0,alpha, ("SP" 1) ("NL" 1) ("lower" 1)]
language	[28,35,28,35,0,0,alpha, ("SP" 1) ("lower" 1)]
processing	[37,46,37,46,0,0,alpha, ("SP" 1) ("lower" 1)]

Table 3.3: Output tree from the dictionary demo file

Dictionary KB location

The dictionary is located in the conceptual grammar hierarchical KB path:

```
concept sys dict
```

Where concept is the root of the hierarchy, sys is its child, and **dict** holds the dictionary subhierarchy. It goes without saying that users should avoid directly modifying the structure of the **sys**, or system-internal, subhierarchy. NLP++ provides built-in functions **addword()** and the equivalent **dictgetword()** to find or add entries to the dictionary. As for attributes, one should check those already present before modifying them. The parse-en-us analyzer's dictionary has only a **pos** attribute, representing a word's possible parts of speech.

The dictionary subsystem uses indexing concepts and hash tables to speed dictionary lookup. Embedding the dictionary within the KB enables words to be treated as full-fledged concepts and allows vocabulary to be added dynamically when analyzing text.

Note: All `.dict` files update the same internal dictionary.

One can dump the entire KB using the **KBFuncs DisplayKB** function with the **findroot()** function in NLP++. This looks like:

```
DisplayKB(findroot(),2);
```

The following is a partial KB dump using the date-time analyzer (discussed in *Chapter 7, Example Analyzers*), obtained by adding the above **DisplayKB** command to the final pass file:

```
concept
  gram
  sys
    vals
    nlp
    mean
    dict
      a
        A
          A
        Z
        a
          a
          aa
          ab
          ac
```

```
            acdt: timezone=1, sign="+", hour=10, min=30, descr="Australian Central Daylight Saving Time"
            acst: timezone=1, sign="+", hour=9, min=30, descr="Australian Central Standard Time"
            act: timezone=1, sign="-", hour=5, ambig=2, descr="Acre Time"
            acwst: timezone=1, sign="+", hour=8, min=45, descr="Australian Central Western Standard Time (unofficial)"
```

As noted, indentation represents the descending levels of the CG hierarchical KB. In the above, we see that the dictionary is located under the path **concept/sys/dict**. Below that are folders for each English letter. Under **dict** is a subhierarchy specific to indexing English words. Under each letter are subhierarchies for the first two letters of a word. An analogous scheme can support other languages.

Looking at the **.dict** files used by the date-time analyzer, we find a dictionary for timezones, as shown in detail in the following code:

```
# Timezone Abbreviations
acdt timezone=1 sign=+ hour=10 min=30 descr="Australian Central Daylight Saving Time"
acst timezone=1 sign=+ hour=9 min=30 descr="Australian Central Standard Time"
act timezone=1 sign=- hour=5 ambig=2 descr="Acre Time"
acwst timezone=1 sign=+ hour=8 min=45 descr="Australian Central Western Standard Time (unofficial)"
adt timezone=1 sign=- hour=3 descr="Atlantic Daylight Time"
```

Knowledge base

The backbone of a conceptual grammar KB is a hierarchy of concepts. A concept is a data structure with attributes and values, as well as pointers to other concepts. Unlike a parse tree, the KB is a permanent store for information. The **.kbb** files used in the latest version of VisualText offer a flexible, human-readable format for representing information.

The root concept of the KB is named concept. The top levels of the hierarchy (i.e., the children of the root concept) hold dictionaries, phrases, system knowledge, domain subhierarchies, and the like.

Knowledge base file

The main file extension for KB files is **.kbb** (KB Beautiful), and the icon for the KB files in VisualText is a human head (refer to the following figure):

Figure 3.5: Icon denoting a KB file

The first versions of NLP++ introduced **.kb** KB files, which used a command language for adding concepts, attributes, and dictionaries to a KB. These were designed by *Amnon Meyers* and were not meant to be manually edited. Rather, one created a KB by reading information via text analyzers, then saving the KB to **.kb** files. Often, a series of analyzers is used to mix in various information sources within a single KB. For example, one analyzer builds a dictionary and a second adds in medical domain knowledge. A KB editor in VisualText offered a powerful way to view the active KB.

In the early 2020s, when *David de Hilster* created the NLP++ Language Extension for VS Code, no analogous KB editor was available, and VS Code limitations necessitated another approach to viewing the KB. To display the state of the KB, David added functions to output a KBB file from any analyzer pass file.

As discussed, the KBB file format consists of one line per concept and its attributes. Increased indentation of a line signifies a deeper level in the concept hierarchy. Syntax and special attributes are introduced in an earlier section. Files in the original **kb** command line format are still used for core parts of the KB hierarchy.

The KB display functions are in the **KBFuncs.nlp** file, as listed in the following table:

Library function	Description
DisplayKB	Dump the state of the KB at an analyzer pass. In the analyzer sequence, the head icon indicates a pass with a KBB file.
SaveKB	Create a KBB file in the output area. Available to other analyzers and KB libraries.

Table 3.4: KB display functions in KBFuncs.nlp file

The call to **DisplayKB** creates a file named **anaNNN.kbb**, where **NNN** is the pass number in the analyzer sequence. A pass with a KBB is displayed in the following figure:

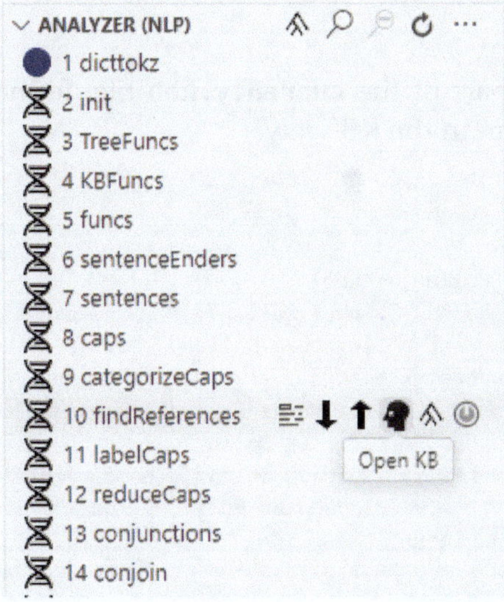

Figure 3.6: Analyzer sequence pass with open KB icon

KB concepts

As designed, the conceptual grammar allows concepts to point to other concepts, in order to support knowledge graphs, beyond the basic CG knowledge hierarchy.

In a KBB file, concept attributes consist of an attribute followed by a concept path. The concept path consists of a square-bracketed list of double-quoted concepts, as in the following example.

In the NLP Fix "nlp" analyzer, we find a concept named **article** whose children are **sentence** concepts that record each person within them. In the KBB file, the **article** concept, as shown in the following figure:

```
article
  sentence001: text="Nathalia Ribas and Eduardo Costa, two programmers from E
    person001: con=["concept" "people" "Nathalia Ribas"]
    person002: con=["concept" "people" "Eduardo Costa"]
    person003: con=["concept" "people" "David de Hilster"]
  sentence002: text="Nathalia is finishing her bachelor's degree at Santa Cat
    person001: con=["concept" "caps" "Nathalia Ribas"]
  sentence003: text="Their project improves AI's understanding of Portuguese,
  sentence004: text="De Hilster is also the founder of the Natural Language L
    person001: con=["concept" "people" "De Hilster"]
```

Figure 3.7: KBB example of concepts pointing to other concepts

The **con** attributes link to concepts under the **people** concept in the knowledge base. This example was generated by the DisplayKB function, but these files can also be manually constructed or constructed by a separate NLP++ analyzer.

KBB example

The following figure shows part of the **currency.kbb** file, found under the **Miscellaneous Libraries** right-click menu item in the KB view:

```
nlpfix-analyzers > nlp > kb > user > currency.kbb
1  # Currency symbols
2  currency
3    $: name=[dollar,escudo]
4      BND: currency="Brunei Dollar", country=Brunei
5      SGD: currency="Singapore Dollar", country=Singapore
6      USD: currency="United States Dollar", country="Timor-Leste"
7      CVE: currency="Cape Verde Escudo", country="Cabo Verde"
8      LRD: currency="Liberian Dollar", country=Liberia
9      NAD: currency="Namibian Dollar", country=Namibia
10     ZWD: currency="Zimbabwean Dollar", country=Zimbabwe
11   Ar: name=ariary
12     MGA: currency="Malagasy Ariary", country=Madagascar
13   CF: name=franc
14     KMF: currency="Comorian Franc", country=Comoros
15   CFA: name=cfa
16     XOF: currency="West African CFA", country=[Benin,"Burkina Fa
17   D: name=dalasi
18     GMD: currency="Gambian Dalasi", country=Gambia
```

***Figure 3.8**: Part of the KBB file for currency names in English*

The KBB file is a hierarchical structure, and indentation is used to distinguish the hierarchical structure, much like Python. Each line represents one concept. The first word or words represent the concept name, which is delineated by end-of-line (*line* 2 above) or a colon. If present, a colon separates the concept name from its attributes (*line* 3).

An attribute comprises the attribute name, an equal sign, and the attribute value. A multi-word value is enclosed in double quotes (*line* 4); otherwise, no quotes are needed (*line* 4).

Creating dictionaries and KBs with NLP++

Many of the library files for dictionaries and KBs are created using NLP++ itself, in what the authors call bootstrapping.

David de Hilster has archived NLP++ analyzers that create various library dictionaries and KBs. The repository is located at:

https://github.com/VisualText/dehilster-analyzers

Folders under this repository, listed in the following table, contain bootstrapping NLP++ analyzers. Associated **README** files link to authoritative internet knowledge and data sources:

Repository	Bootstrap analyzers
`Dictionaries`	`Countries, Currencies, Emoji, FamilyEnglish, FunctionWords, HumanNames, ISOCountries, ISOLanguages, Surnames, TLDs, TelCountryCodes, TwentyThouNames, Wiki`
`KBs`	`PostalSecondaryDesig, PostalDtreetSuffix`
`pt (Portuguese)`	`ConjugSite, DicioLookup, Enderecos, Estados, GenDict, Lograouro, NomesHumanos, Numeros, Pronouns, kb`
`Misc`	`Timezones`

Table 3.5: Repositories for bootstrapping analyzers

Mod files

Module files or **modular files** (**mod files**) bundle together both rule files and KB files, allowing for easy creation and loading. They are built as follows:

1. Right-click on an item in the KB view and choose **Create Mod File**.
2. Type the name of the mod file. It appears in the KB view.
3. Add files by choosing **Add to Mod File** in either the sequence view, the KB view, or the text view.
4. Or, add a file by clicking on its inline mod file icon.
5. Once the **Add to Mod File** command is invoked, the developer can pick a target mod file in the KB view, followed by selecting files to add to it.
6. To load a mod file, import it into the KB view, then right-click on **Load Mod File**.

   For the above steps, refer to the following figure:

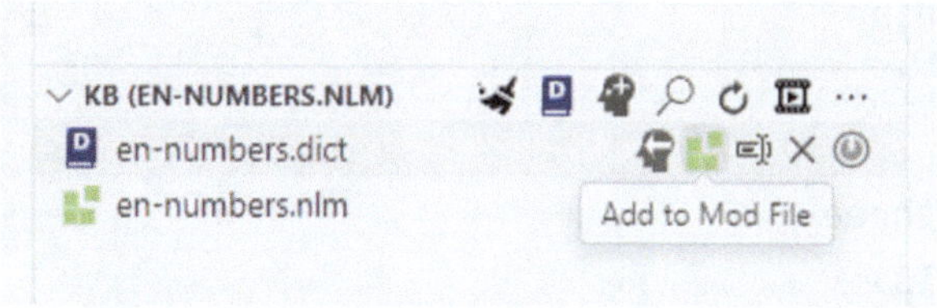

Figure 3.9: Adding files to a mod file in the KB view

Mod files have the extension `.nlm` and contain headers that identify a file and its location, as well as the actual file content. The headers serve to separate each file. In the following code, *lines 2, 12,* and *29* show the separation headers that are automatically added when using the right-click menus in the text view, analyzer view, and KB view.

```
# Convert words to numbers
<modfile kb\user\en-numbers.dict>
# Number words with numeric values

one s=number numeric=1
two s=number numeric=2
three s=number numeric=3
...
million s=number numeric=1000000 power=4
billion s=number numeric=1000000000 power=5
trillion s=number numeric=1000000000000 power=6
<modfile input\numbers.txt>
one
four
ninety seven
eighty-five
seven hundred trillion and three
twenty-nine hundred million
two hundred seven billion four hundred fifteen million
   thirty-nine thousand eight hundred and forty-nine
eight-nine trillion six hundred twenty billion nine
   hundred ninety-nine million and three
six hundred fifty-six thousand seven hundred and ninety-two
nineteen hundred and fifty-nine
nineteen fifty nine
nine twenty
ten sixty-six
twenty twenty three
<modfile spec.nlp>
###############################################
# FILE: numbers
# SUBJ: comment
# AUTH: David de Hilster
# CREATED: 2023-3-2 22:8:25
# MODIFIED:
###############################################
```

```
37
38  @NODES _ROOT
39
40  @POST
41      L("node") = N(1);
42      L("last") = 0;
43      L("final") = 0;
44      "number.txt" << "\n";
45
46      while (L("node")) {
47          L("name") = pnname(L("node"));
48          ...
49
50  @RULES
51  _number <-
52      _xWILD [plus match=(_number   and &)]    ### (1)
53      @@
```

Line 1 in the above listing was added by hand so that when the mod file is listed for the developer to choose, there is a description for that file.

Before you right-click **Add to Mod File**, you must have the mod file selected in the KB, as shown in the following figure:

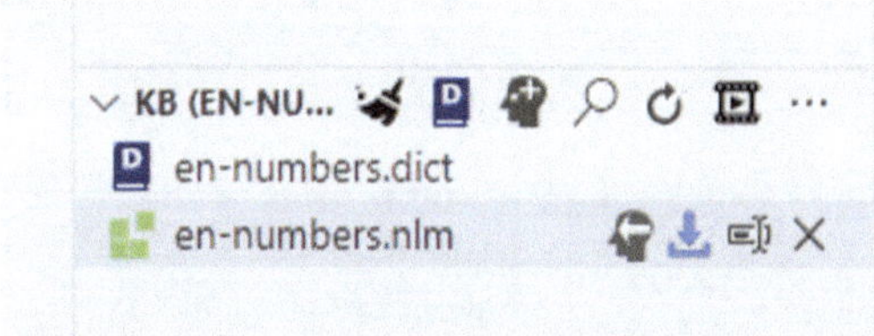

Figure 3.10: Selecting a Mod file before adding to it

The following figure is a sample right-click menu item for adding to mod files:

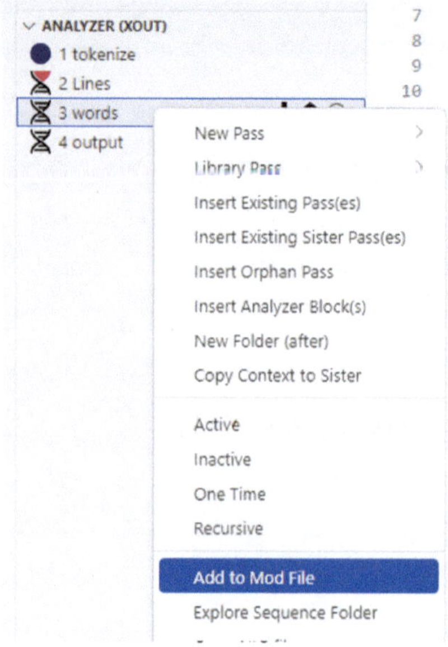

Figure 3.11: Right-click menu item in the analyzer view; Add to Mod File

Loading a module file

Here is an example of loading a modular file; this one is located in the English library.

Right-click on any item in the KB view and choose **Language Library**, as shown in the following figure:

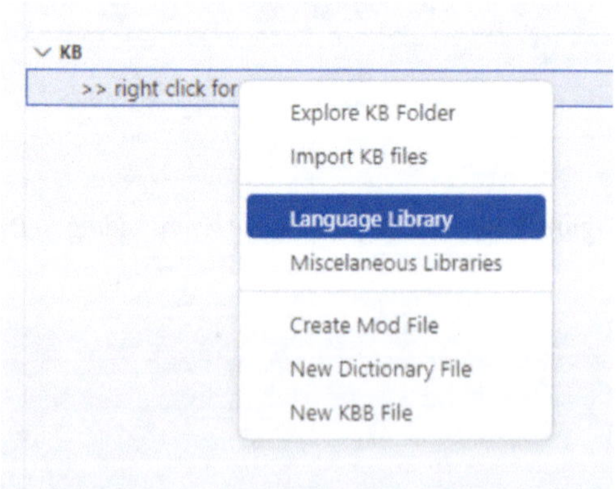

Figure 3.12: Right-click menu item in the KB view; Language Library

Then choose **English**, as shown in the following figure:

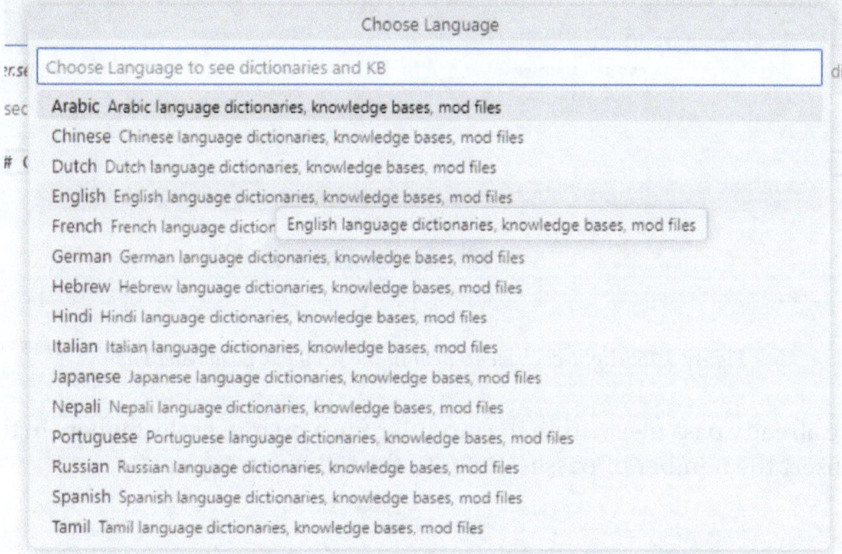

Figure 3.13: Choose Language pop-up menu

Next, choose the **en-numbers.nlm** module file, as shown in the following figure:

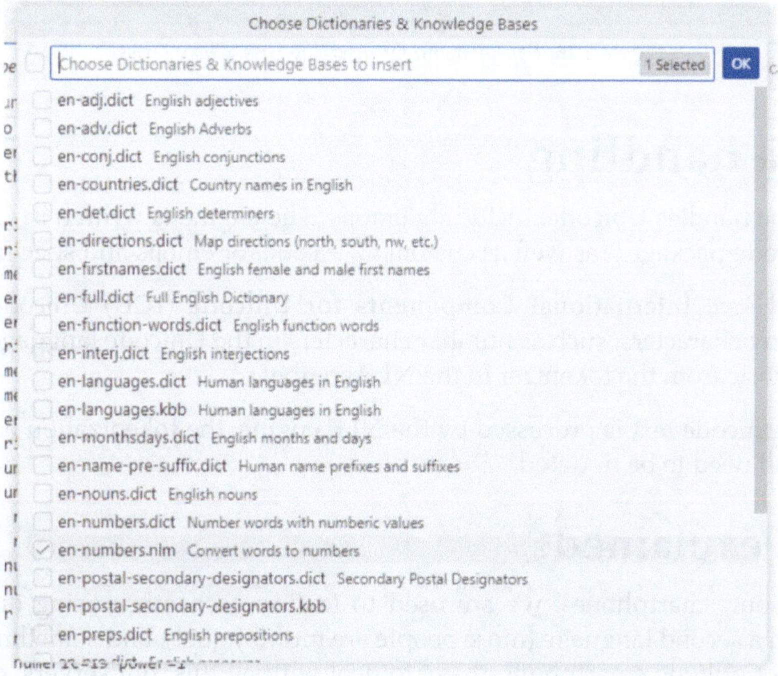

Figure 3.14: Choose dictionaries and knowledge bases menu

The file **en-numbers.nlm** will now appear in the KB view. Right-click on the mod file and choose **Load Mod File**, as shown in the following figure:

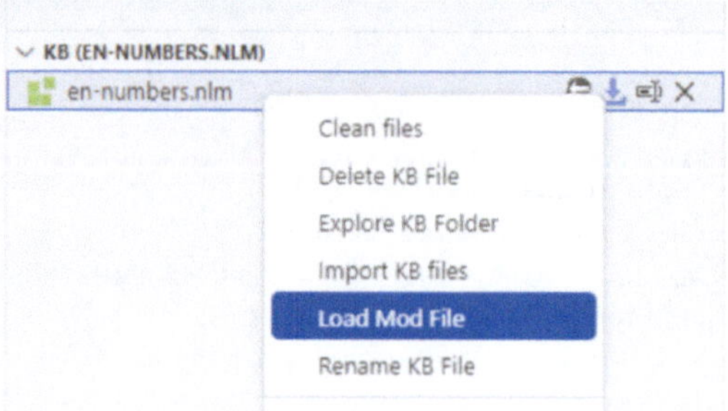

***Figure 3.15**: Right-click menu item in the KB view; Load Mod File*

Since there are already pass files within the modular file, you must select where in the analyzer sequence to insert the number of passes. Refer to the following figure:

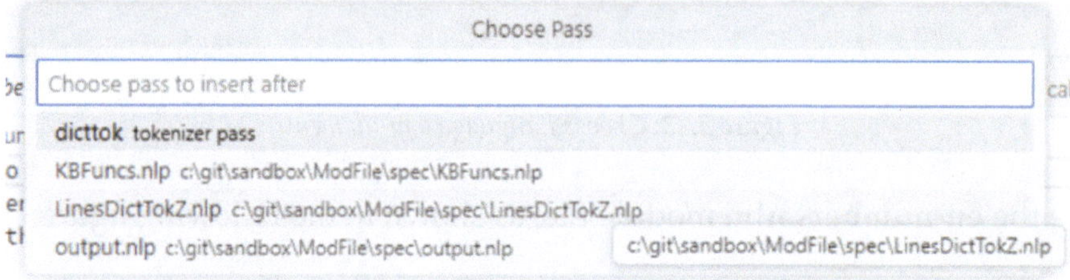

***Figure 3.16**: Pop-up menu for inserting pass: Choose pass*

Unicode handling

The NLP engine handles Unicode, including emojis. The engine is written in C++ and uses a universal Unicode package [1] as well as custom C++ code for emojis and specific languages.

Using the universal **International Components for Unicode** (**ICU**) Unicode C++ library means that many characters, such as number characters in the Unicode languages, are already labeled as numeric from the tokenizer in the NLP engine.

As ever more Unicode text is processed by the NLP engine, the tokenization functions of the NLP engine will need to be updated.

Unicode explained

When we use our smartphones, we are used to texting each other using our own native language, often a second language (more people are multilingual), and something newer than text: emojis. Not only do smartphones have to deal with all this, but servers, databases, text processors, and even machine learning must be able to navigate this strange world of modern text.

This is a world that most programmers do not have to worry about much. With today's UTF-8 standard, data is data. However, as Unicode is applied to an ever-growing domain of characters, the standard is not always updated in a timely manner.

In the beginning, computers dealt only with American English. With one byte (8 bits of 1s and 0s), one could store up to 256 different characters, as depicted in the following figure. That was fine. Some early computers only dealt with all capitalized letters, like the TSR-80 from the late 1970s:

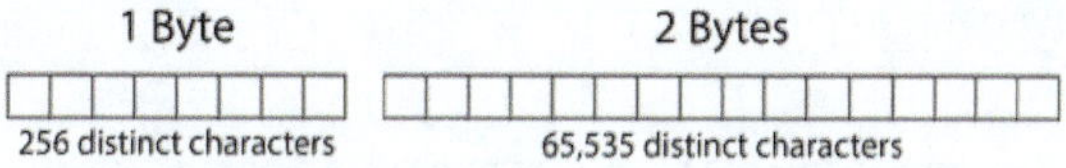

Figure 3.17: Unicode byte comparison

However, as more countries adopted computers, they had to deal with more characters, and when the smartphone came into use, there were emojis, and the number of characters quickly grew past the 256 limit. If 2 bytes were used, one could store up to over 65,000 characters. However, in the modern world of text, such a system is inadequate.

Since most Indo-European languages use the first 128 characters, using two bytes for every character would not only unnecessarily increase the size of files, but also slow down the processing of that text. The second dilemma is to find a method that mixes one, two, three, or more bytes per character as needed. Both dilemmas are represented in the following figure:

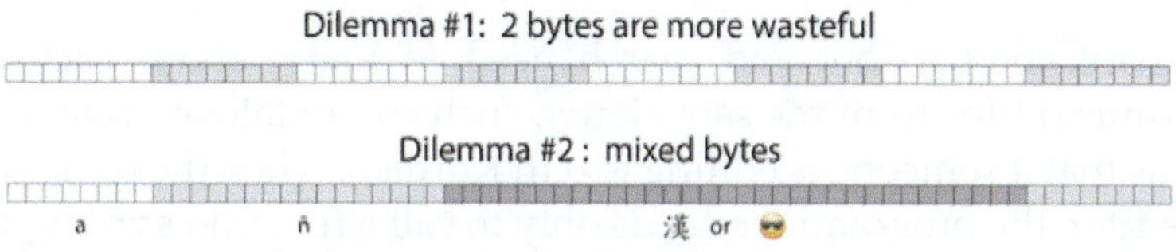

Figure 3.18: Unicode dilemmas

The answer came in July of 1992, when Dave Prosser of Unix System Laboratories submitted a proposal for a faster, more efficient implementation of character storage and reading[2]. The X/Open committee Ox JIG was looking for a better encoding for a universal multi-byte character set. There was a draft for such a character set back in 1989, but the character set was not satisfactory on performance grounds and other concerns. Dave's system was ingenious and one of the forgotten inventions in the computer world that is used now by billions of people worldwide every day without knowing it.

Prosser's idea was to come up with five or more unique codes that would start each 8-byte sequence. If the byte started with a zero, it was a one-byte character that represented the oldest and most commonly used characters for computers. For 2 bytes, the first byte started with a *110*; for three bytes, *1110*; and for four bytes, *11110*. The following extra bytes would all be marked by *10*. There were five codes in total: *0, 10, 110, 1110,* and *11110,* making it clear how many bytes were needed for a particular character. The rest of the bits were left for encoding a specific character. Text files could handle thousands of Chinese characters and still efficiently encode the standard character set. Refer to the following figure:

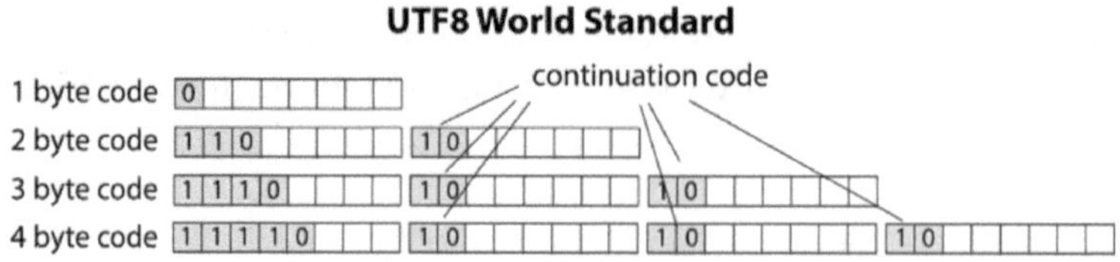

***Figure 3.19**: Unicode UTF8 World Standard*

This was not only an efficient use of space, but performance-wise, it was extremely fast to read. It solved the two main dilemmas. First, the majority of the text that fell into the range of one byte was wasted on bits per byte (8 bits). Second, it allowed for mixed-length byte characters in the same text. This has become even more important given the introduction of emojis into our daily lives.

Most heavy-duty programs that deal with characters, such as texting apps and word editors, use the programming language C++ or Java. Fortunately, there is a Unicode Package for both that is standardized to deal with the multitude of languages used today. The package is the ICU package[3]. This package allows programmers to manipulate text without having to worry about what language is being used.

Capitalization, word comparison, and search need to know about each language. Some languages have different forms of the same letter, such as capitalization or letters with accent marks. This means that if someone is editing text in Kurdish, when the user wants to capitalize the letters in an editor, the programmer needs only to call a function **`string_to_upper`**, which changes all the characters in the selected **`string_to_upper`** case. The ICU package knows how to deal with each language.

The package also deals with date and time formats for each language,an added bonus for programmers.

Emojis

In NLP++, emojis are treated as individual tokens, and the NLP engine deals with them accordingly. Documentation for emojis is sparse[4], and is absent in the C++ Unicode library used by the NLP engine, so this code had to be constructed from scratch.

Specific language functions

So far, the NLP engine has specialized C++ code for only three languages: Chinese, Tamil, and Nepali. Historically, this is because internship projects had to deal with these particular languages. The solutions below may need to be revisited.

Chinese

One of the internship projects needed to separate each Chinese character. Whereas many Indo-European languages separate words with whitespace, Chinese characters must be tokenized as separate characters even when there is no space.

The following is the current code for identifying the Chinese characters. This, like all the language-specific code, may need to be revisited.

```
bool unicu::isChinese(UChar32 c) {
  return (
      (0x4E00 <= c && c <= 0x9FFF) ||
      (0x3400 <= c && c <= 0x4DBF) ||
      (0x20000 <= c && c <= 0x2A6DF) ||
      (0x2A700 <= c && c <= 0x2B73F) ||
      (0x2B740 <= c && c <= 0x2B81F) ||
      (0x2B820 <= c && c <= 0x2CEAF) ||
      (0xF900 <= c && c <= 0xFAFF) ||
      (0x2F800 <= c && c <= 0x2FA1F)
  );
}
```

Nepali

This comes from one of the first intern projects, which involved the Nepali alphabet. To correctly separate Nepali characters, the following function was added:

```
bool unicu::isNepali(UChar32 c) {
  return (
      (0x0900 <= c && c <= 0x097F)
  );
}
```

Conclusion

In this chapter, the reader learned about specific topics relating to NLP++ and VisualText, including recursive passes, human-readable KB and dictionary files, as well as Unicode handling of emojis and particular natural languages (Chinese and Nepali).

In the next chapter, we describe the VisualText integrated development environment, its history, and its latest implementation in the VS Code NLP++ Language Extension. We detail the installation, capabilities, and use of VisualText, as well as the folder structure of an analyzer project.

True or false

1. NLP++ allows executing any rule-based pass as a recursive pass.
2. The NLP engine will always detect that a rule-based system may be infinitely recursive.
3. Users can try to break out of infinite loops in recursive passes via the VisualText interface.
4. The three file types added to NLP++ are "kbb", "dict", and "txxt" files.
5. The dictionary lines "prime number s=phrase type=math" and "prime number type=math" will generate the same tree structure.
6. The only way to invoke the reading of dictionaries and KB files in an analyzer is to use a tokenizer with dict in the name.
7. The difference between dicttok and dicttokz is that dicttokz removes spaces from the tree.
8. Dictionary files can have more than one line for a word.
9. The kbb files stand for kb beautiful files.
10. The "kbb" hierarchy in "kbb" files is designated by dashes.
11. The original kb files were meant to be human-readable files.
12. kbb files are automatically generated for each rule-pass file.
13. kb files are still used by the NLP engine.
14. It is common to write NLP++ analyzers to help build dictionaries and KB files.
15. Mod files can contain only dictionary and kb files.
16. The main function of mod files is to package files that can be stored in one file.
17. The NLP engine has special code for Chinese and Nepali.
18. Emojis cannot be used in NLP++ rules.

Answers

1. True	2. False	3. True
4. True	5. False	6. True
7. True	8. False	9. True
10. False	11. False	12. False
13. True	14. True	15. False
16. False	17. True	18. False

Multiple choice questions

1. **Recursive passes in VisualText are displayed as:**
   a. A circular arrow
   b. Two arrows
   c. A capitalized R
   d. A plus sign
   e. None of the above
2. **When canceling out of a running analyzer, VisualText tries to do the following:**
   a. Reset the VisualText interface back to a resting state
   b. Tries to kill the nlp.exe process on your local computer
   c. Closes the analyzer running pop-up
   d. All of the above
   e. None of the above
3. **The following are file extensions recently introduced to NLP++ (choose all that apply):**
   a. .kb
   b. .kbb
   c. .nlp
   d. .dict
   e. .txxt

4. **The line prime number type=math in a dictionary file will generate what in the parse tree:**

    a. Add an attribute type "math" to the words prime and number that remain separate

    b. Creates a new node "prime number" and adds an attribute type "math" to the new node

    c. Creates a new node "_phrase" with the attribute-value type="math"

    d. None of the above

5. **Which attributes are special in dict files (mark all that apply):**

    a. a

    b. s

    c. phrase

    d. pos

    e. l (lower case L)

6. **For node attributes for a word with multiple parts of speech, which of the following are invalid outputs from the NLP engine:**

    a. google ("pos num" 3) ("verb" 1) ("noun 1") ("adj" 1)

    b. base ("pos num" 2) ("verb" 1) ("noun 1")

    c. run ("pos num" 1) ("verb" 1) ("noun 1")

    d. fun ("pos num" 2) ("adj" 1)

    e. number ("pos num" 2) ("verb" 1) ("noun 1")

7. **When using the DisplayKB function, a file is generated that:**

    a. Is located in the output file directory

    b. Creates a file called "anaNNN.kbb", where NNN is the pass number

    c. Creates a file "displaykb.kbb"

    d. Displays the KB in a pop-up window

    e. None of the above

8. **Which KB lines are valid lines (check all that apply):**

    a. "this and that": type=moose

    b. here and there: attr="fred"

    c. fred: name=["concept" "people" "firstname"]

    d. this attr=a determiner

9. **Which analyzers are available to peruse that were created to build dictionary and KB files (check all that apply):**
   a. Time zones
   b. Countries
   c. Verbs
   d. Numbers
   e. Emoji
10. **Mod files can be added to through the following VisualText views:**
   a. Text view
   b. Analyzer sequence view
   c. KB view
   d. All of the above
   e. None of the above
11. **Which languages does the NLP engine have special Unicode knowledge for (mark all that apply):**
   a. English
   b. Spanish
   c. Chinese
   d. Portuguese
   e. Nepali

Answers

1. c	2. d	3. b d e
4. c	5. b d e	6. c d
7. b	8. a b c	9. a b e
10. d	11. c e	

Short answer questions

1. Define recursion.
2. Describe the two ways that one can construct a phrase tree for multiple-word phrases in the .dict file.

3. Explain the difference in the parse tree between dicttok and dicttokz.
4. Describe where the dictionary is located in the conceptual grammar and how it is organized.
5. Describe how the special attribute "pos" works in a dictionary.
6. What is the difference between a "kb" and a "kbb" file.
7. Describe the difference between the functions DisplayKB and SaveKB.
8. Explain how concept attributes are annotated in a KBB file.
9. Describe how you would make a mod file and give an example.

References

1. **IBM Corporation. International Components for Unicode (ICU). A set of C++ and C libraries for Unicode and globalization support. 2025. URL: https://icu.unicode.org/**
2. **File System Safe UCS—Transformation Format (FSS-UTF) - X/Open Preliminary Specification. Unicode.org. https://www.unicode.org/L2/Historical/wg20-n193-fss-utf.pdf**
3. **IBM Corporation. International Components for Unicode (ICU). A set of C++ and C libraries for Unicode and globalization support. 2025. URL: https://icu.unicode.org/**
4. **HPCC Systems. The Hidden World of Unicode – From Text to Emojis. Accessed: 2025-06-30. 2022. URL: https://hpccsystems.com/resources/the-hidden-world-of-unicode-from-text-to-emojis-2/**

CHAPTER 4
VisualText

Introduction

The best way to start learning NLP++ is to download and use VisualText, an essential platform for developing NLP++ programs. *David de Hilster*, co-creator of VisualText and creator of the NLP engine version, offers his take on the importance of VisualText:

The human brain is a neural network that is great at recognizing faces, but terrible at math and logic. In writing computer programs that read and understand language, we humans need to use the largest part of our brain to visualize the words, their rules, structures, and knowledge in such a way as to easily understand them. We must be able to visualize all these, given the complexity of language understanding. That is why VisualText is essential to writing rule-based and knowledge-based NLP systems.

Interns and students who have used VisualText for their projects have said that, without it, they would not attempt to build rule-based NLP systems. Developers have found that VisualText is the ultimate tool for studying language processing.

Structure

In this chapter, we will discuss the following topics:

- History
- NLP++ analyzer folder structure
- VS Code NLP++ Language Extension

Objectives

By the end of this chapter, the reader will learn about: the VisualText development environment, its history, and its current implementation as a VS Code language extension; and the folder structure of an NLP++ analyzer.

History

VisualText development began in late 1998, with the founding of **Text Analysis International, Inc. (TAI)**, and the system has continuously evolved to the present. De Hilster and Meyers developed a predecessor IDE named **Text Understanding Shell** (**TexUS**) in the early 1990s at a *McDonnell Douglas AI research lab*. The TexUS group participated in MUC-3 and MUC-4 (DARPA Message Understanding Conferences).

The VisualText IDE was developed in tandem with the NLP++ language, initially from 1998 to 2001, in the TAI, California startup company. De Hilster built the IDE, and Meyers coded NLP++ and the conceptual grammar KBMS. VisualText ran only on Windows and employed Windows graphical widgets. World-class TAI customers included *IBM, NASDAQ, Educational Testing Service* (*ETS*), and *Michael Page International*.

The following figure depicts the original version of VisualText:

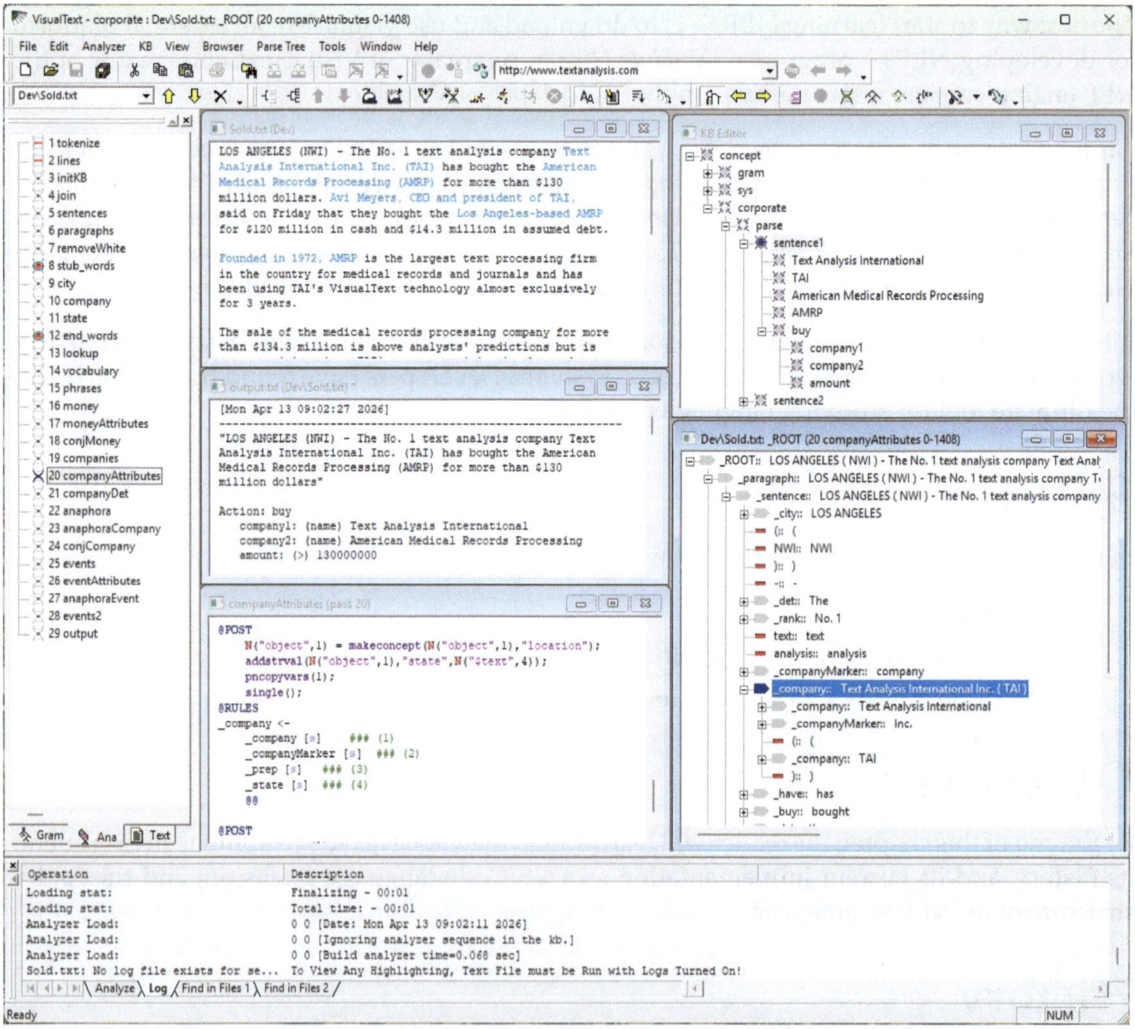

***Figure 4.1:** Windows version of the original VisualText IDE*

NLP++ analyzer folder structure

We describe the Windows VS Code extension for NLP++. The IDE is called VisualText, and the current runtime is the NLP engine. Each NLP++ analyzer is a subfolder within a top-level **`ANALYZERS`** folder, and is named for the current analyzer (e.g., parse-en-us, the general US English parser). An analyzer's subfolders are shown in the following table:

Folder	Description
`input`	Stores input files and folders for the current analyzer.
`spec`	Holds **`.nlp`** pass files and **`analyzer.seq`** pipeline file.
`kb`	Holds **knowledge base** (**KB**) and dictionary files.
`tmp`	Temporary folder for text analyzer.
`output`	Primary output folder.
`logs`	Debugging output (Windows VisualText).
`user`	C++ user functions to extend NLP++ (Windows VisualText).
`run`	Compiled analyzer code. (Windows VisualText).
`bin`	Compiled kb and user code. (Windows VisualText).
`data`	Folder for auxiliary outputs and data. (Windows VisualText).

***Table 4.1**: NLP++ analyzer folder structure*

Familiarity with the folder structure is key to using the VisualText IDE.

Input folder

When the NLP engine runs an analyzer with the debug switch on, it creates a log folder. The folder name is **`<filename>_log`**, where **`<filename>`** is invariably a **`.txt`** input file. Files within help view, debug, and develop the analyzer. These file types appear in the log folder:

- **.tree**: Parse tree for every rule-matching pass in the analyzer.
- **.txt**: Auxiliary output files coded by the programmer.
- **.log**: Log files generated by the VisualText runtime system.
- **.kbb**: Human-readable KB files.

The following figure is a sample log folder listing:

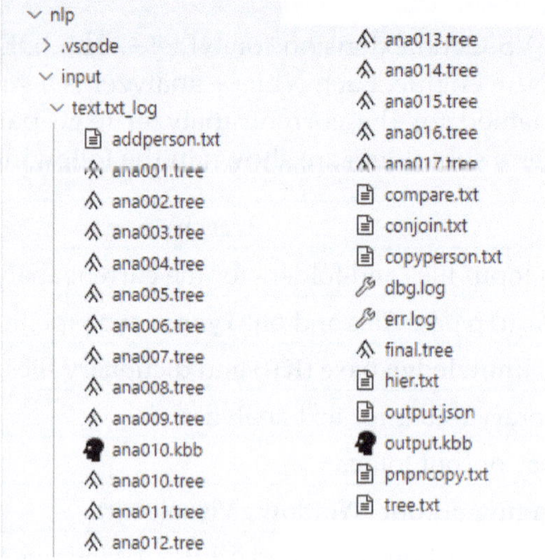

Figure 4.2: Listing of log folder for text.txt input file

Spec folder

The **spec** folder (or sequence folder) holds the analyzer sequence file and pass files:

- **analyzer.seq**: The text file that specifies the analyzer sequence (or pipeline).
- **.nlp**: NLP++ pass files referenced by the analyzer sequence file.

The **spec** folder may include NLP++ files not currently in the analyzer sequence. When a user deletes an NLP++ pass from the pipeline, VisualText retains it as an orphan pass so that it can be retrieved. Clicking the cog icon in the **OUTPUT FILES** view lists the orphans, as shown in the following figure:

Figure 4.3: Clicking on the cog icon to view orphan files

KB folder

The **kb\user** folder holds an analyzer's permanent dictionary and KB files, as exemplified in the following figure:

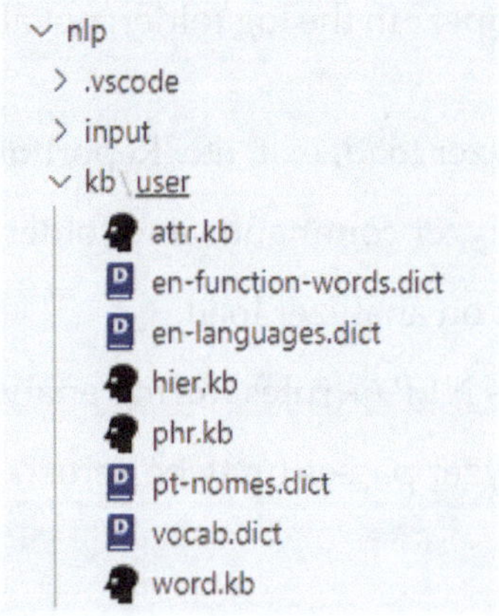

Figure 4.4: Listing of the KB folder

The KB folder holds the file types in the following:

- **.kb**: Legacy KB files used internally (that should not be edited)
- **.dict**: Dictionary files
- **.kbb**: KB files

Temporary folder

The temporary folder (**`tmp`**) is used internally by the NLP engine during processing. It is used primarily by the **`kbdumptree()`** function, and should not be accessed or modified by the user, in general. If necessary, it can be accessed for each analyzer via the **EXPLORER** icon in the leftmost pane of the VS Code window.

Output folder

The output folder holds log files produced when running an analyzer. Timing, loading, and error files are generated and can be viewed by users via the **LOGGING** view. The following figure shows status messages in the **LOGGING** view when loading an analyzer:

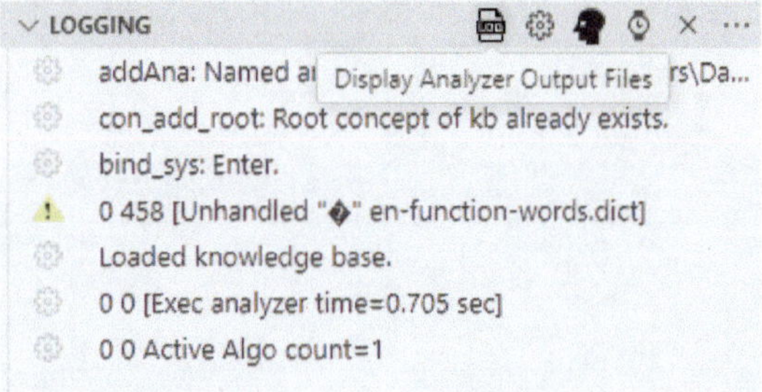

Figure 4.5: Listing the stderr.log from the NLP engine by clicking on the log file icon

The following are files that may appear in the log folder; not all of the files are quickly available in the log view:

- **stderr.log**: Errors on analyzer load, exit, etc. Report on memory leaks.
- **stdout.log**: Report on analyzer commands and folder paths.
- **init.log**: Additional errors on analyzer load.
- **def.log**: Report on various NLP++ rules during analyzer load.
- **dbg.log**: Timings for analyzer passes (may be zeroed out, see the following section).

Logs folder

The **`logs`** folder holds additional verbose output produced when running an analyzer:

- **cgerr.log**: Logs/errors when loading a KB.
- **dbg.log**: Timings for analyzer passes (may be zeroed out).
- **file.log**: Filenames being analyzed.
- **make_ana.log**: Report on building/loading the analyzer.

VS Code NLP++ Language Extension

In 2020, de Hilster recreated VisualText as a language extension in the popular Microsoft VS Code editor, making it available on Windows, Mac, and the Linux X Window system. The VS Code NLP++ extension calls the command line version of the NLP engine, whereas the original Windows version of VisualText integrates the IDE and the runtime. The following figure depicts the VisualText IDE as implemented in the VS Code version:

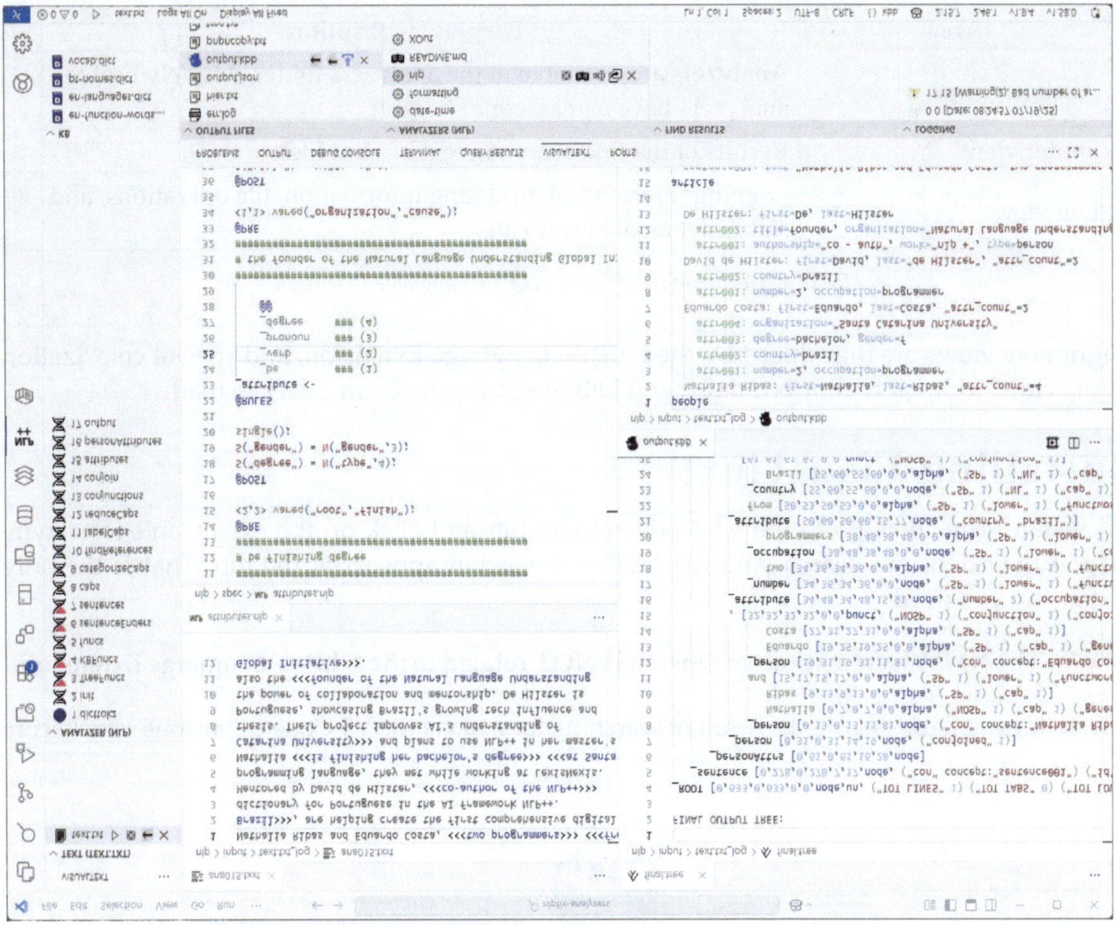

***Figure 4.6**: VisualText IDE the NLP++ Language Extension for VS Code*

The following table describes the views available in the VS Code version of VisualText:

Area	Display description
Activity bar	Vertical bar on the left side of the window, with icons for views and functionalities.
Text view	Text files are available to run with the analyzer.
Sequence view	Analyzer sequence of passes (or pipeline), one per line.
KB view	Dictionary, KB, and mod files.
Edit Window tabs	Tabs at the top represent KB, dictionary, and pass files to edit. Highlighted text files and help pages are also available.
Output view	Output files generated by text analysis, including final tree, debug, KB, JSON files, etc.

Area	Display description
Analyzer view	Analyzers are available in the analyzers folder. Actively usable analyzers have a gear icon.
Finder view	Results of the find search in text or pass files
Log view	Logging information, updating information, file operations, and stats after an analyzer run.

Table 4.2: Views of the VSCode NLP++ Language Extension

Eight new views are introduced by the NLP++ Language Extension, and special colorization is provided for **nlp**, **tree**, **txxt**, **dict**, and **kbb** files, to make them easier to read.

Installing VisualText

To install VisualText, go to the VS Code activity bar and click on the extension's icon, type **nlp** in the extensions search, and the NLP++ extension appears at the top. That is the only extension you need.

Note: The NLP Visualizations extension is NOT related to the NLP++ Language Extension.

The following figure shows the result of searching for **nlp** via the VS Code extensions search icon:

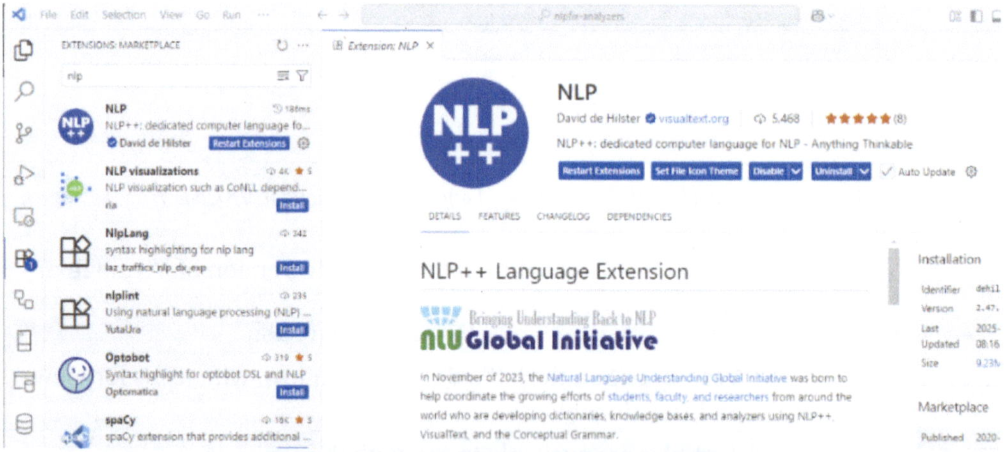

Figure 4.7: NLP++ Language Extension in VS Code

Updating VisualText

There are several ways that VisualText updates:

- When there is a new version of the NLP++ Language Extension.
- When there are new versions of library files associated with VisualText.

New version of VisualText

When a new version of VisualText is available, it also updates the files associated with the language extension in VS Code. This is specific to VisualText. You will see VisualText downloading and installing all the necessary files into the new version folder for VisualText in the log window. It looks like as shown in the following figure:

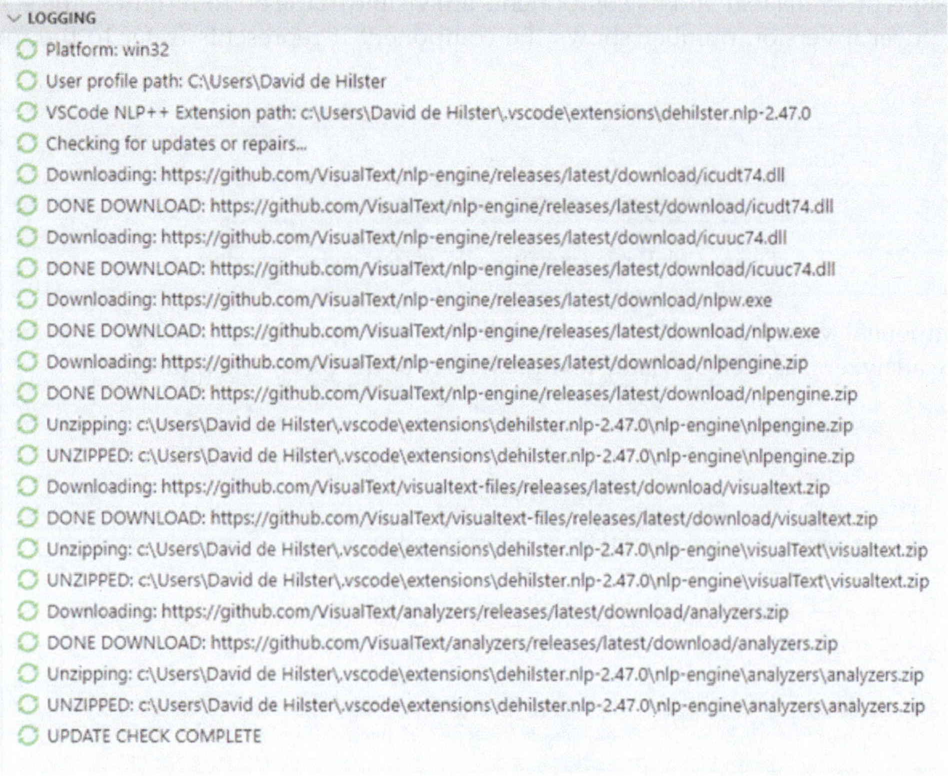

Figure 4.8: *Update messages in the logging view of VisualText*

Updating VisualText library files

Each time you open the NLP++ Language Extension, VisualText checks for new versions of key components. The following figure is what you see if there is nothing to update:

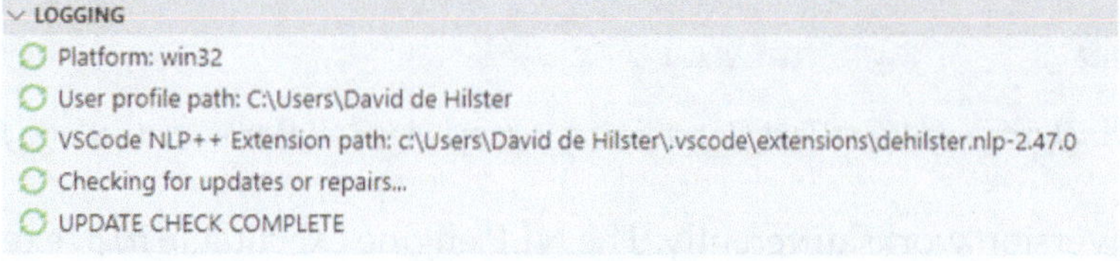

Figure 4.9: *VisualText logging output when loading in VS Code*

VisualText checks for a new version of the following components:

- NLP engine (**`nlp.exe`**)
- VisualText files
- Example analyzers

The versions of VisualText and its components are visible in the bottom right of the status bar. Mousing over a version number shows the component it represents (refer to the following figure):

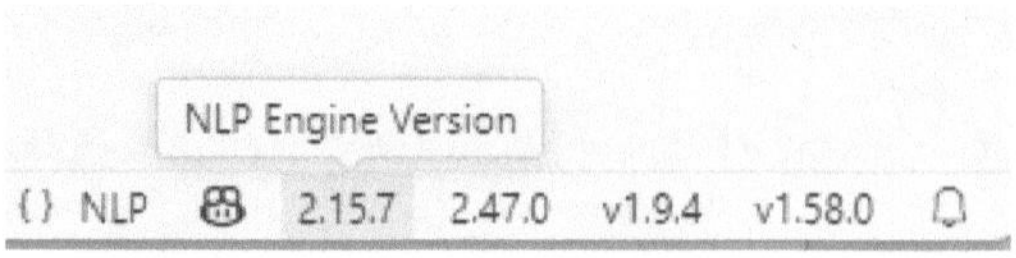

***Figure 4.10**: Version numbers of VisualText and its components*

Two-component versions are stored in the NLP++ settings area, including the example and template analyzers, as well as VisualText files (refer to the following figure):

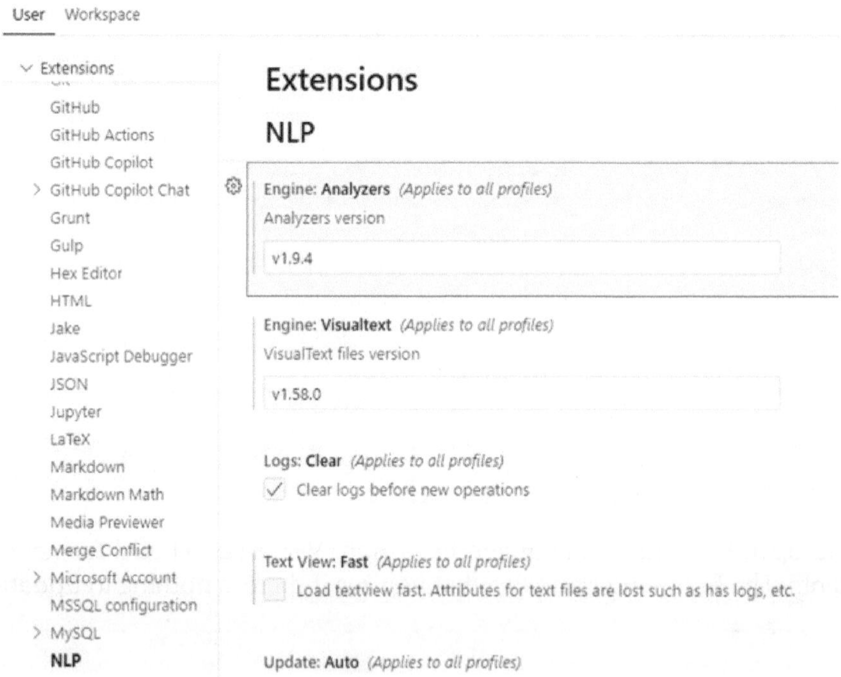

***Figure 4.11**: Analyzers and VisualText file versions are stored in the NLP extension settings for VS Code*

The NLP engine version works differently. The NLP engine executable **`nlp.exe`** has the switch **`-version`**, which, when called on the command line, returns its version:

```
nlp.exe --version
2.15.7
```

When checking the current version of the NLP engine, VisualText executes the command line for the current **nlp.exe** in the VisualText extension folder and compares it with the latest version of the NLP engine repository in GitHub. If they do not match, then the new engine is downloaded.

When there is something to update or repair, you will see the new version of the component being downloaded and installed. This means that everyone is using the latest version of all components of the VisualText programming environment. The following figure is what one sees in the **LOGGING** view if a single component needs updating:

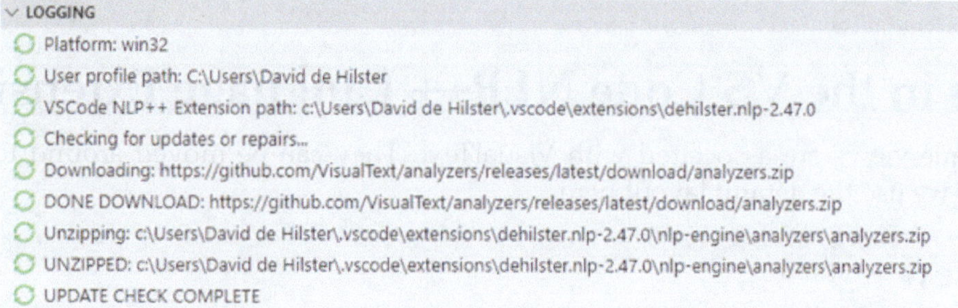

***Figure 4.12**: LOGGING view of VisualText updating the analyzer files version*

Example analyzers

It is very important for you to understand that, when first experimenting with the example analyzers bundled with VisualText, the example analyzers folder is overwritten when a new version of the analyzers is available. The example analyzers are loaded by clicking on the cog in the **ANALYZERS** view (refer to the following figure):

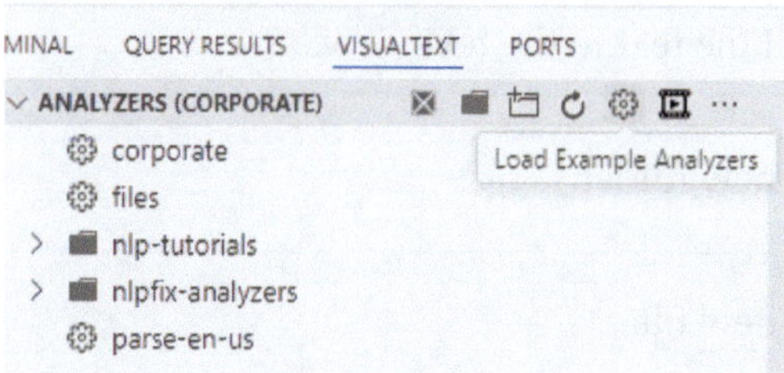

***Figure 4.13**: Loading the example analyzers by clicking on the cog icon in the analyzers view*

It is highly recommended that you immediately copy these analyzers to a safe folder before making any modifications, using the convenient **Copy All Analyzers to Another Folder**, as shown in the following figure:

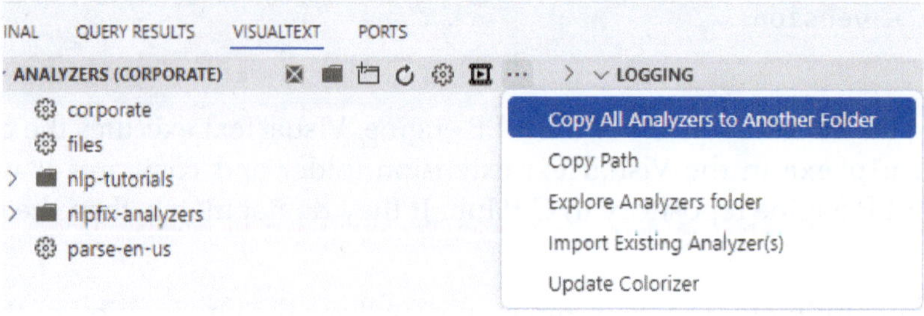

***Figure 4.14**: Convenient right-click copy function for the example analyzers*

This ensures that your work is not overwritten the next time VisualText is automatically updated.

Views in the VS Code NLP++ Language Extension

Eight unique views are associated with VisualText. They can be moved around to a user's liking, but we use the default layout here.

Text view

The text view displays the text files being processed by the NLP++ analyzer. Files that display a solid file icon already have log files generated from a run, whereas file icons that are not filled have not been run and have no log files.

Text view in VisualText

The following table describes the actions available in the text view header bar:

Icon	Description
	Search all the text in the text view.
	Create a new folder.
	Create a new file.
	Refresh the text view.
Fast Load	Toggle **ON** or **OFF**. When the text view has many files, this allows faster loading, but less information is displayed in the text view.

Icon	Description
	Delete the log files after a run.
	Copy the text or folder to another folder.

Table 4.3: Text view items in VisualText

Note: Choosing a folder runs the analyzer on its files. Executing the command line NLP engine on a folder loads the dictionary and KB files only once and then runs the analyzer on every file. For text analysis on a folder, we recommend setting the Development Settings (at the bottom left of the taskbar) to "Final Logs Only" or "All Logging Off".

Fast Load

When working with large text files or with many files, the text view may slow down significantly due to increased preprocessing. To circumvent this, the user can toggle the **Fast Load (ON)** flag by first clicking on the three dots (right-hand side of the text view header bar), as shown in the following figure:

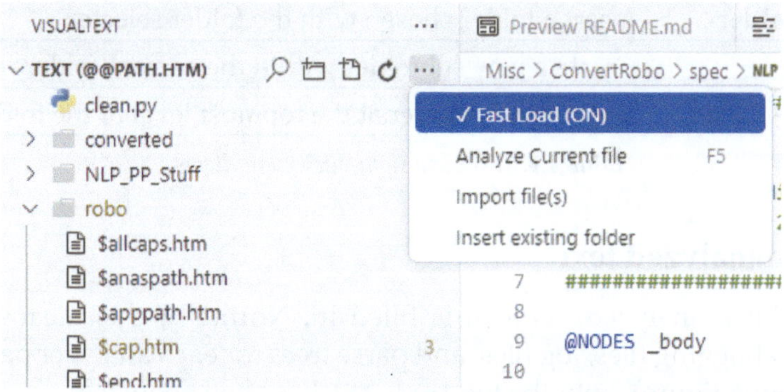

Figure 4.15: Activating Fast Load in the text view

In **`dehilster-analyzers`** repository, one analyzer converts Robo HTML help files:

https://github.com/VisualText/dehilster-analyzers/tree/main/Misc/ConvertRobo

This folder holds hundreds of files. Turning the **Fast Load** flag greatly speeds up listing the files. Right-clicking on any file in the text view invokes a pop-up menu with the following items, listed in the following table:

Menu item	Description
Analyze File	Run the selected text file or folder using the current analyzer.
Open Text Properties	Display metadata and settings related to the text file.
Search	Text search in the current file.
Add to Mod File	Add the selected file to a mod file in the KB view.
Delete File	Delete the selected file or folder.
Import File(s)	Add one or more text files to the current analyzer text view.
New Text File	Create a new text file within the selected area.
New Top Text File	Create a new text file at the topmost level of the folder.
Python Scripts	Access to Python scripts for text analysis and NLP.
Remove Log Files	Delete all log files in the current text analysis session.
Rename File	Rename the selected file.
Explore Current Folder	Open the current folder in the file explorer.
Explore Input Folder	Open the current input folder in the file explorer.
Move to Selected Folder	Move the selected file or folder to a user-selected folder.
Move Up a Folder	Move the selected file or folder one level higher in its tree.
Insert Existing Folder	Insert a folder chosen with the folder selector.
New Folder	Create a new subfolder within the current folder.
New Top Folder	Create a new folder at the topmost level of the folder tree.

***Table 4.4**: Text view right-click menu items*

Analyzed vs. unanalyzed text

When a text has been analyzed, its icon is filled in. Normally, this means that the text is accompanied by debugging files, log files, and parse trees for each analyzer pass. In the sample (refer to the following figure), only the file **`text.txt`** has been analyzed:

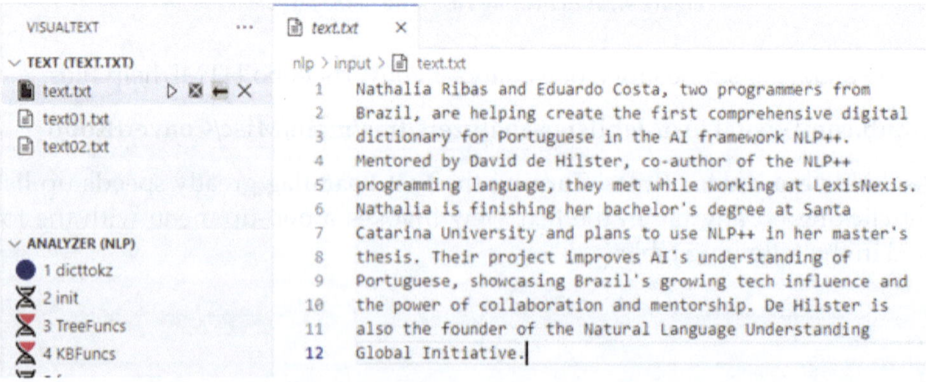

***Figure 4.16**: Text view display when only text.txt has been analyzed*

Notice that a box containing an *x* appears when a text has been analyzed and has log files. It is absent for unanalyzed text files. Clicking on the x box for a text deletes its log files.

The x box can appear in four places:

- An individual text's line icons (shown in *Figure 4.16*).
- The text view's heading bar.
- The analyzer's heading bar.
- An individual analyzer's line icons.

Figure 4.17 depicts an analyzer's **x** box icon in the analyzer view:

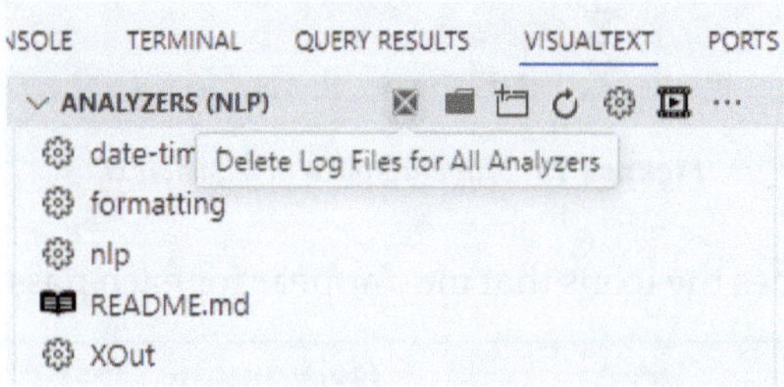

***Figure 4.17**: Delete Log Files icon in the analyzer view*

Clearing logs before archiving

Using the x box in the analyzer view's header line is important prior to archiving or pushing the analyzer to a repository. The number and size of log files, parse tree files (e.g., **`ana001.tree`**), and output files can be quite large. Deleting these helps ensure that only necessary analyzer files are archived, greatly reducing clutter.

Sequence view

The sequence view shows the sequence of pass files (i.e., the pipeline) that defines an analyzer, as exemplified in the following figure. It visually represents the **`analyzer.seq`** file, which can be viewed by clicking on the (always first) tokenizer pass. The sequence file should not be modified directly (unless corrupted).

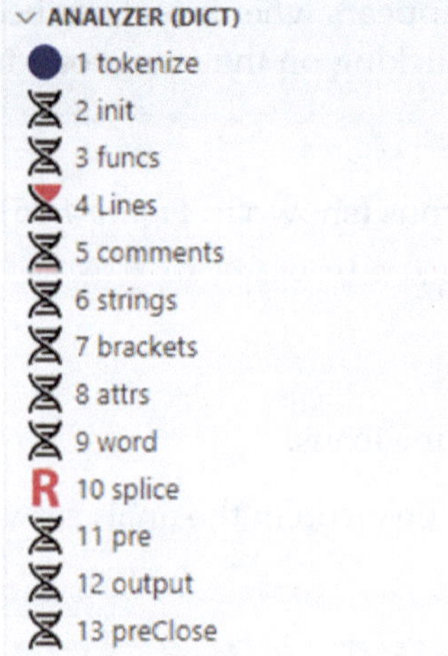

***Figure 4.18**: Sequence view in VisualText*

The following table describes the icons that may appear for each pass of the analyzer sequence:

Icon	Description
	Tokenizer or unrecognized pass. If the **`analyzer.seq`** file is corrupted, analyzer passes may exhibit this icon.
	Pass with the associated NLP++ pass file.
	Pass file copied from the standard library (e.g., **`KBFuncs`**). These can be edited, thereby leading to improving the library.
R	Recursive pass. NLP++ pass file executed as a recursive grammar.
	Folder containing the ordered pass file.

***Table 4.5**: Icons in the analyzer sequence view*

Sequence right-click menu items

The following table describes the right-click menus of the analyzer sequence view. (Note that the sequence folder and spec folder are synonyms):

Menu item	Description
New Pass	Create a new analyzer pass.
Library Pass	Insert a selected library pass.
Insert Existing Pass(es)	Insert any passes from the current analyzer.

Menu item	Description
Insert Existing Sister Pass(es)	Insert passes from analyzers in the current analyzer folder.
Insert Orphan Pass	Insert an orphan pass (one not currently in the sequence).
Insert Analyzer Block(s)	Insert a grouped set of passes.
New Folder (after)	Create a new folder below the selected sequence line.
Active	Mark the pass as active for execution.
Inactive	Mark the pass as inactive, preventing execution.
One Time	Mark the pass to run only once (regular rule matching).
Recursive	Mark the pass as recursive. (Pass repeatedly traverses the parse tree context till no rules match).
Explore Sequence Folder	Open and explore the contents of the sequence folder.
Open NLP file	Open the NLP++ file for the current pass.
Search	Search through all files in the analyzer sequence.
Search Top Level Only	Search only files at the top-level of the analyzer sequence.
Delete pass	Remove selected pass file from sequence, retain as an orphan.
Duplicate pass	Create a duplicate of the selected pass, insert one line lower.
Rename pass	Rename selected pass.
Move Down	Move the selected pass file or folder one line down in sequence.
Move Up	Move the selected pass file or folder one line up in sequence.

Table 4.6: Right-click menu items in the analyzer sequence view

Library passes

Every library pass in an analyzer is distinguished by a partly filled-in DNA icon.

Note: Some generally useful library passes are `KBFuncs` and `Lines`.

Normally, there is no reason to update these passes unless they are buggy. However, sometimes, updates or additions may be useful to the current analyzer. To compare the copied version with the library on the server, use the **Compare with Latest Library File** right-click menu item (refer to the following figure):

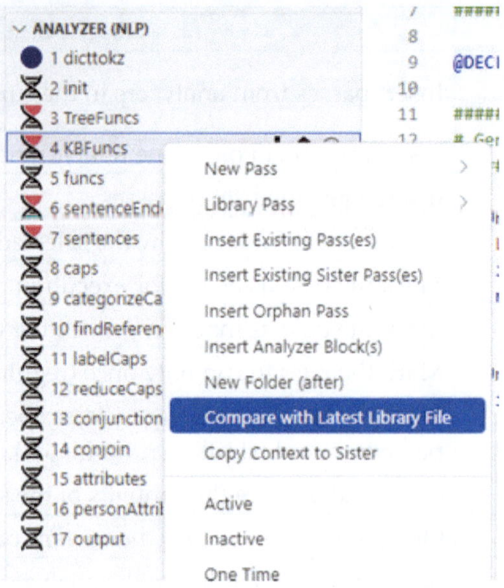

Figure 4.19: Menu item for comparing analyzer library pass with latest version

Once selected, a VS Code file comparison is opened to examine the differences (refer to the following figure):

Figure 4.20: Comparing analyzer library pass with the latest version

At this point, the user can select the desired changes or simply reload the same library function, and the newer version overwrites the current version (refer to the following figure):

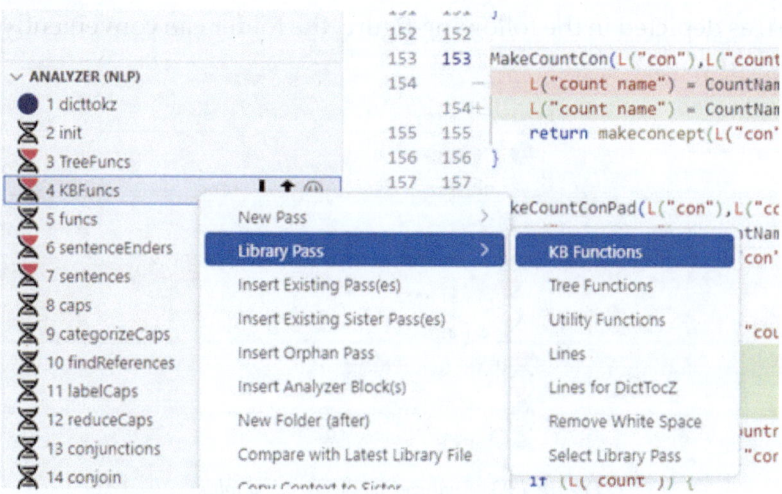

Figure 4.21: Updating analyzer pass with the latest library version

Folders

Folders in the sequence view are not real folders on the computer platform. Creating a folder and adding passes to it in the analyzer sequence results in a virtual folder that is only recorded in the **analyzer.seq** file. One cannot, for example, open the file browser in VS Code and move sequence files there.

Due to restrictions on the classes available to VS Code extension programmers, a fully functional **ListView** that resembles the file browser is not available. With that in mind, the following mechanism was implemented.

When creating and using folders in the analyzer sequence:

- Only one level of folders is allowed.
- Moving files in and out of folders must be done one-at-a-time, using arrows – no multi-selection is available at this time.

For instance, to populate the folder **Initialize** in the NLP example analyzer, we first create the folder, then use the up or down arrows to move files into the folder (refer to the following figure):

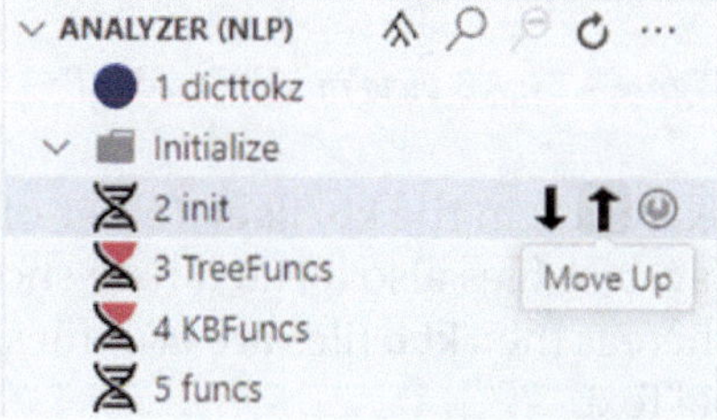

Figure 4.22: Moving a pass into a folder in the analyzer sequence

Once populated, as depicted in the following figure, the folder can conveniently be closed and moved as a single unit:

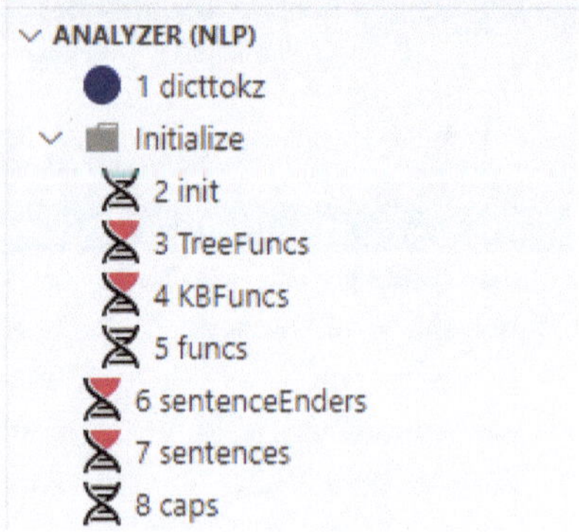

Figure 4.23: Analyzer passes inside a folder

Knowledge base view

The KB view displays dictionary, KB, and module files used by the currently selected NLP++ analyzer. The user may add, delete, edit, and otherwise manipulate these files, which will then be automatically loaded as a first step when analyzing input texts. The following subsections detail the use of the KB view.

KB files

Files include dictionaries, KBs, and module (or Mod) files (as discussed in the *Mod file* section of *Chapter 3, NLP++ Topics*). Dictionary and KB files are only loaded if the tokenizer includes the prefix **`dict`** in the name, as in **`dicttok`** and **`dicttokz`**, as shown in the following figure:

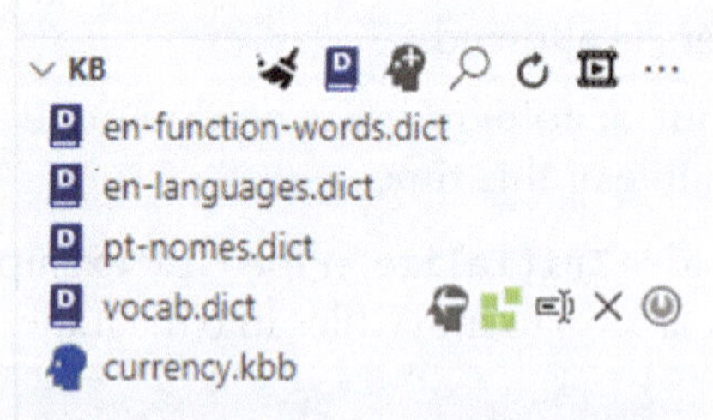

Figure 4.24: KB view in VS Code NLP++

The dictionary and **`.kbb`** KB files reside in the **`kb/user`** folder of an NLP++ analyzer, as in the following figure. Required **`.kb`** system files also located here should not be removed or edited. The **`.kb`** files are system files, whereas the **`.kbb`** files are user files. The **`.kb`** files are hidden from the user in the KB view of VisualText.

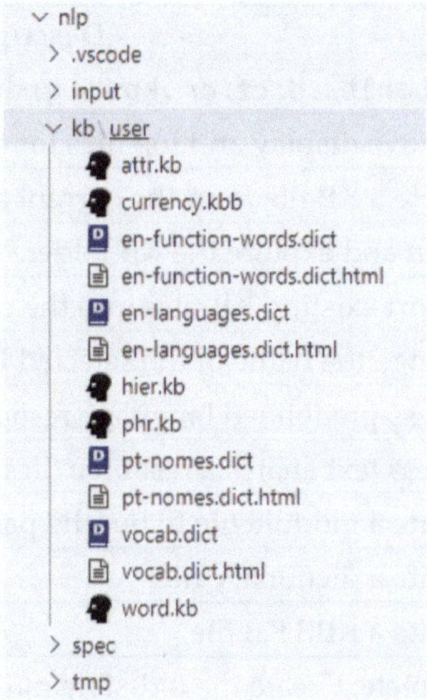

Figure 4.25: Folder listing of a KB folder

Title bar icons

The following table shows are descriptions of the icons in the KB view title bar:

Icon	Description
	Remove display and log files for the current analyzer run.
	Create a dictionary file.
	Create a new **.kbb** file.
	Search the files in the KB.
	Refresh the KB listing.
	Link to a video tutorial on the KB view.

Table 4.7: Icons in the KB view title bar

Right-click menu

The following table lists the right-click menu items as they appear in the KB view:

Menu item	Description
Add to Mod File	Add **.nlp**, **.dict**, or **.kb** file to the module file.
Clean Files	Remove display and log files for the current analyzer run.
Delete KB File	Delete a KB file from the current analyzer.
Explore KB Folder	Open and explore the KB folder.
Import KB Files	Import existing KB files into the current analyzer project.
Rename KB File	Change the name of the selected KB file.
Language Library	Access predefined language resource files.
Miscellaneous Libraries	Access text analysis resource files.
Create Mod File	Create a module file to bundle pass files, dict, and kbb files.
New Dictionary File	Create a dictionary file.
New KBB File	Create a KBB KB file.
Generate main.kb	Obsolete: Create the old-style main KB file.
Merge Dictionary Files	Obsolete: Combine multiple dictionary files into one file.

***Table 4.8**: Right-click menu items in the KB view*

Output view

The output view presents the results of the NLP analysis, including analyzer debug and output files, as well as runtime system log files and error files. Analyzer outputs may include KB files, dictionary files, JSON files, text files, formatted files (e.g., XML/HTML), and so on.

Output view display

Each input file, once analyzed, gets an output folder within the same input folder. The output folder name is formatted as **<input-filename>_log**, e.g., **file01.txt_log**. The following figure shows a typical output folder:

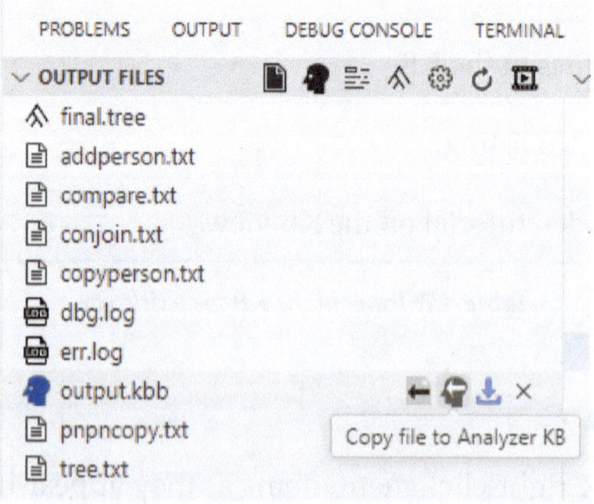

***Figure 4.26**: Output view in VS Code NLP++*

Output view icons

The icons on the **OUTPUT** view header are filters for different types of files (refer to the following figure):

Icon	Description
	List all the output files.
	List the KBB files.
	List the text highlighting files.
	List the tree files.
	List the orphan files.

***Table 4.9:** Output files filter icons*

Analyzer view

The analyzer view manages NLP++ analyzers in the current analyzers folder. Remember: VisualText operates on a folder of analyzer folders. Every analyzer folder name appears with a gear icon. Clicking on an analyzer line selects that as the current analyzer. Clicking on the NLP++ button on the left-hand VS Code panel alternately hides or unhides the sequence view (or whatever pane is immediately to the right of the NLP++ button).

The header lines for the analyzer view and the sequence view are similar. The analyzer view is shown in *Figure 4.27*, with the analyzer name in parentheses. The corresponding sequence view header looks like:

- **ANALYZERS (NLP)**: An analyzer folder holds, at a minimum, an **`input`**, **`spec`**, **`kb`**, and **`tmp`** folder.
- **Analyzer view display**: The analyzer view can include nested analyzer folders (refer to the following figure):

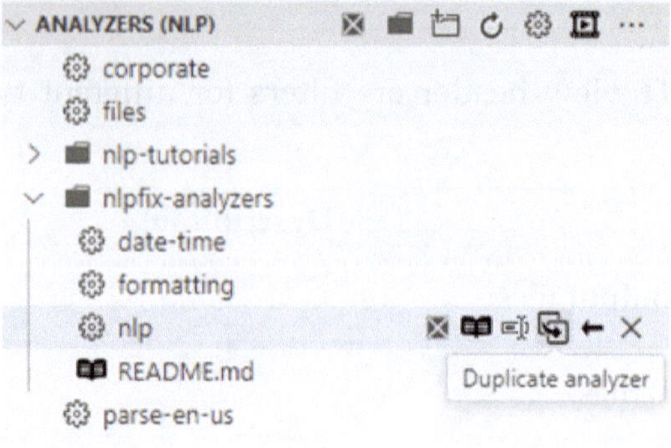

Figure 4.27: Analyzer view with one analyzer selected

- **Analyzer view right-click menu**: The following table lists the right-click menu items available when clicking on a line in the analyzer view:

Menu item	Description
New ECL File	Create a new ECL file (for HPCC Systems plugin).
Copy Analyzer to Another Folder	Copy an analyzer to a user-selected folder.
Delete Analyzer	Permanently remove an analyzer.
Delete Analyzer Logs	Present only when there are log files to delete.
Duplicate analyzer	Create a duplicate copy of an analyzer.
Import Existing Analyzer(s)	Import analyzer(s) into the current analyzers folder.
New Analyzer	Create a new analyzer based on a user-selected template.
Rename Analyzer	Rename the selected analyzer.
Update Colorizer	Update to the latest colorizer file.
Explore Analyzer Folder	Open and explore the selected analyzer folder.
Move to Selected Folder	Move the selected analyzer or file to the selected folder. Select the destination folder, then click on the move icons on the analyzer, folder, or file to be moved.
New Folder	Create a new folder in the analyzers folder.
Edit Parent Folder with VisualText	Reload VisualText at the parent of the analyzers folder.
README Delete File	Delete the `README` file of the selected analyzer.
README Edit/Create File	Edit or create a `README` file for the selected analyzer.
README Open File	Open the analyzer `README` file for viewing.

Table 4.10: Right-click menu items in the analyzer view

- **Analyzer view header icons**: The following table shows the icons that are found in the analyzer view header:

Icon	Description
	Delete Log Files for All Analyzers. This icon appears only if there are log files to delete within the analyzer's folder tree.
	Opens the associated **`README`** file for the analyzer if one exists.
	This allows the user to rename the analyzer and its folder under the analyzers folder.
	Prompt the user to copy the current analyzer folder to another location.
	The right arrow moves the analyzer into the selected folder. The left arrow moves the analyzer up a level out of the current folder. NOTE: **The right arrow appears only when a target folder is selected.**

Table 4.11: Icons in analyzer view header

- **Analyzer view line icons**: The following table lists the icons in the analyzer view line:

Icon	Description
	Delete the log files for the current analyzer. The icon appears only if log files exist in the chosen analyzer.
	Create a new empty folder (not an analyzer folder).
	Create a new analyzer. Prompt the user to choose a template analyzer.
	Refresh the analyzer listing.
	Load the bundled example analyzers. NOTE: **To retain edits, copy the folder to a safe location: click the three dots . . . in the extended header menu, then select "Copy All Analyzers to Another Folder".**

Table 4.12: Icons in analyzer view line

Logging view

The logging view displays logging and diagnostic information for VisualText. This includes information after running the analyzer, updating information when first invoking VisualText, and displaying syntax errors. The following figure shows a typical output after running the analyzer on a text:

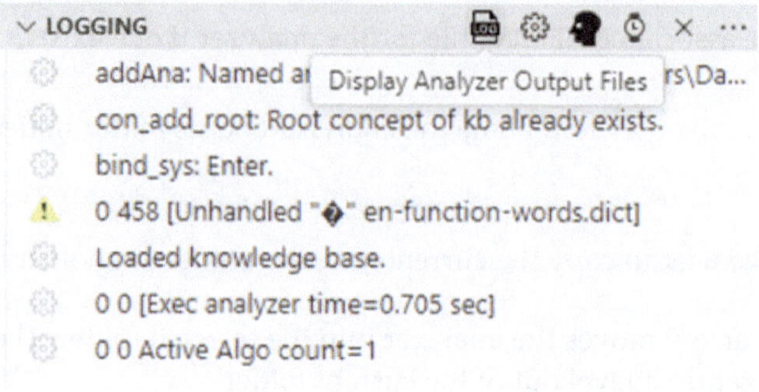

Figure 4.28: *VisualText LOGGING view*

Log view icons

The log view uses the icons, as shown in the following table, to display various types of log files:

Icon	Description
	Display the general log file (the default view).
	Analyzer log output in the err.log file, found in the current input file's **`_log`** folder (e.g., under **`text.txt_log`**).
	KB log, which displays the cgerr.log in the analyzer's **`logs`** folder.
	Displays the timings for the analyzer sequence, from the **`dbg.log`** file in the analyzer's **`logs`** folder.
	Toggle **ON** or **OFF**. When there are many files in the text view, it allows faster loading, but with less information.

Table 4.13: *Logging view icons*

Log view extended menu

The following figure shows the right-click menu for three dots in the header of the **LOGGING** view:

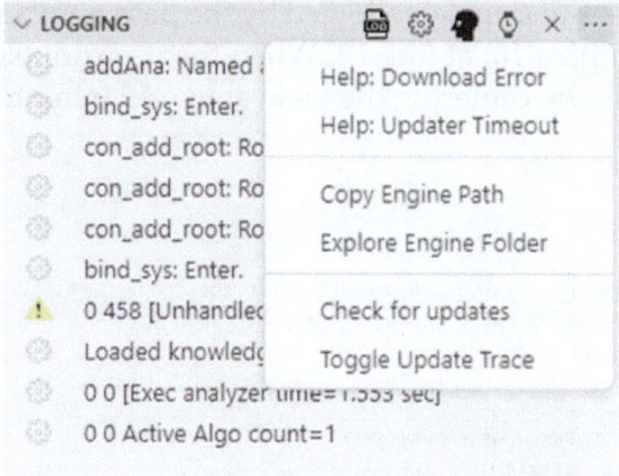

Figure 4.29: LOGGING view extended menu

The following table lists the explanation of each menu item:

Menu item	Description
Help: Download Error	Display a help page for download errors.
Help: Update Timeout	Display a help page for analyzer timeouts.
Copy Engine Path	Copy path to NLP engine (i.e., where **`nlp.exe`** resides).
Explore Engine Folder	Open and explore the NLP engine folder.
Check for Updates	Run the updater, which updates or repairs VisualText files.
Toggle Update Trace	Toggle the update trace to display the updater's work in real-world.

Table 4.14: LOGGING view menu items

Log view syntax warnings and errors

When the NLP engine encounters a syntax error, the error appears in the log view. This normally happens automatically in the log view; otherwise, the user can click on the cog icon to examine the syntax error messages.

In the NLP example analyzer in this book, suppose the user has accidentally misspelled the rule element attribute **match** as **matcher** in pass *16*, **`personAttributes`**. The generated syntax error then appears in the log view pane (refer to the following figure):

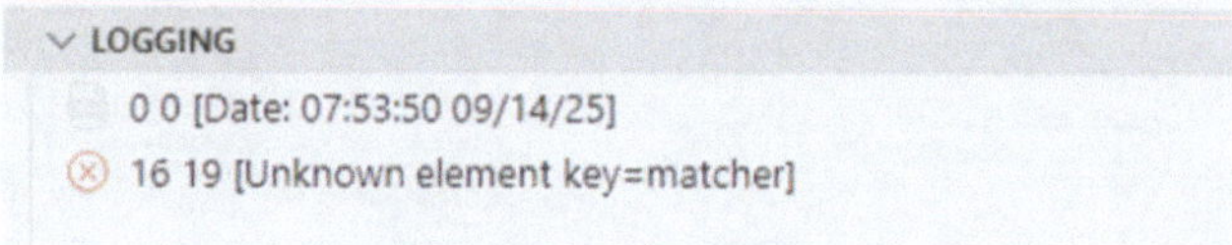

Figure 4.30: Logging view errors and warnings

A syntax error is marked as **x** in a circle, followed by the pass number and line number. In this case, the syntax error is in pass *16*, at line *19*. When the user double-clicks on the error line, VisualText displays pass file *16*, centering the view at line *19* (refer to the following):

```
14
15  @RULES
16  _personAttrs <-
17      _person                                  ### (1)
18      _be                                      ### (2)
19      _xWILD [matcher=(\, also the)]           ### (3)
20      _xWILD [plus match=(_attribute \,)] ### (4)
21      @@
22
23  @POST
24  PersonAttributes(N(1),N(2));
25  single();
26
27  @RULES
28  _personAttrs <-
29      _person                                  ### (1)
30      _xWILD [plus match=(_attribute \,)] ### (2)
31      @@
32
```

Figure 4.31: *Display of the pass file at the line number of the syntax error*

Tracing through an analyzer

A key aspect of VisualText is interconnectivity between the input text, parse tree, pass files, rewrite rules, KB, and dictionaries. We use the date-time analyzer in the **`nlpfix-analyzers`** folder.

View text and tree from analyzer sequence

The following figure shows that, starting with the analyzer sequence, one can display:

1. Highlighted matched text.
2. Updated parse tree for a specific pass.

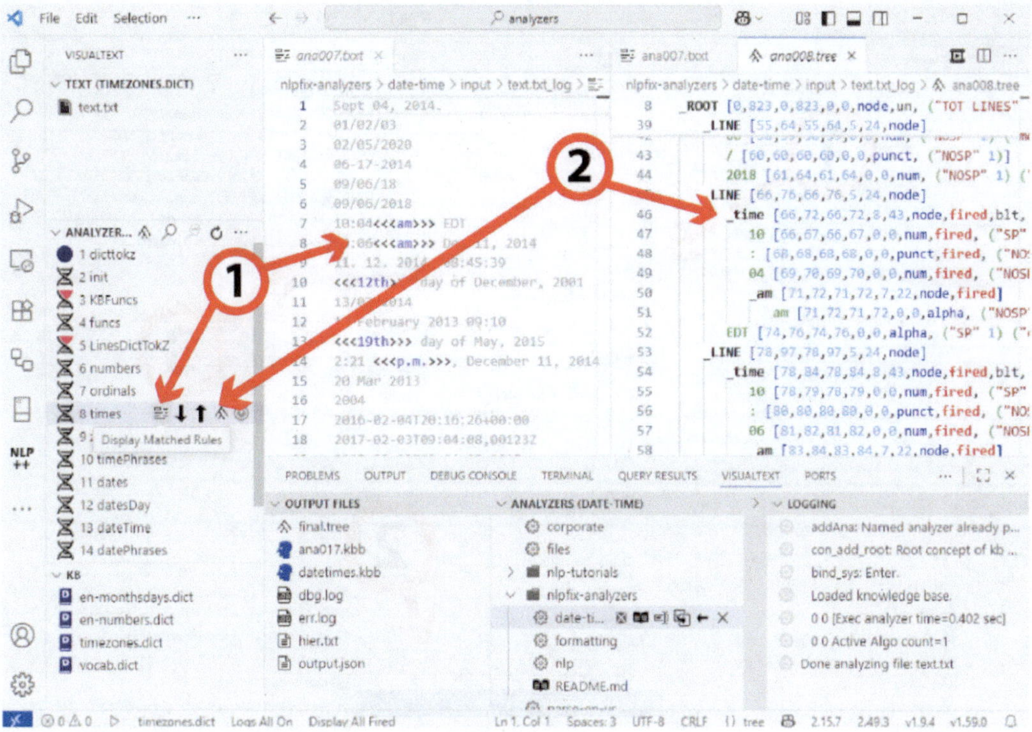

***Figure 4.32**: Analyzer sequence pass highlights matched text and displays the parse-tree-so-far*

One can view the state of the analysis so far at each pass of the analyzer sequence. Each pass in the analyzer sequence provides various ways for the user to visualize its work as well as the state of the analysis so far. If the analyzer was run with logs turned on, the user can click **Display Matched Rules** to highlight text matched by the current pass. Clicking **Open Tree File** shows the state of the parse tree at the selected pass.

View selected tree from text

With larger trees, it is often convenient to look at only a portion of the tree from the text. This option is available in both the text file in the text view and from the rule-match highlighted text (**`.txxt`**) files. Select the desired text, right-click, and choose **View selected tree**. A pop-up window then displays the desired part of the parse tree.

If you are viewing the original text and not a highlighted pass file, then the tree portion derives from the final parse tree. If you are in a highlighted pass file, then the portion of the tree comes from the tree associated with that pass. The following figure shows:

1. Select and highlight the desired text.
2. Choose **View selected tree**.
3. View partial tree.

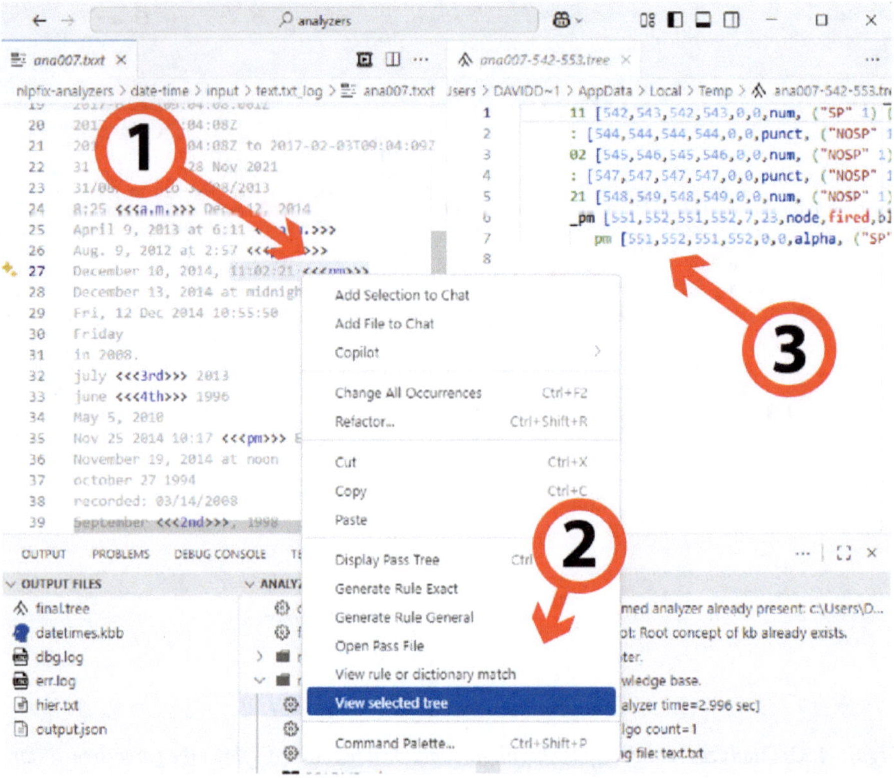

Figure 4.33: View of the partial tree associated with a selected piece of input text

View rule or dictionary match from text

To see which rule matched in the text highlighted window (**.txxt**), right-click on the matched word or phrase and choose **View rule or dictionary match**. A pop-up window displays the matched rule in the current pass file. The following figure shows:

1. Right-click on highlighted text.
2. Choose **View rule or dictionary match**.
3. View rule.

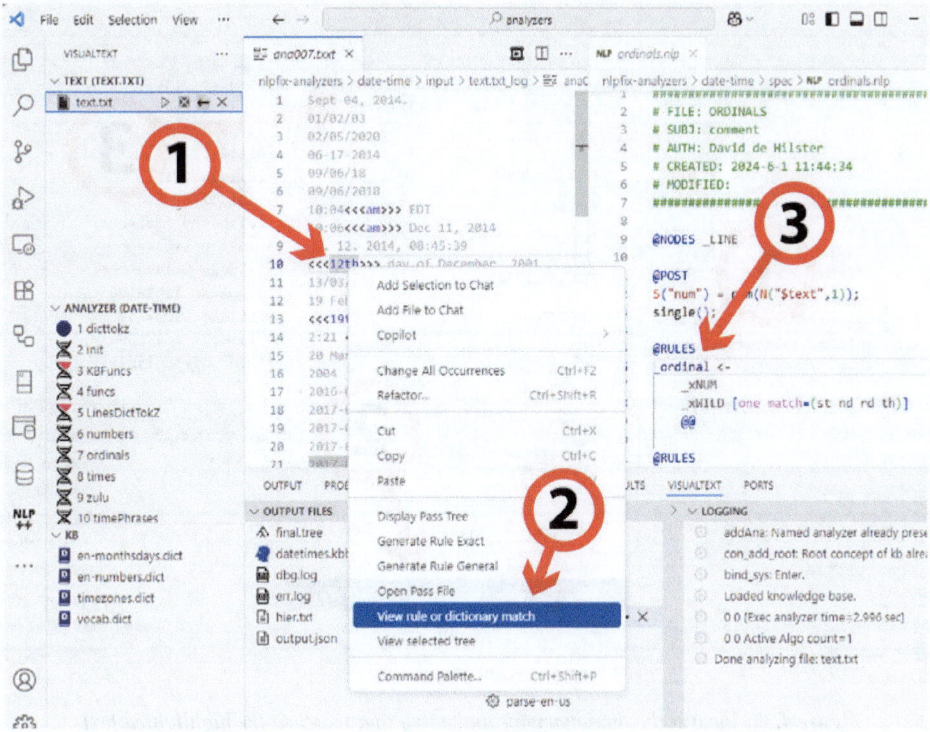

***Figure 4.34**: View of the pass file and rule that matched the highlighted text*

The following figure shows:

1. Right-click on highlighted text.
2. Choose **View rule or dictionary match**.
3. View dictionary.

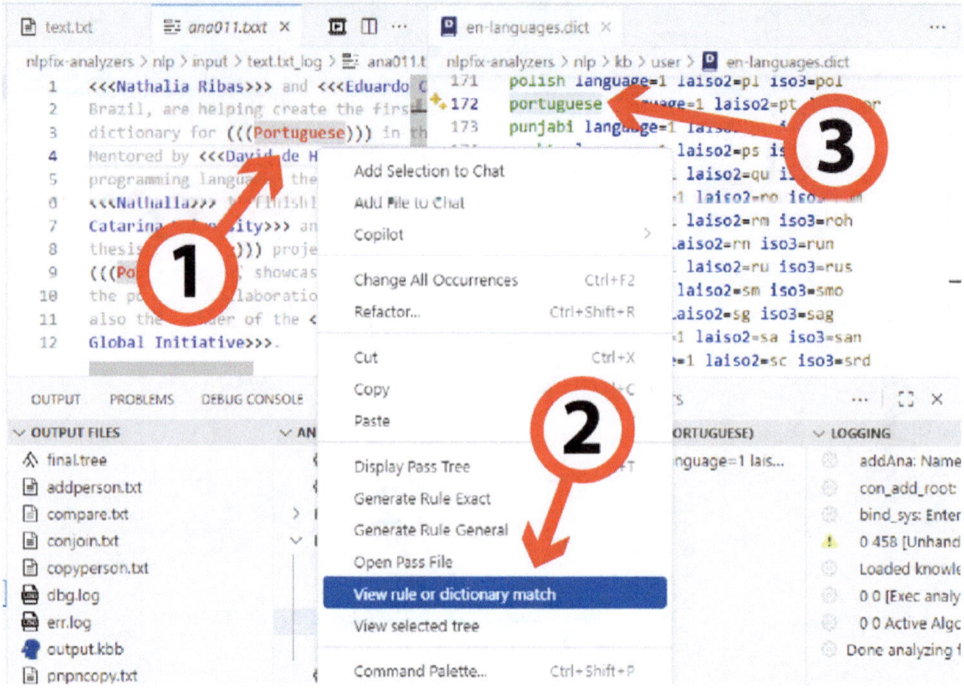

Figure 4.35: *View of the dictionary file and entry that matched the highlighted text*

Display Rule Fired from tree

When examining the tree, one can go directly to the rule that created a node. Click on the desired node line, right-click, and choose **Display Rule Fired** to bring up the rule file. The following figure shows:

1. Right-click on fired node.
2. Select **Display Rule Fired** from the menu.
3. View selected rule.

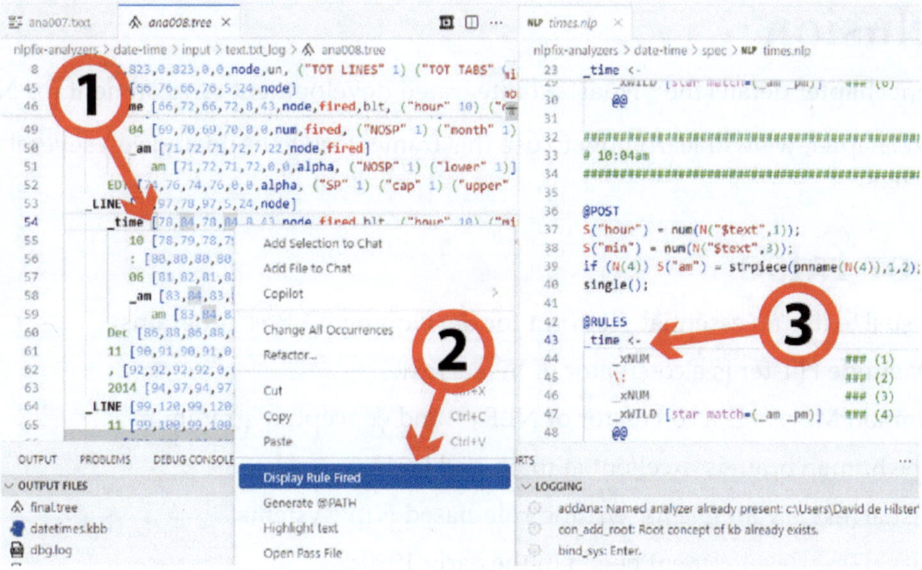

Figure 4.36: View the pass file and rule that created the selected parse tree node

Highlight text from tree

To highlight the text for a portion of the tree, highlight lines of the tree, right-click, and choose **Highlight text**, and a pop-up displays the corresponding text:

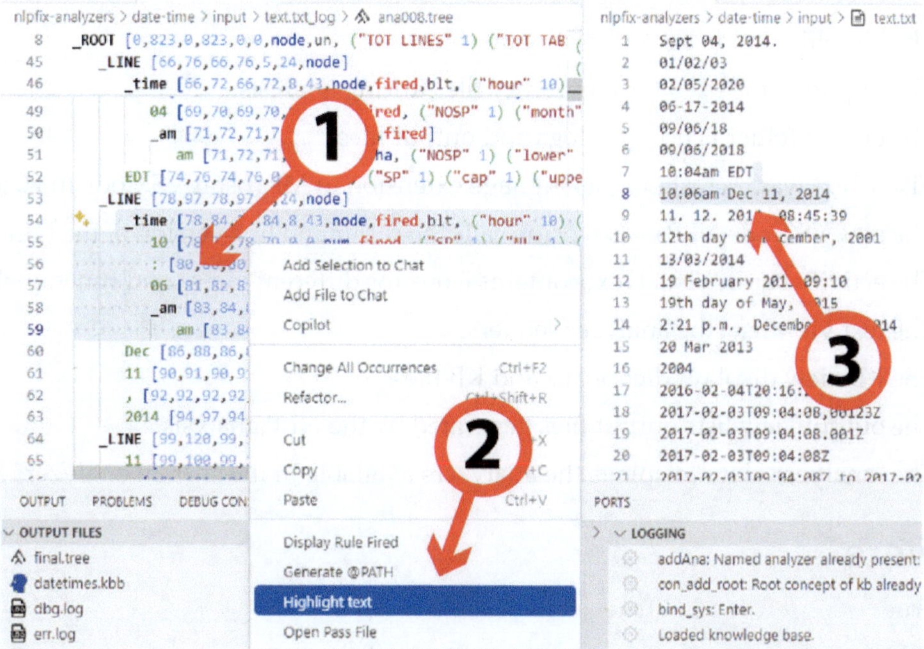

Figure 4.37: View the text associated with the selected lines of the parse tree

Conclusion

The current chapter details the VisualText integrated development environment for NLP++.

In the next chapter, we will learn how to use this framework to build and run several types of text analyzers.

True or false

1. VisualText is an essential platform for developing NLP++ programs.
2. David de Hilster is a co-creator of VisualText.
3. Amnon Meyers is a co-creator of NLP++ and conceptual grammar.
4. The human brain is excellent at math and logic.
5. VisualText is valuable for writing rule-based NLP systems.
6. VisualText development began in the early 1990s.
7. TexUS was developed by de Hilster and Meyers at the McDonnell Douglas AI lab.
8. VisualText ran only on Windows originally.
9. VisualText employs Windows graphical widgets.
10. The NLP++ analyzer folder structure includes a debug folder.
11. The spec folder contains .nlp files.
12. The kb folder holds KB and dictionary files.
13. The tmp folder is used for temporary files during analysis.
14. The output folder is used for logs and output files.
15. VisualText was recreated as a language extension in Microsoft VS Code in 2020.
16. The new VS Code NLP++ extension calls the command line version of the NLP engine.
17. The activity bar in VisualText contains icons for different views and functionalities.
18. The text view lists the analyzer sequence.
19. The KB view displays dictionary and KB files.
20. The output view lists output files generated by the NLP analysis.
21. The "analyzer view" displays the analyzers available in the current analyzers folder.

Answers

1. True
2. True
3. True
4. False
5. True
6. False

7. True 8. True 9. True
10. False 11. True 12. True
13. True 14. True 15. True
16. True 17. True 18. False
19. True 20. True 21. True

Multiple choice questions

1. **What is VisualText?**
   a. A programming language
   b. An essential platform for developing NLP++ programs
   c. A text editor
   d. A database management system
2. **Who are the creators of VisualText?**
   a. John Meyers b. David de Hilster
   c. Michael Page d. IBM
   e. Amnon Meyers
3. **What is the human brain adept at processing?**
   a. Numbers b. Faces
   c. Text d. Logic
4. **When did VisualText development begin?**
   a. Early 1990s b. Late 1998
   c. 2001 d. 2020
5. **What was the predecessor IDE to VisualText?**
   a. TexUS b. NLP++
   c. VOX d. Conceptual grammar KBMS
6. **Which company developed VisualText initially?**
   a. IBM b. NASDAQ
   c. Text Analysis International d. Educational Testing Service
7. **What does the input folder store?**
   a. Rule files b. KB files
   c. Text files d. Log files

8. **What is contained in the spec folder?**
    a. Temporary files
    b. Analyzer sequence file and .nlp files
    c. Dictionary files
    d. KB files
9. **What is the purpose of the tmp folder?**
    a. To store input files
    b. To hold KB files
    c. To store intermediate files during analysis
    d. To store log output files
10. **What does the output folder contain?**
    a. Text files
    b. Rule files
    c. Log files
    d. KB files and dictionaries
11. **In which year was VisualText recreated as a language extension in VS Code?**
    a. 1998
    b. 2001
    c. 2020
    d. 2023
12. **What does the new VS Code NLP++ extension call?**
    a. The command line version of the NLP engine
    b. The graphical version of the NLP engine
    c. The web version of the NLP engine
    d. The mobile version of the NLP engine
13. **What does the activity bar contain?**
    a. Icons for different views and functionalities
    b. List of text files
    c. Analyzer sequence
    d. Output files
14. **What does the text view display?**
    a. Dictionary files
    b. Analyzer sequence
    c. Text files to be processed by the analyzer
    d. Log output files

15. **What does the KB view display?**
    a. Text files
    b. Analyzer sequence
    c. Dictionary and KB files
    d. Log output files
16. **What does the output view list?**
    a. Text files
    b. Analyzer sequence
    c. Dictionary files
    d. Output files generated by the NLP analysis
17. **What does the analyzer view display?**
    a. Text files
    b. Analyzer sequence
    c. Analyzers available in the current analyzers folder
    d. Log output files
18. **What is the purpose of the spec folder?**
    a. To store input files
    b. To hold KB files
    c. To store temporary files during analysis
    d. To contain .nlp files
19. **What is the tmp folder used for?**
    a. To store input files
    b. To hold KB files
    c. To store temporary files during analysis
    d. To store log output files
20. **What does the output folder contain?**
    a. Input files
    b. Grammar rules
    c. Log output files
    d. KB files

Answers

1. b	2. b, e	3. b, c
4. b	5. a	6. c

7. c
8. b
9. c
10. a, c
11. c
12. a
13. a
14. c
15. c
16. d
17. c
18. d
19. c
20. c

Short answer questions

1. What is VisualText and why is it important for NLP++?
2. Who is a co-creator of VisualText and what is his perspective on its importance?
3. Describe the human brain's capabilities in relation to math, logic, and language understanding.
4. When did VisualText development begin and what was its predecessor?
5. What is the significance of the input folder in the NLP++ analyzer folder structure?
6. What types of files are contained in the spec folder?
7. Explain the purpose of the tmp folder in the NLP++ analyzer folder structure.
8. What is the role of the output folder in the NLP++ analyzer folder structure?
9. How was VisualText recreated in 2020 and what platform does it use?
10. What does the activity bar in VisualText contain?
11. Describe the text view in VisualText.
12. What is displayed in the KB view of VisualText?
13. What types of files are listed in the Output View of VisualText?
14. What does the analyzer view in VisualText show?
15. What is the purpose of the spec folder in the NLP++ analyzer folder structure?
16. Describe the function of the tmp folder in the NLP++ analyzer folder structure.
17. What is contained in the output folder of the NLP++ analyzer folder structure?
18. How does the new VS Code NLP++ extension interact with the NLP engine?
19. What is the significance of the activity bar in VisualText?
20. Explain the role of the "text view" in VisualText.

References

1. *Proceedings of the 6th Message Understanding Conference (MUC-6). Defense Advanced Research Projects Agency (DARPA). San Mateo, CA: Morgan Kaufmann Publishers, 1993.*

CHAPTER 5

NLP++ Philosophy and Libraries

Introduction

While NLP++ is a general programming language, it is designed specifically for constructing **natural language processing** (**NLP**) systems. It supports the use of authoritative knowledge, the dynamic creation of knowledge structures to represent the understanding of text, a grammar rule system, and a rich set of predefined library functions, all within a uniform pipeline architecture. As such, NLP++ enables the developer to think like a human or, in other words, to emulate the processes involved in understanding text.

Structure

In this chapter, we will discuss the following topics:

- Thinking like a human
- History
- Library functions

Objectives

By the end of this chapter, the reader will learn about the unique philosophy for the development of NLP systems, as supported by NLP++. As well, the reader will be introduced to the many library functions that accelerate the development of text analyzers. The chapter paves the way for actually developing various types of text analyzers.

Thinking like a human

Thinking like a human means emulating the processes that occur in human text understanding. NLP++ uniquely supports the encoding of such processes by integrating knowledge use and creation as well as grammar rules and actions into a general programming language. The pipeline architecture enables the construction of a best-first understanding of the meaning of the text being analyzed.

Cognitive model

The NLP++ framework, designed by *Amnon Meyers* and *David de Hilster*, supports cognitive models that emulate human reading and understanding of text. The framework includes the following:

- Synergistic, uniform, flexible glass-box pipeline architecture.
- Multi-paradigm NLP (bottom-up, top-down, island-driven, etc.).
- NLP++ language fully integrated with parse tree and KB management.
- Support for rule-based and knowledge-based NLP.
- Construction of a single, best-first parse tree.
- Parse tree system.
- Rule-based pattern matching system.
- NLP support for recursive grammars, tokenizers, and more.
- Hierarchical **knowledge base management system** (**KBMS**) called **conceptual grammar** (**CG**).
- Dictionary system.

David de Hilster, co-creator of NLP++, in a lecture at *Clemson in 2022* [1], defined traditional programming and intelligent programming as follows:

- **Traditional programming**: Think like a computer.
- **Intelligent programming**: Think like a human.

De Hilster facetiously lays out the two most important rules when programming in NLP++:

- Think like a human.
- Think like a human.

Before NLP++, computational linguists and NLP developers were left only with general programming languages not built for text processing, such as C++ and Java. The resulting systems typically featured a pipeline of black-box modules merged from independent programming groups (often students at universities). Substantial effort was needed to get the modules to work together, rather than working on the NLP task at hand.

With the advent of the computer programming language NLP++, developers could build a uniform pipeline of glass-box (i.e., fully transparent) passes, all in the same language and all operating on a single parse tree and KB. System development could now focus on the NLP task, a profound advance in natural language engineering.

With that advance, NLP developers could now consider the methods people use when reading and understanding text. This is a skill that new NLP++ developers have to learn.

Note: Throughout the book, notes like this identify where developers can think about how humans do a certain task with text. This is a major benefit to programming with NLP++.

History

The roots of NLP++ come from its two creators, Amnon Meyers and David de Hilster, who have worked in NLP since the early 1980s. Both have the philosophy of getting computers to understand language in the way that we humans do.

Collaboration

In 1990, de Hilster joined Meyers at the **artificial intelligence** (**AI**) group at *McDonnell Douglas* in *Huntington Beach, California*, where he helped move the Vox program to C++. Their collaboration combined island-driven parsing with the CG KBMS, yielding the **Text Understanding Shell** (**TexUS**) system. They applied TexUS to the **Third Message Understanding Conference** (**MUC-3**) and **Fourth Message Understanding Conference** (**MUC-4**) workshops sponsored by the *Defense Advanced Research Projects Agency* (*DARPA*) [2] in the early 1990s. They placed fourth among 12 participating groups that included *MIT*, *SRI*, *BBN*, and *Carnegie Mellon*.

In the mid-1990s, both joined the AI group at *TRW Space Park*. De Hilster's work inspired the creation of the company *ISearch*, which electronically processed resumes. De Hilster joined ISearch in 1997, converting their NLP system to the C language.

In 1998, Meyers co-founded *Text Analysis International* and, with de Hilster, created NLP++, VisualText, and a new CG KBMS. VisualText is an IDE comprising a uniform pipeline architecture specifically tailored to NLP++, its tree structures, and its KB. Meyers implemented both the NLP++ runtime system and CG KBMS in C++.

NLP++ goes open-source

During the 2000s and 2010s, the technology was privately owned and was licensed by private companies to process medical, social media, historical documents, and real estate text. In December 2018 Text Analysis International dissolved and the technology went open-source, so that the NLP engine is now available as open-source freeware.

Starting in 2018, de Hilster created the NLP engine, consisting of a new version of VisualText housed as a VS Code language extension, and including human-readable dictionary and KB files.

De Hilster, working at *LexisNexis Risk* (years 2016-2024), created an NLP++ plug-in for the *HPCC Systems* supercomputer. He also mentored NLP projects for interns and international university students.

The collaborations with students and universities culminated in the creation of the **Natural Language Understanding Global Initiative** (**NLUGI**), founded in 2023 to promote NLP++ as a universal programming language for rule-based NLP systems. This led to the first master's thesis using NLP++ as the main technology[3]. Plans are underway for a university course to teach rule-based NLP and NLP++.

VisualText comes with an ever-growing library of useful functions and passes, accessed via the KB panel in VisualText. (**Library location**: **https://github.com/VisualText/visualtext-files**).

Library functions

Right-clicking in the **KB** panel brings up the menu (refer to the following figure):

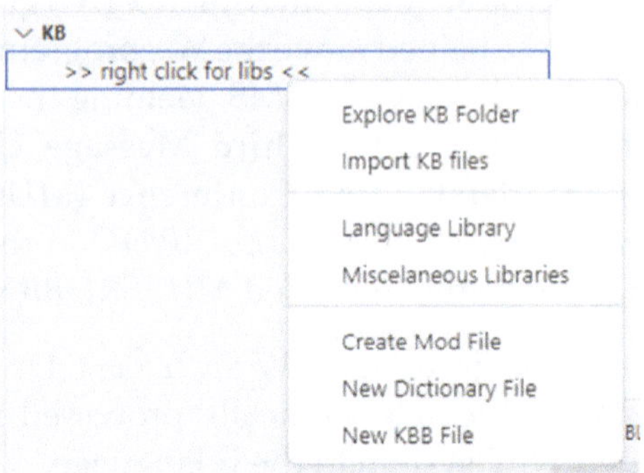

***Figure 5.1**: Right-click menu in the KB panel*

Currently, the libraries are categorized according to human languages, refer to the following figure:

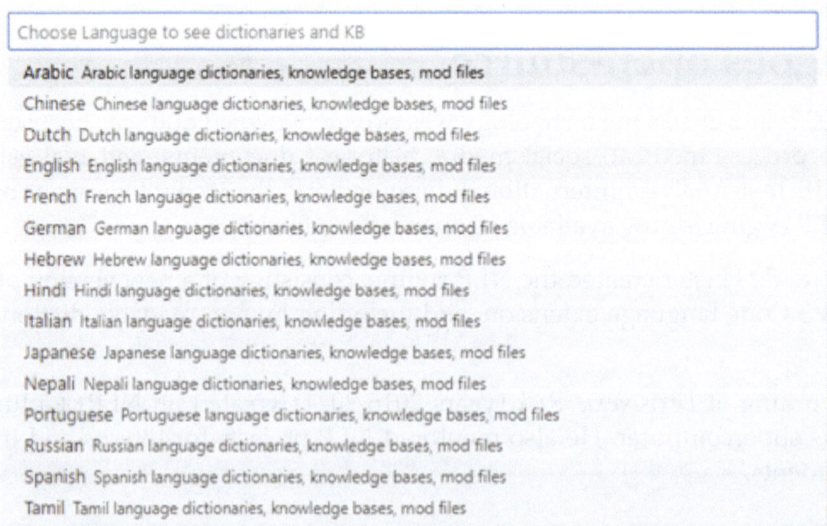

***Figure 5.2**: Language library selections currently available*

Choosing the **English** line brings up the following, as listed in the following figure:

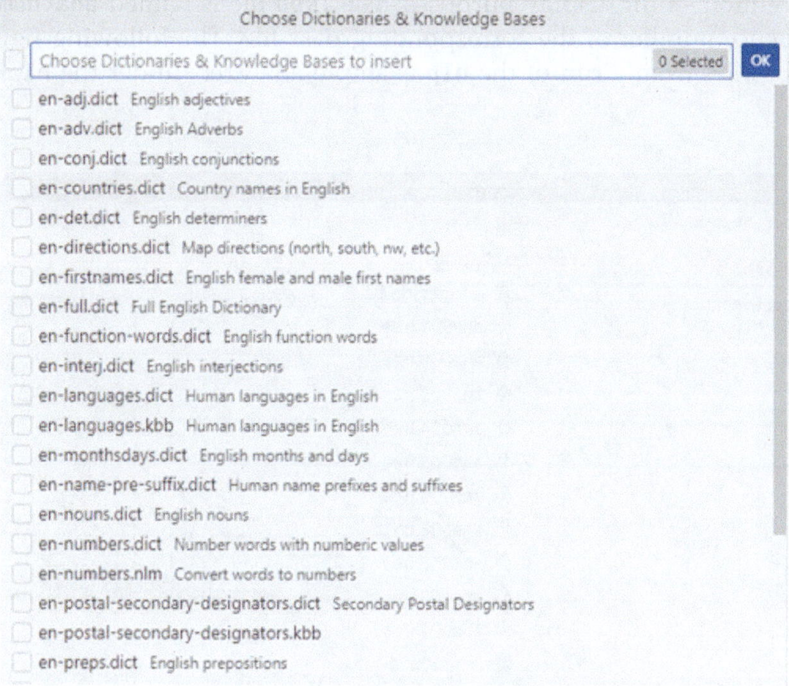

***Figure 5.3**: English pop-up library in VisualText*

Knowledge base functions

In early versions of the VS Code NLP++ Language Extension (what is currently called VisualText), de Hilster created KB functions and others, useful to his interns. This yielded the `KBFuncs` function library, found in the right-click menu under **Library Functions**, within the analyzer sequence view.

The original VisualText, implemented with Microsoft Visual C++, runs exclusively on Windows, bundled with the NLP engine. There, the CG KBMS is accessible as an interactive window. In the second incarnation of VisualText, a VS Code language extension , this is no longer possible. The VS Code version calls the nlp.exe executable and in that way accesses the internal memory of an analyzer run. The only way to view the state of the KB is to manually dump it to a readable file.

Due to this limitation, de Hilster coded the `DisplayKB` function to print out the KB in human-readable form. The user can dump any part of the KB at any pass of the analyzer pipeline. Since, the file extension `.kb` was already in use for KB command files, so the new file extension `.kbb` was created for human-readable KB files, facetiously called **KB beautiful files**.

The **DisplayKB** function, in order to coordinate with the current analyzer pass, uses the following convention -- for display purposes: The **.kbb** file is named **ana<num>.kbb**, where **num** is the sequence number of the corresponding pass file. The following figure shows the listing of the log files from a run of the **nlp** example analyzer (under the **nlpfix-analyzers** folder):

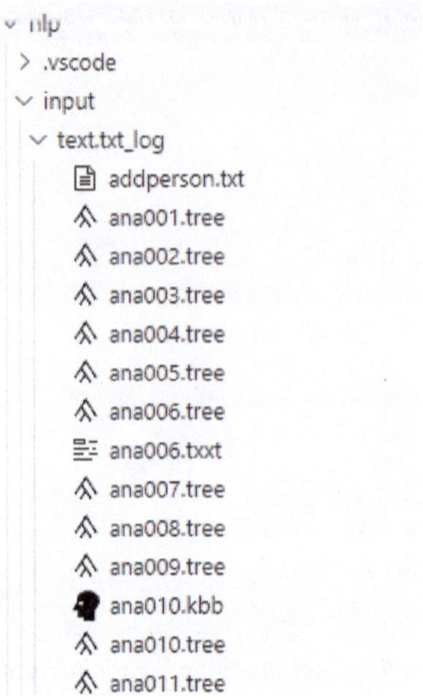

Figure 5.4: Listing of log files with a KBB dump file

The following figure shows the **OUTPUT FILES** view, which lists text files created by the analysis of the current input, as well as files created by the runtime system (such as the final text tree, named **final.tree**.):

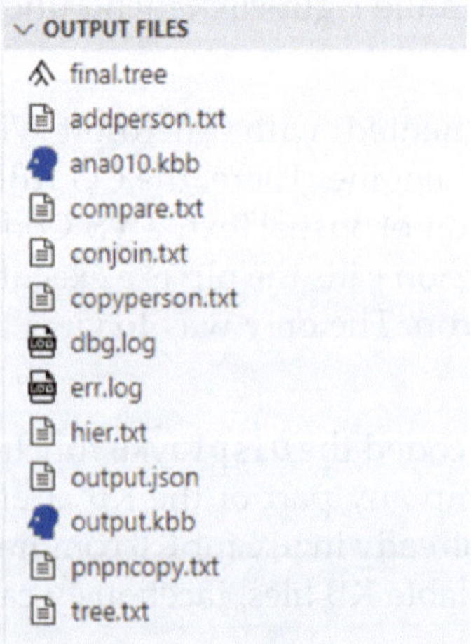

Figure 5.5: Output view for the NLP example analyzer

The following figure shows the compact view of the KB, as generated via the **DisplayKB** function:

```
caps
  Nathalia Ribas: sent=["concept" "article" "sentence001"], "person_count"=1, pn="2 1"
  Eduardo Costa: sent=["concept" "article" "sentence001"], "person_count"=1, pn="2 3"
  Portuguese: sent=["concept" "article" "sentence001","concept" "article" "sentence003"], pn=["2 4","12 14"]
  AI: sent=["concept" "article" "sentence001","concept" "article" "sentence003"], pn=["2 5","12 13"]
  David de Hilster: sent=["concept" "article" "sentence001"], "person_count"=1, pn="2 6"
  LexisNexis: sent=["concept" "article" "sentence001"], pn="2 7"
  Nathalia: sent=["concept" "article" "sentence002"], "person_count"=1, pn="9 8", full=["concept" "caps" "Nathalia Ribas"]
  Santa Catarina University: sent=["concept" "article" "sentence002"], pn="9 10", "person_count"=1, "school_count"=1
  Their: sent=["concept" "article" "sentence003"], pn="12 11"
  De Hilster: sent=["concept" "article" "sentence004"], pn="16 15", full=["concept" "caps" "David de Hilster"]
  Natural Language Understanding Global Initiative: sent=["concept" "article" "sentence004"], pn="16 17", "cause_count"=1
```

Figure 5.6: DisplayKB with display type 2, or compact

The following figure shows the normal KB view, also available via the **DisplayKb** function:

```
caps
  Nathalia Ribas:
    sent=["concept" "article" "sentence001"]
    "person_count"=1
    pn="2 1"
  Eduardo Costa:
    sent=["concept" "article" "sentence001"]
    "person_count"=1
    pn="2 3"
  Portuguese:
    sent=["concept" "article" "sentence001","concept" "article" "sentence003"]
    pn=["2 4","12 14"]
  AI:
    sent=["concept" "article" "sentence001","concept" "article" "sentence003"]
    pn=["2 5","12 13"]
  David de Hilster:
    sent=["concept" "article" "sentence001"]
    "person_count"=1
    pn="2 6"
  LexisNexis:
    sent=["concept" "article" "sentence001"]
    pn="2 7"
  Nathalia:
    sent=["concept" "article" "sentence002"]
    "person_count"=1
    pn="9 8"
    full=["concept" "caps" "Nathalia Ribas"]
  Santa Catarina University:
    sent=["concept" "article" "sentence002"]
    pn="9 10"
    "person_count"=1
    "school_count"=1
  Their:
    sent=["concept" "article" "sentence003"]
    pn="12 11"
  De Hilster:
    sent=["concept" "article" "sentence004"]
    pn="16 15"
    full=["concept" "caps" "David de Hilster"]
  Natural Language Understanding Global Initiative:
    sent=["concept" "article" "sentence004"]
    pn="16 17"
    "cause_count"=1
```

Figure 5.7: DisplayKB example with normal format

The following tables describe the functions available in the **KBFuncs** library. They are concerned with displaying, loading, and saving the KB, as well as manipulating its component concepts.

Table 6.1 describes the KB display functions:

Function	Description
DisplayAttributes (file, con, type, level)	Display **con** attributes.
DisplayFileName ()	Return display file name for current pass.
DisplayKB (top con, display type)	Display KB to file with given display type.
DisplayKBRecurse (file, parent, lev-el, **display type)**	Recursively display the KB hierarchy.
KBHeader (text)	Write a header to display the file.

***Table 5.1**: KBFuncs library,display functions*

Table 6.2 describes the functions that load and save the KB:

Function	Description
DumpKB (con, file)	Dump the KB hierarchy to a file.
SaveKB (file, top con, display type)	Save KB to a file with the given display type.
SaveToKB (con, name)	Save **con** to **.kbb** file.
TakeKB (filename)	Load KB from file.

***Table 5.2**: KBFuncs library—KB management functions*

Table 6.3 describes the functions that output the KB in the JSON format:

Function	Description
JsonAttributes (file, con, level)	Output **con** attributes as JSON.
JsonKB (file, con)	Output KB in JSON format.
JsonKBRecurse (file, parent, level)	Recursively output KB as JSON.
JsonStr (str)	Escape and quote string for JSON output.

***Table 5.3**: KBFuncs library—JSON output functions*

Table 6.4 describes the KB dictionary functions:

Function	Description
DictionaryEnd()	Close dictionary attributes file.

Function	Description
`DictionaryStart()`	Open the dictionary attributes file for writing.
`DictionaryWord (word, attrName, value, attrType)`	Write word and its **attr** to the dictionary file.
`OrderByCount (words, order)`	Order words by their count **attr**.

***Table 5.4**: KBFuncs library—KB dictionary functions*

Table 6.5 describes the functions that manage KB concepts:

Function	Description
`AddUniqueCon (con, name)`	Add a unique con with the given name under the given **con**.
`AddUniqueConVal (con, attr, val)`	Add a unique concept **val** to **con attr**.
`AddUniqueNum (con, attr, val)`	Add a unique numeric **val** to **con attr**.
`AddUniqueStr (con, attr, val)`	Add a unique string **val** to **con attr**.
`AmbigCopyAttrs (con, node, pos)`	Copy **attr** from **con** to **node**, excluding **pos**.
`AmbigTrimPOS (node, pos)`	Trim ambiguous **pos** from the **node**.
`AttrValues (con, attr)`	Return values of **con attr**.
`CopyAttr (from, to, attr)`	Copy string **attr** from **con** to **con**, if absent.
`CopyAttrNew (from, to, attr from, attr to)`	Copy string **attr** from **con** to **con**, rename.
`CopyConAttr (from, to, attr)`	Copy **attr** from **con** to **con**, if absent.
`CopyConAttrs (from, to)`	Copy all **attr** from **con** to **con**.
`IncrementCount (con, countname)`	Increment and return **con countname**.
`LastChild (parent)`	Return the last child of **con**.
`PathToConcept (parent, hier)`	Navigate or create a path of concepts from the parent, using a hierarchy string.

***Table 5.5**: KBFuncs library—KB concept functions*

Table 6.6 describes the KB count functions:

Function	Description
`ChildCount (con)`	Count **con** children
`CountName (con, root, pad)`	Generate a counted name for **con**, with optional padding.
`IsCountCon(str, con)`	Check if a **con** is a counted **con**.
`MakeCountCon (con, count name)`	Create a child of **con** with a **count name.**

Function	Description
MakeCountConPad (con, countname, pad)	Create a child of **con** with a padded **countname**.
SeparateConCount (conname)	Separate the counted **conname** into base and count.
ValCount (vals)	Count **vals** in list.

***Table 5.6**: KBFuncs library—KB count functions*

Table 6.7 describes the string functions:

Function	Description
IsPOS (pos)	Check if the string is a **POS**
PadStr (num str, pad str, pad len)	Pad string with another string to the specified length
QuoteIfNeeded (str)	Quote string if it contains spaces or punctuation
RepeatStr (num, str)	Repeat a string a given number of times
SpacesStr (num)	Return a string of spaces for indentation
StripEndDigits (name)	Remove trailing digits from a string

***Table 5.7**: KBFuncs library—string functions*

Tree functions

In the following table, **pn_path_str** refers to a list of unique ID numbers, converted to a string, that represents the path to a specific parse tree node. (For example, **3, 7** means, start at the parse tree root and find its child node with **id** equal **3**. Then find that **node** child with **id** equal **7**). A KB concept's **pn** attribute may refer to one or more parse tree nodes as a list of **pn_path_str** strings, and each parse tree node has a unique ID number in its **id** attribute. (See KB references to the Parse tree section in *Chapter 6, Developing Text Analyzers*).

Function	Description
PNCopyAttrsToCPn (from_pn, to_pn)	Copy all attributes from **from_pn** to **to_pn**. Analogous to **pncopyvars(from_pn, to_pn)**.
PNCopyAttrsToCon (pn, con)	Copy all attributes from **pn** to **con**, handling types.
PNIncrement (pn, var)	Increment/Create num-valued **var** on **pn**.

Function	Description
`AddTreeID (con, pn)`	Assign unique IDs to the **id** attribute of **pn** and its ancestors. Create and add **pn_path_str** to the **pn** attribute of **con**.
`TreeNodeID (pn_path_str)`	Find the parse tree node designated by **pn_path_str**.
`TreeNodeWithID (pn, id)`	Find a node with a specific ID among siblings.
`MarkFired (con)`	Mark **con** associated parse tree node as fired, using **con pn** attribute.

Table 5.8: Listing of KB to parse tree functions

Conclusion

In this chapter, the reader learned about the philosophy of developing analyzers with NLP++, as well as the various library functions that help accelerate analyzer development.

In the next chapter, the reader will apply the acquired NLP++ background to developing several types of text analyzers.

True or false

1. NLP++ is a programming language designed for general-purpose programming.
2. David de Hilster and Amnon Meyers co-founded Text Analysis International in 1998.
3. Before NLP++, computational linguists primarily used the Python programming language for text processing.

Answers

1. False
2. True
3. False

Multiple choice questions

1. **What is the main focus of NLP++?**

   a. Image processing
   b. Text analysis
   c. Data analysis
   d. Web development

2. **Which of the following systems is NOT part of the NLP++ architecture?**
   a. Tokenizers
   b. Neural networks
   c. Parse tree system
   d. Knowledge base system
3. **Who defined traditional programming as "think like a computer" and intelligent programming as "think like a human"?**
   a. Amnon Meyers
   b. David de Hilster
   c. Alan Turing
   d. John McCarthy

Answers

1. b
2. b
3. b

Short answer questions

1. What are the two most important rules when programming in NLP++, according to David de Hilster?
2. Name one of the early text analysis systems developed by Amnon Meyers.
3. What is the main advantage of NLP++ over previous programming languages used for NLP tasks?
4. In what year did NLP++ technology change to open-source?
5. Pick a task that humans perform when reading and understanding text. Explain how a human performs that task and how that could be translated into an NLP++ analyzer.
6. Pick a task that computers do very well and that humans do not. Then choose a task that humans do well, and computers do not. Compare and contrast.
7. Explain why it is not natural for a computer programmer to examine how humans do tasks, and what the difficulties are in learning to think like a human when it comes to reading and understanding text.

References

1. *David de Hilster. Lecture at Clemson University. YouTube video*. Available at **https://www.youtube.com/watch?v=RD21vl5-sJo**. 2022.
2. *Proceedings of the 6th Message Understanding Conference (MUC-6). Defense Advanced Research Projects Agency (DARPA). San Mateo, CA: Morgan Kaufmann Publishers, 1993.*
3. *Ashton Williamson, David de Hilster, Amnon Meyers, Nina Hubig, and Amy Apon. 2024 Low Resource ICD Coding of Hospital Discharge Summaries. In Proceedings of the 23rd Workshop on Biomedical Natural Language Processing, pages 548-558, Bangkok, Thailand. Association for Computational Linguistics.*

CHAPTER 6

Developing Text Analyzers

Introduction

VisualText and NLP++ comprise a unique framework for developing text analyzers. Multiple NLP++ passes provide a 100% transparent, uniform, and modifiable analyzer pipeline, while Visualtext offers powerful visualization tools for step-by-step elaboration of a single best-first parse tree. The associated KB supports all needed linguistic and domain knowledge, as well as enabling the dynamic construction of semantic and conceptual representations of the text being analyzed.

Structure

This chapter discusses the following topics:

- VisualText
- Text view
- Trees
- Tree vs. knowledge base
- Output
- Creating an analyzer
- NLP++ editor
- Text highlights
- Ambiguity

Objectives

By the end of this chapter, the reader will learn the basics of using VisualText and NLP++ to construct text analyzers. The reader will also gain an understanding of issues and tradeoffs attending the analyzer development process.

VisualText

VisualText, when combined with the NLP++ programming language and the **conceptual grammar** (CG) hierarchical **knowledge base management system** (KBMS), is a powerful IDE for **natural language processing** (NLP). From simple analyzers for calendar dates to full-blown natural language understanding systems, the IDE is ideal for any text analysis system because it is not tied to a particular NLP paradigm or technique.

VisualText is well-suited to the following areas:

- Rule-based NLP.
- Knowledge-based NLP.
- Specific applications, tasks, and domains.
- Computational linguistics.
- Text corpus study.

Rule-based NLP has largely disappeared from universities and industry, due to the immense popularity of self-training statistical systems over hand-built systems. With the growing recognition of the limitations of statistical methods in critical flow operations, ever more developers are looking for alternatives. NLP++ is helping revive rule-based NLP both in universities and industry. Universities can start teaching rule-based NLP in computer science and linguistics departments and create a new area of study, a new profession, and new computer applications.

Creating an analyzer

VisualText is the ultimate sandbox for creating text analyzers. It provides a developer with a set of tools that make the process of developing analyzers a visual experience.

The largest and most developed part of our brain and thinking processes is dedicated to vision. This differs greatly from the language part of our brain. Our neural network-like brain is not naturally adept at math, logic, and language. These must be learned via years of study. Human language requires about 4 to 14 years to master, depending on the language. Developing accurate and complete text analyzers is next to impossible without visual tools.

Bottom-up approach

VisualText provides a sandbox in which a developer can immediately grab an input text, run an analyzer, and examine the tokenized parse tree. Next, the developer creates passes and rules for logical token patterns, generating a new tree. In each development cycle, the developer creates rules for larger-scale linguistic units, moving from words to lexical phrases, syntactic patterns, sentence constituents, sentences, and onward to semantic, domain, and task-oriented processing.

Knowledge about words is needed, so the developer can start with an existing dictionary or build a customized one from scratch.

As the analyzer develops, the developer adds needed knowledge to an existing KB library or again builds from scratch.

VisualText is well-suited to bottom-up analyzer development, starting with a single text and generalizing the analyzer by successfully processing each successive text. This approach has worked well for rapid prototyping and proof-of-concept systems, as well as transitioning from these to commercially deployed text analyzers.

Top-down approach

After building a bottom-up prototype analyzer, the developer should re-examine the task as a whole in a top-down fashion.

The number 1 and 2 rules of NLP++ are: *think like a human*. In assessing the text analyzer, the developer assesses the scope of knowledge and methods needed for the end product. Developers need to think about how a person reads and understands the text, and start designing and implementing NLP++ code to mimic this task.

A simple example of this is capitalization. If the input text has mixed capitalization, one can find possible entity names by examining capitalization patterns. Otherwise (for all-lower or all-uppercase text), more expansive development of knowledge, dictionaries, context, and methods may be needed.

Using templates

When creating a new analyzer, the developer is offered a list of template analyzers with which to start. These are located in the **`visualtext-files`** repository under the GitHub VisualText project.

After entering the new analyzer name, this pop-up is given to allow the developer to choose one of the templates as shown in the following figure:

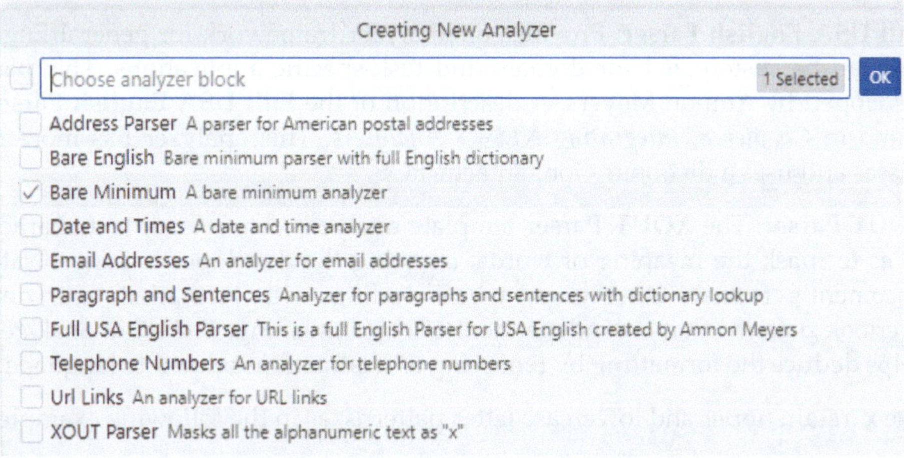

***Figure 6.1**: Template analyzers Available in VisualText*

Available analyzers are described in the following table:

Template analyzer	Description
Address Parser	A parser for American postal addresses.
Bare English	Bare minimum parser with full English dictionary.
Bare Minimum	A bare minimum analyzer.
Date and Times	A date and time analyzer.
Email Addresses	An analyzer for email addresses.
Paragraphs Sentences	Analyzer for paragraphs and sentences with dictionary lookup.
Full USA English Parser	A full English parser for USA English created by Amnon Meyers.
Telephone Numbers	An analyzer for telephone numbers.
URL Links	An analyzer for URL links.
XOUT Parser	Masks all the alphanumeric text as x.

Table 6.1: Template analyzer descriptions

A few of these analyzers are explained further:

- **Bare Minimum**: The **Bare Minimum** is the smallest template analyzer available. It has no passes or KB. This is the most-used analyzer type, as the other options are specialized.
- **Bare English**: The **Bare English** parser features a full English dictionary with more than 190,000 words and syntactic features, including **part of speech** (**POS**) attributes.
- **Full USA English Parser**: Provides an analyzer framework for general English text, and can be customized for domain and task-specific applications. This parser was developed by Amnon Meyers. A description of the **Full USA English Parser** can be found in *Chapter 8, Integrating NLP++ Analyzers*. This analyzer has more than 130 passes and uses a dictionary for syntactic POS.
- **XOUT Parser**: The **XOUT Parser** template analyzer converts all text characters to *x* so as to mask the meaning of words, allowing the developer to concentrate on the document's format. Oftentimes, when dealing with formatted text, developers overlook patterns that are independent of word meaning. The XOut analyzer output helps deduce the formatting by removing all distractions related to language.

  The **x** retain upper and lowercase letter patterns, as in the following example:

```
2
Xxxxxxxx& | Xxxxx xxx xxxxxxxxxxxx: Xxxxx xxxxxxx xx xxxxx xxx xxx
xx xxx xxxxxxx xxxx xxxxxxxxxx xxx xxxxxxx
```

```
3    Xxxx xxx xxxxx xxxxxxx xxxx xxx xxxx xxxxxx xxx xxxxx xxxxxxxx xx
     xxx xxxxx xxxx xxx xxxx xxxx
4    xxxxxxx xxxxxxx xxxxxxxxxx xxxxxx xxxx xxxx xxxxxxxxxxx xxxxx xx
     x xxxxxxx:
5    1. Xxxxxxx Xxxxxxxx Xxxxxxxxxx
6    Xxxxxxxxxxx xxxx xxxxxx xxxxxxxx xxxxx xxxxxx xxx xxx xxxxx xxxx x
     xx xxxxxxx. Xx
7    xxxxxx xxxxxxxx, xxxxxxxx xxxxx xx xxx xxxxx xxxxxxxx xxxxxxx.
8    Xxxx xxx xx xxxxxxxxx xxxx xxxxxxx xx xx xxxxxx xxxx xxxxxx xxxxxx
     xxx xxxxx xxxx xxxxxxxxxx.
9    1. Xxx xxx xxxx xxxxxxxx xxxxxxx? Xxxx'x xxxxxxxx xx xxxx xxxxxxx
     , xxxxxxxx, xxx
10   xxxxxxxxxxx? Xxxx xxxxxx xx xxxxxxxxxx xxxx xxxxxxxxxxx?
11   2. Xxxx xxxxxx xxx xxxxxxx xxxx xxxxxxxxx xx x xxxx-
     xxxxxxxx xxxxx?
12   3. Xxx xxx xxxxxxxxxx xxx xxx xxxxxx xxxx xxxxxxxxxx xxxxx xx xx x
     xxxxx xxxx xxxxxx xxxx xx
13   xxxxx xx xxxx xxxxx xxxxxx? Xxxx xxxx xxxx xxxxxxxxxxx xxxxxxxxx
     xx?
14   4. Xxx xxx xxxxxxxxx xxxxxx xx xxxxx xxx xxxxxx? Xxxxx xx xxx xxx
     x xx xxxxx xxxx xx xxx
15   xxxx xxx xxxxx xx xxxxxxxx xxxxx xx xxxxx-
     xxxxxxxx xxxxxxxxxxxxxxx?
16   Xxxxx xxxxxxxxx xxxxxx xxxx xxx xxxxxxx xxxxx xxxx xxx xxxx-
     xxxxx - xxx xxxxxxx xx
17   xxxxxxxx xxxx xxxxxxxxxxxxx xxxx xxxxxxxxxx xx xxx xxxxxx. Xxxxxxx
     x xxxx xx xxxxx xxxxx xxxxx
18   xxxxxx xxxx xx xxxxxx xxxx xxx xxxxxxx, xxxx xxxxxxxxxx xxx xxx xx
     xxx xxxxxxxxx xx xxxxxx
```

Text view

The text view area is where your development text set is located. Texts should be chosen to help develop the best text analyzer possible. Since NLP++ is a programming language and not a statistical system, the ability of the developer to generalize is very important, and the development text set is key to efficiently developing accurate and complete text analyzers.

NLP++ editor

The NLP++ file editor is replete with functionality to create and debug NLP++ code. The following figure depicts the right-click menu:

Figure 6.2: *Right-click menu in NLP++ file editor*

The following table is a listing of the menu items and a description of their function:

Menu item	Description
Comment Line	[Toggle] Comment or uncomment the selected line(s).
Duplicate Line	Duplicate (copy/paste) the selected line. *Ctrl* + *Shift* + *D*.
Go to Function	Jump to the definition of the selected function.
Reformat Rule	Reformat selected rule to default rule format.
Reformat Rule Long Parens	Reformat long lists in a rule to one token per line.
Reformat Rule to One Line	Compress rule into a single line layout.

Menu item	Description
Search	Open a search interface to locate specific text or code.
Display Final Tree	Show the final syntax tree generated by the parser.
Display Matched Rules	Display rules matching the selected text.
Display Pass Tree	Display the parse tree so far for the current pass.
Lookup Word	Search and display help for the given word in VS Code.
Lookup Word in Browser	Search and display help for the word in the local browser.
Open Full Windows Help	Launch the RoboHelp file (from original VisualText) [available only on Windows].
Open Browser Function Help	Open help for NLP++ functions in the local browser.
Open Browser Variable Help	Open help for NLP++ variables in the local browser.
Change to Lowercase	Convert the selected text to lowercase.
Copy Context from Pass Above	Copy parsing context from previous pass.
Generate Rule Exact	Create a literal rule from selected text.
Generate Rule General	Create a general rule from selected text, using **_xALPHA** and **_xNUM**.
Remove Accents	Remove accent marks in selected text.
Reveal Sequence Number	Display the sequence number for the selected file in the **LOGGING** view (There is no way to programmatically select items in VS Code ListView widgets).
Sort & Unique text lines	Sort selected lines, removing duplicates.

Table 6.2: NLP++ file editor; menu items

Reformatting rules

Reformatting rules can promote readability. The reformatting code is written in TypeScript and is part of the NLP++ Language Extension for VS Code.

Rule formatting is a convention established by *David de Hilster* in the first versions of VisualText.

Default rule format

The default rule format (or standard rule format) places each phrase element on a separate line, with a comment indicating its numerical order. Numbering starts at **1** to conform to NLP++ numbering of rule phrase elements.

The following example illustrates the default rule format:

```
1    @POST
2    PersonAttributes(N(1),N(4));
3    single();
4
5    @RULES
6    _personAttrs <-
7        _person                                ### (1)
8        _be                                    ### (2)
9        _xWILD [match=(\, also the)]           ### (3)
10       _xWILD [plus match=(_attribute \,)]    ### (4)
11       @@
```

The phrase elements in the **_personAttrs** rule above are placed on separate lines (*lines 7* to *10*) with comments indicating element numbers. This default rule format helps rule writing, as these numbers are referenced in the various rule regions (**PRE**, **CHECK**, and **POST**). In *line* 2 above, elements 1 and 4 are passed to the function **PersonAttributes** via node variable **N** and its element number, **N(1)** and **N(4)**, for nodes matching elements **1** and **4**.

One line rule format

Simple, short, and repeating rules are sometimes placed on a single line. If we click on any of the *lines* 6 to *10* in the above rule and select *Reformat Rule to One Line* in the NLP editor window's right-click menu, the rule now looks like:

```
1    @POST
2    PersonAttributes(N(1),N(4));
3    single();
4
5    @RULES
6    _personAttrs <-_person _be _xWILD [match=(\, also the)] _
     xWILD [plus match=(_attribute \,)]      @@
```

Line 6 now holds the entire rule.

Parens rule format

Rules often contain a long list of node names to match, making it preferable to display each list item on a separate line. This often happens with the match, fail, and except modifiers of a phrase element.

Reformatting the above rule to the Parens format looks like:

```
1   @POST
2   PersonAttributes(N(1),N(4));
3   single();
4
5   @RULES
6   _personAttrs <-
7       _person                 ### (1)
8       _be                     ### (2)
9       _xWILD [match=(
10          \,
11          also
12          the
13          )]                  ### (3)
14      _xWILD [plus match=(
15          _attribute
16          \,
17          )]                  ### (4)
18      @@
```

The element modifiers in *lines 9* and *14* have list items on separate lines. This can help readability and debugging of long item lists. Note that the ordering is kept as it is.

Note: Long parenthetical lists may also be organized based on semantics, alphabetical ordering, literals vs nonliterals, and any other way that suits the developer. (This may reduce the length of printouts as well.

The following matches a calendar month in various ways:

```
_xWILD [one match=(
    _month
    January February March April May June July August
    September October November December
    Jan Feb Mar Apr May Jun Jul Aug Sep Sept Oct Nov Dec
    )]                                                     ### (1)
```

The **_month** nonliteral may represent misspelled months, numeric variants, and the like.

Warning: The reformatting functions work well for most, but not all, strings.

Auto-generate rules

The NLP++ file editor can automatically generate rules from a string. The developer can cut and paste any string into an NLP++ file editor, highlight the string, and choose the right-click menu items **Generate Rule Exact** or **Generate Rule General**. The idea is to *kickstart* the rule-writing process, enabling developers to quickly type in strings and generate rules that they can then manually edit.

In the following figure, the developer highlighted the date string **`December 14, 2023`** and then selected each autogenerate menu item. With **Generate Rule Exact**, the phrase literally matches the string. With **Generate Rule General**, **`_xALPHA`** and **`_xNUM`** abstract the word and numbers:

```
December 14, 2023

@RULES
_newNode <-
    dec     ### (1)
    14      ### (2)
    \,      ### (3)
    2023    ### (4)
    @@

@RULES
_newNode <-
    _xALPHA ### (1)
    _xNUM   ### (2)
    \,      ### (3)
    _xNUM   ### (4)
    @@
```

Figure 6.3*: NLP++ File Editor; auto-generating rules from string*

Help

Help for NLP++ comes from the original VisualText RoboHelp HTML files. These are available locally in the NLP++ Language Extension for VS Code. However, because VS Code does not allow for links when displaying HTML files inside an editor window, the same help functions and files are available online at **https://www.textanalysis.com/help/help.htm**.

Note: New functions in the NLP engine may not have associated help files.

Lookup Word

Lookup Word is the fastest way to get help on a particular NLP++ function or variable. This finds the local html help file and displays it in a new editor window (as in the following figure). It is fast, but the links within a file do not work:

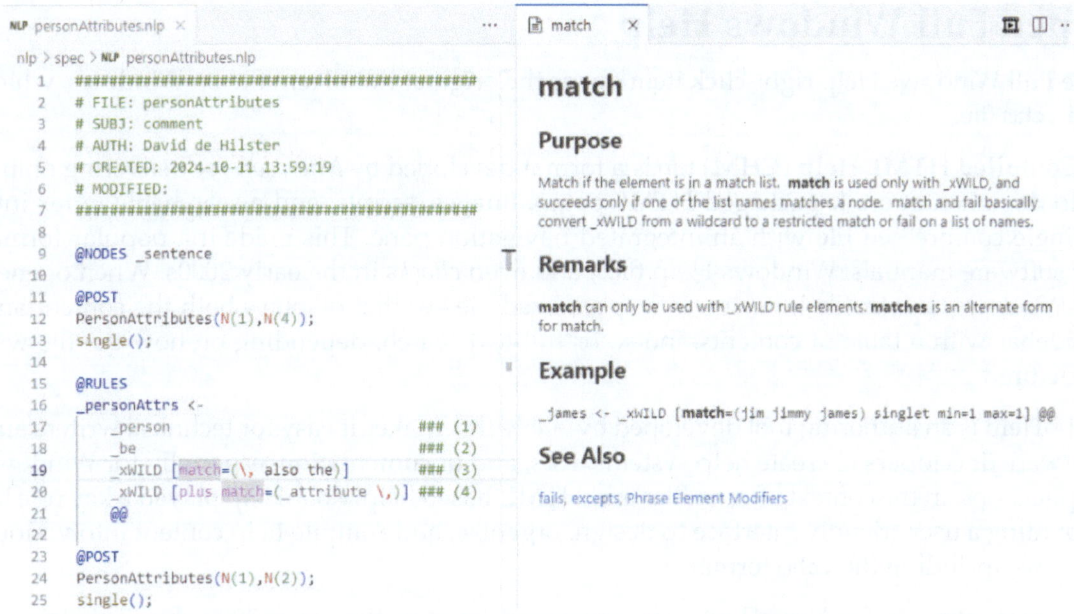

Figure 6.4: Lookup Word selected after right-clicking match

Lookup Word in browser

Lookup Word in browser is identical to Lookup Word except that it opens up the local help file in a local browser. The reason for this is that all the hyperlinks in the browser work, whereas those in a VS Code edit window do not. Here is what the help looks like using a local file in the browser (refer to the following figure):

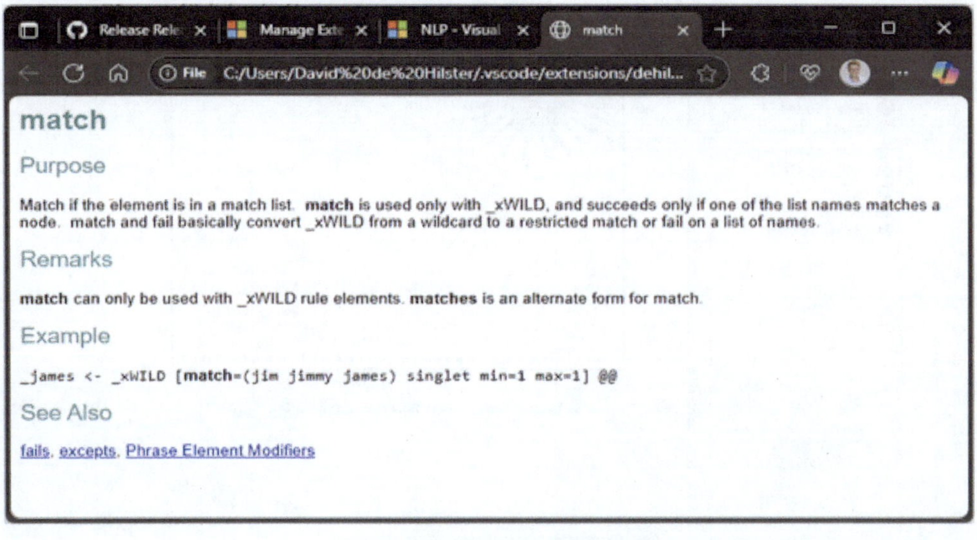

Figure 6.5: Online help selected

Open Full Windows Help

The Full Windows Help right-click item opens the original RoboHelp file on Windows, which is a `.chm` file.

A **Compiled HTML Help** (CHM) file is a format developed by *Microsoft* for delivering online help documentation. It packaged HTML pages, images, scripts, and a searchable index into a single compressed file with an integrated navigation pane. This made it a popular format for software manuals, Windows Help files, and even *eBooks* in the early 2000s. When opened on Windows, a `.chm` file launches in a specialized viewer that displays both the content and a sidebar with a table of contents, index, or full-text search, depending on how the file was structured.

RoboHelp is an authoring tool developed by *Adobe* that makes it easy for technical writers and software developers to create help systems, KBs, and documentation, especially for Windows applications. In the context of `.chm` files and HTML-based help, RoboHelp played a key role by providing a user-friendly interface to design, organize, and compile help content into various formats, including the `.chm` format.

The **`help.chm`** file for VisualText was developed back in the early 2000s by *Text Analysis International* and is currently the most extensive help available for VisualText and NLP++.

It is our intention in the future to convert the HTML help files to markdown files so that they can be used locally with links.

The following figure shows the compiled html help file opened for VisualText:

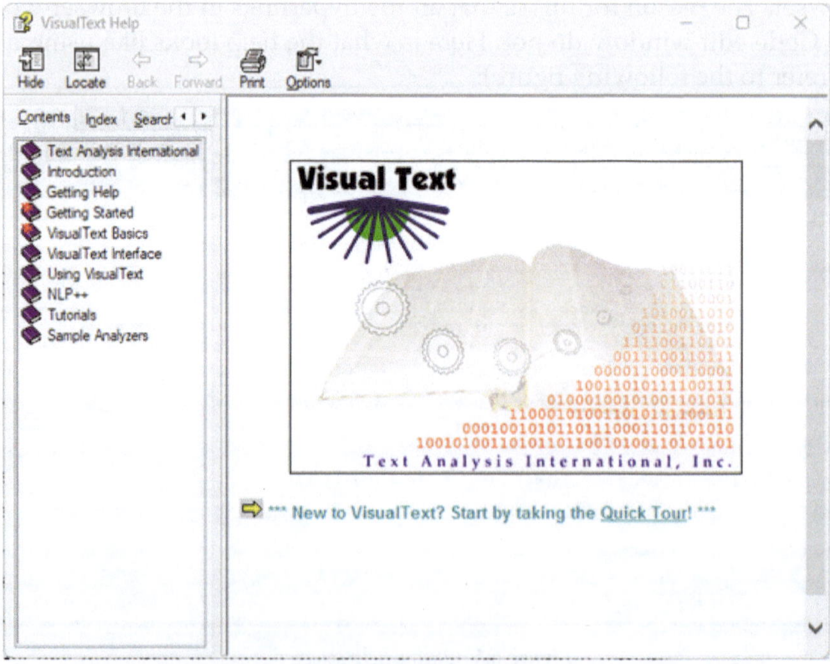

Figure 6.6: *Comprehensive help for original VisualText Windows version*

Open browser function help

This menu choice opens the webpage, as shown in the following figure in a local browser, where links do work:

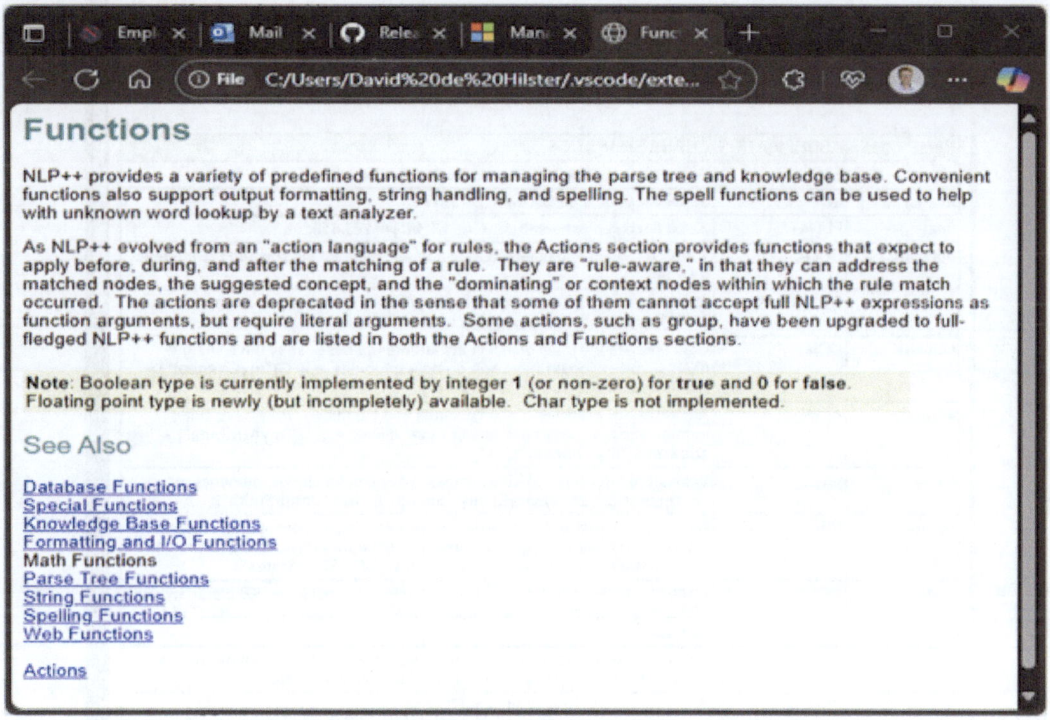

Figure 6.7*: Web browser help page for NLP++ functions*

Open browser variable help

This right-click menu choice opens the webpage (as shown in the following figure) in a local browser for variable help. The reason for opening it up in a browser is that the links work in an external browser:

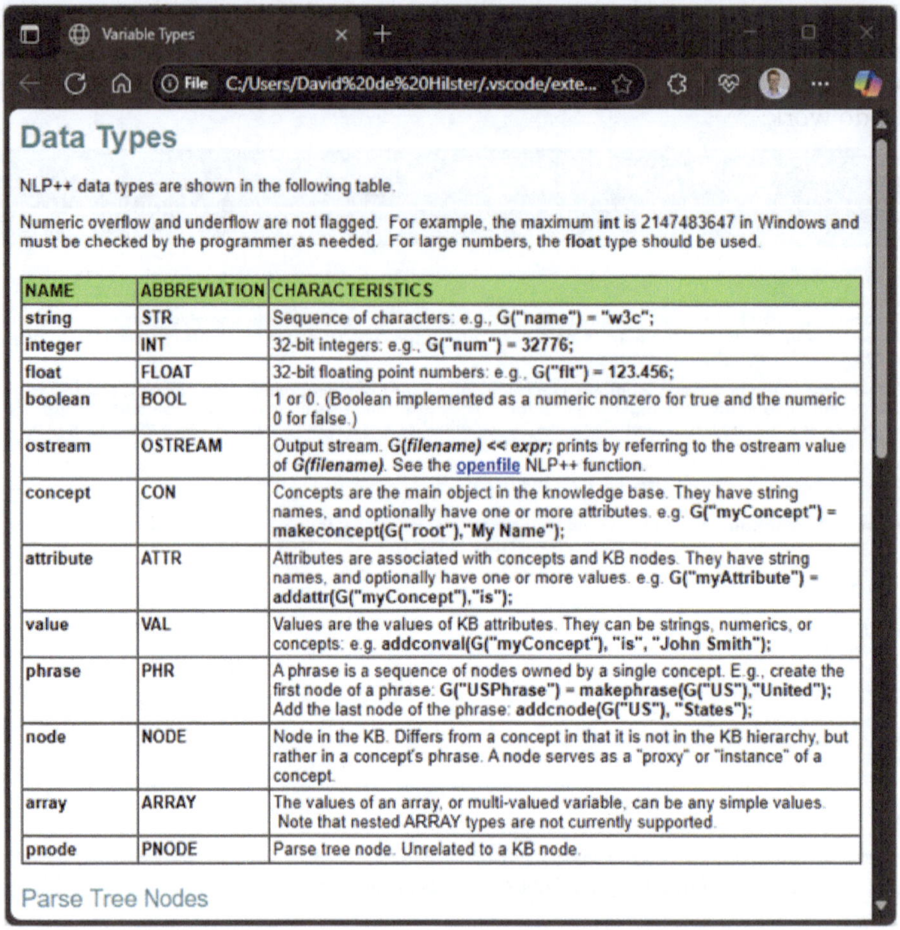

Data Types

NLP++ data types are shown in the following table.

Numeric overflow and underflow are not flagged. For example, the maximum **int** is 2147483647 in Windows and must be checked by the programmer as needed. For large numbers, the **float** type should be used.

NAME	ABBREVIATION	CHARACTERISTICS
string	STR	Sequence of characters: e.g., **G("name") = "w3c";**
integer	INT	32-bit integers: e.g., **G("num") = 32776;**
float	FLOAT	32-bit floating point numbers: e.g., **G("flt") = 123.456;**
boolean	BOOL	1 or 0. (Boolean implemented as a numeric nonzero for true and the numeric 0 for false.)
ostream	OSTREAM	Output stream. **G(*filename*) << *expr;*** prints by referring to the ostream value of ***G(filename)***. See the openfile NLP++ function.
concept	CON	Concepts are the main object in the knowledge base. They have string names, and optionally have one or more attributes. e.g. **G("myConcept") = makeconcept(G("root"),"My Name");**
attribute	ATTR	Attributes are associated with concepts and KB nodes. They have string names, and optionally have one or more values. e.g. **G("myAttribute") = addattr(G("myConcept"),"is");**
value	VAL	Values are the values of KB attributes. They can be strings, numerics, or concepts: e.g. **addconval(G("myConcept"), "is", "John Smith");**
phrase	PHR	A phrase is a sequence of nodes owned by a single concept. E.g., create the first node of a phrase: **G("USPhrase") = makephrase(G("US"),"United");** Add the last node of the phrase: **addcnode(G("US"), "States");**
node	NODE	Node in the KB. Differs from a concept in that it is not in the KB hierarchy, but rather in a concept's phrase. A node serves as a "proxy" or "instance" of a concept.
array	ARRAY	The values of an array, or multi-valued variable, can be any simple values. Note that nested ARRAY types are not currently supported.
pnode	PNODE	Parse tree node. Unrelated to a KB node.

Parse Tree Nodes

Figure 6.8: *Help web page for variable data types*

Shortcuts

The following table lists the shortcuts available for NLP++ rule files. They all start with *Ctrl* + *Shift*:

Function	Shortcut	Description
Duplicate line	*Ctrl* + *Shift* + *D*	Duplicate the line containing the cursor.
Reformat rule default	*Ctrl* + *Shift* + *R*	Convert rule to default rule format.
Reformat rule 1 line	*Ctrl* + *Shift* + *Q*	Compact rule to one line.
Reformat rule Parens	*Ctrl* + *Shift* + *A*	Convert match lists to one name per line.
Show pass tree	*Ctrl* + *Shift* + *A*	Open parse tree for the current pass.

Table 6.3: *Shortcut keys for NLP++ rule files*

Trees

VisualText analyzers build and use a single parse tree (or tree, for short), which is a data structure that tracks the patterns that have matched within the input text. Building parse trees is similar to the sentence diagramming taught in elementary school.

The first pass of every analyzer tokenizes the text, that is, it converts a stream of characters to a parse tree in which alphabetic, numeric, whitespace, punctuation, and control chars are grouped into units called **nodes**. The following figure shows a parse tree as displayed in the parse tree viewer:

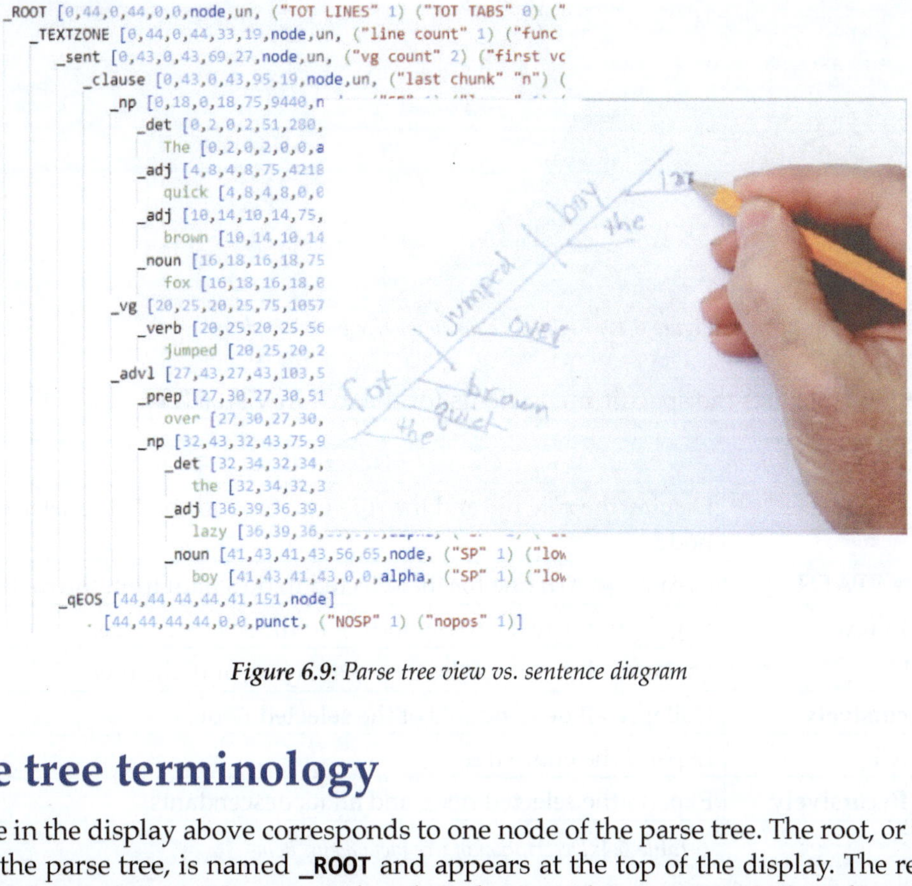

Figure 6.9: Parse tree view vs. sentence diagram

Parse tree terminology

Each line in the display above corresponds to one node of the parse tree. The root, or top-level node of the parse tree, is named **_ROOT** and appears at the top of the display. The remaining nodes are descendants of the root. Other than the root, the ancestor of all, each node has an (immediate) parent and zero or more (immediate) children. Generations, or levels, of nodes in the parse tree are indicated by indentation. The phrase or list of children (under one parent) is siblings.

A token, literal, leaf, or terminal node usually represents a literal word (or equivalent cluster). A nonterminal (or abstract) node is one with descendants. We say that a nonterminal node dominates its descendant nodes.

Tree right-click menu

The following figure shows the right-click menu for the tree view window:

***Figure 6.10**: Right-click menu for tree view Window*

The following table lists the specific menu items for the tree in VisualText:

POS	Description
POS	Display the rule file and the rule that fired to create the selected node.
Generate @PATH	Create a **@PATH** line for the selected node's path from the root.
Highlight text	Highlight the text corresponding to the selected node(s).
Fold All	Collapse all nodes of the tree, displaying only the root.
Fold Recursively	Collapse all descendants of the selected node.
Unfold All	Expand the entire tree.
Unfold Recursively	Expand the selected node and all its descendants.

***Table 6.4**: Description of tree view menu items*

Fold and unfold

Several handy menu items help navigate a parse tree. The fold and unfold menu items help to examine the overall structure of the parse tree. This is because parse trees are displayed using indentation, and one can easily focus on a subtree of interest.

A common trick is to fold all, then reopen one level at a time, giving the developer a top-down view of the evolving parse tree.

```

FINAL OUTPUT TREE:

_ROOT [0,633,0,633,0,0,node,un, ("TOT LINES" 1) ("TOT TABS" 0) ("TOT LOWERS" 79) ("TOT C
   _sentence [0,278,0,278,7,17,node, ("con" concept:"sentence001") ("id" 2)]···
   _sentence [280,398,280,398,7,17,node, ("con" concept:"sentence002") ("id" 9)]···
   _sentence [400,545,400,545,7,17,node, ("con" concept:"sentence003") ("id" 12)]···
   _sentence [547,633,547,633,7,17,node, ("con" concept:"sentence004") ("id" 16)]
      _personAttrs [547,632,547,632,16,16,node]
         _person [547,556,547,556,11,81,node, ("con" concept:"De Hilster") ("id" 15)]
            De [547,548,547,548,0,0,alpha, ("SP" 1) ("cap" 1)]
            Hilster [550,556,550,556,0,0,alpha, ("SP" 1) ("cap" 1)]
         _be [558,559,558,559,0,0,node, ("SP" 1) ("lower" 1) ("person" 3) ("tense" "pres
         also [561,564,561,564,0,0,alpha, ("SP" 1) ("NL" 1) ("lower" 1) ("functword" 1)
         the [566,568,566,568,0,0,alpha, ("SP" 1) ("lower" 1) ("functword" 1) ("articles
         _attribute [570,632,570,632,15,42,node, ("title" "founder") ("organization" "Na
            _title [570,576,570,576,0,0,node, ("SP" 1) ("lower" 1)]···
            of [578,579,578,579,0,0,alpha, ("SP" 1) ("lower" 1) ("functword" 1) ("prepos
            the [581,583,581,583,0,0,alpha, ("SP" 1) ("lower" 1) ("functword" 1) ("artic
            _organization [585,632,585,632,11,22,node, ("organization" "cause") ("con" c
      _endSent [633,633,633,633,6,15,node]···
```

Figure 6.11: Using the fold and unfold right-click menus in the tree view window

Tree files

Tree files are designated by **.tree** and are particular to NLP++. These files are generated by the NLP engine. If the debug flag is set, the NLP engine generates an output tree for every pass (or **.nlp**) file that modifies the tree. A final parse tree file is always generated.

Analyzer sequence view

In the analyzer sequence view, one can open the final tree or click on a tree associated with a particular pass. This is important when trying to understand and debug an analyzer and to see how the passes affected the parse tree at each step.

You can view the final tree by clicking on the tree icon in the header of the **ANALYZER** sequence view. You can also see the final tree by the shortcut *Ctrl + Shift + F* (refer to the following figure):

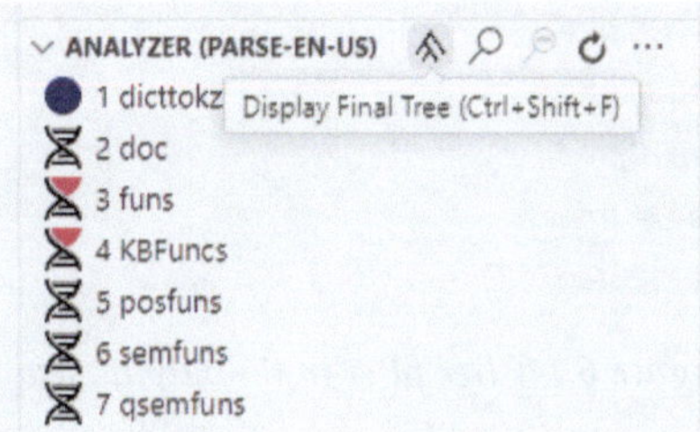

Figure 6.12: Final tree icon in the analyzer sequence view

If debugging is on, tree icons appear on passes containing rule files. When mousing over a pass in the analyzer sequence, if a tree icon is present, the developer can click on that and see the state of the tree after that pass has executed. Here is what that looks like in VisualText (refer to the following figure):

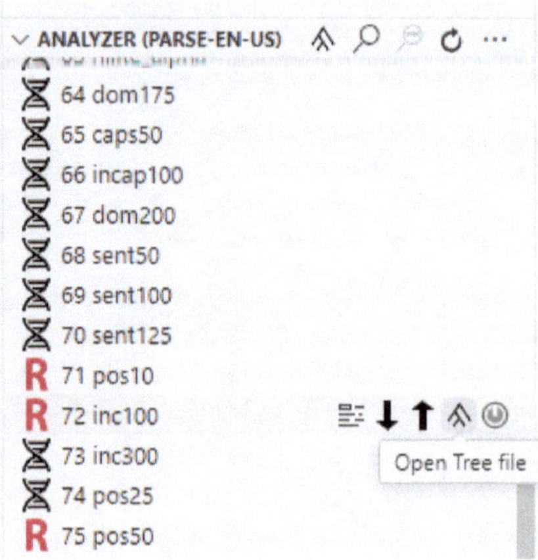

Figure 6.13: *Tree icon for a rule-containing pass*

Output view

The output view has a filter to allow for the display of all of the tree files for a run on a file. By clicking on the tree icon in the *Output View Header*, one gets all the tree files listed (refer to the following figure), allowing a developer to see the changes in the tree corresponding to each pass:

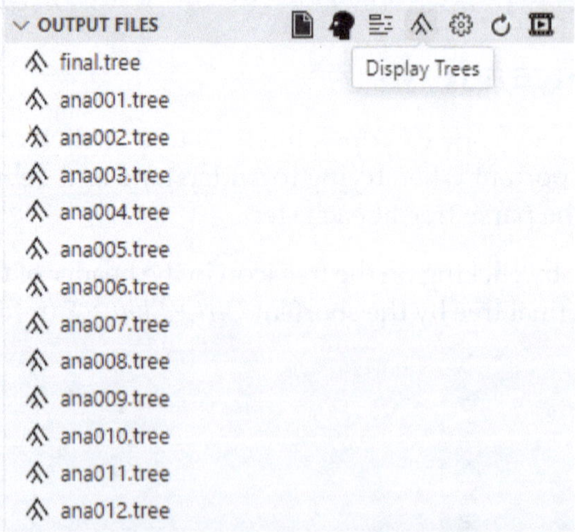

Figure 6.14: *Tree filter in the output view*

Tree nodes

Tree nodes are tokens that represent words, numbers, whitespace, and punctuation. The format for the display of a tree node is as follows:

```
nodename [num1,num2,num3,num4,num5,num6,node_type,info1,info2,info3 ("attr" "val")...)
```

Here is a tree display for the sentence **Happy me ⍰⍰ Yea!!!** using the full English parser:

```
parse-en-us > input > tweet.txt_log > ana069.tree
1  |
2  ***************
3      PASS 69 (sent100)
4  ***************
5
6  PAT OUTPUT TREE:
7
8  _ROOT [0,21,0,17,0,0,node,un, ("TOT LINES" 1) ("TOT TABS" 0) ("TOT
9     _TEXTZONE [0,21,0,17,33,19,node,un, ("line count" 1)]
10       _sent [0,18,0,14,69,27,node,un,fired,blt]
11          _adj [0,4,0,4,56,65,node,fired, ("NOSP" 1) ("cap" 1) ("ad
12             Happy [0,4,0,4,0,0,alpha, ("NOSP" 1) ("cap" 1) ("adj"
13          _pro [6,7,6,7,51,74,node,fired, ("sem" "person") ("stem"
14             _proObj [6,7,6,7,51,74,node]
15                me [6,7,6,7,0,0,alpha, ("SP" 1) ("lower" 1) ("pro"
16          😆 [9,14,9,10,0,0,emoji,fired, ("SP" 1)]
17          Yea [16,18,12,14,0,0,alpha,fired, ("SP" 1) ("cap" 1) ("no
18       _qEOS [19,21,15,17,41,151,node,fired]
19          ! [19,19,15,15,0,0,punct, ("NOSP" 1)]
20          ! [20,20,16,16,0,0,punct, ("NOSP" 1)]
21          ! [21,21,17,17,0,0,punct, ("NOSP" 1)]
```

Figure 6.15: Parse tree for the sentence Happy me 😆 Yea!!!

Parse tree node numbers

There are six numbers for every **parse tree node (pn)**, as in *line 16*, copied here:

```
[9, 14, 9, 10, 0, 0, emoji, fired, ("SP" 1)]
```

The numbers hold the following values, as listed in the following table:

Position	Example	Description
num1	**9**	Starting byte in input text buffer
num2	**14**	Ending byte in the input text buffer
num3	**9**	Starting display character in text
num4	**10**	Ending display character in text
num5	**0**	Pass the number of the rule that matched, if any
num6	**0**	Line number of the rule that matched, if any

Table 6.5: Explanation of pn number format

Notice that the ending byte number and the ending display number are different. This is because the NLP engine (runtime) needs to know the actual byte location of the token, whereas VisualText (GUI) needs to know the display location. When dealing with an emoji, these differ. Even though we see only one emoji, internally in the file, it occupies 6 bytes. However, VisualText, which displays the tree file, uses **num3** and **num4**.

Next, we examine *line 10*, where **_sent** was created by a rule match (in pass file *69, line 27*):

```
_sent [0,18,0,14,69,27,node,un,fired,blt]
```

The rule match is shown in the following figure:

```
15  @POST
16    if (N("sent end",3))
17      S("sent end") = N("sent end",3);
18
19    if (pnname(N(3)) == "_qEOS")
20      {
21      setlookahead(3);
22      singler(1,2);
23      }
24    else # _EOS
25      singler(1,3);  # Include the _EOS node.
26  @RULES
27  _sent [unsealed] <-
28      _xWILD [one fail=(_qEOS \" \( \< \[ _EOS)]
29      _xWILD [star fail=(_qEOS _EOS)]
30      _xWILD [one match=(_qEOS _EOS)]
31      _xWILD [star match=( \) \] \> \" \' )]
32      @@
```

***Figure 6.16**: Full USA English Parser*

Type and info

After the numbers in the matched **_sent** node, the type of the node is listed, as well as zero to three node flags, e.g., fired.

The node type identifies the type of token. The type may be: **node** (for nonliteral), **alpha** (for alphabetic), **num** (for number), **white** (for whitespace), **punct** (for punctuation), **emoji**, etc. Information about the node follows the node type. Flag settings such as unsealed (or un), built, and fired may be shown in abbreviated form. Attributes and values attached to the node may be displayed on the node line as well. Each variable and value-list is a parenthesized list of the form **("varname" "value1" "value2" ...)**.

The node flags mark a parse tree node in a successfully matched rule. The flags are: un, for a suggested node getting the unsealed flag, fired, for every node matched, and blt for a suggested node built by the matched rule. The fired and built flags are present only in passes where the node was successfully matched. However, the unsealed flag is permanent, enabling subsequent passes to *look inside* the flagged node. The **@NODES** context selector only operates in nodes with the unsealed flag, enabling *hiding* subtrees as a speed optimization.

Tree node attributes and values

The last part of the node line in the tree file is the attributes (also called **variables**) for that node. Attributes are formatted as follows:

```
("attribute_name" value) . . .
```

The attribute name is always quoted, and values may be numeric, string, or concept types.

Concept values appear in the following; they only display the concept name and not the KB location. This saves space but still provides information about the concept. The following is the attribute name **con** and its value, **Nathalia Ribas**:

```
("con" concept:"Nathalia Ribas")
```

The following figure is a tree with several **concept** attributes. They are located on *lines 5, 8,* and *12*:

```
nlpfix-analyzers > nlp > input > text.txt_log > final.tree
1
2   FINAL OUTPUT TREE:
3
4   _ROOT [0,644,0,644,0,0,node,un, ("TOT LINES" 1) ("TOT TABS" 0) ("TOT LOWERS" 79) ("TOT CAPS'
5      _sentence [0,282,0,282,7,17,node, ("con" concept:"sentence001") ("id" 2)]
6         _personAttrs [0,62,0,62,16,28,node]
7            _person [0,31,0,31,14,19,node, ("conjoined" 1)]
8               _person [0,13,0,13,11,81,node, ("con" concept:"Nathalia Ribas") ("person" 1) (":
9                  Nathalia [0,7,0,7,0,0,alpha, ("NOSP" 1) ("cap" 1) ("genero" "f") ("pessoa" 1
10                 Ribas [9,13,9,13,0,0,alpha, ("SP" 1) ("cap" 1)]
11              and [15,17,15,17,0,0,alpha, ("SP" 1) ("lower" 1) ("functword" 1) ("coordinating(
12              _person [19,31,19,31,11,81,node, ("con" concept:"Eduardo Costa") ("person" 1) ('
13                 Eduardo [19,25,19,25,0,0,alpha, ("SP" 1) ("cap" 1) ("genero" "m") ("pessoa"
14                 Costa [27,31,27,31,0,0,alpha, ("SP" 1) ("cap" 1)]
15           , [32,32,32,32,0,0,punct, ("NOSP" 1) ("conjunction" 1) ("conjoin" 1)]
16           _attribute [34,48,34,48,15,91,node, ("number" 2) ("occupation" "programmer")]
17              _number [34,36,34,36,0,0,node, ("SP" 1) ("lower" 1) ("functword" 1) ("cardinalNu
18                 two [34,36,34,36,0,0,alpha, ("SP" 1) ("lower" 1) ("functword" 1) ("cardinalNu
19              _occupation [38,48,38,48,0,0,node, ("SP" 1) ("lower" 1) ("count" "plural") ("roo
20                 programmers [38,48,38,48,0,0,alpha, ("SP" 1) ("lower" 1) ("count" "plural")
21           _attribute [50,61,50,61,15,77,node, ("country" "brazil")]
22              from [50,53,50,53,0,0,alpha, ("SP" 1) ("lower" 1) ("functword" 1) ("preposition:
23              _country [56,61,56,61,0,0,node, ("SP" 1) ("NL" 2) ("cap" 1)]
24                 Brazil [56,61,56,61,0,0,alpha, ("SP" 1) ("NL" 2) ("cap" 1)]
25           , [62,62,62,62,0,0,punct, ("NOSP" 1) ("conjunction" 1)]
26        are [64,66,64,66,0,0,alpha, ("SP" 1) ("lower" 1)]
27        helping [68,74,68,74,0,0,alpha, ("SP" 1) ("lower" 1)]
28        create [76,81,76,81,0,0,alpha, ("SP" 1) ("lower" 1)]
```

Figure 6.17*: Tree nodes with concept attributes in lines 5, 8, and 12*

Highlight text from tree

It is because the tree contains information about the position of a node and its text, the developer can choose any part of the tree and highlight its corresponding text. This comes in very handy when developing and debugging text analyzers.

Here is an example of highlighting a portion of a tree and viewing the resulting window, which opens and highlights the corresponding text:

Figure 6.18: Choosing highlight text in the tree view

Text highlights

Text highlight files have the file extension **.txxt** and are generated for a pass when a user clicks on icon or select **Display Matched Rules**.

Rules that fired and modified the tree are highlighted in blue, surrounded by three angle brackets **<<< .... >>>**. Rules that matched a portion of text but did not modify the tree are highlighted in red and surrounded by three parentheses **(((...)))**.

The reasoning for using **<<<** and **(((** is that oftentimes, the input text itself contains **<** and **(** characters. VS Code language extensions use TextMate syntax for highlighting, and to distinguish rule matches, we surround the words with tags.

The following figures show two displays:

- The first shows normal prose (full English sentences) with both types of highlighting.
- The second is from an analyzer that converts HTML Robo help files to markdown files.

```
nlpfix-analyzers > nlp > input > text.txt_log > ana011.txxt
<<<Nathalia Ribas>>> and <<<Eduardo Costa>>>, two programmers from
Brazil, are helping create the first comprehensive digital
dictionary for (((Portuguese))) in the (((AI))) framework NLP++.
Mentored by <<<David de Hilster>>>, co-author of the NLP++
programming language, they met while working at (((LexisNexis))).
<<<Nathalia>>> is finishing her bachelor's degree at <<<Santa
Catarina University>>> and plans to use NLP++ in her master's
thesis. (((Their))) project improves (((AI)))'s understanding of
(((Portuguese))), showcasing Brazil's growing tech influence and
the power of collaboration and mentorship. <<<De Hilster>>> is
also the founder of the <<<Natural Language Understanding
Global Initiative>>>.
```

Figure 6.19 (a): Text highlighting with tree-modifying matches (in blue) and non-modifying matches (in red)

```
C: > Users > DAVIDD~1 > AppData > Local > Temp > ana018-1013-1126.tree
1       _bodyStart [1013,1018,1013,1018,2,12,node]
2          < [1013,1013,1013,1013,0,0,punct, ("SP" 1) ("NL" 3)]
3          body [1014,1017,1014,1017,0,0,alpha, ("NOSP" 1) ("lower" 1)]
4          > [1018,1018,1018,1018,0,0,punct, ("NOSP" 1)]
5       _headerOne [1021,1050,1021,1050,18,16,node,fired,blt, ("text" "Functio
6          _hOneStart [1021,1024,1021,1024,2,15,node,fired]
7             < [1021,1021,1021,1021,0,0,punct, ("SP" 1) ("NL" 2)]
8             h [1022,1022,1022,1022,0,0,alpha, ("NOSP" 1) ("lower" 1)]
9             1 [1023,1023,1023,1023,0,0,num, ("NOSP" 1)]
10            > [1024,1024,1024,1024,0,0,punct, ("NOSP" 1)]
11         Functions [1025,1033,1025,1033,0,0,alpha,fired, ("NOSP" 1) ("cap" 1
12         and [1035,1037,1035,1037,0,0,alpha,fired, ("SP" 1) ("lower" 1)]
13         Actions [1039,1045,1039,1045,0,0,alpha,fired, ("SP" 1) ("cap" 1)]
14         _hOneEnd [1046,1050,1046,1050,2,16,node,fired]
15            < [1046,1046,1046,1046,0,0,punct, ("NOSP" 1)]
16            / [1047,1047,1047,1047,0,0,punct, ("NOSP" 1)]
17            h [1048,1048,1048,1048,0,0,alpha, ("NOSP" 1) ("lower" 1)]
18            1 [1049,1049,1049,1049,0,0,num, ("NOSP" 1)]
19            > [1050,1050,1050,1050,0,0,punct, ("NOSP" 1)]
20      _headerTwo [1053,1070,1053,1070,18,30,node,fired,blt, ("text" "Functio
21         _hTwoStart [1053,1056,1053,1056,2,17,node,fired]
22            < [1053,1053,1053,1053,0,0,punct, ("SP" 1) ("NL" 2)]
23            h [1054,1054,1054,1054,0,0,alpha, ("NOSP" 1) ("lower" 1)]
24            2 [1055,1055,1055,1055,0,0,num, ("NOSP" 1)]
25            > [1056,1056,1056,1056,0,0,punct, ("NOSP" 1)]
26         Functions [1057,1065,1057,1065,0,0,alpha,fired, ("NOSP" 1) ("cap" 1
27         _hTwoEnd [1066,1070,1066,1070,2,18,node,fired]
```

Figure 6.19 (b): Tree example showing matched rule highlighting

The second example is from the Robo HTML help file conversion analyzer (**ConvertRobo**) in the **dehilster-analyzers** located in the **Misc** folder. It shows the highlighting of the header rules. Above is the tree for the headers pass (pass 18):

```
_headerOne [1021,1050,1021,1050,18,16,node,fired,blt, ("text" "Functions and Actions")]
```

Line 5 has the **fired** attribute and the numbers **18** and **16** as the 5th and 6th numbers representing *pass 18, line 16*. The first two numbers in *line 5* are **1021** and **1050**. These are the character positions of the head node.

These character position numbers from the tree file are then used to generate the **`.txxt`** file when the user clicks on the **Display Matched Rules** for *pass 18*. This produces the following file, as shown in the figure:

```
ConvertRobo > input > text01.htm_log > ana018.txxt

<!--(Body)=================================================================-->


<body>

<<<<h1>Functions and Actions</h1>>>>

<<<<h2>Functions</h2>>>>

<p>NLP++ supports function calls, which have a similar form to other programming
 languages (such as C/C++): </p>

<p><!--kadov_tag{{<spaces>}}-->    <span style="font-weight: bold;"
 .... argN)</span> </p>

<p>where functionName is constrained to be alphabetic and where each argument
 to the function may be an NLP++ expression.</p>

<p>Only call-by-value arguments are supported at present. <!--kadov_tag{{<spaces>}}-->&
 means that when a variable is used as an argument, its value is not changed
 by a change to the local variable that it becomes associated with in the
 function.</p>
```

***Figure 6.20**: Highlight of matched rules by the ConvertRobo analyzer in the dehilster-analyzers Misc folder*

Tree vs. knowledge base

When designing a text analyzer using NLP++, a key question is: when do you put information in the parse tree, and when in the KB? Some analyzers only need to keep information in the tree structure, while others require the KB.

> Note: **The NLP engine dictionaries are embedded within the KB, but could, in principle, be implemented separately. Also, accessing the KB is simpler than dynamically building knowledge within it.**

Complexity

In general, the simpler the analyzer, the less likely the KB will be needed. For example, the date-time analyzer (in *Chapter 7, Example Analyzers*) needs no KB. The dictionaries and rules are sufficient to parse and understand dates and times, and all the information found can be stored in the parse tree. (The dictionary knowledge could be stored in the analyzer code as well.)

In the following figure, all the information about dates and times is stored in the parse tree:

```
C: > Users > DAVIDD~1 > AppData > Local > Temp > ana015-99-121.tree
_dateTime [99,120,99,120,13,17,node, ("date" pnode:"_date") ("time" pnode:"_time")]
   _date [99,110,99,110,11,82,node, ("month" 11) ("day" 12) ("year" 2014)]
      11 [99,100,99,100,0,0,num, ("SP" 1) ("NL" 1) ("month" 1) ("day" 1) ("year" 1)]
      . [101,101,101,101,0,0,punct, ("NOSP" 1)]
      12 [103,104,103,104,0,0,num, ("SP" 1) ("month" 1) ("day" 1) ("year" 1)]
      . [105,105,105,105,0,0,punct, ("NOSP" 1)]
      2014 [107,110,107,110,0,0,num, ("SP" 1) ("year" 1)]
   , [111,111,111,111,0,0,punct, ("NOSP" 1)]
   _time [113,120,113,120,8,23,node, ("hour" 8) ("min" 45) ("sec" 39)]
      08 [113,114,113,114,0,0,num, ("SP" 1) ("month" 1) ("day" 1) ("year" 1)]
      : [115,115,115,115,0,0,punct, ("NOSP" 1)]
      45 [116,117,116,117,0,0,num, ("NOSP" 1) ("year" 1)]
      : [118,118,118,118,0,0,punct, ("NOSP" 1)]
      39 [119,120,119,120,0,0,num, ("NOSP" 1) ("year" 1)]
```

***Figure 6.21**: Date and time information stored entirely in the parse tree*

However, when the task is more complex, as in the NLP example analyzer, it is simpler to build areas in the KB for storing information during parsing. For example, it is preferable to use the KB to track capitalized names occurring in prose. The KB can help track coreferences, e.g., using a first name like **`Nathalia`** after having used the full name **`Nathalia Ribas`**.

Bottom-up prototyping without KB

When building an analyzer, we often use a bottom-up methodology that starts without the KB. During development, we assess when and where the KB may better support the analysis, tracking, storage, and access of information.

Output

The KB is often used for producing output. For example, to generate JSON, the KB can help organize the needed knowledge.

The date-time analyzer does not need the KB to parse dates and times. However, in order to create a JSON output, NLP++ already has built-in KB functions. It is easy to make a couple of passes that match the date and time nodes in the parse tree, create a KB, and then use the KB with JSON library functions for output (see passes 16 and 17 in the date-time analyzer).

Parse tree references to the KB

It is often advantageous to store pointers to the KB inside the tree itself. In the NLP example analyzer, the KB has a place for tracking sentence information.

In the *sentence pass*, when a sentence node is constructed in the parse tree, a concept representing that sentence is created in the KB, and a pointer from the **`_sentence`** node to that concept is stored as an attribute. The *S* suggested variable assignment stores the created concept, as seen in *line 12* in the following figure:

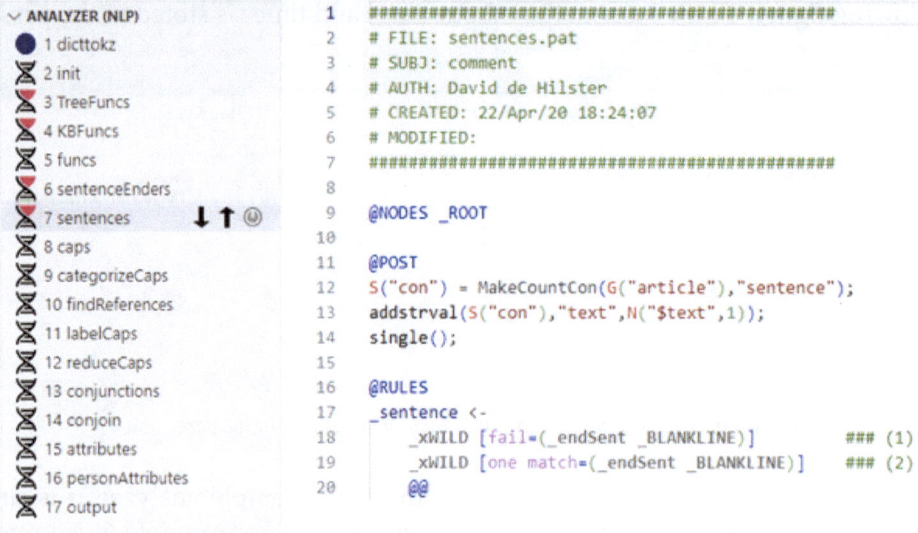

Figure 6.22: *Sentences pass in the NLP example analyzer store concept pointers in the parse tree*

This produces a tree with a *con* attribute (the user can name it otherwise), as shown in the following figure:

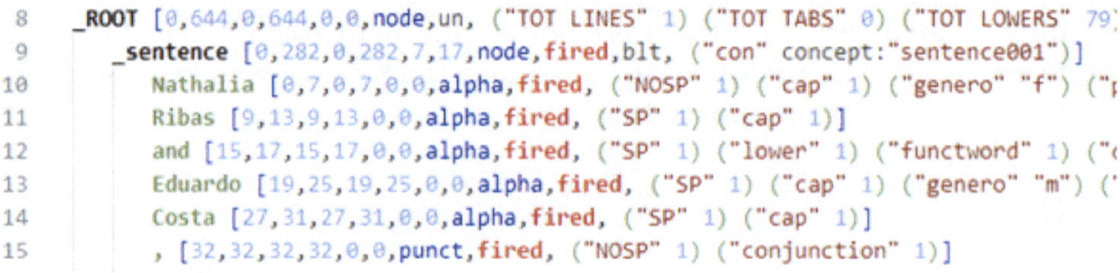

Figure 6.23: *Parse tree from the NLP example analyzer showing a concept pointer in line 9*

KB references to the parse tree

Storing backpointers from the KB to the parse tree is tricky:

- A parse tree is temporary.
- It changes as the analyzer pipeline progresses.
- When nodes are deleted, pointers to them become invalid.
- When a parse tree is deleted, all pointers to it become invalid.

Given these issues, the NLP++ runtime has no built-in scheme for such backpointers. However, given a need, de Hilster implemented (in 2024) a method for backpointers in the NLP engine, via user functions in the **TreeFuncs** library.

The key function **AddTreeID** takes a concept and the parse tree node it points to as arguments, and does the following:

- For the node pointed to, create an attribute named *id*, with a unique ID number (converted to a string) as its value.
- Traverse from the node to the parse tree root, adding an *id* attribute and a unique ID number value to each ancestor, as needed. The parse tree root *id* is always *0*.
- For the pointing concept, create or add to an attribute named *pn*, whose values are a list of *numeric paths* to nodes in the parse tree (Such a path is dubbed **pn_path_str** in this book). Add the node's unique parse tree path as a new list value of the attribute *pn*. For example, ["3 2 1"] is a parse tree path (implicitly starting at root node *0*) to child 3, then to child 2, then to child 1.

> Note: **That the unique ID numbers may be in mixed order, as a parse tree is typically built-in a bottom-up fashion.**

The scheme is not efficient, but it works. And if a path is invalid, the analyzer will not crash, as it would with a bad pointer.

In the following figure example, the KB concept is retrieved in *line 12* from the `_cap` context node (3rd in the `@PATH` context on *line* 9). On *line 27*, the function `AddTreeID` is called with the `cap` concept and the sentence node that it represents.

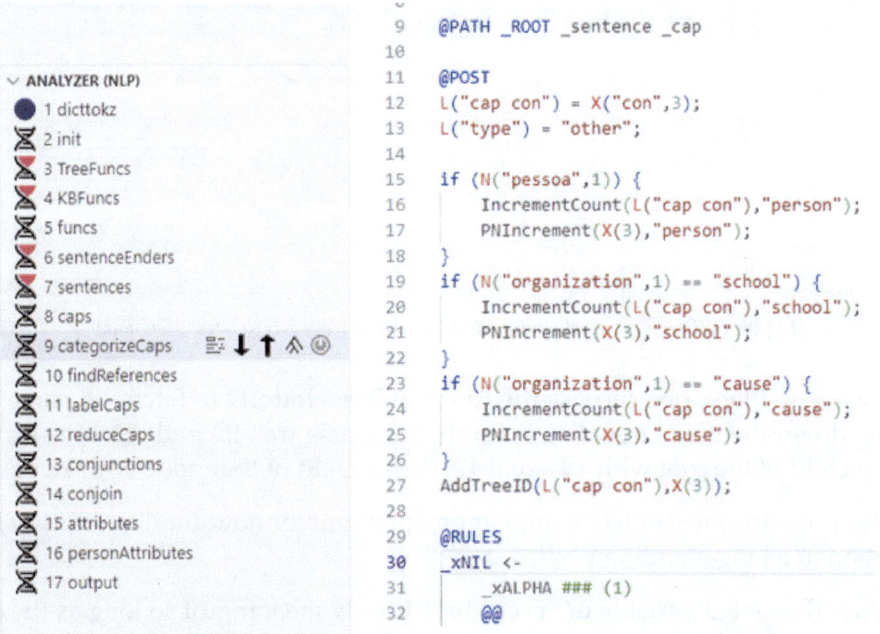

***Figure 6.24**: AddTreeID creates a backpointer from the cap concept to the cap node*

What makes this work is that **AddTreeID** adds unique IDs to the node and all the parent nodes (**_ROOT** is assumed to be zero). In the following figure, tree on *line 10*, the id for **_cap** on *line 10* is set to **1**. **AddTreeID** increments a global tree id variable by executing **++G("tree id")** and assigns that to the given node. **AddTreeID** then travels up the parse tree putting IDs on all the ancestors, as needed. In this case, there is only one parent, so one can see that on *line 9*, the sentence node has **id** equal to 2.

This repeats, and you can see that on *line 14*, the **id** is now 3 and, since its parent already has an **id** attribute, traversing up the parse tree can stop.

```
8   _ROOT [0,633,0,633,0,0,node,un, ("TOT LINES" 1) ("TOT TABS" 0) ("TOT LOWERS" 79) ("TOT CAPS
9     _sentence [0,278,0,278,7,17,node, ("con" concept:"sentence001") ("id" 2)]
10      _cap [0,13,0,13,8,31,node, ("con" concept:"Nathalia Ribas") ("person" 1) ("id" 1)]
11        Nathalia [0,7,0,7,0,0,alpha,fired, ("NOSP" 1) ("cap" 1) ("genero" "f") ("pessoa" 1
12        Ribas [9,13,9,13,0,0,alpha,fired, ("SP" 1) ("cap" 1)]
13      and [15,17,15,17,0,0,alpha, ("SP" 1) ("lower" 1) ("functword" 1) ("coordinatingConjur
14      _cap [19,31,19,31,8,31,node, ("con" concept:"Eduardo Costa") ("person" 1) ("id" 3)]
15        Eduardo [19,25,19,25,0,0,alpha,fired, ("SP" 1) ("cap" 1) ("genero" "m") ("pessoa"
16        Costa [27,31,27,31,0,0,alpha,fired, ("SP" 1) ("cap" 1)]
17      , [32,32,32,32,0,0,punct, ("NOSP" 1) ("conjunction" 1)]
18      _number [34,36,34,36,0,0,node, ("SP" 1) ("lower" 1) ("functword" 1) ("cardinalNumeral
```

Figure 6.25: NLP example analyzer tree for the categorizeCaps pass, showing node IDs

On the KB side, the function **AddTreeID** adds the unique tree id path as an attribute called **pn** on the concept. As discussed, the **pn** attribute value(s) are one or more lists of numeric paths down the parse tree (e.g., see the line that starts with AI).

```
caps
  Nathalia Ribas: sent=["concept" "article" "sentence001"], "person_count"=1, pn="2 1"
  Eduardo Costa: sent=["concept" "article" "sentence001"], "person_count"=1, pn="2 3"
  Portuguese: sent=["concept" "article" "sentence001","concept" "article" "sentence003"], pn=["2 4","12 14"]
  AI: sent=["concept" "article" "sentence001","concept" "article" "sentence003"], pn=["2 5","12 13"]
  David de Hilster: sent=["concept" "article" "sentence001"], "person_count"=1, pn="2 6"
  LexisNexis: sent=["concept" "article" "sentence001"], pn="2 7"
  Nathalia: sent=["concept" "article" "sentence002"], "person_count"=1, pn="9 8"
  Santa Catarina University: sent=["concept" "article" "sentence002"], pn="9 10", "person_count"=1, "school_cou
  Their: sent=["concept" "article" "sentence003"], pn="12 11"
  De Hilster: sent=["concept" "article" "sentence004"], pn="16 15"
  Natural Language Understanding Global Initiative: sent=["concept" "article" "sentence004"], pn="16 17", "caus
```

Figure 6.26: KB dump showing the PN pointer from KB to parse tree node

Once the IDs are in place, one can use the function **TreeNodeID** to fetch the parse tree node by searching down the parse tree. For example, the parse tree ID path *12 14* is traversed by looking for a child of the root with **id** equal 12, then a child of that node with **id** equal 14.

As noted, this is not the most efficient implementation. But for now, the Tree Library Functions offer a solution to a long-standing need.

This is because the global variable **G("tree id")** is only meaningful so long as the parse tree exists, placing this variable on the parse tree's root node is a good alternative.

Ambiguity

Ambiguity as a linguistic term refers to words that have more than one meeting. Currently, most ambiguity in NLP++ is handled on a case-by-case basis, but some mechanisms exist to help when building a text analyzer. *Tutorial 15* in the NLP++ online tutorials handles ambiguity using library functions. This particular solution requires a dictionary and a KB named identically (e.g., **ambig.dict** and **ambig.kbb**).

First, let us take a look at the text:

```
1   Did you google his friend?
2   He works at Google.
```

Here, the ambiguous word is **google**. In *sentence 1*, **google** is a verb. In *sentence 2*, **Google** is a noun. We construct our dictionary with the various parts of speech for the word **google** using the name **ambig.dict**:

```
google pos=verb
google pos=noun
google pos=adj

at pos=prep
his pos=pro
```

Here is the KB called **ambig.kbb**:

```
dictionary
  google
    m01: pos=verb, syn=search
    m02: pos=noun, entity=company
```

There are functions in the **KBFuncs.nlp** that are dedicated to resolving ambiguity using the current English dictionary and the way it uses POS. The main function is called **AmbigTrimPOS** and can be called when an ambiguity is resolved. This all can be seen in *Tutorial 15*. Here is the rule file that uses **AmbigTrimPOS**:

```
@NODES _ROOT

# He works at google.

@PRE
<1,1> var("prep");
```

```
7    <2,2> var("noun");
8    <2,2> vargt("pos num",1);
9
10   @POST
11   AmbigTrimPOS(N(2),"noun");
12
13   @RULES
14   _xNIL <-
15       _xALPHA    ### (1)
16       _xALPHA    ### (2)
17       @@
18
19   # Did you google his friend?
20
21   @PRE
22   <1,1> var("verb");
23   <1,1> vargt("pos num",1);
24   <2,2> var("pro");
25
26   @POST
27   AmbigTrimPOS(N(1),"verb");
28
29   @RULES
30   _xNIL <-
31       _xALPHA    ### (1)
32       _xALPHA    ### (2)
33       @@
```

In *lines 11* and *27*, the ambiguous node in the parse tree is passed along with the unambiguous POS as a string. In the first rule, the **PRE** check from *lines 6* to *8* states that if there is a preposition in front of an ambiguous node that could be a noun, then in *line 11*, the function **AmbigTrimPOS** is called to disambiguate the word. The second rule states in the **PRE** that a verb node that is ambiguous, followed by a pronoun, is disambiguated to become a verb.

The way that **AmbigTrimPOS** can do this is because the **ambig.dict** and **ambig.kbb** are coordinated so that when a final POS is decided, then the function can place all the appropriate attributes onto the word in the tree, including semantic information. The tree before disambiguation looks like this:

```
1   ***************
2       PASS 1 (dicttokz)
3   ***************
4   _ROOT [0,45,0,45,0,0,node,un, ("TOT LINES" 1) ("TOT TABS" 0) ("TOT LOWERS" 7) ("TOT CAPS" 2) ("TOT UPPERS" 0) ("TOT NUMS" 0)]
5      Did [0,2,0,2,0,0,alpha, ("NOSP" 1) ("cap" 1)]
6      you [4,6,4,6,0,0,alpha, ("SP" 1) ("lower" 1)]
7      google [8,13,8,13,0,0,alpha,fired, ("SP" 1) ("lower" 1) ("meaning" concept:"google") ("verb" 1) ("noun" 1) ("adj" 1) ("pos num" 3)]
8      his [15,17,15,17,0,0,alpha,fired, ("SP" 1) ("lower" 1) ("pro" 1) ("pos num" 1)]
9      friend [19,24,19,24,0,0,alpha, ("SP" 1) ("lower" 1)]
10     ? [25,25,25,25,0,0,punct, ("NOSP" 1)]
11     He [27,28,27,28,0,0,alpha, ("SP" 1) ("NL" 1) ("cap" 1)]
12     works [30,34,30,34,0,0,alpha, ("SP" 1) ("lower" 1)]
13     at [36,37,36,37,0,0,alpha,fired, ("SP" 1) ("lower" 1) ("prep" 1) ("pos num" 1)]
14     google [39,44,39,44,0,0,alpha,fired, ("SP" 1) ("lower" 1) ("meaning" concept:"google") ("verb" 1) ("noun" 1) ("adj" 1) ("pos num" 3)]
15     . [45,45,45,45,0,0,punct, ("NOSP" 1)]
```

In *lines 7* and *14*, the words are ambiguous with three different POS. After the disambiguation pass, the final tree now has the attributes from the **ambig.kbb** for the proper meaning of the word.

```
1
2   FINAL OUTPUT TREE:
3
4   _ROOT [0,45,0,45,0,0,node,un, ("TOT LINES" 1) ("TOT TABS" 0) ("TOT LOWERS" 7) ("TOT CAPS" 2) ("TOT UPPERS" 0) ("TOT NUMS" 0)]
5      Did [0,2,0,2,0,0,alpha, ("NOSP" 1) ("cap" 1)]
6      you [4,6,4,6,0,0,alpha, ("SP" 1) ("lower" 1)]
7      google [8,13,8,13,0,0,alpha, ("SP" 1) ("lower" 1) ("meaning" concept:"m01") ("verb" 1) ("pos num" 1) ("syn" "search")]
8      his [15,17,15,17,0,0,alpha, ("SP" 1) ("lower" 1) ("pro" 1) ("pos num" 1)]
9      friend [19,24,19,24,0,0,alpha, ("SP" 1) ("lower" 1)]
10     ? [25,25,25,25,0,0,punct, ("NOSP" 1)]
11     He [27,28,27,28,0,0,alpha, ("SP" 1) ("NL" 1) ("cap" 1)]
12     works [30,34,30,34,0,0,alpha, ("SP" 1) ("lower" 1)]
```

```
13    at [36,37,36,37,0,0,alpha, ("SP" 1) ("low-
er" 1) ("prep" 1) ("pos num" 1)]
14    google [39,44,39,44,0,0,alpha, ("SP" 1) ("lower" 1) ("meaning"
concept:"m02") ("noun" 1) ("pos num" 1) ("entity" "company")]
15    . [45,45,45,45,0,0,punct, ("NOSP" 1)]
```

Line 7 is now a verb meaning **search**, and *line 14* is now a noun meaning **company**. Here is the function that makes this happen:

```
##################################################
# Ambiguity Functions
##################################################

AmbigTrimPOS(L("node"),L("pos")) {
    L("meaning") = pnvar(L("node"),"meaning");
    if (!L("meaning")) {
        return;
    }
    L("con") = down(L("meaning"));
    while (L("con")) {
        L("p") = strval(L("con"),"pos");
        if (L("p") == L("pos")) {
            AmbigCopyAttrs(L("con"),L("node"));
            pnreplaceval(L("node"),"pos num",1);
            pnreplaceval(L("node"),"meaning",L("con"));
        }
        L("con") = next(L("con"));
    }

    L("names") = pnvarnames(L("node"));
    while (L("names")[L("ii")]) {
        L("name") = L("names")[ L("ii") ];
        if (IsPOS(L("name")) && L("name") != L("pos")) {
            pnremoveval(L("node"),L("name"));
        }
        L("ii")++;
    }
}
```

```

AmbigCopyAttrs(L("con"),L("node")) {
    L("attrs") = findattrs(L("con"));

    while (L("attrs")) {
        L("vals") = attrvals(L("attrs"));
        L("name") = attrname(L("attrs"));
        L("type") = attrtype(L("con"),L("name"));

        if (L("name") != "pos") {
            while (L("vals")) {
                if (L("type") == 1) {
                    pnmakevar(L("node"),L("name"),getnumval(L("vals")));
                } else if (L("type") == 2) {
                    pnmakevar(L("node"),L("name"),getconval(L("vals")));
                } else if (L("type") == 3) {
                    pnmakevar(L("node"),L("name"),getfltval(L("vals")));
                } else {
                    pnmakevar(L("node"),L("name"),getstrval(L("vals")));
                }
                L("vals") = nextval(L("vals"));
            }
        }

        L("attrs") = nextattr(L("attrs"));
    }
}

IsPOS(L("pos")) {
    if (L("pos") == "noun" || L("pos") == "verb" || L("-
pos") == "adj" || L("pos") == "adv" || L("pos") == "prep" || L("-
pos") == "pron" || L("pos") == "conj" || L("pos") == "det" || L("-
pos") == "num" || L("pos") == "int" || L("pos") == "art" || L("-
pos") == "pro" || L("pos") == "punct")
        return 1;
    return 0;
}
```

This is meant to show how ambiguity can be handled more than to provide a final solution. Real-world solutions to ambiguity are more complex but can be handled using NLP++.

Output

An NLP++ analyzer can output to a stream, file, or buffer. NLP++ has some legacy ODBC code, but that is beyond the scope of the present book.

Output to files

Output to files uses the NLP++ **<<** piping symbol.

Local file

The simplest way to output to a file is to specify a file name and pipe output to that file. These are heavily used in NLP++ to help with debugging, given the fact that VisualText does not allow for stepping into an NLP++ analyzer and executing it line-by-line. Instead, NLP++ developers make heavy use of local debug files.

Here is the general format for piping to a local output file, C++-style:

```
"filename.ext" << text1 << text2 << text3;
```

The first argument when piping to a local file is the file name placed between double quotes. It can take any name and extension, like **output.txt** or **output.json**.

All the arguments that are piped or output to the file must be strings or numbers. NLP++ does not output complex variables such as arrays, concepts, or parse tree nodes.

When using a simple double-quoted file name, the files end up in the output folder for that text and appear in the output view in VisualText. Here is the debugging output file **nesting.txt** in the Recursion tutorial analyzer. You can see that on *line 17* in the **nestHeaders.nlp** file that pertinent information is piped to the **nesting.txt** file, as shown in the following figure:

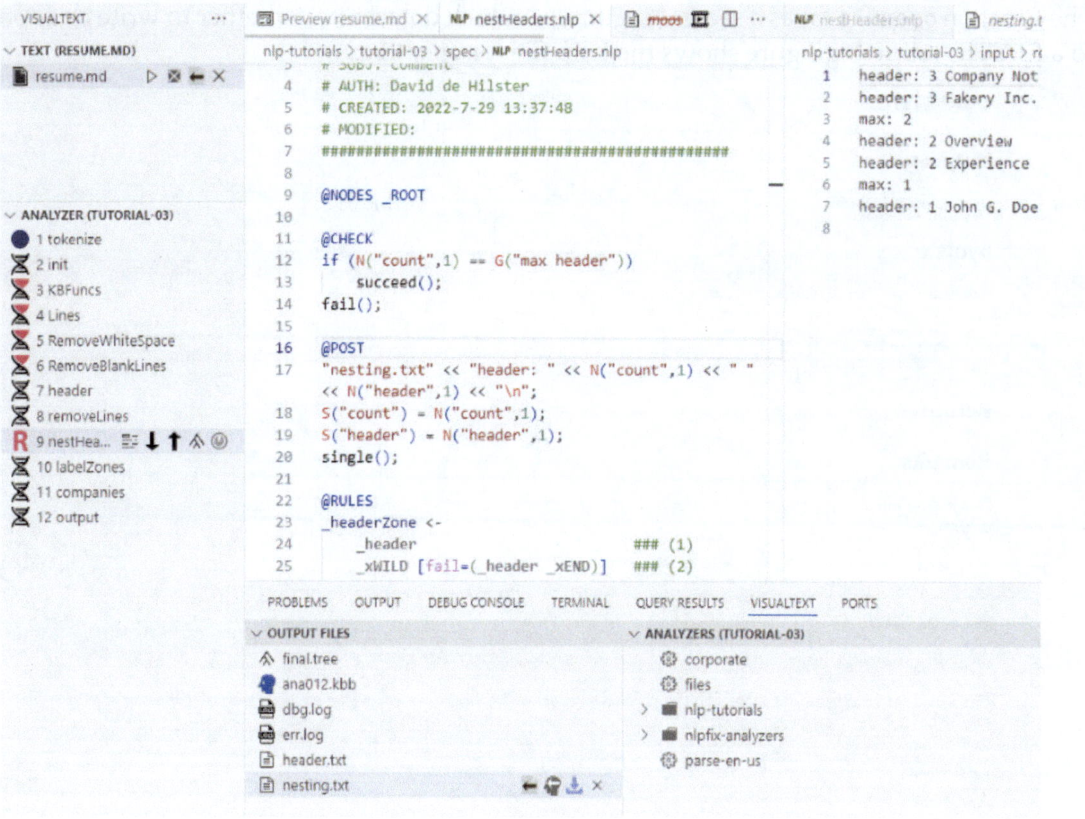

Figure 6.27: Piping output to the debug file nesting.txt

Openfile to output

NLP++ also allows you to pipe output into any file on your system using the **openfile** function. It works by storing the output of the **openfile** function into a variable and then piping the **output** to that variable:

```
G("output") = openfile("file-path");
G("output") << "hello world!" << "\n";
closefile(G("output"));
```

The function **openfile** takes a second argument, which determines whether to write or append to a file. The following figure shows the help file for **openfile**:

openfile

Purpose

Open output file stream.

Syntax

```
returnedOstream = openfile(path_str [, mode_str [, mode_str [, mode_str]]] )

      returnedOstream - type: ostream
      path_str - type: str
      mode_str - type: str
```

Returns

Remarks

Zero to three mode strings selected from: 1) "app" = append; 2) "ate" = special C++ append; 3) "binary" = open in binary mode (text is default).

`openfile` is analogous to C++ open file function.

WARNING: Default mode is OVERWRITE, not APPEND. Unlike `fileout()`, does not create a global variable for the file stream.

In specifying file names, double slashes should be used. To specify output.txt use `c:\\output.txt`, not `c:\output.txt`.

Files should not be placed in the application's input folder since VisualText wipes out the files after each text analysis. For example, a file called blob.txt in the folder c:\\apps\input\\eg1.txt_log will get deleted each time the text gets analyzed.

Example

```
@CODE
G("file") = openfile("c:\\tmp.txt");
closefile(G("file"));
@@CODE
```

See Also

closefile, Formatting and I/O Functions

Figure 6.28: openfile

A good way to learn about outputting to files is to look at the files analyzer in the **ANALYZERS** folder that comes with VisualText (refer to Figure 6.29). Simply click on the cog icon to view the files analyzer, as shown in the following figure:

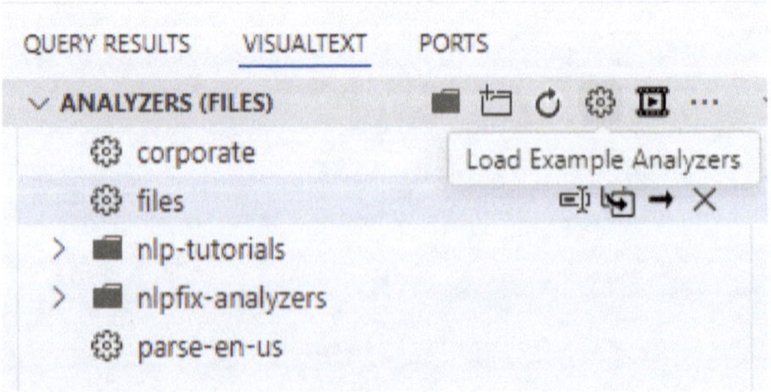

Figure 6.29: Cog icon lists files analyzer and others bundled with VisualText

Special characters

NLP++ uses C/C++ -like syntax for special characters like newline and tab. Newlines are **`\n`** and tabs are **`\t`**, as shown in the following:

```
"output.txt" << "Hello world!\nHow you doing?";
```

Outputs:

```
Hello word!
How you doing?
```

JSON output

As JSON is now a common NLP++ provides functions to support it.

The easiest way to output JSON is to build the output data into the KB, then use tailored output functions in the **`KBFuncs`** library. We examine the date-time analyzer in the **`nlpfix-analyzers`** folder of VisualText example analyzers.

In the last pass of the date-time analyzer, the output file has two lines, one to dump the KB, and the other to output the KB to a JSON file:

```
@CODE
SaveKB("datetimes.kbb",G("datetimes"),2);
JsonKB("output.json",G("datetimes"));
@@CODE
```

Both the **`SaveKB`** and **`JsonKB`** functions reside in the **`KBFuncs`** library. **`JsonKB`** outputs any KB in JSON format. The following figure shows the two outputs side-by-side:

nlpfix-analyzers > date-time > input > text.txt_log > datetimes.kbb

```
datetimes
  dates: "date_count"=37
    date001: month=9, day=4, year=2014
    date002: month=1, day=2, year=3
    date003: month=2, day=5, year=2020
    date004: month=6, day=17, year=2014
    date005: month=9, day=6, year=18
    date006: month=9, day=6, year=2018
    date007: month=12, day=11, year=2014, "time_count"=1
      time001: hour=10, min=6, am=am
    date008: month=11, day=12, year=2014, "time_count"=1
      time001: hour=8, min=45, sec=39
    date009: day=12, month=12, year=2001
    date010: month=13, day=3, year=2014
    date011: day=19, month=2, year=2013, "time_count"=1
      time001: hour=9, min=10
    date012: day=19, month=5, year=2015
    date013: month=12, day=11, year=2014, "time_count"=1
      time001: hour=2, min=21, am=pm
    date014: day=20, month=3, year=2013
    date015: year=2004
```

nlpfix-analyzers > date-time > input > text.txt_log >

```
{
  "datetimes": {
    "dates": {
      "date_count": "37",
      "date": [
        {
          "id": "001",
          "month": "9",
          "day": "4",
          "year": "2014"
        },
        {
          "id": "002",
          "month": "1",
          "day": "2",
          "year": "3"
        },
        {
          "id": "003",
          "month": "2",
          "day": "5",
          "year": "2020"
        },
```

Figure 6.30: KB file and corresponding JSON output file

Output to a stream

NLP++ can also output to a stream, when called from the NLP++ C++ library. Stream I/O is required when using the **NLP_ENGINE** C++ class, because there is no size limit to the I/O.

The NLP++ function for outputting to a stream is **cout**, for use in embedded and standalone analyzers. The user may supply an output stream to an API call, such as **nlp->analyze()**, where **nlp** is an instantiated subclass of the **NLP_ENGINE** class in C++. See the following example:

```
@CODE

G("out") = cout();
G("out") << "Hello output stream!" << "\n";

@@CODE
```

Let us first examine calling the NLP_ENGINE C++ class without streams.

If you look at the file **main.cpp** in the **nlp** folder under the VisualText **nlp-engine** repository on GitHub, you will see the code for calling the **NLP_ENGINE** C++ class without the stream. None of the variables being passed is a return-value variable. The output variable is the output folder being specified, not the return output from the analyzer. The code calling the analyzer must know where and how to use the output files:

```
_TCHAR *analyzerpath = 0, *input = 0, *output = 0, *workdir = 0;
// These strings are filled with the appropriate values

NLP_ENGINE *nlpEngine = new NLP_ENGINE(workdir);
nlpEngine->analyze(analyzerpath, input, output, develop, silent, compiled);

// No output is returned. Output files were created somewhere.
delete nlpEngine;
```

Now let us examine calling the **NLP_ENGINE** using input and output streams.

The call is in the **main.cpp** file, under the **test** folder within the VisualText **nlp-engine** repository. Notice that, unlike the code above, the **nlp | analyze** function call includes an input and output stream. Here, the output is returned in the **sso1** variable and is written to the standard output (*line 10* in the following):

```
1   std::istringstream ssi1(str);
2   std::ostringstream sso1;
3   _TCHAR workdir[1001];
4
5   GetCurrentDir(workdir, FILENAME_MAX);
6   NLP_ENGINE *nlpEngine = new NLP_ENGINE(workdir);
7   nlpEngine->analyze(anaParse,&ssi1,&sso1);
8
9   // The output is returned in the ss01 stream variable.
10  std::_t_cout << _T("[output: ") << sso1.str() << _T("]") << std::endl;
11
12  delete nlpEngine;
```

Conclusion

The current chapter describes the basics of creating and developing text analyzers using VisualText. It covers text analysis approaches, the graphical NLP++ editor, the integrated help, viewing the parse tree, and various types of output.

The next chapter presents library functions and passes available to the analyzer developer.

True or false

1. NLP++ builds multiple parse trees for an input text.
2. NLP++ supports both bottom-up and top-down analysis.
3. The NLP++ file editor can generate rules from selected text.
4. All NLP++ analyzers must use the KB.
5. Concepts in the KB may point to parse tree nodes.
6. NLP++ is well-suited to handle language ambiguity.
7. NLP++ can build a best-first parse tree.
8. NLP++ can only output to files.

Answers

1. False	2. True	3. True
4. False	5. True	6. True
7. True	8. False	

Multiple choice question

1. **NLP++ is best-suited to which of these analyzer types:**
   a. General
   b. Rule-based
   c. Domain-specific
   d. Text corpus
   e. Machine learning and statistical
   f. Neural network
2. **Which template analyzers are bundled with NLP++:**
   a. Address parser
   b. English parsers
   c. Bare minimum
   d. Date and time
   e. Email
   f. All of the above
   g. None of the above

3. **The NLP++ file editor can:**
   a. Remove accent marks
   b. Sort and deduplicate text lines
   c. Report on text size and line length
   d. All of the above
   e. None of the above
4. **The VisualText interface these capabilities:**
   a. Help documentation and lookup
   b. Artificial intelligence help view
   c. Shortcut keys
   d. Right-click menus for views and navigating among views
   e. An analyzer sequence view
   f. All of the above
   g. None of the above

Answers

1. b c d
2. f
3. a b
4. a c d e

Short answer questions

1. What are the two most important rules when programming in NLP++, according to David de Hilster?
2. What is the main advantage of NLP++ over previous programming languages used for NLP tasks?
3. Describe the tradeoffs of using the KB to store information when analyzing a text.
4. Pick a task that humans perform when reading and understanding text. Explain how a human performs that task and how that could be translated into an NLP++ analyzer.
5. Describe prototyping an analyzer with bottom-up and top-down analysis methods.
6. Explain some ways to handle ambiguity with NLP++.
7. What are the issues with allowing the KB to point to the parse tree?
8. Describe the various ways to format NLP++ rules.

Join our Discord space

Join our Discord workspace for latest updates, offers, tech happenings around the world, new releases, and sessions with the authors:

https://discord.bpbonline.com

Chapter 7
Example Analyzers

Introduction

In this chapter, we study three typical analyzers using NLP++. These represent three different levels of human understanding of text: simple patterns, formatting, and entity understanding.

When humans read and understand text, many levels are involved. The common focus is on understanding people, places, things, or actions. Rarely do humans study text formatting and organization. Yet the latter is exactly suited to NLP++, without which, the task of processing previously formatted text is extremely difficult.

Structure

In this chapter, we will discuss the following topics:

- Typical tasks for NLP++ analyzers
- REGEX vs. NLP++
- Date-time analyzer
- Formatted text analysis
- NLP entity extraction
- Full English parser

Objectives

By the end of the chapter, the reader will gain practical experience in reading, executing, and modifying text analyzers. A few distinct analyzers will be studied, starting with simple ones and ending with a substantial English parser. With these examples, the reader will better understand the use of NLP++ and the VisualText development environment.

Typical tasks for NLP++ analyzers

The following table presents typical text analysis tasks suitable for NLP++ analyzers. Among these, analyzers that extract entity information may range from the simple to the highly complex, the latter involving issues such as reference resolution (sometimes called **anaphoric resolution**):

Analyze	Description
Small patterns	Dates, times, emails, URLs, telephone numbers, etc., are handled elsewhere via **regular expression** (**REGEX**)
Text formatting	English words for numbering and organizing text
Entities	Extracting and consolidating information about people, places, and things across sentences and paragraphs

***Table 7.1**: Three types of typical tasks for NLP++*

We use the analyzers found in the **`nlpfix-analyzers`** folder, within the sandbox area of the VS Code NLP++ Language Extension. To access those analyzers, click on the gear icon in the **ANALYZERS** view.

REGEX vs. NLP++

Before delving into the three analyzers, we compare REGEX to NLP++ rules.

Ask any computer programmer who has used REGEX, and you will find that it is almost universally disliked. Various disadvantages of this pattern language are:

- **Cryptic syntax**:
    - REGEX patterns often resemble unreadable symbols.
    - Even when you write a correct pattern, interpreting it later can be extremely challenging.
- **Maintenance issues**:
    - Small changes can break existing functionality.
    - For example, a REGEX intended to match email addresses might fail when encountering edge cases (**`user@domain.com`** vs. **`user@sub.domain.com`**).
- **Lack of modularity**:
    - REGEX patterns are often dense one-liners.
    - Debugging requires re-reading the entire expression instead of modifying structured logic.
- **Hard to scale beyond simple cases**:
    - As complexity increases, REGEX patterns become unreadable.
    - For example, parsing nested structures (like HTML or JSON) becomes a nightmare or is, in all practical senses, impossible.

Use of NLP++

Unlike REGEX, NLP++ operates via human-readable rules that are constructed in steps. Some advantages are as follows:

- **Readable syntax:**
  - Rules are human-readable and therefore self-explanatory
  - Rules have **@PRE**, **@CHECK**, and **@POST** regions, allowing for human-readable rule conditions and actions
- **Modular and maintainable**:
  - You can reuse analyzer passes, making building new analyzers painless
  - Parsing logic is layered, allowing the pattern matching to be broken up into hierarchical steps
  - VisualText allows for stepping through the pattern matching step-by-step, simplifying the debugging process
- **Handles complexity without becoming unreadable**:
  - NLP++ uses multi-step parsing instead of forcing everything into a single cryptic REGEX pattern
  - NLP++ multi-step analysis supports any level of complexity, from simple patterns to full-blown **natural language processing** (**NLP**)

The following are the key differences between human intuition and symbolic processing:

- **REGEX**: Requires pattern memorization, trial-and-error debugging, and deep knowledge of special symbols.
- **NLP++**: Enables structured reasoning, modular development, and a logical approach to text analysis.

REGEX is great for quick searches, but NLP++ is superior for building rule-based NLP systems that need to scale while remaining understandable. (Without needing to decipher arcane symbols).

Parsing dates is a simple application in which NLP++ significantly outperforms REGEX in terms of readability, scalability, and maintainability. Let us break it down by comparing both approaches.

Approach 1: Using REGEX

Regular expressions attempt to match patterns based on rigid character sequences. While powerful for simple extractions, they quickly become unreadable when handling variations like different date formats (e.g., `MM/DD/YYYY`, `YYYY-MM-DD`, `DD-MMM-YYYY`).

Here is a REGEX pattern to capture common date formats:

```
regex
(?:(?:0?[1-9]|1[0-2])[-](?:0?[1-9]|[12][0-9]|3[01])
[-](?:19|20){2}|(?:19|20){2}[-](?:0?[1-9]|1[0-2])
[-](?:0?[1-9]|[12][0-9]|3[01])|
(?:0?[1-9]|[12][0-9]|3[01])[-]
(?:Jan|Feb|Mar|Apr|May|Jun|Jul|Aug|Sep|Oct|Nov|Dec)
[-](?:19|20){2})
```

The following are the challenges with REGEX:

- **Unreadable and hard to modify**: If you come back later, parsing the pattern is difficult.
- **Lack of hierarchical structure**: REGEX does not provide logical separation for parts of the date (day, month, year).
- **Fragile for edge cases**: Adding leap year detection or accounting for typos is nearly impossible without rewriting the entire expression.
- **No meaningful labels**: REGEX only matches text but does not assign structured information like month, day, and year as separate entities.

Approach 2: Using NLP++ rule-based parsing

NLP++ is designed for structured NLP and makes data parsing readable, maintainable, and scalable. It replaces cryptic REGEX patterns with clear rules that explicitly match concepts in text.

NLP++ example, Date parsing:

Here is a rule for matching a date using NLP++. Notice that readability is not an issue when coming back to the code or seeing it for the first time:

```
@PRE # Require these attributes to match the rule’s phrase.
<1,1> var("day");
<3,3> var("day");
<4,4> var("month");
<5,5> var("year");

@POST # The new _date node gets info from the matched pattern.
S("weekday") = N("day",1);
S("day") = num(N("$text",3));
```

```
S("month") = N("month",4);
S("year") = num(N("$text",5));
single();

@RULES
_date <-
    _xALPHA    ### (1)
     [opt]     ### (2)
    _xNUM      ### (3)
    _xALPHA    ### (4)
    _xNUM      ### (5)
    @@
```

The second thing that makes NLP++ superior to REGEX is the ability to build patterns from previous patterns. Here is a later rule in the date-time analyzer that puts together dates and times, after these were matched in previous passes. You can see that **_date** and **_time** are matched rules in previous passes and are now used in the **_dateTime** rule:

```
@POST
S("date") = N(1);
S("time") = N(3);
single();

@RULES
_dateTime <-
    _date                    ### (1)
    _xWILD [match=( t at)]   ### (2)
    _time                    ### (3)
    @@
```

Date-time analyzer

The date-time analyzer shows how an NLP++ analyzer can parse dates and times. This is a common task usually done by using REGEX. Those who know NLP++ prefer it over REGEX in that it gives coders the confidence that the pattern matching is solid, readable, and can easily be modified, no matter what complexities may arise in the future.

Before we start, we must follow the first and second rules of NLP++, think like a human:

When humans parse dates and times, they see numbers that have meaning. A number like 31 can be a day of the month, whereas 32 cannot. Numbers like 1959 look like a year to us, while 3240 does not. When programming in NLP++, we can capture this same idea.

A common technique for numbers used in NLP++ is to write a function to classify numbers for a particular domain. NLP++ enables using the same ideas in different analyzers, e.g., to tailor numeric attributes to the specific task at hand. We can write rules that look for specific types of numbers, making the rules more accurate.

For the date-time analyzer, the **NumberType** function looks for numbers that are possible days, months, and years. With this, the rules can restrict the numbers to include in a date:

```
@DECL

NumberType(L("node"),L("num")) {
   if (L("num") >= 1 && L("num") <= 12) {
      pnmakevar(L("node"),"month",1);
   }
   if (L("num") >= 1 && L("num") <= 31) {
      pnmakevar(L("node"),"day",1);
   }
   if (L("num") >= 1900 && L("num") <= 2050) {
      pnmakevar(L("node"),"year",1);
   }
   if (L("num") >= 0 && L("num") <= 99) {
      pnmakevar(L("node"),"year",1);
   }
}
```

Notice that numbers can have more than one date attribute. For instance, 11 can be a day, a month, or a year. However, in an extended pattern, only one of these meanings usually matches.

KB dictionary files

The date-time analyzer uses three library dictionaries (available in VisualText) and one small vocabulary dictionary specific to this task (as in the following table). These dictionaries are automatically accessed by the **dicttokz** tokenizer pass (i.e., tokenizer using the dictionary and building a parse tree with zero whitespace).

Pass	Description
`en-monthsdays.dict`	English month and day words
`en-numbers.dict`	English words for numbers
`timezones.dict`	Words and abbreviations for time zones
`vocab.dict`	Custom vocabulary for this analyzer

Table 7.2: KB dictionary files for the date-time analyzer

Analyzer sequence

One of the important qualities of NLP++ is its multi-pass pipeline (often used for bottom-up and island-driven parsing). This allows for building phrases from smaller pieces. In a date like *10:45 AM, December 12, 2024,* it makes sense to build up the date and times separately and then combine them in a later pass.

Not only is this a logical way to build a date, but it also provides a user-friendly visual environment for tracking the evolving analysis, one pass at a time. The following table presents the analyzer sequence for the date-time analyzer:

Pass	Description
`dicttokz`	Tokenize, remove whitespace, lookup in dictionary
`init`	Initializes the KB
`KBFuncs`	Standard KB library functions
`funcs`	Custom functions
`LinesDictTokZ`	Processes lines for the `dicttokz` tokenizer
`numbers`	Handles numeric values
`ordinals`	Processes ordinal numbers
`times`	Analyzes time expressions
`zulu`	Handles `zulu` time format
`timePhrases`	Processes time-related phrases
`dates`	Analyzes date expressions
`datesDay`	Processes day-specific date expressions
`dateTime`	Combines date and time
`datePhrases`	Handles date-related phrases
`splice`	Removes `_LINE` to make the tree more readable
`kb`	Moves date-time attributes from the tree to the KB

Pass	Description
output	Generates the final output

Table 7.3: Analyzer sequence (pipeline) of the date-time analyzer

We assume the input consists of the date: *10:06 AM, December 11, 2014*

dicttokz analyzer pass

Every tokenizer converts a text input to a parse tree. The current one accesses the dictionary (embedded in the KB) and produces a parse tree that omits whitespace, shown in the following table:

Node	Description
10	[0,1,0,1,0,0,num, ("NOSP" 1)]
:	[2,2,2,2,0,0,punct, ("NOSP" 1)]
06	[3,4,3,4,0,0,num, ("NOSP" 1)]
am	[5,6,5,6,0,0,alpha, ("NOSP" 1) ("lower" 1)]
Dec	[8,10,8,10,0,0,alpha,fired, ("SP" 1) ("cap" 1) ("month" 12)]
11	[12,13,12,13,0,0,num, ("SP" 1)]
,	[14,14,14,14,0,0,punct, ("NOSP" 1)]
2014	[16,19,16,19,0,0,num, ("SP" 1)]

Table 7.4: The date-time analyzer: dicttokz pass

Note: `Dec` has been given the (tentative) attribute `month`, with value `12`.

Numbers analyzer pass

During the number pass, numbers are categorized, and you can see that **`10`** is labeled as a possible **`day`**, **`month`**, or **`year`**, as shown in the following table:

Node	Description
10	[0,1,0,1,0,0,num,fired, ("NOSP" 1) ("month" 1) ("day" 1) ("year" 1)]
:	[2,2,2,2,0,0,punct, ("NOSP" 1)]
06	[3,4,3,4,0,0,num,fired, ("NOSP" 1) ("month" 1) ("day" 1) ("year" 1)]
am	[5,6,5,6,0,0,alpha, ("NOSP" 1) ("lower" 1)]
Dec	[8,10,8,10,0,0,alpha, ("SP" 1) ("cap" 1) ("month" 12)]

11	[12,13,12,13,0,0,num,fired, ("SP" 1) ("month" 1) ("day" 1) ("year" 1)]
,	[14,14,14,14,0,0,punct, ("NOSP" 1)]
2014	[16,19,16,19,0,0,num,fired, ("SP" 1) ("year" 1)]

Table 7.5: The date-time analyzer: numbers pass

Times analyzer pass

In the following table, we see a **_time** rule being matched while the date has not yet been processed:

Node	Description
10	[0,1,0,1,0,0,num,fired, ("NOSP" 1) ("month" 1) ("day" 1) ("year" 1)]
:	[2,2,2,2,0,0,punct, ("NOSP" 1)]
06	[3,4,3,4,0,0,num,fired, ("NOSP" 1) ("month" 1) ("day" 1) ("year" 1)]
am	[5,6,5,6,0,0,alpha, ("NOSP" 1) ("lower" 1)]
Dec	[8,10,8,10,0,0,alpha, ("SP" 1) ("cap" 1) ("month" 12)]
11	[12,13,12,13,0,0,num,fired, ("SP" 1) ("month" 1) ("day" 1) ("year" 1)]
,	[14,14,14,14,0,0,punct, ("NOSP" 1)]
2014	[16,19,16,19,0,0,num,fired, ("SP" 1) ("year" 1)]

Table 7.6: The date-time Analyzer: times pass

This is the rule that fired. In the first row of the table above, you can see the numbers **[0,6,0,6,8,43]**, and the 5th and 6th numbers are the pass number and line number, and points to this rule:

```
@POST
S("hour") = num(N("text",1));
S("min") = num(N("text",3));
S("sec") = num(N("text",5));
if (N(6)) S("am") = strpiece(pnname(N(6)),1,2);
single();

@RULES
_time <-
```

```
    _xNUM    ### (1)
    \:       ### (2)
    _xNUM    ### (3)
    \:       ### (4)
    _xNUM    ### (5)
    _xWILD [star match=(_am _pm)]    ### (6)
    @@
```

Dates analyzer pass

This pass matches dates. You can see the **_date** node created in the following table, and the **_time** node:

Node	Description
_time	[0,6,0,6,8,43,node, ("hour" 10) ("min" 6) ("am" "am")]
10	[0,1,0,1,0,0,num, ("NOSP" 1) ("month" 1) ("day" 1) ("year" 1)]
:	[2,2,2,2,0,0,punct, ("NOSP" 1)]
06	[3,4,3,4,0,0,num, ("NOSP" 1) ("month" 1) ("day" 1) ("year" 1)]
_am	[5,6,5,6,7,22,node]
am	[5,6,5,6,0,0,alpha, ("NOSP" 1) ("lower" 1)]
_date	[8,19,8,19,11,128,node,fired,blt, ("month" 12) ("day" 11) ("year" 2014)]
Dec	[8,10,8,10,0,0,alpha,fired, ("SP" 1) ("cap" 1) ("month" 12)]
11	[12,13,12,13,0,0,num,fired, ("SP" 1) ("month" 1) ("day" 1) ("year" 1)]
,	[14,14,14,14,0,0,punct,fired, ("NOSP" 1)]
2014	[16,19,16,19,0,0,num,fired, ("SP" 1) ("year" 1)]

Table 7.7: The date-time analyzer: dates pass

Date-time analyzer pass

In this pass, the time and date area are combined, as shown in the following table:

Concept	Attributes
_dateTime	[0,19,0,19,13,29,node,fired,blt, ("date" pnode:"_date") ("time" pnode:"_time")]

Concept	Attributes
_time	[0,6,0,6,8,43,node,fired, ("hour" 10) ("min" 6) ("am" "am")]
10	[0,1,0,1,0,0,num, ("NOSP" 1) ("month" 1) ("day" 1) ("year" 1)]
:	[2,2,2,2,0,0,punct, ("NOSP" 1)]
06	[3,4,3,4,0,0,num, ("NOSP" 1) ("month" 1) ("day" 1) ("year" 1)]
_am	[5,6,5,6,7,22,node]
am	[5,6,5,6,0,0,alpha, ("NOSP" 1) ("lower" 1)]
_date	[8,19,8,19,11,128,node,fired, ("month" 12) ("day" 11) ("year" 2014)]
Dec	[8,10,8,10,0,0,alpha, ("SP" 1) ("cap" 1) ("month" 12)]
11	[12,13,12,13,0,0,num, ("SP" 1) ("month" 1) ("day" 1) ("year" 1)]
,	[14,14,14,14,0,0,punct, ("NOSP" 1)]
2014	[16,19,16,19,0,0,num, ("SP" 1) ("year" 1)]

Table 7.8: The date-time analyzer: dateTime pass

Output analyzer pass

The output is a KBB file, as shown in the following table:

Concept	Attributes
datetimes	
dates:	"date_count"=1
date001:	month=12, day=11, year=2014, "time_count"=1
time001:	hour=10, min=6, am=am

Table 7.9: The date-time analyzer: output pass

Formatted text analysis

Standard NLP and computational linguistics courses focus on analyzing prose. However, text in the real world is often formatted. Even worse, analyzing a human-readable text requires conversion from PDF, MS Word, HTML/XML, or a similar format. The resulting previously formatted text is messy, requiring cleanup before one can analyze its prose content. Common source documents include employment resumes, government documents, and published papers.

Dealing with ill-formed and garbled text can be extremely difficult, and therefore is not usually done by automated analysis. We know that NLP++ allows developers to encode how humans read and understand text, and that includes understanding text formatting.

Previously formatted text

There is a previously formatted text example in the following section. It is displayed in a small font to emphasize format rather than content. We observe that it was previously formatted with enumerations, colon headers, and page breaks.

Text

The text in the following figure can be obtained from the formatting analyzer available with the example analyzers and also within the **nlpfix-analyzers** folder, with the filename **text.txt**. The following are the steps to process this text:

1. Create the **XOut** template analyzer.
2. Navigate to the **input** folder of the formatting analyzer.
3. Copy the **text.txt** file from there to the **XOut\input** folder.
4. Run **XOut** on **text.txt** and find the output file in **XOut\input\X\text.txt**.

```
2
Broadway&    |    After the intermission: Three actions to reset the stage and reshape your production for success
Here are three actions that can help refine the right elements in the right ways and help your
musical theater production emerge from this intermission ready for success:
 1. Revisit Creative Priorities
 Productions that emerge stronger after breaks are not those that cut corners. To
emerge stronger, redirect focus to the right creative drivers.
Step one in achieving this balance is to answer some simple questions about your production.
 1. How has your audience changed? What's happened to your patrons, sponsors, and
competitors? What trends or disruptors have accelerated?
2. What themes and stories look promising in a post-pandemic world?
 3. Can you articulate the few things your production needs to do better than anyone else in
order to meet those themes? What will your competitive advantage be?
```

```
 4. Are you invest-
ing enough in those few things? Where do you need to spend less so you
have the funds to redirect focus to value-creating differentiation?
 These questions should help you quickly frame your few
must-haves - the handful of
elements that differentiate your production in the market.
Doubling down in these areas helps
ensure that no matter what the outcome, your
production has the right strengths to emerge
stronger.
Keep in mind that what was differentiating your production before the
intermission may no longer be
working. (See Exhibit). Think how your competitors are already
prepared to respond in areas
such as:
   Long-term shifts in audience preferences: People expect greater
options with digital
experiences, so expectations around live performances will
fundamentally change.
  A more volatile and ambiguous entertainment environment: Theater
leaders are investing
as a way to withstand strong external forces and quickly
recover from setbacks. They're
committing to dynamic strategies that can help them become more
resilient. They're testing
and tweaking assumptions, so they can adjust without
losing speed or getting knocked off
course.
 Broadway&    |    After the intermission: Three actions to
reset the stage and reshape your production for success
 3
  A shift in the nature of work: Producers are moving from fixed and
predictable cast and crew
models to more flexible, virtual and diversified models that support
autonomy, flexibility and
more.
```

XOut template analyzer

As noted, XOut is available as a template analyzer when creating a new NLP++ analyzer. It replaces all alphabetical characters with an *X* or *x*, depending on the original letter case.

After performing the steps described above, the output corresponding to the above input text looks like:

```
2
Xxxxxxxx& | Xxxxx xxx xxxxxxxxxxxx: Xxxxx xxxxxxx xx xxxxx xxx xxxxx xx x xxxxxxx xxxx xxxxxxxxxx xxx xxxxxxx
Xxxx xxx xxxxx xxxxxxx xxxx xxx xxxx xxxxxx xxx xxxxx xxxxxxxx xx xxx xx xxx xxxx xxx xxxx xxxx
xxxxxxx xxxxxxx xxxxxxxxxx xxxxxx xxxx xxxx xxxxxxxxxxx xxxxx xxx xxxxx xx:
1. Xxxxxxx Xxxxxxxx Xxxxxxxxxx
Xxxxxxxxxx xxxx xxxxxx xxxxxxxx xxxxx xxxxxx xxx xxx xxxxx xxxx xxx xxx xxxx. Xx
xxxxxx xxxxxxxx, xxxxxxxx xxxxx xx xxx xxxxx xxxxxxxx xxxxxxx.
Xxxx xxx xx xxxxxxxxx xxxx xxxxxxx xx xx xxxxxx xxxx xxxxxx xxxxxxxxx xx xxx xxxx xxxxxxxxxx.
1. Xxx xxx xxxx xxxxxxxx xxxxxxx? Xxxx'x xxxxxxxx xx xxxx xxxxxxx, xxxxx xxx, xxx
xxxxxxxxxxx? Xxxx xxxxxx xx xxxxxxxxxx xxxx xxxxxxxxxxx?
2. Xxxx xxxxxx xxx xxxxxxx xxxx xxxxxxxxx xx x xxxx-xxxxxxxx xxxxx?
3. Xxx xxx xxxxxxxxxx xxx xxx xxxxxx xxxx xxxxxxxxxx xxxxx xx xx xxxxxx xxxx xxxxxx xxxx xx
xxxxx xx xxxx xxxxx xxxxxx? Xxxx xxxx xxxx xxxxxxxxxxx xxxxxxxxx xx?
4. Xxx xxx xxxxxxxxx xxxxxx xx xxxxx xxx xxxxxx? Xxxxx xx xxx xxxx xx xx xxx xxxx xx xxx
xxxx xxx xxxxx xx xxxxxxxx xxxxx xx xxxxx-xxxxxxxx xxxxxxxxxxxxxxx?
Xxxxx xxxxxxxxx xxxxxx xxxx xxx xxxxxxx xxxxx xxxx xxx xxxx-xxxxx - xxx xxxxxxx xx
xxxxxxxx xxxx xxxxxxxxxxxxx xxxx xxxxxxxxxx xx xxx xxxxxx. Xxxxxxxx xxx x xx xxxxx xxxxx xxxxx
xxxxxx xxxx xx xxxxxx xxxx xxx xxxxxxx, xxxx xxxxxxxxxx xxx xxx xxxxx xx xxxxxxx xx xxxxxx
xxxxxxxx.
Xxxx xx xxxx xxxx xxxx xxx xxxxxxxxxxxxxxx xxxx xxxxxxxxxx xxxxxx xxx xx xxxxxxxxxx xxx xx xxxxxx xx
xxxxxxx. (Xxx Xxxxxxx). Xxxxx xxx xxxx xxxxxxxxxxx xxx xxxxxxx xxxxxxx xx xxxxxxx xx xxxxx
xxxx xx:
Xxxx-xxxx xxxxxx xx xxxxxxxx xxxxxxxxxxx: Xxxxxx xxxxxx xxxxxxx xxxxxxx xxxx xxxxxxx
```

```
xxxxxxxxxxx, xx xxxxxxxxxxxx xxxxxx xxxx xxxxxxxxxxxx xxxx xxxxxxxxxxxx x xxxxxx.
X xxxx xxxxxxxx xxx xxxxxxxxx xxxxxxxxxxxx xxxxxxxxxxx: Xxxxxxx xxxxxx x xxx xxxxxxxxx
xx x xxx xx xxxxxxxxx xxxxxx xxxxxxxx xxxxxx xxx xxxxxxx xxxxxxx xxxx xx xxxxxx. Xxxx'xx
xxxxxxxxxx xx xxxxxxx xxxxxxxxxx xxxx xxx xxxx xxxx xxxxxx xxxx xxxxxxxxx. Xxxxâ€™xx xxxxxxx
xxx xxxxxxxx xxxxxxxxxxx, xx xxxx xxx xxxxxx xxxxxxx xxxxxx xxxxx xx xxx xxxx xxxxxxx xxx
xxxxxx.
Xxxxxxxx& | Xxxxx xxx xxxxxxxxxxxx: Xxxxx xxxxxxx xx xxxxx xxx xxxxx xx x xxxxxxx xxxx xxxxxxxxxx xxx xxxxxxx
3
X xxxxx xx xxx xxxxxx xx xxxx: Xxxxxxxx xxx xxxxxx xxxx xxxxx xxx xxxxx xxxxxx xxxx xxx xxxx
xxxxxx xx xxxx xxxxxxxx, xxxxxxx xxx xxxxxxxxxxx xxxxxx xxxx xxxxxxx xxx xxxxx, xxxxxxxxxxx xxx
xxxx.
```

Formatting analyzer

We use the formatting analyzer as an exercise for students learning to write NLP++ analyzers for previously formatted text, e.g., from resumes, papers, and government documents with sections, chapters, enumerations, etc. Replacing the content allows students to concentrate on formatting.

When you look at previously formatted text, we humans can study the physical location, capitalization, and general word distribution of a text. We can *tease out* the titles, headers, enumerations, lists, and prose (i.e., full sentences) regions.

Note: **When building an analyzer to reconstruct the formatting from pure American Standard Code for Information Interchange (ASCII) text, we must think about how we humans read such a text and distinguish between formatting and prose. VisualText and NLP++ enable us to encode our thinking directly in a text analyzer.**

Analyzer sequence

The following table lists the analyzer sequence for the formatting analyzer. We discuss some important passes in more detail:

Pass	Description
`dicttokz`	Tokenize, remove whitespace, dictionary lookup
`init`	Initialize KB variables
`KBFuncs`	KB functions from library
`funcs`	Custom functions for this analyzer
`LinesDictTokZ`	Library pass matching lines for **`dicttokz`**
`numbered`	Handle numbered lines
`pageNumber`	Match page numbers
`pageTitle`	Match page titles
`pageHeader`	Match page headers
`lineAttrs`	Generate line attributes
`headers`	Match header lines
`colonHeaders`	Match colon headers
`prose`	Find prose text using line attributes
`stragglers`	Handle straggling text
`paragraphBreaks`	Detect paragraph breaks
`enumerateBlock`	Find enumerated blocks
`colonBlock`	Find colon-separated blocks
`proseBlock`	Find prose blocks
`spliceLines`	Remove line nodes (no longer needed)
`sentenceEnders`	Find sentence-ending punctuation
`sentences`	Find sentences
`sentEnum`	Process enumerated sentences
`sentColon`	Process colon-separated sentences
`enumerate`	Process enumerated blocks
`colon`	Process colon blocks
`output`	Generate output

***Table 7.10**: Formatting analyzer sequence*

colonHeaders analyzer pass

A common formatting clue consists of colon headers. These are lines with a single colon. The rule in the following checks if the first word is capitalized (*line* 4) and then collects all the words up to a colon (see *line 15*):

```
@NODES _LINE

@PRE
<2,2> cap();

@POST
X("colon",2) = 1;
group(2,3,"_colonText");
single();

@RULES
_colonHeader <-
    _xSTART                  ### (1)
    _xALPHA                  ### (2)
    _xWILD [fail=(:)]        ### (3)
    :                        ### (4)
    @@
```

VisualText highlights the text matched by the rule, as shown in the following figure:

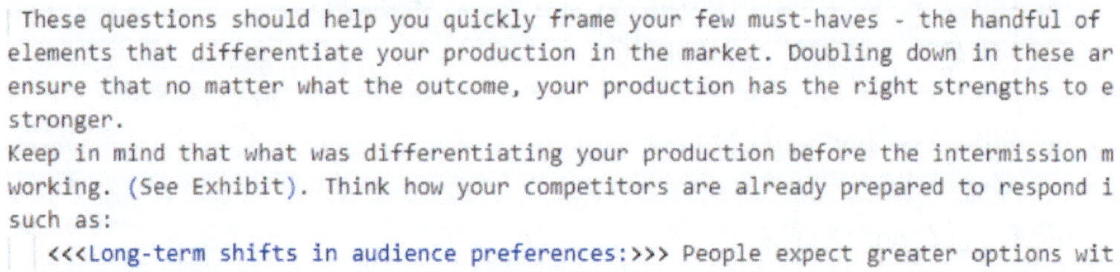

These questions should help you quickly frame your few must-haves - the handful of
elements that differentiate your production in the market. Doubling down in these ar
ensure that no matter what the outcome, your production has the right strengths to e
stronger.
Keep in mind that what was differentiating your production before the intermission m
working. (See Exhibit). Think how your competitors are already prepared to respond i
such as:
<<<Long-term shifts in audience preferences:>>> People expect greater options wit
experiences, so expectations around live performances will fundamentally change.
<<<A more volatile and ambiguous entertainment environment:>>> Theater leaders are
as a way to withstand strong external forces and quickly recover from setbacks. They
committing to dynamic strategies that can help them become more resilient. They're t
and tweaking assumptions, so they can adjust without losing speed or getting knocked
course.
Broadway& | After the intermission: Three actions to reset the stage and reshap
3
<<<A shift in the nature of work:>>> Producers are moving from fixed and predictab
models to more flexible, virtual and diversified models that support autonomy, flexi
more.

***Figure 7.1**: Highlighted for the colonHeader pass*

Note: This example analyzer is not a complete solution for previously formatted text. Each document type presents its own challenges. It is exactly this type of problem that distinguishes NLP++: one can customize analyzers to specific domains, tasks, and file types, in stark contrast to generic NLP toolkits.

The realities of real-world text have forced many programmers to abandon this type of text analysis altogether. However, with NLP++ and VisualText, analyzing previously formatted text, as well as other complex challenges, can be tackled successfully.

Prose analyzer pass

We now examine the **lineAttrs**, **prose**, and **stragglers** passes.

The **lineAttrs** pass calls the **LineAttrs** function located in the **funcs** pass.

Note: When studying previously formatted text, we note various features of lines: length, number of words, number of upper and lowercase words. Can you think of other useful features?

In the following is the function **LineAttrs**. To the given line node, it adds attributes for length, number of lowercase and uppercase words, and sentence-ending punctuation mark, if present.

```
LineAttrs(L("line")) {
    L("len") = strlength(pnvar(L("line"),"text"));
    pnmakevar(L("line"),"length",L("len"));

    L("node") = pndown(L("line"));
    L("first") = 1;
    while (L("node")) {
        L("name") = pnname(L("node"));
        if (L("first")) {
            if (strisupper(L("name"))) {
                pnmakevar(L("line"),"first upper",1);
            }
            L("first") = 0;
        }
        if (L("name") != "_enum") {
            if (strcontains(L("name"),",.:;!?")) {
                IncrementPN(L("line"),"lower");
            }
            else if (pnvar(L("node"),"lower")) {
```

```
                IncrementPN(L("line"),"lower");
            } else if (strisupper(L("name"))) {
                IncrementPN(L("line"),"upper");
            }
            IncrementPN(L("line"),"words");
        }
        if (!pnnext(L("node"))  IsCharPunct(L("name"))) {
            pnmakevar(L("line"),"sent end",1);
        }
        L("node") = pnnext(L("node"));
    }
}
```

The **line** attributes are used in the **prose** pass, remembering that **prose** refers to fully grammatical sentences, in contrast to headers. In the following prose pass code, the single rule checks every **_LINE** node in the parse tree, qualifying a line as **prose** using either of these two simplistic criteria:

- Are all the words in the line lowercase, and are there at least 2 of them?
- Are there at least 5 words and at least 5 lowercase words

However, this is an oversimplification for demonstration purposes.

```
@POST
if ((N("words") == N("lower") && N("words") > 2) ||
'       (N("words") >= 5 && N("lower") >= 5)) {
    N("prose") = 1;
}

@RULES
_xNIL <-
    _LINE    ### (1)
    @@
```

Stragglers analyzer pass

Stragglers are short lines ending a sentence. The following single rule in the stragglers pass checks line attributes to see if the words are all lowercase, another overly simple test. (One could also check for a sentence-ending punctuation mark here.) The **@PRE** conditions require that the line has not already been assigned a type. If successful, the line is marked as prose:

```
@PRE
<1,1> varz("prose");
<1,1> varz("enum");
<1,1> varz("page");

@POST
if (N("words",1) == N("lower",1))
   N("prose",1) = 1;

@RULES
_xNIL <-
   _LINE ### (1)
   @@
```

The following parse tree fragment precedes the stragglers pass. The two highlighted lines show the difference between a straggler (*lines 1 to 3*) and a prose line (starting at *line 4*). *Line 1* in the following file listing does not have the **prose** attribute yet, while *line 4* does. Comparing the above rule with the attributes in *line 1* shows that the requirements for a straggler are met:

```
1  _LINE [1361,1369,1361,1369,5,28,node,fired, ("NL" 1) ("length" 9) ("lower" 2) ("words" 2) ("sent end" 1)]
2     stronger [1361,1368,1361,1368,0,0,alpha, ("SP" 1) ("NL" 1) ("lower" 1)]
3     . [1369,1369,1369,1369,0,0,punct, ("NOSP" 1)]
4  _LINE [1372,1470,1372,1470,5,28,node,fired, ("NL" 1) ("length" 99) ("first upper" 1) ("upper" 1) ("words" 16) ("lower" 15) ("prose" 1)]
5     Keep [1372,1375,1372,1375,0,0,alpha, ("SP" 1) ("NL" 1) ("cap" 1)]
6     in [1377,1378,1377,1378,0,0,alpha, ("SP" 1) ("lower" 1)]
7     mind [1380,1383,1380,1383,0,0,alpha, ("SP" 1) ("lower" 1)]
8     that [1385,1388,1385,1388,0,0,alpha, ("SP" 1) ("lower" 1)]
9     what [1390,1393,1390,1393,0,0,alpha, ("SP" 1) ("lower" 1)]
10    was [1395,1397,1395,1397,0,0,alpha, ("SP" 1) ("lower" 1)]
11    differentiating [1399,1413,1399,1413,0,0,alpha, ("SP" 1) ("lower" 1)]
12    your [1415,1418,1415,1418,0,0,alpha, ("SP" 1) ("lower" 1)]
13    production [1420,1429,1420,1429,0,0,alpha, ("SP" 1) ("lower" 1)]
14    before [1431,1436,1431,1436,0,0,alpha, ("SP" 1) ("lower" 1)]
```

```
the [1438,1440,1438,1440,0,0,alpha, ("SP" 1) ("lower" 1)]
intermission [1442,1453,1442,1453,0,0,alpha, ("SP" 1) ("lower" 1)]
may [1455,1457,1455,1457,0,0,alpha, ("SP" 1) ("lower" 1)]
no [1459,1460,1459,1460,0,0,alpha, ("SP" 1) ("lower" 1)]
longer [1462,1467,1462,1467,0,0,alpha, ("SP" 1) ("lower" 1)]
be [1469,1470,1469,1470,0,0,alpha, ("SP" 1) ("lower" 1)]
```

After running the stragglers pass, *line 1* of the following tree now has the **prose** attribute:

```
1   _LINE [1361,1369,1361,1369,5,28,node,fired, ("NL" 1) ("length" 9)
    ("lower" 2) ("words" 2) ("sent end" 1) ("prose" 1)]
2      stronger [1361,1368,1361,1368,0,0,alpha, ("SP" 1) ("NL" 1)
    ("lower" 1)]
3      . [1369,1369,1369,1369,0,0,punct, ("NOSP" 1)]
4   _LINE [1372,1470,1372,1470,5,28,node, ("NL" 1) ("length" 99) ("first
    upper" 1) ("upper" 1) ("words" 16) ("lower" 15) ("prose" 1)]
5      Keep [1372,1375,1372,1375,0,0,alpha, ("SP" 1) ("NL" 1) ("cap" 1)]
6      in [1377,1378,1377,1378,0,0,alpha, ("SP" 1) ("lower" 1)]
7      mind [1380,1383,1380,1383,0,0,alpha, ("SP" 1) ("lower" 1)]
8      that [1385,1388,1385,1388,0,0,alpha, ("SP" 1) ("lower" 1)]
```

The highlights in the VisualText **Display Matched Rules** (txxt file), as shown in the following figure, correspond to rule matching in the stragglers pass:

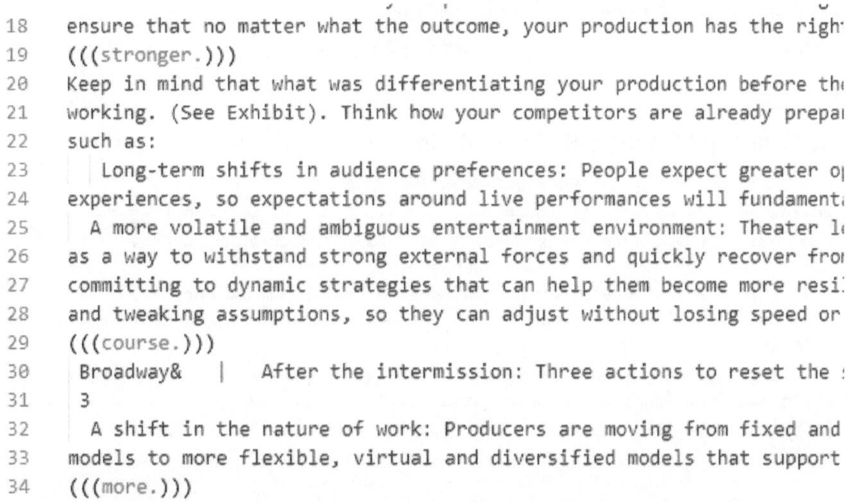

Figure 7.2: *Formatting analyzer display of matched stragglers*

Grouping passes

A late stage of the formatting analyzer groups the individual parts, comprising headers, numbered areas, and prose paragraphs. When successful, the analyzer recreates the intended format of the original document.

Next, we describe the two passes for enumerated regions.

The **`sentEnum`** analyzer pass in the following, the single rule of the **`sentEnum`** pass traverses sentences within an enumerated block (context *line 1*). When it encounters an **`_enum`** (e.g., **1**, **2**), it collects the sentence text into a **`_text`** node (*line 6*), thus separating it from the **`_enum`**.

```
1   @PATH _ROOT _enumerateBlock _sentence
2
3   @POST
4   X("enum",3) = N("enum",2);
5   X("text",3) = N("$text",3);
6   group(3,3,"_text");
7
8   @RULES
9   _xNIL <-
10      _xSTART                      ### (1)
11      _enum                        ### (2)
12      _xWILD [star fail=(_xEND)] ### (3)
13      _xEND                        ### (4)
14      @@
```

The VisualText **Display Matched Rules** view is shown in the following figure:

```
emerge stronger, redirect focus to the right creative drivers.
Step one in achieving this balance is to answer some simple questions about your production.
 (((1.))) <<<How has your audience changed?>>> What's happened to your patrons, sponsors, and
competitors? What trends or disruptors have accelerated?
(((2.))) <<<What themes and stories look promising in a post-pandemic world?>>>
 (((3.))) <<<Can you articulate the few things your production needs to do better than anyone else in
order to meet those themes?>>> What will your competitive advantage be?
 (((4.))) <<<Are you investing enough in those few things?>>> Where do you need to spend less so you
have the funds to redirect focus to value-creating differentiation?
 These questions should help you quickly frame your few must-haves - the handful of
elements that differentiate your production in the market. Doubling down in these areas helps
```

Figure 7.3: Formatting analyzer matching of enumerated sentences

- The enumerate analyzer pass the enumerate pass traverses the sentences of an enumerated block (context *line 1*). When it finds a sentence with an **enum** (**PRE** condition *line 4*), it gathers that and the following unnumbered sentences (**PRE** condition *line 5*) into a subregion named **_enumerate** (*line 12*):

```
1   @PATH _ROOT _enumerateBlock
2
3   @PRE
4   <1,1> var("enum");
5   <2,2> varz("enum");
6
7   @POST
8   S("enum") = N("enum",1);
9   single();
10
11  @RULES
12  _enumerate <-
13      _sentence                          ### (1)
14      _xWILD [star match=(_sentence)]    ### (2)
15      @@
```

Final tree

When the formatting analyzer succeeds, the final parse tree (refer to the following figure) reflects the intended format of the original document (PDF, MS Word, XML/HTML, and so on).

This example analyzer is for instructional use only, demonstrating that VisualText and NLP++ belong in every programmer's toolkit and that with these, no task is too difficult.

A deployable application requires a development effort with a substantial set of input texts targeted to a specific language, domain, and task.

```
FINAL OUTPUT TREE:

_ROOT [0,2428,0,2428,0,0,node,un, ("TOT LINES" 1) ("TOT TABS" 0) ("TOT LOWERS" 333) ("T
   _prose [0,285,0,285,18,15,node]
      _sentence [0,285,0,285,21,17,node, ("con" concept:"sentence001")]…
   _header [288,317,288,317,11,17,node]…
   _prose [320,463,320,463,18,25,node]
      _sentence [320,396,320,396,21,17,node, ("con" concept:"sentence002")]…
      _sentence [398,463,398,463,21,17,node, ("con" concept:"sentence003")]…
   _prose [466,557,466,557,18,25,node]
      _sentence [466,557,466,557,21,17,node, ("con" concept:"sentence004")]…
   _enumerateBlock [560,1088,560,1088,16,17,node]…
   _prose [1091,1369,1091,1369,18,25,node]
      _sentence [1091,1232,1091,1232,21,17,node, ("con" concept:"sentence013")]…
      _sentence [1234,1369,1234,1369,21,17,node, ("con" concept:"sentence014")]…
   _prose [1372,1573,1372,1573,18,25,node]
      _sentence [1372,1480,1372,1480,21,17,node, ("con" concept:"sentence015")]…
      _sentence [1482,1495,1482,1495,21,17,node, ("con" concept:"sentence016")]…
      _sentence [1497,1573,1497,1573,21,17,node, ("con" concept:"sentence017")]…
   _colonBlock [1578,2428,1578,2428,17,17,node]
      _colon [1578,1743,1578,1743,25,21,node, ("colon" "Long-term shifts in audience pr
         _sentence [1578,1743,1578,1743,21,17,node, ("con" concept:"sentence018") ("col
      _colon [1749,2114,1749,2114,25,21,node, ("colon" "A more volatile and ambiguous e
         _sentence [1749,1915,1749,1915,21,17,node, ("con" concept:"sentence019") ("col
         _sentence [1917,1999,1917,1999,21,17,node, ("con" concept:"sentence020")]…
         _sentence [2001,2114,2001,2114,21,17,node, ("con" concept:"sentence021")]…
      _colon [2117,2428,2117,2428,25,21,node, ("colon" "A shift in the nature of work:"
         _sentence [2117,2428,2117,2428,21,17,node, ("con" concept:"sentence022") ("col
```

***Figure 7.4**: Final parse tree of formatting analyzer*

NLP entity extraction

The entity extraction analyzer discussed here is called simply NLP and resides with the example analyzers under the **nlpfix-analyzers** folder.

The current example analyzer identifies entities in text and also tackles coreference resolution, a well-known and challenging NLP task. From *Google AI Overview*:

Coreference resolution is a Natural Language Processing (NLP) task that identifies all words or phrases (mentions) in a text that refer to the same real-world entity.

For example, a news article may refer to a person by first and last name in the first instance, then use only the first or only the last name in subsequent references to the same person.

This is considered a difficult task in computational linguistics, but with the framework NLP++ provides, it becomes simpler and more natural to implement.

NLP++ supports cognitive models that recognize that **natural language understanding** (**NLU**) requires knowledge, dictionaries, rules, parsing, and short and long-term memory, all working together. To construct an NLP++ analyzer that handles coreference, we again must think about the methods people use to understand text (i.e., *think like a human*).

Note: When we read text, we keep track of people, places, things, and events as we read. We do bookkeeping of these things so that later in the text, when we encounter a pronoun or a last name, we can go back to our short-term memory and associate that reference with something we read earlier in the text (i.e., anaphoric reference).

The following is the text to be analyzed, highlighting references to people:

```
Nathalia Ribas and Eduardo Costa, two programmers from
Brazil, are helping create the first comprehensive digital
dictionary for Portuguese in the AI framework NLP++.
Mentored by David de Hilster, co-author of the NLP++
programming language, they met while working at LexisNexis.
Nathalia is finishing her bachelor's degree at Santa
Catarina University and plans to use NLP++ in {her} master's
thesis. Their project improves AI's understanding of
Portuguese, showcasing Brazil's growing tech influence and
the power of collaboration and mentorship. De Hilster is
also the founder of the Natural Language Understanding
Global Initiative.
```

Dictionaries

For this example analyzer, we use several dictionaries from the VisualText library: two from English and one from Portuguese. The last dictionary, **`vocab.dict`**, is specific to this analyzer. As always, this is a demo analyzer, not a comprehensive solution, as listed in the following table:

KB files	Description
`en-function-words.dict`	English function words
`en-languages.dict`	English words for human languages
`pt-nomes.dict`	Portuguese names
`vocab.dict`	Custom vocabulary for this analyzer

***Table 7.11**: KB and DICT files*

Dynamic knowledge base

The CG KBMS can help emulate what people do when they read: use knowledge to understand the current text, and dynamically store new information.

The entity extraction analyzer uses global variables to point to KB locations for tracking entities and related information. (NLP++ implementation tip: another way to store analyzer-wide pointers and attributes is to place them on the parse tree root.)

Note: **When reading text that tells a story" like a news article, we humans immediately start constructing story concepts that keep track of people, places, things, and actions or events. When building an NLP++ analyzer, programmers must decide what concepts need to be remembered in the KB. A programmer can think of this as a brain that stores information as it reads.**

Analyzer sequence

The analyzer sequence (reference the following table) consists of seventeen passes, surprisingly few for what is deemed a difficult task. This is because the NLP++ framework includes a parse tree, KB, pattern matching rules, and functions, allowing developers to concentrate on the task at hand.

Note: **As always, this analyzer is for instructional use and is not a complete solution.**

Node	Description
`dicttokz`	Tokenize, remove whitespace, dictionary lookup.
`init`	Initialize KB with our bookkeeping areas.
`TreeFuncs`	Tree library functions.
`KBFuncs`	KB library functions.
`funcs`	Analyzer-specific functions.
`sentenceEnders`	Identify sentence boundaries.
`sentences`	Find sentences.
`caps`	Process capitalization.
`categorizeCaps`	Categorize capitalized words.
`findReferences`	Find references in text.
`labelCaps`	Label capitalized words.
`reduceCaps`	Splice capitalization branches.
`conjunctions`	Handle conjunctions.
`conjoin`	Conjoin the conjunctions.

Node	Description
attributes	Find interesting attributes.
personAttributes	Handle person attributes.
output	Generate output.

Table 7.12: Analyzer sequence for entity extraction

Dictionary lookup

The following table shows a portion of the tree resulting from the dictionary lookup during tokenization. **Nathalia** and **Eduardo** are labeled as names with a gender, the function words **and** and **from** are labeled, the number **two** reduces to a **_number** node, and **Brazil** reduces to a **_country** node.

Node	Description
Nathalia	[0,7,0,7,0,0,alpha,fired, ("NOSP" 1) ("cap" 1) ("genero" "f") ("pessoa" 1)]
Ribas	[9,13,9,13,0,0,alpha, ("SP" 1) ("cap" 1)]
and	[15,17,15,17,0,0,alpha,fired, ("SP" 1) ("lower" 1) ("functword" 1) ("coordinatingConjunctions" 1) ("pos num" 1) ("conjunction" 1)]
Eduardo	[19,25,19,25,0,0,alpha,fired, ("SP" 1) ("cap" 1) ("genero" "m") ("pessoa" 1)]
Costa	[27,31,27,31,0,0,alpha, ("SP" 1) ("cap" 1)]
,	[32,32,32,32,0,0,punct,fired, ("NOSP" 1) ("conjunction" 1)]
_number	[34,36,34,36,0,0,node,fired, ("SP" 1) ("lower" 1) ("functword" 1) ("cardinalNumerals" 1) ("pos num" 1) ("value" 2)]
two	[34,36,34,36,0,0,alpha, ("SP" 1) ("lower" 1) ("functword" 1) ("cardinalNumerals" 1) ("pos num" 1) ("value" 2)]
_occupation	[38,48,38,48,0,0,node,fired, ("SP" 1) ("lower" 1) ("count" "plural") ("root" "programmer")]
programmers	[38,48,38,48,0,0,alpha, ("SP" 1) ("lower" 1) ("count" "plural") ("root" "programmer")]
from	[50,53,50,53,0,0,alpha,fired, ("SP" 1) ("lower" 1) ("functword" 1) ("prepositions" 1) ("pos num" 1)]
_country	[55,60,55,60,0,0,node,fired, ("SP" 1) ("NL" 1) ("cap" 1)]
Brazil	[55,60,55,60,0,0,alpha, ("SP" 1) ("NL" 1) ("cap" 1)]

Table 7.13: Tree after dictionary lookup

Init analyzer pass

The **init**, or initialization, of the following pass code builds three main subtrees in the KB:

- **Article concept**: Stores sentences and their content
- **Caps concept**: Stores capitalized words
- **People concept**: Gathers information about people

```
@CODE

G("article") = getconcept(findroot(),"article");
G("caps")    = getconcept(findroot(),"caps");
G("people")  = getconcept(findroot(),"people");

@@CODE
```

Subsequent passes use these concepts to do bookkeeping and build up information about the people referenced in the current text.

Sentences analyzer pass

We use the KB's article subtree to track relevant information in each sentence.

Note: When reading text that tells a "story", such as a news article, people keep track of relevant information. To mirror that process, the analyzer creates concepts in the KB for items found in each sentence. It can then identify references to people's names and attributes, e.g., by resolving the referents of pronouns.

Line 4 in the following sentence pass code constructs a numbered sentence concept under the KB **article** concept, named e.g., **sentence001**. *Line 5* adds the sentence text to that concept, for convenience when viewing and outputting the KB.

```
1   @NODES _ROOT
2
3   @POST
4   S("con") = MakeCountCon(G("article"),"sentence");
5   addstrval(S("con"),"text",N("$text",1));
6   single();
7
8   @RULES
9   _sentence <-
```

```
        _xWILD [fail=(_endSent _BLANKLINE)]         ### (1)
        _xWILD [one match=(_endSent _BLANKLINE)]    ### (2)
        @@
```

The following table is a KB dump at this point in the analysis:

Node	Description
sentence001	**text="Nathalia Ribas and Eduardo Costa, two programmers from Brazil, are helping create the first comprehensive digital dictionary for Portuguese in the AI framework NLP++. Mentored by David de Hilster, co-author of the NLP++ programming language, they met while working at LexisNexis."**
sentence002	**text="Nathalia is finishing her bachelor's degree at Santa Catarina University and plans to use NLP++ in her master's thesis."**
sentence003	**text="Their project improves AI's understanding of Portuguese, showcasing Brazil's growing tech influence and the power of collaboration and mentorship."**
sentence004	**text="De Hilster is also the founder of the Natural Language Understanding Global Initiative."**

***Table 7.14**: First view of sentence concepts*

Caps analyzer pass

The **caps** pass (in the following code figure) operates inside sentences (context *line 1*) and has two rules. The first (*lines 4 to 14*) is more specific than the second (*lines 17 to 25*). The ordering of rules inside a pass file and among multiple passes is important to understand. The NLP engine matches rules in the order they appear in a pass file. Specific rules should be placed ahead of more general rules; the specific rules may become inaccessible to the pattern matcher. Similarly, rules and knowledge with higher confidence should be applied first.

The first rule applies specifically to names with embedded definite articles (**de**, **las**, **los**), matches *David de Hilster*, adds that under the KB **caps** concept (*line 5*), and reduces the matched tree nodes to the suggested **_cap** node (*lines 7 and 10*). (This rule could also record the presence of definite articles, signifying a name.)

The more generic rule simply matches a set of capitalized-word nodes and repeats the actions of the first rule.

In addition, both rules have the KB concept for the current sentence pointed to by the **_cap** tree node within (*lines 6 and 19*). This is a powerful aspect of NLP++: parse tree nodes can point to KB concepts. Text inputs are structured by a parse tree, which dynamically works in tandem with the KB to build and access a conceptual representation of the text.

```
@NODES _sentence

### David de Hilster ############################
@POST
S("con") = getconcept(G("caps"),phrasetext());
addconval(S("con"),"sent",X("con",2));
single();

@RULES
_cap <-
    _xCAP [plus]                        ### (1)
    _xWILD [plus match=(de las los)] ### (2)
    _xCAP [plus]                        ### (3)
    @@

##############################################
@POST
S("con") = getconcept(G("caps"),phrasetext());
addconval(S("con"),"sent",X("con",2));
single();

@RULES
_cap <-
    _xCAP [plus]        ### (1)
    @@
```

Text with mixed capitalization is far easier to analyze than all-caps and all-lowercase text, because it distinguishes proper names and potential entities of interest from prose words.

The following table lists the KB after the **caps** pass:

Concept	Attributes
Nathalia Ribas	**sent=["concept" "article" "sentence001"]**
Eduardo Costa	**sent=["concept" "article" "sentence001"]**
Portuguese	**sent=["concept" "article" "sentence001","concept" "article" "sentence003"]**
AI	**sent=["concept" "article" "sentence001","concept" "article" "sentence003"]**

Concept	Attributes
David de Hilster	sent=["concept" "article" "sentence001"]
LexisNexis	sent=["concept" "article" "sentence001"]
Nathalia	sent=["concept" "article" "sentence002"]
Santa Catarina University	sent=["concept" "article" "sentence002"]
Their	sent=["concept" "article" "sentence003"]
De Hilster	sent=["concept" "article" "sentence004"]
Natural Language Understanding Global Initiative	sent=["concept" "article" "sentence004"]

Table 7.15: Concepts under the KB caps concept

categorizeCaps analyzer pass

The **categorizeCaps** pass traverses the capitalized phrases found earlier (under the **_cap** nodes of context *line 1* in the following code). It looks for specific attributes from the dictionary, including **pessoa** (*person*, in Portuguese), **school**, and **cause** (organization with a cause). The functions **IncrementCount** and **PNIncrement** are KB functions in **KBFuncs.nlp** that increment the count of an attribute in the KB and parse tree, respectively. For instance, if two words in a capitalized phrase are found to be human names (like **John** and **Smith**), then the count is at least two. Finding such attributes raises confidence in a person's name, school, etc.

NLP++ developers have options for storing information: mainly parse tree vs. KB, or both. Some analyzers use the parse tree alone. The more complex the task, the more likely that the KB will be useful.

```
1   @PATH _ROOT _sentence _cap
2
3   @POST
4   L("cap con") = X("con",3);
5   L("type") = "other";
6
7   if (N("pessoa",1)) {
8       IncrementCount(L("cap con"),"person");
9       PNIncrement(X(3),"person");
10  }
11  if (N("organization",1) == "school") {
12      IncrementCount(L("cap con"),"school");
```

```
13      PNIncrement(X(3),"school");
14  }
15  if (N("organization",1) == "cause") {
16      IncrementCount(L("cap con"),"cause");
17      PNIncrement(X(3),"cause");
18  }
19  AddTreeID(L("cap con"),X(3));
20
21  @RULES
22  _xNIL <-
23      _xALPHA     ### (1)
24      @@
```

It is easy to create pointers from the parse tree to the KB using the function **addconval**. But there is no built-in mechanism for concepts in the KB to point back to the parse tree. Instead, the **TreeFuncs** pass provides a function to accomplish this. **AddTreeID** (called in *line 19* above) creates a pointer from the KB cap concept, in **L("cap con")**, to its corresponding **_cap** parse tree node (context *line 1* above). (See the section KB references to the *Parse tree*, in *Chapter 6, Developing Text Analyzers* for a detailed discussion that uses the **categorizeCaps** pass as an example.)

In the following table, the **_cap** node (*line* 2) has **id** value **1**, while its parent **_sentence** (*line 1*) gets **id** value **2**, due to the actions performed by **AddTreeID**:

Node	Attributes
_sentence	[0,278,0,278,7,17,node, ("con" concept:"sentence001") ("id" 2)]
_cap	[0,13,0,13,8,31,node, ("con" concept:"Nathalia Ribas") ("person" 1) ("id" 1)]
Nathalia	[0,7,0,7,0,0,alpha,fired, ("NOSP" 1) ("cap" 1) ("genero" "f") ("pessoa" 1)]
Ribas	[9,13,9,13,0,0,alpha,fired, ("SP" 1) ("cap" 1)]
and	[15,17,15,17,0,0,alpha, ("SP" 1) ("lower" 1) ("functword" 1) ("coordinatingConjunctions" 1) ("pos num" 1) ("conjunction" 1)]
_cap	[19,31,19,31,8,31,node, ("con" concept:"Eduardo Costa") ("person" 1) ("id" 3)]
Eduardo	[19,25,19,25,0,0,alpha,fired, ("SP" 1) ("cap" 1) ("genero" "m") ("pessoa" 1)]
Costa	[27,31,27,31,0,0,alpha,fired, ("SP" 1) ("cap" 1)]

Table 7.16: Parse tree display for categorizeCaps pass

The following table lists the KB at the **categorizeCaps** pass. Notice the attribute **pn** (parse tree node) and the path of tree ID numbers (dubbed **pn_path_str** in this book). As discussed, this allows KB concepts to point to parse tree nodes:

Concept	Attributes
`Nathalia Ribas`	`sent=["concept" "article" "sentence001"], "person_count"=1, pn="2 1"`
`Eduardo Costa`	`sent=["concept" "article" "sentence001"], "person_count"=1, pn="2 3"`
`Portuguese`	`sent=["concept" "article" "sentence001","concept" "article" "sentence003"], pn=["2 4","12 14"]`
`AI`	`sent=["concept" "article" "sentence001","concept" "article" "sentence003"], pn=["2 5","12 13"]`
`David de Hilster`	`sent=["concept" "article" "sentence001"], "person_count"=1, pn="2 6"`
`LexisNexis`	`sent=["concept" "article" "sentence001"], pn="2 7"`
`Nathalia`	`sent=["concept" "article" "sentence002"], "person_count"=1, pn="9 8", full=["concept" "caps" "Nathalia Ribas"]`
`Santa Catarina University`	`sent=["concept" "article" "sentence002"], pn="9 10", "person_count"=1, "school_count"=1`
`Their`	`sent=["concept" "article" "sentence003"], pn="12 11"`
`De Hilster`	`sent=["concept" "article" "sentence004"], pn="16 15", full=["concept" "caps" "David de Hilster"]`
`Natural Language Understanding Global Initiative`	`sent=["concept" "article" "sentence004"], pn="16 17", "cause_count"=1`

Table 7.17: KB display in categorizeCaps pass

The findReferences analyzer pass

The **findReferences** pass uses the following code to traverse the subhierarchy of capitalized phrases under **G("caps")**. If one text is a substring of another (*line 9*), then the corresponding texts are assumed to be coreferences. For example, **Nathali** is a substring of **Nathalia Ribas**, so these are assumed to be references to the same person, and the concept corresponding to **Nathalia** gets the attribute **full** (*line 14*), whose value is the concept for **Nathalia Ribas**.

```
1    @CODE
2
3    L("con") = down(G("caps"));
```

```
4   while (L("con")) {
5       L("name") = strtolower(conceptname(L("con")));
6       L("child") = down(G("caps"));
7       while (L("child")) {
8           L("n") = strtolower(conceptname(L("child")));
9           if (L("n") != L("name") && strcontains(L("n"),L("name"))) {
10              MarkFired(L("child"));
11              MarkFired(L("con"));
12              "compare.txt" << "Found: " << L("name") <<
13                  ": " << L("n") << " " << L("unique") << "\n";
14              addconval(L("child"),"full",L("con"));
15          }
16          L("child") = next(L("child"));
17      }
18      L("con") = next(L("con"));
19  }
20
21  @@CODE
```

The code performs two interesting tasks:

- Find any capitalizations that are contained in larger capitalizations
- Mark the coreferences for display in VisualText

The first task is found on *line 9* above, as noted. This checks to make sure that the strings are not equal and that the one string is contained in another.

The second task is to mark the tree node corresponding KB concept as **fired**. The attribute **fired** signifies that a rule fired for a given node in the current pass. But no rules have actually fired, so we use the following **TreeFuncs** library function called **MarkFired** to mark the tree nodes pointed to by KB concepts as fired. This enables highlighting in the text view (third figure below). (Recall that in *Table 7.17*, KB displays in **categorizeCaps** pass, KB concepts for capitalized phrases pointed to the corresponding phrases in the parse tree.)

```
MarkFired(L("concept")) {
    L("pn str") = strval(L("concept"),"pn");
    L("pn") = TreeNodeID(L("pn str"));
    pnsetfired(L("pn"),1);
}
```

In the following KB output table, notice that the **concept Nathalia** has a new **full** attribute pointing to **Nathalia Ribas**, and **De Hilster** has a new full attribute pointing to the **David de Hilster** concept:

Node	Description
Nathalia Ribas	sent=["concept" "article" "sentence001"], "person_count"=1, pn="2 1"
David de Hilster	sent=["concept" "article" "sentence001"], "person_count"=1, pn="2 6"
Nathalia	sent=["concept" "article" "sentence002"], "person_count"=1, pn="9 8", full=["concept" "caps" "Nathalia Ribas"]
De Hilster	sent=["concept" "article" "sentence004"], pn="16 15", full=["concept" "caps" "David de Hilster"]

Table 7.18: KB view in findReferences pass

The following figure highlights the name references matched in the input text:

```
(((Nathalia Ribas))) and Eduardo Costa, two programmers from
Brazil, are helping create the first comprehensive digital
dictionary for Portuguese in the AI framework NLP++.
Mentored by (((David de Hilster))), co-author of the NLP++
programming language, they met while working at LexisNexis.
(((Nathalia))) is finishing her bachelor's degree at Santa
Catarina University and plans to use NLP++ in her master's
thesis. Their project improves AI's understanding of
Portuguese, showcasing Brazil's growing tech influence and
the power of collaboration and mentorship. (((De Hilster))) is
also the founder of the Natural Language Understanding
Global Initiative.
```

Figure 7.5: Text highlights in findReferences pass

Full English parser

VisualText comes with a full English parser using a dictionary of 190,000 words. It was constructed in a bottom-up fashion by the co-creator of NLP++, *Amnon Meyers*. Meyers has used the parser as the starting point for various text analyzers over the years.

The English parser can serve as a skeletal analyzer that can be tailored to particular domains and applications. It is available for use as a 100% modifiable template analyzer.

See a detailed specification of passes and functions in *Appendix D, Full English Parser Reference*.

Loading the full English parser

The full English parser is one of the templates available, as depicted in the following figure, when creating a new analyzer:

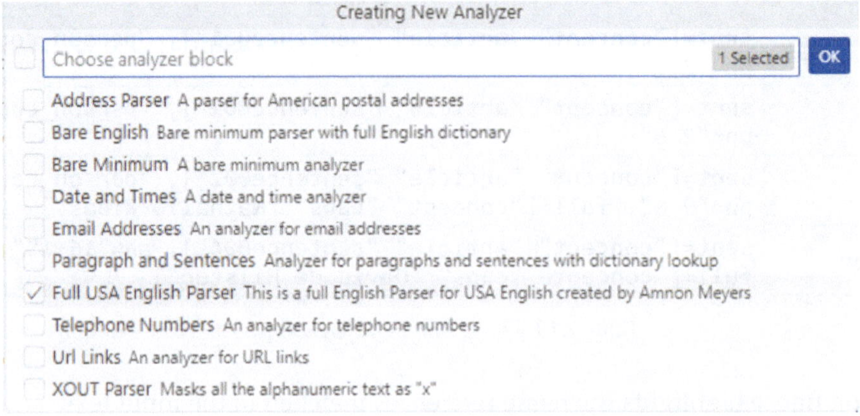

Figure 7.6: *Selecting the full USA English parser template*

Tutorial on using the full English parser

If you have examined *Appendix D, Full English Parse Reference,* you may find parse-en-us to be daunting, with more than 130 passes and a host of functions. So in the following sequence of numbered steps, we will introduce you to using the analyzer for a simple task, namely, enhancing the processing of a well-known input sentence (already in the `test.txt` input file of the example analyzer), namely:

The quick brown fox jumped over the lazy boy.

1. **Duplicate analyzer**: First, fetch all the example analyzers and copy them, if not already done.

   Next, select **parse-en-us**, click **Duplicate Analyzer**, and name this copy, e.g., **parse-en-us_01**.

2. **Add a documentation pass:** In the **ANALYZER** view, right-click the first pass, **dicttokz**, and select **New Pass**, giving it a name like `doc_01`. You can use comments (lines starting with a hash mark **#**) to document your customization of the analyzer.

3. **Analyze the input file**: In the **TEXT** view, find the `test.txt` input file (which you can also click to view), and analyze that file by clicking the right-facing arrow on its line.

   In the **OUTPUT FILES** view, click on the `final.tree` file to examine the final parse tree. A simplified version is shown in the following:

```
_ROOT
  _TEXTZONE
    _sent
      _clause
        _np
          _det  The
          _adj  quick
          _adj  brown
          _noun fox
        _vg
          _verb jumped
        _advl
          _prep over
          _np
            _det  the
            _adj  lazy
            _noun boy
```

You may want to examine the other output files as well.

While this parse may be grammatically correct, Meyers prefers a pattern better-suited to a semantic or conceptual understanding, along the lines of actor act object. Many practical analyzers use triplets of this type, which better conform to the dictum *think like a human*. So, let us build that.

4. **Search the analyzer**: In the **ANALYZER** view, click the magnifying glass (**Search**) and type **`prepositional`**. For complete results, use the Search magnifying glass in the left panel, restrict to **`.nlp`** files.

   Similarly, you can search for phrasal and for items like actor, act, and object. With these, you can explore what is already present in the analyzer. For our example, in the **FIND RESULTS** view, these functions are of interest, as we can view jumped over as a prepositional verb phrase:

   ```
   phrprepverbq(L("nverb"),L("nprep"))
   phrasalverbq(L("nverb"),L("nprep"))
   prepositionalverbq(L("nverb"),L("nprep"))
   ```

   Examining these, we see that the dictionary would have an entry **`jump`** with attribute **`over`**, and one of these values:

```
1 = phrasal
2 = prepositional
3 = both
```

5. **Add attributes to dictionary entries**: In the KB view, click to open the **`all.dict`** file. Find the verb forms of **`jump`** and edit them to look like:

```
jump pos=verb over=2
jumps pos=verb over=2
jumping pos=verb over=2
jumped pos=verb over=2
```

6. **Reanalyze the input file:** Before reanalyzing, we recommend clearing the log files, because outputs are appended by default. In the **TEXT** view, click the X-box (remove log files) for **`test.txt`** and confirm deletion by pressing *Enter*.

   On reanalyzing **`test.txt`**, we see that the final tree has been modified automatically to:

```
_ROOT
  _TEXTZONE
    _sent
      _clause
        _np
          _det  The
          _adj  quick
          _adj  brown
          _noun fox
        _vg
          _verb jumped
          _prep over
        _np
          _det  the
          _adj  lazy
          noun boy
```

This is more in line with our desire to parse the input sentence as an instance of an actor-act-object triplet. In the **OUTPUT FILES** view, we can examine the **`final.tree`** file. Placing the cursor on the **`_vg`** (or verb group) node, we can right-click **Display Rule Fired**. However, rather than seeing the rule that grouped jumped over, we see a rule that merely created a simple verb group for jumped. As the pass is **`pos50`**, a recursive pass, more than one rule has matched here, and VisualText does not track all the rule reductions in a recursive pass.

To overcome the tracking limitation, let us examine the **_vg** node. In particular, note these attributes:

```
_vg [. . . ("pos50 v-p-check" 1) ("pos50-v-p-n" 1) ("pos50 vg4" 1)]
```

The rules are coded to be self-documenting (*line 607* below). When a rule matches, a unique attribute name is placed on matched nodes, starting with the pass name. The following figure rule matches jumped over (extensive **@CHECK** region omitted). Note that the **listadd** action (*line 617*) causes the matched **_vg** node to also cover the preposition (**over**). *Lines 612 to 615* use the 1-2-3 scheme mentioned above to tag the **part of speech** (**POS**) of the **_prep** node:

```
606   @POST
607      N("pos50 v-p-n",2) = 1; # Loop guard.
608      fixvg(N(2), "active",0);
609      N("pos50 vg4",2) = 1;
610      if (!N("mypos",4))
611         {
612         if (S("p") == 1 || S("p") == 3)
613            chpos(N(4),”RP”); # prep/RP
614         else
615            chpos(N(4),"IN"); # prep/IN
616         }
617      listadd(2,4,"true");  # vg prep -> vg
618   @RULES
619   _xNIL <-
620      _xWILD [one fail=(\,)]            ### (1)
621      _vg                               ### (2)
622      _xWILD [star match=(_adv _advl)] ### (3) # FIX. 10/05/25 AM.
623      _prep                             ### (4)
624      _xWILD [star match=(_adv _advl)] ### (5)
625      _np                               ### (6)
626   @@
```

The following figure depicts the same code as it appears in the NLP++ editor:

```
606  @POST
607    N("pos50 v-p-n",2) = 1; # Loop guard.
608    fixvg(N(2),"active",0);
609    N("pos50 vg4",2) = 1;
610    if (!N("mypos",4))
611      {
612      if (S("p") == 1 || S("p") == 3)
613        chpos(N(4),"RP"); # prep/RP
614      else
615        chpos(N(4),"IN"); # prep/IN
616      }
617    listadd(2,4,"true");  # vg prep -> vg
618  @RULES
619  _xNIL <-
620    _xWILD [one fail=(\,)]          ### (1)
621    _vg                             ### (2)
622    _xWILD [star match=(_adv _advl)] ### (3) # FIX. 10/05/25 AM.
623    _prep                           ### (4)
624    _xWILD [star match=(_adv _advl)] ### (5)
625    _np                             ### (6)
626    @@
```

***Figure 7.7**: Rule matching jumped over*

The fix in element 3 (*line 622*) removed the lookahead modifier. Since elements 2 through 4 would be consumed by the **listadd** action, the earliest valid lookahead would be at element 5.

As **pos50** is a recursive pass, lookahead is irrelevant (when a rule matches, recursion continues at the start of each context in the parse tree). However, if this rule were copied, or if the pass were changed to non-recursive, lookahead would determine where matching continues.

Finally, note that *line 607* has a **Loop guard** comment. In a recursive pass, placing an attribute on a matched node can be used to guard against the same nodes matching the same rule more than once, resulting in an infinite loop:

```
@PRE
<2,2> varz("pos50 v-p-n"); # Loop guard.
```

7. **Add a dictionary phrase**: Another way to encode jumped over is to add it as a phrase to the dictionary.

   In the KB view, click to open **all.dict** dictionary file.

   Next to the existing entry for jumped, add a new line as follows:

```
jumped over s=verb pos=verb sem="jump_over"
```

Reanalyze the input text and reexamine the **final.tree** file. Note that the parse tree nodes for jumped over have now been created via the above dictionary entry. The **s** in **s=verb** is a special attribute to reduce jumped over and name the suggested node as **`_verb`**. Other attribute-value pairs are up to the developer, as in the **`sem`** semantic attribute above.

There are trade-offs among the various ways to treat phrases in an analyzer. In building the full English parser, Meyers gave the developer control over every aspect, including the timing and conditions for phrase matching. In the original TAIParse version, a phrase subhierarchy is implemented separately from the dictionary subhierarchy of the KB.

Examine the output files

While building an analyzer, it is useful to periodically examine the **OUTPUT FILES** view. The English parser is mainly concerned with the semantics of named entities, such as *John Smith*. As our simple sentence does not contain these, the output files are not very interesting.

The reader can, as an exercise, produce an output triple for the actor, act, and object roles of the input sentence.

This tutorial offers a simple introduction to the full English parser. We note that this is by no means a *finished product*, but it can serve as a skeletal analyzer that can be customized for tasks requiring full analysis of English prose.

Much can be done to improve the analyzer, starting with comprehensive updates to the dictionary and KB. The various linguistic stages are present in the analyzer, comprising format/zoning, lexical, syntactic, semantic, and conceptual analysis. When more specific knowledge or rules are available, they can be placed in passes that precede the more general processing. In this way, the NLP++ pipeline yields analyzers that build a best-first parse and exhibit graceful degradation from specific to general processing.

Conclusion

In this chapter, we learned about several types of NLP++ analyzers, tasks, and methods. The analyzers presented a range of difficulty, from simple pattern matching tasks to full English language parsing.

In the next chapter, we will learn about ways to integrate NLP++ analyzers into other computer programs and computer languages. C++ and Python are the main systems to be covered.

True or false

1. A previously-formatted text is one that was converted from Word, PDF, or other standard format.
2. REGEX is a system for writing complete NLP analyzers.
3. The date-time analyzer does not use KBs.
4. The XOut analyzer modifies only the alphabetic characters of a text.

5. The entity extraction analyzer omits coreference resolution.
6. The Full English parser can be used without studying all of its passes.

Answers

1. True	2. False	3. False
4. True	5. False	6. True

Multiple choice questions

1. **The number 10 can represent:**
   a. A day
   b. A month
   c. A year
   d. None of the above
2. **The XOut analyzer retains:**
   a. Punctuation
   b. Capitalization
   c. Spacing
   d. Proper names
   e. None of the above
3. **The KB is dynamic because it supports (multiple options):**
   a. Storing information
   b. Accessing information
   c. Error checking
   d. Dictionary information
   e. Math functions
   f. Pointers to the parse tree
4. **A common semantic representation in NLP consists of:**
   a. Doublets
   b. Triplets
   c. Quadruplets
   d. None of the above
5. **For complete text search results, use:**
   a. ANALYZER view search
   b. File search in the VS Code panel
   c. Either of the above
   d. None of the above
6. **When analyzing an input text:**
   a. First, the OUTPUT FILES view is automatically cleared
   b. Output is appended to existing files

Answers

1. a, b, c
2. a, b, c
3. a, b, d, f
4. b
5. b
6. a

Short answer questions

1. What are the main advantages of NLP++ over REGEX?
2. What is the purpose of the XOut analyzer?
3. Discuss some dangers of pointing from the KB to the parse tree.
4. Describe how you might use an existing NLP++ analyzer as a starting point for a specific task.
5. Describe how the full English parser records reductions in a recursive pass.
6. Select a document (e.g., a computer language manual) and build an NLP++ analyzer to enclose embedded computer code with <do_not_translate> HTML tags.
7. Convert informational webpages to structured data. Compare the NLP++ analyzer to, e.g., the Python package Beautiful Soup. Which one is simpler for which types of webpages? Which is more readable and maintainable?
8. Resumes embed similar content in wildly varying formats. In contrast to most formatted-document analysis, here, the content helps deduce the format! Can be a group programming task.
9. Use NLP++ to parse the wiki text format and extract content from Wiktionary and Wikipedia pages. (see article and papers)
10. Write an NLP++ analyzer to resolve anaphora (i.e., multiple references to an entity) in text. Helps teach methods that humans use to understand text. One can start by fixing anaphora capabilities in parse-en-us.

Join our Discord space

Answers

1. b, c [illegible] 2. a, b [illegible] a, b, d, e [illegible]
4. b [illegible] b

Short answer questions

1. What are the main advantages of NLP [illegible] RegEx?
2. What is the purpose of the [illegible] analysis?
3. Discuss some [illegible] of [illegible] the [illegible]
4. Describe how [illegible] and [illegible] specific [illegible]
5. [illegible]
6. [illegible]
7. Consider [illegible] to use the Python package [illegible] types of [illegible] more [illegible]
8. [illegible] programming tasks.
9. Use [illegible] Wikipedia [illegible]
10. What [illegible] NLP [illegible]

Join our Discord space

Join our Discord workspace for latest updates, offers, tech happenings around the world, new releases, and sessions with the authors:

https://discord.bpbonline.com

Chapter 8
Integrating NLP++ Analyzers

Introduction

There are numerous ways to integrate NLP++ analyzers into other computer programs, via: the NLP engine executable **`nlp.exe`**, NLP++ packages written in other programming languages, various class packages using the command line NLP engine, C++ libraries, and even and a supercomputer plugin.

Each analyzer consists of a folder structure, which must be studied and understood in order to integrate and deploy NLP++ analyzers. This is covered in detail in *Chapter 4, VisualText*, in the section *NLP++ Analyzer folder structure*.

We will then discuss the NLP engine command line, followed by detailed discussions of integrating NLP++ analyzers with VS Code, Python, and **High Performance Computing Cluster** (**HPCC**) programming environments.

Structure

In this chapter, we will discuss the following topics:

- NLP engine command line
- VS Code and NLP engine
- Python package and class
- TypeScript class
- C++ library packages
- HPCC Systems supercomputer

Objectives

By the end of the chapter, the reader will learn about the practical issues and knowledge required to integrate NLP++ analyzers with popular programming environments, including

C++, Python, and *HPCC Systems*. Prerequisites to such integration are knowledge of analyzer folder structure and an understanding of the NLP++ command line arguments and their use.

NLP engine command line

The NLP engine command line executable is available on GitHub for Windows, Linux (three versions), and macOS. Here is the help that prints out with the **`--help`** switch when calling **`nlp.exe`**:

```
nlp.exe --help

usage: nlp [--version] [--help]
       [-INTERP][-COMPILED] INTERP is the default
       [-ANA analyzer] name or path to NLP++ analyzer folder
       [-IN infile] input text file path
       [-OUT outdir] output directory
       [-WORK workdir] working directory
       [-DEV][-SILENT] -DEV generates logs,
             -SILENT (default) does not
       [infile [outfile]] when no -IN or -OUT specified

Directories in the nlp.exe files:
   data         nlp engine bootstrap grammar
   analyzers    default location for nlp++ analyzer folders
   visualtext   common files for the VisualText IDE
```

When VisualText processes a text, it creates a command line string and argument array to send directly to the **`nlp.exe`** executable. The following is a sample set of arguments, in a TypeScript array, that VisualText produces via an analyzer in the **`dehilster-analyzers`** repository:

```
[
-ANA
"c:\\git\\dehilster-analyzers\\Dictionaries\\Countries\\",
 -WORK,
 "c:\\Users\\User Name \\.vscode\\extensions\\dehilster.nlp-2.49.6\\nlp-engine\",
 "c:\\git\\dehilster-analyzers\\Dictionaries\\Countries\\input\\countries.txt",
 -DEV
]
```

Line 2 is the **`-ANA`** or analyzer switch, whose value is *line* 3, the full path to the **`Countries`** analyzer in the **`Dictionaries`** folder. The -**`WORK`** switch on *line* 4, whose value is *line* 5, specifies the path of the NLP engine folder that will run the text analyzer. This path varies depending on the operating system (Windows, Linux, or macOS).

Line 6 specifies the path to the input text to be analyzed, and the developer switch on *line* 7 tells the analyzer to generate verbose log files.

The **`nlp.exe --version`** switch is used by VisualText to check the current version of the NLP engine.

Command line executables

There are three command line repositories on GitHub for each operating system. These are key when using either the Python or TypeScript NLP engine class that calls the NLP command line.

- **Window NLP engine repository**: **https://github.com/VisualText/nlp-engine-windows**
- **Linux NLP engine repository**: **https://github.com/VisualText/nlp-engine-linux**
- **macOS NLP engine repository**: **https://github.com/VisualText/nlp-engine-mac**

VS Code and NLP engine

The VS Code NLP++ Language Extension uses the **`nlp`** command line executable (**`nlp.exe`**) to process text. The NLP engine is downloaded by the VS Code extension, allowing for dynamic updates when new versions are available.

The NLP engine is located in the VS Code extensions folder, located in the **`.vscode`** folder under the **`user`** folder. On Windows, it is under the .**`vscode`** folder, while on Linux and macOS, it is located in the .**`vscode-server`** under the **`user`** folder.

You can open the folder using the **LOGGING** list in the bottom VS Code panel, as shown in the following figure:

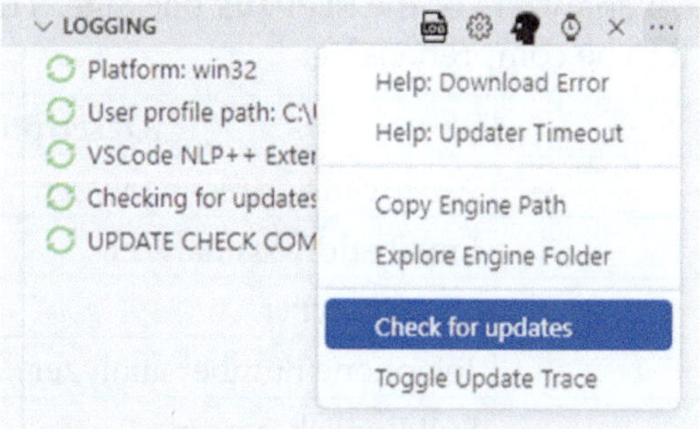

Figure 8.1: Using Explore Engine Folder to find the nlp.exe executable

Python package and class

There are two ways to call NLP++ analyzers in Python:

- The native Python **NLPPlus** package
- The **NLPEngine** Python class that calls the nlp.exe via the command line

Each of these is discussed in detail in the following sections. Integration, issues, and differences between the two methods will also be covered.

NLPPlus package

An **NLPPlus** Python package can be loaded using **pip**:

```
pip install NLPPlus
```

The following is a sample Python script using the **NLPPlus** package:

```
import NLPPlus
import json

NLPPlus.set_analyzers_folder("your path to analyzers folder")
text = "My phone number is 123-456-7890. Call me
                at (123) 456-7890 or 123.456.7890."
results = NLPPlus.engine.analyze(text,"Telephone Numbers")
json_obj = json.loads(results.output_json)

for telephone in json_obj["telephones"]["telephone"]:
    print(f"Telephone: {telephone}")
```

NLPPlus package analyzers

The following table lists the 5 analyzers of the **NLPPlus** package. These are modifiable starter analyzers and are not meant to be comprehensive:

Analyzer	Description
`address-parser`	American address analyzer
`emailaddress`	Email address analyzer
`links`	URL analyzer
`telephone`	Telephone number analyzer
`parse-en-us`	Full English parser

Table 8.1: Analyzers of the NLPPlus package

Purpose and design

`NLPPlus` is designed to allow Python scripts to load, execute, and interact with NLP++ analyzers without invoking command line processes. Instead, the package links directly to the underlying C++ NLP engine, providing:

- Higher performance than shelling out to the command line engine.
- A clean Python API for loading analyzers and processing text.
- Crossplatform support (Linux, Windows, macOS).
- A fully rulebased, transparent NLP workflow, consistent with the philosophy of NLP++.

The package is part of the broader open-source NLP++ ecosystem, which emphasizes long-term maintainability, transparency, and modifiability. NLP++ analyzers remain glass-box systems,every rule is visible, editable, and shareable.

Core concepts

The following subsections detail the practical aspects of setting up, applying, and running the **`NLPPlus`** package. Features that help develop text analyzers are described, as well as typical application areas.

Analyzers folder

`NLPPlus` expects an **`analyzers`** folder, which contains one or more NLP++ analyzers. Each analyzer is a directory with the standard NLP++ structure (**`.nlp`**, **`.pat`**, **`.seq`**, **`.dict`**, etc.). The Python API allows you to specify the location of this folder, so that the engine can load and execute the appropriate analyzer. If no analyzer folder is set, Python will use the analyzer folder in the **`NLPPlus`** package itself, which contains the 5 starter analyzers.

Input text and output directory

The engine processes text either from:

- A file
- A string passed directly to the engine

Output is written to the analyzer's output directory, following the same conventions used by VisualText and the command line engine.

Basic usage

The typical workflow consists of:

1. Importing the engine
2. Setting the **`analyzers`** folder

3. Selecting an analyzer
4. Providing input text
5. Running the analyzer
6. Retrieving output

The API also supports analyzing files, clearing output directories prior to a new analysis, and copying analyzer libraries when needed.

Functions and variables

The following *Table 8.2*, lists the functions and variables available in the **NLPPlus** package. These enable managing the text analysis environment and running the selected analyzer.

Name	Type	Description
`engine`	`var`	An **engine** instance created at import time
`set_working_folder(folder, initialize)`	`fn`	Set the working folder for the NLP engine
`set_analyzers_folder(analyzer_name)`	`fn`	Set the analyzer folder path
`set_analyzers_folder(analyzer_path)`	`fn`	Set the analyzer folder path
`copy_library_analyzers(dir, overwrite)`	`fn`	Copy the built-in analyzers to the **dir** directory, optionally overwriting existing files
`copy_library_analyzers(analyzer_path, overwrite)`	`fn`	Convenience function calling the engine's **copy_library_analyzers** function
`input_text(analyzer_name, file_name)`	`fn`	Read the file from the analyzer **input** directory
`analyze(text, analyzer_name, develop)`	`fn`	Analyze the text and return a **Results** object
`final_tree`	`fn`	Return the final parse tree **final.tree**
`output_json`	`fn`	Returns the raw JSON output text **output.json**
`output`	`fn`	Return the JSON output as a Python object

Table 8.2: Functions and variables of the NLPPlus package

Development features

Recent updates to the package include:

- A develop flag for analyzer runs, enabling developmentmode behavior
- Automatic clearing of the output directory before each analysis

- Utility functions for copying analyzer libraries
- Direct text-input support (**`input_text`**)

These features streamline iterative development and testing of NLP++ analyzers inside Python environments such as Jupyter Notebooks, VS Code, or automated pipelines.

Use cases

`NLPPlus` is particularly useful when:

- Embedding NLP++ analyzers inside larger Python applications.
- Integrating rule-based NLP with machine learning pipelines.
- Running analyzers as part of web services or microservices.
- Automating batch processing of large text corpora.
- Teaching NLP++ in environments where Python is already the dominant language.

Because the engine remains fully rule-based, **`NLPPlus`** enables deterministic, explainable NLP workflows, an important contrast to opaque statistical models.

Python NLP engine class

A simple Python class exists for calling the NLP engine, using the **`nlp.exe`** executable (see **https://github.com/VisualText/python**). The NLP engine must already be installed. The following table describes the functions and variables included in the Python NLP engine class:

Signature	Type	Description
`engineDir`	`var`	Folder for the NLP engine executable.
`analyzersDir`	`var`	Holds the folder containing NLP analyzers.
`--init-- (engineDir, analyzersDir)`	`fn`	Initialize the NLP engine instance with the engine and analyzer folders.
`analyzerPath (analyzerFolder)`	`fn`	Return the path to a specific analyzer folder.
`kbPath (analyzerFolder)`	`fn`	Return the KB path for an analyzer.
`specPath (analyzerFolder)`	`fn`	Return the specification folder path by joining `analyzerPath(analyzerFolder)` and `spec`.
`outputDir (analyzerFolder, textPath)`	`fn`	Return the output folder path for the analyzer's text file.
`outputFileContents (analyzerFolder, filename, outputFile)`	`fn`	Read and return the contents of the analyzer output file.

Signature	Type	Description
`inputFileDir (analyzerFolder, textPath)`	**`fn`**	Return the input folder.
`analyzeFile (analyzerFolder, textPath, dev=False)`	**`fn`**	Run the analyzer on the text in the text path. Develop (**`dev`**) flag, when true, generates log files.
`analyzeStr (analyzerFolder, filename, textStr)`	**`fn`**	Write **`textStr`** to the input file in an analyzer file.
`isAnalyzerFolder (analyzerFolder)`	**`fn`**	Return true if the folder contains the required analyzer subfolders (**`spec`**, **`input`**, **`kb/user`**).
`clearLogFiles (analyzerFolder)`	**`fn`**	Traverse the **`log`** folder. Remove **`-log`** subfolders.
`createInputDir (analyzer, inputFolder, clearFolder=True)`	**`fn`**	Create (and optionally clear) an input folder for analysis, and return the folder path.

Table 8.3: Functions of the Python NLP engine class

Python example

The following Python code exemplifies the use of the NLP engine class:

```
engineDir = os.path.join(os.getcwd(),"nlp-engine-windows")
    nlp = NLPEngine(engineDir,os.path.join(os.getcwd(),
"nlpfix-analyzers"))
nlp2 = NLPEngine(engineDir,os.path.join(os.getcwd(),"colorizers"))

analyzer_folders = [name for name in os.listdir(nlp.analyzersDir)
        if os.path.isdir(os.path.join(nlp.analyzersDir, name))]
for analyzer in analyzer_folders:
    analyzerPath = nlp.analyzerPath(analyzer)
    if not nlp.isAnalyzerFolder(os.path.join(nlp.analyzersDir,
        analyzer)):
        continue

    # if analyzer != "date-time":
    #     continue
```

```

    deleteHightlightFiles(analyzerPath)
    print(f"Processing {analyzer}...")
    nlp.analyzeInput(analyzer, "text.txt", True)

    colorizer_folders = [name for name in os.listdir("colorizers")
        if os.path.isdir(os.path.join("colorizers", name))]
    for colorizer in colorizer_folders:
        if colorizer in ["tree", "nlp", "dict", "kb"]:
            print(f"  Processing {colorizer}...")
            colorizerPath = nlp2.analyzerPath(colorizer)
            htmlPath = nlp2.createInputDir(colorizer,"html",True)
            filesPath = nlp2.createInputDir(colorizer,"files",True)

        if colorizer == "tree":
            sourcePath = nlp.inputTextLog(analyzer, "text.txt")
            moveFiles(sourcePath, ".tree", filesPath)
            nlp2.analyzeInput(colorizer, "files", True)
            moveFiles(htmlPath, ".html", sourcePath)
        elif colorizer == "nlp":
            sourcePath = nlp.specPath(analyzer)
            moveFiles(sourcePath, ".nlp", filesPath)
            nlp2.analyzeInput(colorizer, "files", True)
            moveFiles(htmlPath, ".html", sourcePath)
        elif colorizer == "dict":
            sourcePath = nlp.kbPath(analyzer)
            moveFiles(sourcePath, ".dict", filesPath)
            nlp2.analyzeInput(colorizer, "files", True)
            moveFiles(htmlPath, ".html", sourcePath)
        elif colorizer == "kb":
            # KBB files in the KB folder
            sourcePath = nlp.kbPath(analyzer)
            moveFiles(sourcePath, ".kbb", filesPath)
            nlp2.analyzeInput(colorizer, "files", True)
            moveFiles(htmlPath, ".html", sourcePath)

```

```
                # KBB files text.txt_log folder
                sourcePath = nlp.inputTextLog(analyzer, "text.txt")
                moveFiles(sourcePath, ".kbb", filesPath)
                nlp2.analyzeInput(colorizer, "files", True)
                moveFiles(htmlPath, ".html", sourcePath)

print("Done!")
```

Memory use

There is an important difference between the Python **NLPPlus** package and the Python class.

When using the **NLPPlus** package, the NLP engine can be initialized once and then used throughout the Python script without having to initialize it again. This is important when there are dictionaries and knowledge bases that must be loaded each time you initialize the NLP engine.

With the Python class that uses **nlp.exe**, each time you call nlp.exe, it loads the dictionaries and knowledges bases before analyzing the text.

TypeScript class

The TypeScript NLP engine class allows for the use of the **nlp.exe** executable via convenient functions. The following table describes the functions and variables comprising the class:

Name	Type	Description
engineDir	**str**	Folder holding the NLP engine executable.
analyzersDir	**str**	Folder holding analyzers.
analyzerPath (analyzerFolder)	**fn**	Return analyzer path.
kbPath (analyzerFolder)	**fn**	Return the KB path for the analyzer.
specPath (analyzerFolder)	**fn**	Return sequence folder (i.e., **spec** folder) path.
outputDir (analyzerFolder, textPath)	**fn**	Return the output logs folder for the analyzer's text.
outputFileContents (analyzerFolder, filename, outputFile)	**fn**	Read contents of output file.
inputFileDir (analyzerFolder, textPath)	**fn**	Return the path to the analyzer's input folder.

Name	Type	Description
analyzeFile (analyzerFolder, textPath, dev)	fn	Execute the NLP engine on the given input file.
analyzeStr (analyzerFolder, filename, textStr)	fn	Analyze the given text string by first writing it to an input file.
isAnalyzerFolder (analyzerFolder)	fn	Check if the folder has the required analyzer subfolders.
clearLogFiles (analyzerFolder)	fn	Clear log folders generated during analysis.
createInputDir (analyzer, inputFolder, clearFolder)	fn	Create an input folder for an NLP analysis session.
createInputFile (analyzer, filename, text)	fn	Create a text input file for NLP processing.

Table 8.4: *Functions and variables of the TypeScript NLP engine class*

Here is an example of calling the TypeScript NLP engine class:

```
app.post("/api/nlp", async (req: express.Request<unknown, unknown,
        ApiRequest>, res: express.Response<ApiResponse>) => {
  try {
    let text = req.body.text;
    let analyzer = req.body.analyzer;
    const parentPath = path.dirname(__dirname);
    const engineDir = path.join(parentPath, 'nlp-engine-linux');
    const analyzersDir = path.join(parentPath, 'nlp-engine-linux',
       'analyzers');

    const filename = "text.txt";
    const nlpEngine = new NLPEngine(engineDir, analyzersDir);
    nlpEngine.analyzeStr(analyzer, filename, text);

    const outputContents = nlpEngine.outputFileContents(analyzer,
      filename, 'codes.json');
    // console.log("Analysis Output:", outputContents);

    res.status(200).json({ message: outputContents, sql: '',
        error: '' });
```

```
    }
    catch (error) {
      console.error('Error fetching records:', error);
      res.status(500).json({ message: 'Internal Server Error',
         sql: '', error: (error as Error).message });
    }
  });
```

C++ library packages

The NLP engine has C++ libraries that allow it to be integrated natively into other software programs. Currently, the C++ packages are being used in the Python **NLPPlus** package as well as the HPCC Systems NLP++ plugin. A future use of the NLP engine C++ libraries will be the **NLPPlus** package for TypeScript.

NLP engine test folder

The NLP engine repository has a test program that shows how to integrate the NLP engine natively into C++. It is located at:

https://github.com/VisualText/nlp-engine/tree/master/test

Here you will find a **CMake** file and a **text.cpp** file that uses the NLP++ libraries' functions. This example expects the user to correctly manage the folders and paths of the folder for the NLP engine repository, its *include files,* and the **parser-en-us** analyzer.

Here is the **CMakeLists.txt** file for the test C++ program that calls the NLP engine. It works for both Windows and Linux:

```
if(WIN32)
    add_definitions(-DMSVC_VERSION=${MSVC_VERSION}
        -D_CRT_SECURE_NO_WARNINGS)
else()
    add_definitions(-DLINUX -Wno-write-strings -Wno-deprecated)
endif()

if(NOT DEFINED CMAKE_BUILD_TYPE)
    set(CMAKE_BUILD_TYPE Debug)
endif()

if(NOT WIN32)
```

```
    find_library(DL_LIBRARY dl)
endif()

if(WIN32)
    add_executable(test-nlp main.cpp)
    target_link_libraries(test-nlp prim kbm consh words lite)
else()
    add_executable(test-nlp.exe main.cpp)
    target_link_libraries(test-nlp.exe prim kbm consh words
        lite ${ICU_LIBRARIES} {DL_LIBRARY})
endif()
```

Here is the example C++ code that calls the NLP engine. *Lines 1* and 2 are the includes for the NLP engine libraries, *line 32* is the initialization of the NLP engine object, and *line 40* is the calling of the NLP engine. The resulting executable **test-nlp.exe** takes no arguments and runs a simple sentence using the full English parser and returns its output.

```
1   #include "lite/nlp_engine.h"
2   #include "lite/vtrun.h"
3
4   #ifdef LINUX
5   #include <unistd.h>
6   #define GetCurrentDir getcwd
7   #else
8   #include <direct.h>
9   #define GetCurrentDir _getcwd
10  #endif
11  #include<iostream>
12
13  #ifdef LINUX
14  int main(
15  #else
16  int _tmain( // 09/23/20 AM.
17  #endif
18     int argc,
19     _TCHAR *argv[],
20     _TCHAR *envp[]
21     )
```

```
{
_TCHAR anaParse[1001];
_TCHAR workingFolder[1001];

_stprintf(anaParse,"%s",_T("parser-en-usa"));
_stprintf(workingFolder,"%s",_T("./"));

std::_t_cout << _T("[Create runtime manager.]") << std::endl;
getcwd(workingFolder, FILENAME_MAX);
std::string current_working_dir(workingFolder);
NLP_ENGINE *nlpEngine = new NLP_ENGINE(workingFolder);

char *str = "The quick brown fox jumped over the lazy boy";

std::istringstream ssi1(str);
std::ostringstream sso1;
std::_t_cout << _T("[analyzer: ") << anaParse << _T("]") << std::endl;
std::_t_cout << _T("[input: ") << ssi1.str() << _T("]") << std::endl;
nlpEngine->analyze(anaParse,&ssi1,&sso1);
std::_t_cout << _T("[output: ") << sso1.str() << _T("]") << std::endl;
std::_t_cout << _T("[end: ") << anaParse << _T("]") << std::endl;
```

HPCC Systems supercomputer

The HPCC Systems NLP++ plugin was designed and coded by *David de Hilster* while working at *LexisNexis Risk*. It allows those using the HPCC Systems supercomputing framework to natively call NLP++ analyzers inside of **Enterprise Control Language** (**ECL**), the native programming language for the HPCC Systems supercomputing platform. ECL is the HPCC Systems database language.

HPCC Systems platform overview

The HPCC Systems platform is an open-source, massively parallel-processing computing platform designed for large-scale data processing and analytics. It offers an enterprise-ready supercomputing environment that rivals Hadoop by providing a single architecture, a single programming language, and optimized parallel execution across commodity clusters.

Open-source innovation has been at the core of HPCC Systems for over a decade. Backed by *LexisNexis Risk Solutions*, the platform's codebase is available under the Apache License

2.0, and a vibrant community contributes to its continual evolution. You can explore and download the source from GitHub or the HPCC Systems website to run your own clusters or contribute enhancements.

Core components

HPCC Systems comprises two primary cluster types:

- **Thor (data refinery cluster)**:
    - Batch-oriented processing of raw data
    - **Extract, transform, and load** (ETL), sorting, indexing, linking
    - Distributed file system with parallel job execution
- **Rapid Online XML Inquiry Engine (Roxie)**:
    - High-performance online query processing.
    - Serves indexed data via REST, SOAP, HTTP, or XML interfaces.
    - Supports thousands of concurrent queries with sub-second response times.

These clusters can operate independently or together. Thor prepares and refines massive datasets, while Roxie delivers them for real-time query and analytics workloads.

Enterprise Control Language

ECL is HPCC Systems' declarative, dataflow-oriented programming language. Key characteristics include:

- **Implicit parallelism**: Queries are compiled into optimized C++ and executed across all available nodes.
- **Declarative syntax**: Users specify what to compute, not how, leading to concise code.
- **Modular, reusable definitions**: Each ECL attribute builds on prior ones, forming a dictionary of transformations.

ECL's design allows developers to write complex data manipulations and analytics with minimal boilerplate, focusing on business logic and data relationships rather than low-level execution details.

HPCC NLP++ plugin

The HPCC plugin uses the C++ libraries for the NLP engine and is compiled directly with the HPCC C++ ECL code. When writing ECL, the code and all the needed included files are sent to the server, where the ECL is translated to C++ code, which is then compiled and executed.

The repository for the HPCC Systems NLP plugin is found at:

https://github.com/hpcc-systems/HPCC-Platform/tree/master/plugins/nlp

De Hilster has created a repository folder for a working example for building analyzers for the HPCC System. It is part of his repository of analyzers he has built over the years:

https://github.com/VisualText/dehilster-analyzers/tree/main/HPCC

Installing HPCC and NLP++ plugin

These are instructions on how to install the HPCC platform with the NLP++ plugin on **Windows Subsystem for Linux** (**WSL**) and use it with the NLP++ Language Extension for VS Code. This is for Windows, which has WSL installed.

Clone dehilster-analyzers

The **`HPCC`** folder in the repository **`dehilster-analyzers`** contains everything one needs to install and run an HPCC server with the NLP++ plugin. The **`README.md`** file provides a step-by-step procedure on how to do everything.

1. Open up **PowerShell**.
2. Connect to the folder where you want to clone the **`dehilster-analyzers`**.
3. Type **`git clone https://github.com/visualtext/dehilster-analyzers`**.
4. Open the **`HPCC`** folder in VS Code.

Create and launch HPCC server

Now create and launch the HPCC server on WSL.

1. Open up **PowerShell**.
2. Type **`wsl --install -d Ubuntu`** (if you want to reset your WSL to start fresh, type in **`wsl --unregister Ubuntu`**).
3. Enter your username and password.
4. Type **`sudo su -`** and enter your password.
5. Type **`wget http://visualtext.org/downloads/hpccnlp.sh`**.
6. Type **`sh hpccnlp.sh`** and wait until complete (it can take between 1 and 2 minutes).

Add data file to server

In HPCC Systems, you must import data into the HPCC Systems database. To do this, you use the HPCC dashboard using a browser:

1. Open in a browser **`127.0.0.1:8010`**.
2. Click on the **Files** icon on the left icons panel.
3. Click on **Landing Zones**.
4. Click on **Upload** and find the file **`DOJArticles.xml`** under the folder **`dehilster-analyzers/HPCC/analyzers/Entities/input`**.
5. Click on **Upload**.
6. Select the file **DOJArticles.xml** in the **Landing Zones** area that has now appeared.
7. Click on **Import: ... XML**.
8. Type **`doj::articles`** in the **Target Scope** field and choose **UTF-8** in the **Format** field.
9. Click on **Import**.

Run the Enterprise Control Language code

With the HPCC server up and running with the data and the NLP++ plugin, we are ready to run and execute the ECL code using the ECL VS Code extension:

1. Open VS Code.
2. Install the ECL and NLP++ extensions by searching for **`ECL`** and **`NLP`**.
3. Open the folder **`dehilster-analyzers/HPCC/`** in VS Code.
4. Click on the **NLP++** Icon in the left-hand vertical bar.
5. Click on the file **entities.ecl** in the **ANALYZERS** list under.
6. Right-click on **entities.ecl** and choose **Generate HPCC Manifest File**.
7. Click on the **entities.ecl** and click on the run button in the top right corner of the editing window.
8. Wait for the processing to finish to see the results in the HPCC vertical panel at the bottom.

Conclusion

In this, the final chapter, the reader was introduced to methods for integrating NLP++ analyzers into various popular programming environments. The nlp-engine serves to execute analyzers within the VS Code, Python, TypeScript, and HPCC Systems environments.

The reader may refer to the appendices at the back of the book for tables of functions as well as additional topics not detailed in the main body of the text.

True or false

1. The nlp.exe executable is available for download only on PCs and Linux.
2. The nlp.exe command line interface can process a folder of analyzers.
3. The NLPPlus Python package calls the nlp.exe executable, which is not native to Python.
4. The Python and TypeScript classes call the nlp.exe executable to run the NLP engine.
5. The advantage of using the Python class for nlp.exe is that it can load the dictionaries and knowledge bases once and execute many times.
6. The NLPPlus package includes several ready-to-use text analyzers.
7. The Python and TypeScript classes do not require a command line NLP engine.
8. There are two ways to call the NLP engine using Python.
9. The NLP engine test folder in the C++ code folder is for testing NLP++ analyzers.
10. The NLP++ C++ libraries can be integrated anywhere that C++ runs, in order to use the NLP engine.
11. HPCC Systems is an open-source super computing system that includes an NLP++ plugin.
12. The HPCC Systems NLP++ plugin is separate from and is not compiled with the ECL C++ code.
13. VisualText includes specific functionality for ECL files.

Answers

1. False	2. True	3. False
4. True	5. False	6. True
7. False	8. True	9. False
10. True	11. True	12. False
13. True		

Multiple choice questions

1. **The -WORK switch in the nlp.exe command line is responsible for:**
   a. The version of the NLP engine
   b. The path to the text file
   c. The path to the NLP engine folder
   d. Is a flag for debugging

2. **The nlp.exe is called by the following:**
   a. Python class
   b. TypeScript class
   c. The NLP++ Language Extension for VS Code
   d. All of the above
3. **Which text analyzer is not included in the NLPPlus python package:**
   a. Telephone number analyzer
   b. Email analyzer
   c. Entity analyzer
   d. Address analyzer
   e. Full English parser
4. **What is not true about the NLPPlus package for Python:**
   a. It is integrated with Python using the C++ NLP libraries
   b. It calls the nlp.exe executable
   c. It includes 5 library analyzers
   d. It is available using pip
5. **Which function or variable is not part of the Python class:**
   a. engineDir
   b. analyzeFile
   c. analyzerFolder
   d. kbPath
   e. createInputDir
6. **Which function or variable is part of the TypeScript class:**
   a. logDir
   b. isAnalyzerFolder
   c. analyzeFolder
   d. createAnalyzer
   e. deleteAnalyzer
7. **The NLPPlus package includes functions except for:**
   a. analyze
   b. set_working_folder
   c. copy_libary analyzers
   d. input_text
   e. load_dictionaries

8. **The HPCC Systems NLP++ plugin is:**
   a. A C++ class that can be integrated with ECL
   b. Compiled with the ECL C++ code
   c. Can be used in stand-alone fashion
   d. Does not enable VisualText to upload NLP++ analyzers to the HPCC server

Answers

1. c	2. d	3. c
4. b	5. c	6. c
7. e	8. b	

Short answer questions

1. Describe methods to call the nlp.exe in a script (you choose the scripting language)?
2. Compare the NLPPlus Python package with the Python class library?
3. Describe the basic usage of the NLPPlus Python package via an example task?
4. Discuss the use of the C++ libraries of the NLP engine?
5. Describe the use of the NLP++ plugin for HPCC as compared to using the NLP++ Language Extension for VS Code?
6. Contribute to the NLPPlus library analyzers: have students find a specific Python package that parses something like telephone numbers or other simpler patterns. Recreate that in NLP++ and submit it to GitHub to be included in the NLPPlus library of analyzers that can be used in edited by Python programmers.

Join our Discord space

Join our Discord workspace for latest updates, offers, tech happenings around the world, new releases, and sessions with the authors:

https://discord.bpbonline.com

Appendix A
Resources

Discussion topics and projects

The following sections list discussion topics and projects that may be used in coursework related to VisualText and NLP++. The NLP approach described in the present textbook fundamentally differs from statistical, machine learning, and frameworks such as REGEX, and so, the discussion topics and projects suggested here can help elucidate the tradeoffs among these frameworks.

Discussion topics

NLP++ can motivate classes, discussions, homework assignments, and long-term projects.

The following are the ethics and environment topics:

- **Ethical implications of statistical NLP methods**: Copyright and access to private data are legal problems that plague statistical endeavors. The huge cost of **large language models** (**LLMs**) makes them accessible only to large tech companies, leaving others behind.
- **Environmental implications of statistical methods**: In order to increase accuracy and coverage, ever more tokens and ever larger systems are needed. The monetary and environmental costs are substantial and wasteful, given that statistical models are often inadequate.
- **Ethical NLP development**: NLP++ was developed with these issues in mind: privacy, bias, and AI ethics. Its transparent (glass-box) approach supports responsible and fair NLP applications.
- **Practical applications:** VisualText or NLP++ is not merely a research tool. It is a framework built for real-world conditions. It is scalable across various industries, including healthcare, legal, and finance, where the **`-ilities`** such as accuracy and traceability are paramount.
- **Educational impact**: NLP++ serves as an educational tool, helping students and developers understand the intricacies of human language processing. It bridges the gap between theoretical linguistics and practical NLP development, making it an invaluable resource for learning.

- **Singularity**: Will statistical methods eventually lead to uncontrolled AI and, conversely, will NLP++ allow us to forestall the singularity?

The following sections are the **knowledge base** (**KB**) and LLM topics.

Knowledge migration to computers

Discuss what David de Hilster calls the Fifth Linguistic Revolution (see **https://nluglob.org/the-next-revolution-in-human-language**). Why must computers be given certain knowledge, and why is statistical processing insufficient? Discuss how we erroneously assign meaning to statistical relationships and responses from LLMs:

- **NLP++ output to Python**: How do you write an NLP++ analyzer to take input from Python and return output? Talk about generating JSON strings and objects using the `NLPPlus` Python package.
- **NLPPlus Python package**: How to use the NLP++ Python package? Talk about how the package loads the dictionaries and KBs on initialization, and then calls an analyzer multiple times.
- **Untrustworthiness of statistical NLP methods**: Discuss statistical methods such as machine learning, neural networks, and LLMs and their limited usefulness in industry. Contrast that to rule-based and knowledge-based methods as supported by NLP++.
- **NLPPlus Python package to create self-learning systems**: Learn how NLP++ supports trustworthy data and trustworthy NLP. Discuss that erroneous outputs of statistical systems are *random* and *illogical*, so that automated correction is not feasible. Discuss using the `NLPPlus` Python package to create automatic learning systems that build authoritative KBs and dictionaries.
- **Visual versus hidden problems**: Discuss NLP++ enables visualization and correction of text analysis problems, while statistical methods provide no logical means to fix errors. Discuss applying NLP++ to erroneous data from LLMs and other sources enables humans to build automated checking and correction in a logical way.

NLP++

The following are topics relating to the NLP++ programming language, its implementation, and comparison with alternative systems for language processing:

- **History of NLP++**: Discuss the journey of authors *Amnon Meyers* and *David de Hilster* that led to VisualText, NLP++, and conceptual grammar **KB management system** (**KBMS**). Discuss the way in which a multi-pass pipeline, parse tree, rules, code, and a KB work together to emulate human reading and understanding of text.
- **Comparing NLP++ with REGEX**: Discuss the limitations of REGEX. Discuss the advantages of NLP++ and the associated pipeline architecture in promoting readability and maintainability.

- **Comparing NLP++ with traditional NLP Python packages**: Discuss the problems with generic NLP and the difficulty of modifying traditional packages.
- **NLP++ Language Extension for VS Code**: Download the NLP++ Language Extension and discuss the text view, analyzer view, KB view, and bottom panel output, analyzer, find, and log views. Discuss the ability of VisualText to visualize and step through the analysis of text.
- **NLPPlus Python package**: Discuss using the NLP++ Python package and the NLP analyzers bundled with it. Discuss building NLP++ analyzers that return usable data back to Python, via the `output.json` file and the JSON functions in `KBFuncs.nlp`.

Long-term projects

The following is a list of projects, each of which can span the length of a course:

- **Snail mail addresses**: This is a great exercise for students building their first analyzer with NLP++. The address analyzer can utilize existing dictionaries bundled with NLP++
- **Sentiment analysis**: These analyzers demonstrate to students that sentiment analysis is extremely specific to subject matter and task, a good reason to use NLP++. Everyone in class can build a sentiment analyzer from scratch, and the variety of these analyzers is limitless see **https://nluglob.org/category/sentiment-analyzer/**).
- **Resume processing**: While the domain of resumes (academics, experience, skills) is relatively simple, every job applicant endeavors to make their resume unique, so that deducing diverse formatting is challenging, and so it may be suitable as a group project.
- **Wiki to dictionary and KBB files**: Students can use NLP++ to parse the wiki text format, in order to extract authoritative content from Wiktionary and Wikipedia pages. See the `dehilster-analyzers` repository for examples.
- **Named-entity recognition**: Have students tackle this difficult task (or aspects of it) as a group.
- **Anaphora**: Write an NLP++ analyzer to resolve anaphora (e.g., pronoun references) in text. One can use the parse-en-us analyzer and fix the bare bones anaphoric resolution mechanism there.
- **Personal assistant**: Have students choose a topic for a personal assistant, such as a doctor, contractor, lawyer, real estate agent, or build an assistant for the average person who deals with friends, family, addresses, etc. Have the student create some fictitious dialogs and write an analyzer that reads and understands a statement from a user and creates knowledge in a KB. For instance, if someone says: *my grandmother's birthday is December 7, 1963*, then the analyzer reads this and stores a person in the KB with the family member type and birthdate. Then the student can parse a second user input: *when is my grandmother's birthday?*

Quick start or workshop

This chapter can help create a 4-hour hands-on workshop using NLP++. It is doable and can work with participants who are not programmers. The reason that NLP++ can be used by non-programmers is that everyone is an expert at speaking some human language.

Setup

Here are the things you need for the workshop:

- A computer for every participant.
- A computer for the leader and a projection of the computer screen for the participants to follow.
- Connection to the internet.
- The ability to download the VS Code editor freeware from Microsoft.

Workshop description

The workshop is constructed to be a hands-on experience for the participants. The leader can be almost anyone who takes the time to tinker with NLP++ and preview the workshop.

This is a possible marketing blurb for the workshop:

Unlock the power of natural language processing with our 4-hour hands-on workshop using NLP++! This innovative workshop is designed for anyone with an interest in computers and human language. Some experience with computer programming is helpful.

Discover how to encode human knowledge and automate tasks that only people used to do. Join us for an engaging and interactive session where you'll learn the fundamentals of NLP++ and see how it can revolutionize the way we interact with technology. Don't miss this opportunity to expand your skills and explore the future of human-computer understanding of language!

Ready to dive in? Sign up now and take the first step towards mastering NLP++!

Workshop 4-hour schedule

Here is a suggested workshop schedule:

- **Hour one**: Download VS Code and the NLP++ Language Extension. The leader shows how to load, run, and trace through example analyzers. Participants play with example analyzers themselves.
- **Hour two**: Give participants a task. This could be a common task or a chosen task from a list. Start work on the task.

- **Hour three**: A small break, and the participants continue to work on their tasks. They can ask for help or work in groups.
- **Hour four**: Participants (or volunteering participants) present their work to the group, with the leader summing up the importance of NLP++ at the end.

Download VS Code and NLP++

Ask participants to download VS Code to their computers. Once they have done that, they can click on the extensions task icon on the left and search for `nlp`. NLP++ will appear at the top of the choices. Refer to the following figure:

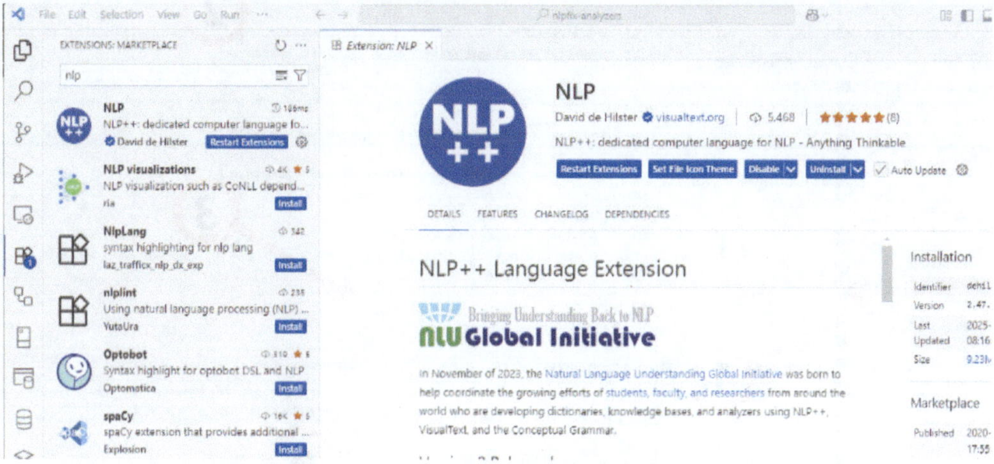

Figure appendix A.1: Downloading VS Code NLP++ extension

Once NLP++ is installed, have students click on the **VISUALTEXT** tab in the bottom panel and click on the cog icon in the **ANALYZERS** view. When they do, the analyzers appear in the **ANALYZERS** view, as shown in the following figure:

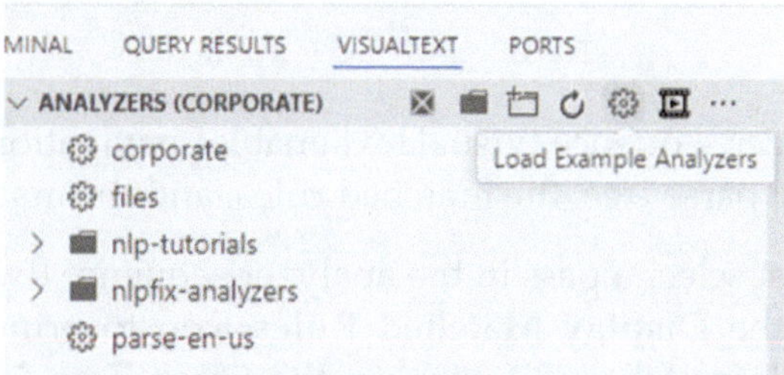

Figure appendix A.2: Loading the example analyzers

The VS Code window, with the VisualText **integrated development environment** (**IDE**), should look similar to the following (the output and find views have been collapsed). The steps are repeated here and numbered in the following figure:

1. Click on the NLP++ icon.
2. Open the bottom panel.
3. Click on the VisualText tab.
4. Click on an example analyzer.

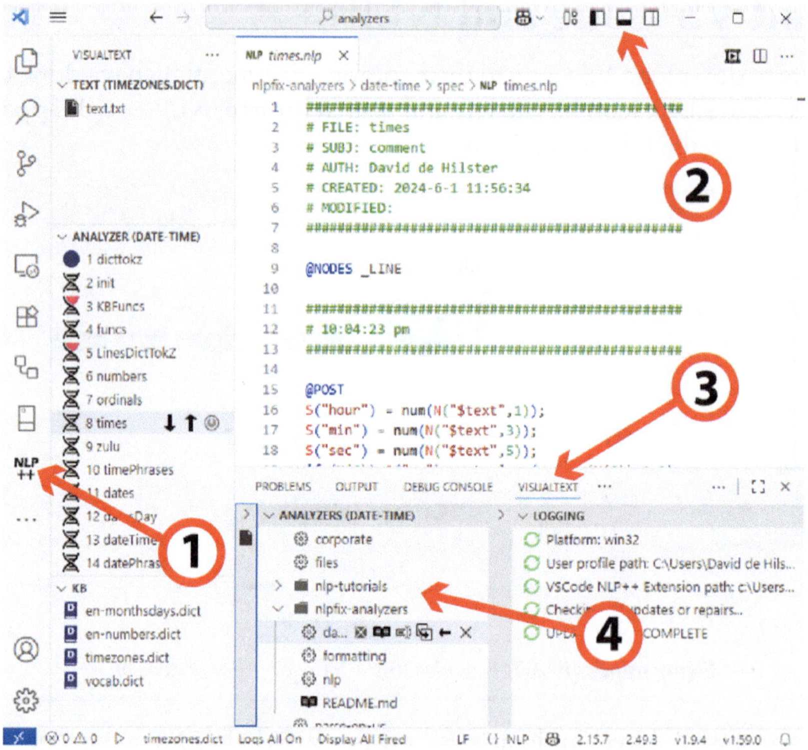

Figure appendix A.3: Steps in setting up VisualText and selecting an analyzer

Tracing

For each pass in the analyzer sequence, VisualText enables navigation (or tracing) among the matched text, the modified parse tree, the matched rules, and the matched dictionary entries.

In the following figure, first select a pass in the analyzer sequence (by clicking in the leftmost pane), then: (1) click on the **Display Matched Rules** icon to bring up the input text file containing highlighted rule matches. (2) click on the **Open Tree File** icon to bring up the current view of the parse tree.

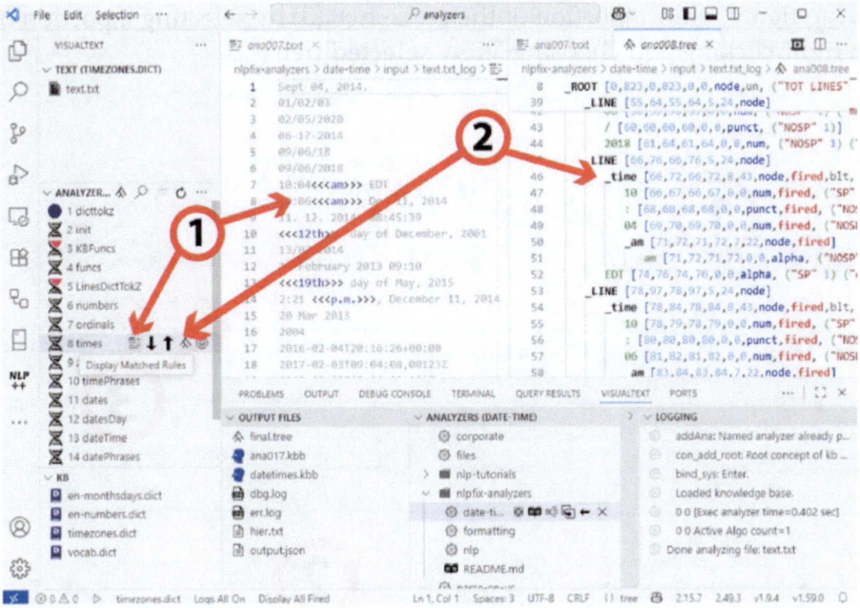

Figure appendix A.4: Analyzer pass; display highlighted text and parse tree views

In the following figure, view a matched rule (3) by right-clicking on a highlighted text snippet (1), then selecting **View rule or dictionary match** (2):

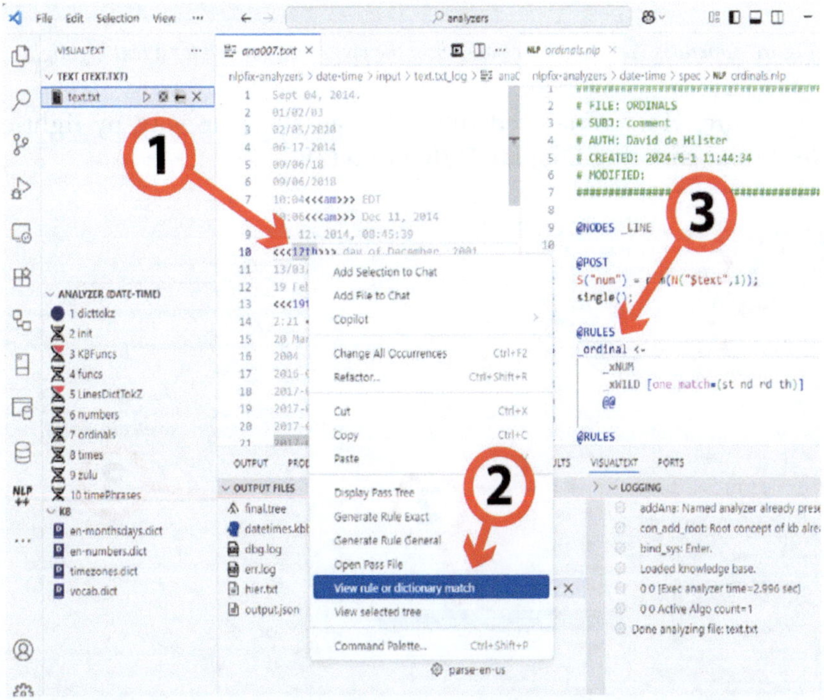

Figure appendix A.5: Analyzer pass; view the rule that matched a highlighted text

In the following figure, view a portion of the parse tree (3) by selecting a portion of the input text (1), then right-clicking and choosing **View selected tree** (2):

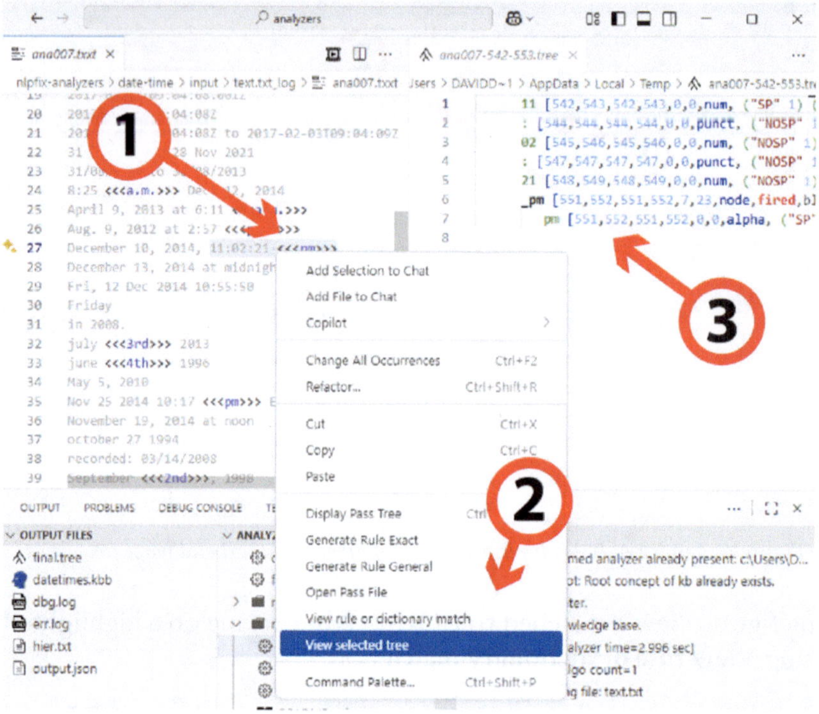

Figure appendix A.6: *Analyzer pass; view the parse tree portion for a text highlight*

In the following figure, view a matched rule (3) in an alternate way, by right-clicking on a parse tree node (1) and choosing **Display Rule Fired** (2):

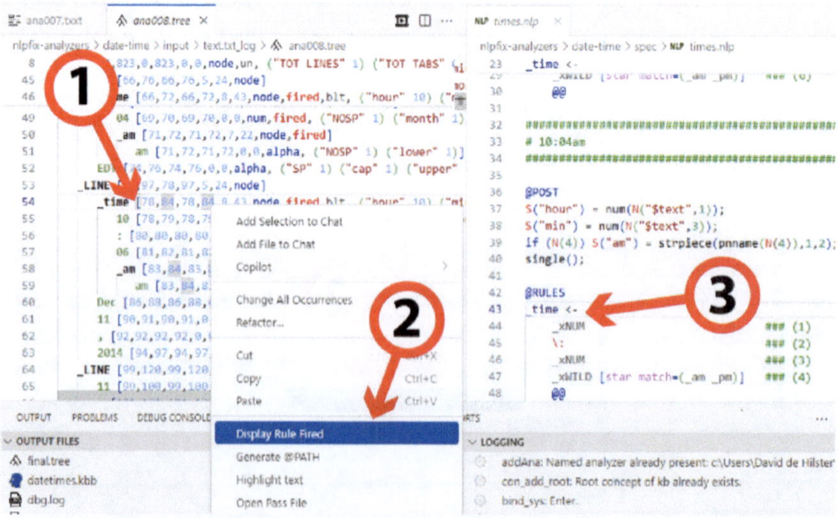

Figure appendix A.7: *Analyzer pass; view the rule that created a parse tree node*

In the following figure, view the text corresponding to a portion of the parse tree (3), by selecting that portion (1), then right-clicking and choosing **Highlight text** (2).

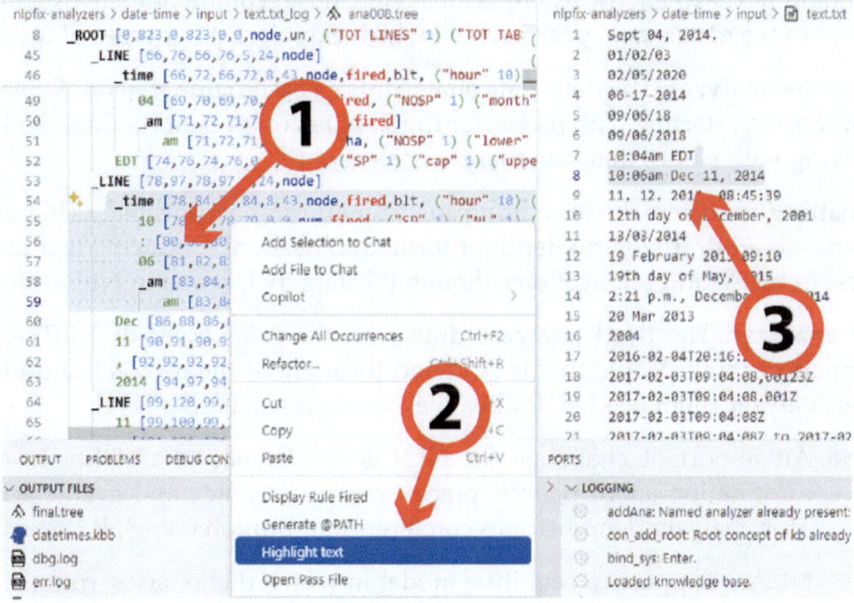

Figure appendix A.8: Analyzer Pass; view text associated with parse tree portion

In the following figure, view a matched dictionary entry (3) by right-clicking on a portion of text highlighted in red (1), then choosing **View rule or dictionary match** (2):

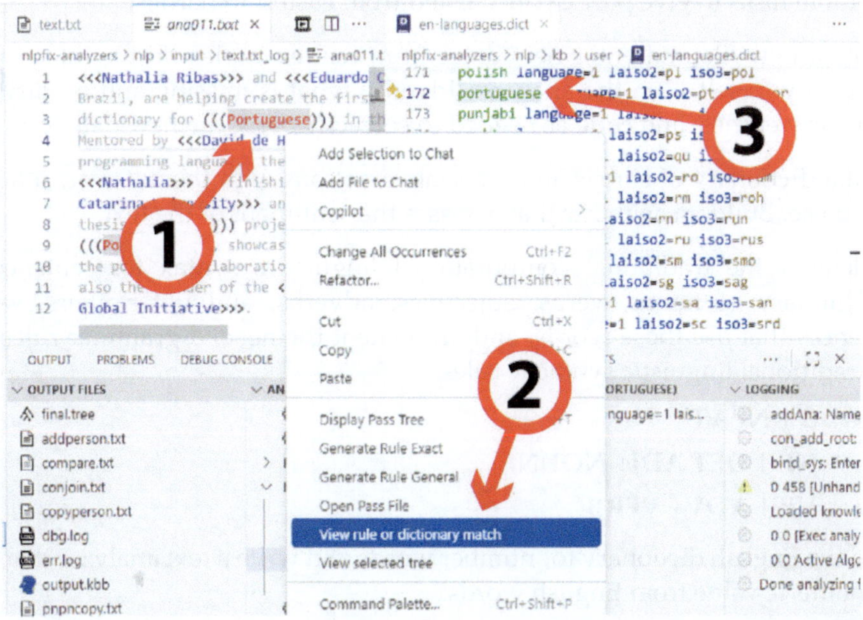

Figure appendix A.9: Analyzer pass; view dictionary entry that matched a highlighted text

Explain the example analyzers

The leader should next explain the example analyzers. It is recommended to use the following three analyzers in the **nlpfix-analyzers** folder, which exhibit distinct types of text analysis:

- **Date-time analyzer**: The date-time analyzer is easiest to understand. Explain bottom-up processing, starting with passes for the smaller components of dates and times, and following with passes that cover larger constructs.
- **Formatting analyzer**: The formatting analyzer is more complicated, as it uses recursion to parse an arbitrarily large depth of formatted headers. Deducing text formatting is critical in real-world applications, though it is largely ignored in NLP courses.
- **NLP analyzer**: The third analyzer draws on the full power of NLP++. It gathers information about people that is scattered throughout the text. A full understanding of the analyzer is not needed. Rather, we explain it at a higher level:
    - An important challenge for NLP is coreference: the ability to consolidate information about people, places, companies, etc., and events across a text. This analyzer demonstrates coreference resolution using NLP++.
    - NLP++ supports a cognitive model in which dictionaries, rules, a parse tree, knowledge, and short- and long-term memory all work together.

Tasks for participants

Here are possible tasks to give participants, listed from easiest to hardest:

1. Create a new file and enter new dates from real examples on the internet, or make them up yourself. Run the analyzer. Identify what is missing and modify the rules, dictionary entries, and code as needed to correctly parse the new date format.

   Build a dictionary of emojis and associate emotions with them. Create a text file that uses these. Build an analyzer that assesses the sentiment of the text.

2. Implement the traditional computational linguistics syntax for sentences. Create a dictionary of nouns, verbs, adjectives, adverbs, and determiners, write some sentences that use those words, and implement the needed grammar rules. Here are the traditional linguistic syntactic rules:
    - **S | NP VP**
    - **NP | DET ADJ+ NOUN**
    - **VP | ADV+ VERB**
3. Load the English dictionary for number words and write a text analyzer that calculates the numeric value from English words.

4. Choose any library dictionary, create text that uses those words, and write rules to analyze that text.
5. Make text with simple math equations. Create a dictionary for those equations and write rules to parse and calculate those equations.

The leader can wrap up the workshop by asking these questions:

1. One of the creators of NLP++, David de Hilster, says that traditional programming is *thinking like a computer*, whereas intelligent programming requires *thinking like a human*. To what extent do you think you have used either type of thinking? Do you find that NLP++ programming differs substantially from what you are used to?
2. If you write a text analyzer that understands text like a human, is that program *intelligent* for the given task?
3. Large language models like ChatGPT do not understand what they are saying. They simply react to input using patterns they learned from training on text. How is this different from a program written in NLP++?
4. Discuss the advantages of using NLP++ over systems that require huge amounts of data and resources.
5. Discuss the difference between systems that learn on their own versus systems that are written by coders. Which one is least likely to take over the world (viz., the singularity)?
6. Discuss the difference between systems that are trained and those that use rules and logic, when it comes to critical decisions and fixing problems. Can probabilistic systems like ChatGPT always have their errors corrected? How does that contrast with rule-based systems?

VisualText repository

The NLP++ environment is open-source, and all the code can be found under the VisualText repository on GitHub. Included are the VisualText and NLP++ source code, the example analyzer repository, and a number of auxiliary repositories of knowledge, dictionaries, analyzers, and code.

Main repositories

The main repositories comprise the core VisualText and NLP++ source code, which are largely written in the C++ programming language. The original versions of the core code date back as early as 1999, the first full year following the founding of *Text Analysis International, Inc.*

NLP engine

The NLP engine is the runtime system that executes NLP++ code, both interpreted and compiled. The current VisualText IDE does not yet support compiled analyzer code. The following repositories hold the core NLP engine code and platform-specific code that supports Windows, Linux, and MacOS versions of the NLP engine.

- **Main repository**: The **`nlp-engine`** repository holds all the C++ code for the NLP engine.

  When a new version is merged, the GitHub YML files compile and create versions of the **`nlp.exe`** engine for Windows, macOS, and several versions for Linux. All the generated files are then attached to the release, where the NLP++ Language Extension for VS Code (VisualText) updates the NLP engine version, as needed. When VisualText is loaded in VS Code, it checks the current version of the local NLP engine and compares it with the latest version in GitHub. It then downloads these assets, attached to the release number on GitHub, in order to update the engine.

- **Platform repositories:** When an update is made to the NLP engine code, the GitHub YML files also trigger the update of three other standalone repositories, for those wanting to use the NLP engine as an executable, namely, as **`nlp.exe`**.

  The repositories are:

  - **`nlp-engine-windows`**
  - **`nlp-engine-linux`**
  - **`nlp-engine-mac`**

  These repositories exist for those who want to use the NLP engine and nlp.exe in command line scripts.

VisualText IDE repository

The repository that holds the code for the current version of VisualText is found in the **`vscode-nlp`** repository.

Launched in 2020, VisualText is the name used for the NLP++ Language Extension for VS Code. It is written in TypeScript and runs on all three platforms: Windows, Linux, and macOS.

VisualText uses the command line form of the NLP engine and automatically downloads the correct version depending on the platform.

Updating versus submodules

Instead of using submodules (pointers to other repositories), the VisualText code has an elaborate updater that checks for new versions of the NLP engine, VisualText files, and analyzer versions.

Analyzers repository

The **`Analyzers`** repository contains example analyzers and tutorial analyzers. These are located in the folder of the NLP++ Language Extension itself. They can be accessed by clicking on the cog icon in the analyzer view. Refer to the following figure:

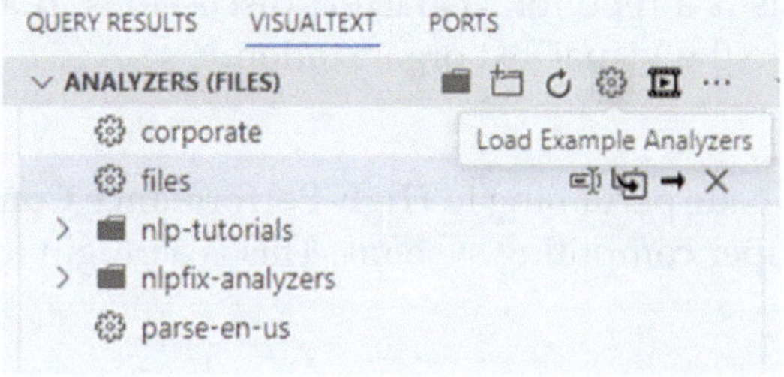

***Figure appendix A.10**: View of the example analyzers included with VisualText*

List of VisualText repositories

Following is a comprehensive list of the repositories within the VisualText repository on GitHub. All the repositories are public, and some are not listed because they are not currently used:

- **amnon-analyzers**:
  - **Public**: Analyzers by Amnon Meyers
- **analyzers**:
  - **Public**: Text Analyzers written in NLP++
- **analyzers-misc**:
  - **Public**: Miscellaneous analyzers
- **dehilster-analyzers**:
  - **Public**: Analyzers built by David de Hilster
  - **Language:** HTML
- **dict-en-us**:
  - **Public**: Analyzers and generated files, creating and enhancing the US English dictionary
- **dict-ne:**
  - **Public**: Nepali dictionary
- **dict-pt-br**:
  - **Public**: Portuguese dictionary for Brazil
  - **Language:** Python

- **dict-zh**:
    - **Public**: Chinese dictionary
    - **Language:** Python
- **discussions**:
    - **Public**: This is a repo for VisualText discussions. It also can hold documents important to the VisualText organization.
- **hpcc**:
    - **Public**: All code pertaining to **High-Performance Computing Cluster** (**HPCC**) systems, super computing systems. This is a plugin for HPCC systems.
- **kb**:
    - **Public**: Useful KBs
- **Legacy**:
    - **Public**: Legacy code, including vtcore and the Windows version of VisualText
    - **Language**: C++
- **Lexers**:
    - **Public**: This is where code for lexers for the NLP++ programming language would go.
    - **Language**: C++
- **Linux**:
    - **Public**: Linux scripts that use the NLP engine
- **llm**:
    - **Public**: Using LLMs to generate knowledge for NLP++
    - **Language:** Python
- **nlp-engine**:
    - **Public**: NLP engine code
    - **Tags:** `nlp, natural-language-processing, natural-language, natural-language-understanding, vscode`
    - **Language**: C++
- **nlp-engine-linux**:
    - **Public**: NLP engine code ready to run
- **nlp-engine-mac**: Public
- **nlp-engine-windows**: Public

- **nlp-tutorials**:
  - **Public**: Analyzers used in the NLP tutorial videos
  - **Language**: Python
- **nlpfix**:
  - **Public**
  - **Language**: TypeScript
- **nlpfix-analyzers**:
  - **Public**
  - **Language**: HTML
- **parse-en-us:**
  - **Public**: Full parser for English for the *United States,* as developed by Amnon Meyers
- **py-package-nlpengine**:
  - **Public**: Code for the **`NLPPlus`** Python package for the NLP engine
  - **Language:** Python
- **Python**:
  - **Public**: Python class for the command line NLP engine executable
  - **Language:** Python
- **ts-nlp-engine**:
  - **Public**: Typescript class for the NLP engine that calls the nlp.exe command line
  - **Language**: TypeScript
- **visualtext-files**:
  - **Public**: Files that go into the **`visualtext`** folder of the **`nlp-engine`**
  - **Tags**: **`nlp`**
  - **Language**: HTML
- **visualtext.github.io**: Public
- **vscode-nlp**:
  - **Public**: VS Code language extension for NLP++
  - **Tags**: **`nlp, natural-language-processing`**
  - **Language**: TypeScript

Join our Discord space

Join our Discord workspace for latest updates, offers, tech happenings around the world, new releases, and sessions with the authors:

https://discord.bpbonline.com

Appendix B
NLP++

Introduction

This appendix contains:

- Built-in actions
- Built-in functions
- User-defined functions

The original VisualText IDE documentation appears at:

http://www.textanalysis.com/help/help.htm

Not all actions and functions are documented in the present book. Check to see if they exist and work correctly. For example, some may not handle Unicode characters.

Chapter 2, NLP++ Architecture and Language includes additional tables listed in the following. Some tables are discussed in *Chapter 2, NLP++ Architecture and Language,* and repeated in this appendix, for convenience:

- Tokenizer types
- Attributes in whitespace-free parse tree
- Regions in pass file
- Token Syntax in **@RULES** region
- Syntax of large structures in **@RULES** regions
- Rewrite rule components
- Number of nodes to match for an element
- Element constraints and modes of matching
- Element actions after matching
- Suggested element modifiers in rewrite rule
- Types of values for rule element modifiers
- Special rule elements
- Post actions for a matched rewrite rule [repeat]
- Parse tree node actions in **@POST** region [repeat]

- Print actions in the **@POST** region [repeat]
- Legacy variable actions [obsolete]
- Actions in **@PRE** region [repeat]
- Actions in **@CHECK** region [repeat]
- NLP++ variable types
- Special runtime variables
- Special file variables
- Special parser variables
- Special text variables
- Special letter-case variables
- Special test variables
- NLP++ variable data types
- Built-in math functions [repeat]
- NLP++ operators

Rule region actions

Actions and functions in the **@RULE** regions operate in the midst of rule matching algorithms. Care must be taken to minimize modifying the parse tree structure in an ad hoc fashion. Adding, removing, and modifying nodes can cause an analyzer to error, fail, and crash.

For example, parse tree functions like **pninsert()**, which inserts a node in the parse tree, may wreak havoc if used while rules are being matched.

Recommendations are as follows:

- Use actions whenever possible, rather than functions, to modify the parse tree. Actions are aware of the ongoing rule-matching process in the **@RULE** regions, while functions are not.
- When feasible, modify the parse tree in the **@CODE** region.

The following table lists the pre-actions:

Pre-action	Description
uppercase()	Succeed if the leaf token is all uppercase.
lowercase()	Succeed if the leaf token is all lowercase.
cap()	Succeed if the leaf token has a capitalized first letter.
length (num)	Succeed if the leaf token has a length exactly equal to num.

Pre-action	Description
`lengthr (num1,num2)`	Succeed if leaf token length is in the range of lengths `(num1,num2)`, inclusive.
`numrange (num1,num2)`	Succeed if the leaf token is numeric in the given range.
`unknown()`	Succeed if the leaf token is an unknown word. Meaningful only if a prior pass has performed the `@CODE` action `lookup()` [obsolete].
`regexp (str)`	Succeed if the regular expression str matches. str may include characters, with `?` meaning a single char, `*` meaning 0 or more chars.
`regexpi (str)`	Like `regexp`, but case insensitive.
`var (str)`	Succeed if the matched node has a variable called `str` with a non-zero value.
`vareq (str,str-or-num)`	Succeed if the matched node has a variable called `str` whose value equals a string or numeric value in `str-or-num`.
`varne (str,strornum)`	Succeed if the matched node has a variable called `str` whose value does not equal a string or numeric value in `strornum`.
`varz (str)`	Succeed if the matched node has a variable called `str` with a 0 value (or lacks the variable altogether).
`debug()`	Succeed unconditionally. Used to place a C++ breakpoint at a particular rule.

Table appendix B.1: Actions specific to the @PRE region

Check actions

The following table shows the check and post actions:

Check action	Return type	Description
`fail()`	`NONE`	Reject and immediately exit the rule match.
`succeed()`	`NONE`	Accept rule match and immediately go to the `@POST` region, if present. [Empty or absent `@POST` region executes implicit `single()` reduce action.]
`or(num1,num2)`	`NONE`	[Obsolete][broken]

Table appendix B.2: Actions specific to the @CHECK region

Post actions

The following table lists the post actions that modify the structure of the parse tree:

Post action	Description
`setlookahead (num)`	Set the node that the rule matcher will continue with, after the current rule match is done. `num` node is the lookahead.
`single()`	Single-tier reduce. Reduce the entire set of nodes that matched a rule phrase.
`singler (num1,num2)`	Single-tier reduce of a range of rule elements. For example, if finding a period to be end-of-sentence in context, we only want to reduce the period to end-of-sentence, not the whole context.
`singlex (num1,num2)`	Single-tier reduce of a range of rule elements. All nodes not in the range are `EXCISED`. For example, if matching a named html tag, we only want to reduce the name and zap the rest of the tag.
`singlezap()`	Single-tier reduce. Excise all the nodes in the matched phrase.
`merge()`	Single-tier reduction that `DISSOLVES` each top-level node in the matched phrase.
`merger (num1,num2)`	Single-tier reduction that `DISSOLVES` each top-level node in the matched range.
`listadd (olist,oitem [, keep])`	Add a new node to a list node's children. If the item occurs after the list (`olist $<$ oitem`), it is added as the last child. If the item occurs before the list, it is added as the first child. The optional keep argument can be `"true"` or `"false"`. If `"true"` or absent, it keeps the nodes between the list and the item as children of the list. If `"false"`, it excises all the intervening nodes.
`excise (num1,num2)`	Excise the nodes matching the range of elements from the parse tree. Multiple excise actions must be ordered such that the `excise` with the highest `num1` is listed first, and so on.
`splice (num1,num2)`	`DISSOLVE` the top-level nodes of the given range.
`group (num1,num2,labelstr)`	Reduce the range of rule elements (`num1,num2`) and name the group node `label-str`. Unlike other reduce actions, this one can be repeated. Warning: **The rule element numbers change after each group action, so subsequent post actions must account for the new numbering of the rule elements. Reimplemented as an NLP++ function so that** `args` **can be NLP++ expressions.**
`noop ()`	Perform no `@POST` reduce action. This is a convenience to disable the default `single()` reduce action.

Table appendix B.3: Post actions for a matched rewrite rule

Most of the post actions listed above perform reduce actions. These create a new suggested node for the left-hand side of a rewrite rule. Using **group()** actions enables the developer to perform multiple reductions on the matched phrase.

The following table lists the auxiliary post actions, that is, those that do not modify the structure of the parse tree:

Post action	Description
pncopyvars(pnode1,pnode2)	Copy vars from **pnode1** to **pnode2**. [General function, not tied to rule region, shown for completeness.]
pncopyvars(pnode)	Copy variables from the **pnode** to the suggested node.
pncopyvars(num)	Copy variables from the numth phrase node to the suggested node.
pncopyvars(0)	Copy variables from the last phrase node to the suggested node.
pncopyvars()	Same as **pncopyvars(0)**.
setbase (num, bool)	Set the base attribute of the numth node to **true** or **false**.
setunsealed (num, bool)	Set the unsealed **attr** of the numth node to **true** or **false**.
xrename (name [, num])	Rename the numth context node to name. If **num** is absent or **0**, rename the last context node.

Table appendix B.4: Parse tree node actions in the @POST region

The table above includes actions that may be used in the **@CHECK** region as well as the **@ RULES** region.

The form **pncopyvars(pnode1,pnode2)**, copying variables from one node to another, is a general parse tree function not constrained to **@RULE** regions. Repeated here for comparison.

The bool arguments here are rarely used. 1 and 0 usually represent true and false, respectively (A future NLP++ version may include an explicit Boolean type).

Print actions

Many of the functions in the following table are [obsolete][deprecated], and are retained for backward compatibility. Regular NLP++ code now handles printing with the C/C++ **<<** output operator and the G, L, X, N, and S variable types:

Print action	Description
`print (str)`	Print the literal string str to standard output.
`printr (num1,num2)`	Print the text for the rule element range from **num1** to **num2** to standard output.
`prchild (file, num, name)`	Look for **name** immediately under the node matching rule element **num**. Print its text to **file**, if found.
`prtree (file, num, name)`	Look for **name** anywhere under the node matching rule element **num**. Print its text to **file**, if found.
`prxtree (filename, prestr, ord, name, poststr)`	To **filename**, print the first node called **name** found in the **ord**th element's tree, preceded by **prestr** and followed by **poststr**. If the named node is not found, nothing is printed out. E.g., **prxtree ("out.txt", "date: ", 3, "_date", "\n")** prints out a line like "date: **3/9/99**" if a **_date** node is found within the subtree of element **3**.
`prlit (file, str)`	Print the literal string **str** to **file**.
`fprintnvar (file, var, ord)`	To **file**, print the value of the variable **var** in the **ord**th element's node.
`fprintxvar (file, var, ord)`	To **file**, print the value of the variable **var** in the **ord**th context node.
`fprintgvar (file, var)`	To **file**, print the value of the global variable **var**.
`gdump (file)`	Dump all the global variables and their values to **file**.
`xdump (file, ord)`	Dump all the variables in the **ord**th context node and their values to **file**.
`ndump (file, ord)`	Dump all the variables in the **ord**th phrase element's node and their values to **file**.
`sdump (file)`	Dump all the variables in the suggested node and their values to **file**.
`prrange (file, num1,num2)`	Print the text under the range of rule elements (**num1,num2**) to **file**.
`pranchor (file,num1,num2)`	Print a web URL to **file**. Treat the range (**num1,num2**) as a URL. Use the global variable named **base** to resolve and print complete relative URLs (A prior pass must find the base HTML tag and set **base** appropriately. Not using the file's URL, so not handling cases where the base itself is a relative URL).

Table appendix B.5: Deprecated and obsolete print actions

Variable actions

The following variable actions are deprecated or obsolete, and are retained for backward compatibility:

Variable action	Description
addstrs	Add a string to the multi-string global variable **var**. Fetch the string from the nodes matching the rule element num. var should have been declared using the code action **varstrs()** [removed]. Use NLP++ array syntax instead.

Table appendix B.6: Legacy variable actions

Parse tree functions

Parse tree functions enable fetching and modifying information within parse tree nodes, as well as traversing and modifying the structure of the parse tree. As noted elsewhere, functions that modify the structure of the parse tree should not be used in the **@CHECK** and **@POST** regions of a pass file, as that will wreak havoc with the rule-matching algorithms.

The **group()** function below is the only approved reduce function for the **@POST** region. The **pndetelechilds()** and **pninsert()** functions should not be used in the **@POST** region for the reason cited above.

The following table lists and describes the available parse tree functions:

Function	Type	Description
eltnode (num)	**pnode**	Fetch first node matching numth elt of rule.
lasteltnode(num)	**pnode**	Fetch the last node matching numth elt of the rule.
group (startn,endn,namestr)	**pnode**	Reduce nodes matching phrase elts **startn** to **endn**. Intern, name and return the new node **namestr**.
phrasetext()	**str**	Fetch cleaned-up text that matched the rule phrase.
phraseraw()	**str**	Fetch raw text that matched the rule phrase.
pncopyvars (pnode1,pnode2)	**none**	Copy vars from **pnode1** to **pnode2**. General function analogous to **pncopyvars()** rule region actions.
pndeletechilds (pnode)	**none**	Delete children of **pnode**. [not in **@POST**]
pninsert (name, pnode, flag)	**pnode**	Create a nonliteral node with a name. Insert before **pnode** if flag is 0, after if flag is 1. [not in **@POST**]
pnmakevar (pnode, varstr, val)	**none**	In **pnode**, make variable **varstr** with value **val**.
pnname (pnode)	**str**	Fetch the name of the **pnode**.

Function	Type	Description
`pnnext (pnode)`	`pnode`	Fetch **pnode** right sibling, if any.
`pnprev (pnode)`	`pnode`	Fetch **pnode** left sibling, if any.
`pnrename (pnode, str)`	`str`	Rename **pnode** to **str**. Intern and return **str**.
`pnroot()`	`pnode`	Fetch the root of the parse tree.
`pndown (pnode)`	`pnode`	Fetch the child of the parse tree **pnode**.
`pnsingletdown (pnode)`	`pnode`	Fetch the farthest descendant of **pnode**, moving down the singlet chain (i.e., stop before any branching and stop when a **pnode** has a base attribute).
`pnup (pnode)`	`pnode`	Fetch **pnode** parent (if not root). Warning: **Only the left-most pnode in its list has a parent link. To get any pnode parent, use pnparent().**
`pnvar (pnode, varstr)`	`array`	Fetch value(s) of pnode's var named **varstr**.
`pnvarnames (pnode)`	`array`	Fetch the pnode's variable names as an array.
`varinlist (varstr, num)`	`array`	Find **varstr** variable's value(s) in any **pnode** that matched the **num**th **PHRASE ELEMENT**.

Table appendix B.7: Parse tree functions

Knowledge base functions

The **knowledge base** (**KB**) functions consist of groups that read and write the KB, fetch information, create/modify information, and traverse the KB.

A KB concept may also manage a private data structure called a **phrase**, consisting of one or more nodes in a linear linked list. These are unrelated to phrases and nodes of the parse tree, and are little-used in the current version of NLP++ and VisualText.

Note: **Strings are case-sensitive unless indicated otherwise.**

Command file functions

Command file functions are tasked with loading and writing out text files that represent the content of the KB. The **take()** function reads a command language dating to the creation of VisualText and NLP++, while the **kbdumptree()** function outputs a more human-readable representation of the KB. Both of these file types are still in use in the latest versions of the NLP engine. The following table lists the command file functions:

Function	Return type	Description
`kbdumptree (root-con, file-str)`	`bool`	Create a dump file of KB concepts.
`take (file-str)`	`bool`	Execute commands in a KB command file (`.KB` file)

Table appendix B.8: Command file functions for the KB

Functions that find and fetch

NLP++ provides a host of functions for retrieving information from the KB concepts, their attributes, and values. Some functions search up and down the hierarchy for specific information, and some manage dictionary information, which is also stored within the KB. The tables in this section list and describe these functions.

The following table describes KB functions that fetch concepts:

Function	Type	Description
`conceptname (con)`	`str`	Fetch the name of the given concept.
`conceptpath (con)`	`str`	Fetch the entire path of the given concept as a string.
`findconcept (con, num)`	`con`	Find concept number `num` under parent `con`.
`findconcept (con, str)`	`con`	Find the concept named `str` under the parent `con`.
`findhierconcept (name, hier)`	`con`	Find a concept in the subhierarchy of a given concept. e.g: `G("returnedConcept") = findhierconcept("child",G("ancestor"));` finds the concept named `child` anywhere under the concept pointed to by `G("ancestor")`.
`findroot()`	`con`	Get the root concept of KB (named concept).
`pathconcept (str)`	`con`	Fetch concept, given the path `str`.
`down (con)`	`con`	Fetch the first child of the given concept.
`next (con)`	`con`	Fetch the right or next sibling of the concept.
`prev (con)`	`con`	Fetch the left or previous sibling of the concept.
`up (con)`	`con`	Fetch the parent of the given concept.

Table appendix B.9: Functions fetching KB concepts

The following table describes KB functions that fetch concept attributes and values:

Function	Type	Description
`attrexists (hier, attr_s, val_s)`	`bool`	Find an attribute and a value pair in the subhierarchy of a concept.
`attrname (attr)`	`str`	Fetch the attribute's name.
`attrvals (attr)`	`val`	Fetch the attribute's list of values.
`attrwithval (con, attr_s, val_s)`	`bool`	Check if the concept's attribute has the given value.
`findattr (con, str)`	`attr`	Fetch attribute named str belonging to concept con.
`findattrs (con)`	`attr`	Fetch the concept's list of attributes.
`findvals (con, name)`	`val`	Fetch the list of values for a concept's attribute.
`conval (con, name)`	`con`	Fetch concept-value of attribute (must be first).
`fltval (con, name)`	`flt`	Fetch float value of attribute (must be first).
`numval (con, name)`	`num`	Fetch the numeric value of the named attribute (must be first).
`strval (con, name)`	`str`	Fetch the string value of the attribute (must be first).
`getconval (val)`	`con`	Fetch concept from value.
`getnumval (val)`	`int`	Fetch number from numeric **`VAL`**.
`getstrval (val)`	`str`	Fetch the string value from a KB value object.
`getsval (val)`	`str`	Fetch value from an attribute value and convert to a string.
`inheritval (con, name, topCon)`	`str`	Find the first named attribute's string value by looking up the hierarchy. con is the current concept, **`topCon`** is the highest concept to search. If **`topCon==0`**, search to the root KB concept.
`nextattr (attr)`	`attr`	Fetch the next attribute in a list of attributes.
`nextval (val)`	`val`	Fetch the next value in a list of values.

***Table appendix B.10**: Functions fetching KB concept attributes and values*

The following table describes KB functions that fetch dictionary objects:

Function	Type	Description
`dictfindword (str)`	`con`	Find the dictionary concept in the dictionary hierarchy of the KB.
`dictfirst()`	`con`	Fetch the first word-concept in the KB dictionary hierarchy.

Function	Type	Description
`dictnext (con)`	`con`	Fetch the word following the given word in the KB dictionary hierarchy.
`findwordpath (str)`	`str`	Find the entire path of the dictionary concept for the given string. (If not present, don't add the word.).
`wordpath (str)`	`str`	Get the entire path of the dictionary concept for the given string. (If not present, add the word.).
`wordindex (str)`	`con`	Fetch index concept for the dictionary concept named by **`str`**.

Table appendix B.11: Functions fetching KB dictionary objects

Functions that create

NLP++ provides built-in KB functions to create concepts, attributes, and values. The dictionary is implemented as a specialized subhierarchy within the KB, and so it can utilize the same functions that manage concepts.

The following table includes functions that create concepts, attributes, and values:

Function	Return type	Description
`makeconcept (parent, name [, num] )`	`con`	Make a concept under the given parent concept. Optionally, as the **`num`**th child of the parent. **`num==0`** or absent places concept at the end of the list of children. The name is the name of the new concept.
`addattr (con, attrs)`	`attr`	Add an attribute with no value to the given concept.
`addsval (con, name, num)`	`none`	Add the numeric value num as a string to concept con's attribute called name.
`addstrval (con, name, str)`	`none`	Add **`str`** as a string value to concept con's attribute called **`name`**.
`addnumval (con, name, num)`	`none`	Add **`num`** as a numeric value to concept con's attribute called name.
`addconval (con, name, conval)`	`none`	Add concept value con**`val`** to the concept's name attribute.
`getconcept (parent, name)`	`con`	Get or make a named concept under the parent.
`addword (str)`	`con`	Add the dictionary concept to the dictionary within the KB, if not present. In either case, fetch the dictionary concept for the word.
`dictgetword (str)`	`con`	Same as **`addword`**; more principled function name.

Table appendix B.12: Functions that create KB objects

Functions that move, replace, and remove

Once KB objects are created, the programmer requires the means to manage them. The following table provides built-in functions to move, replace, and sort concepts, attributes and values within the hierarchical KB:

Function	Type	Description
`rmconcept (con)`	bool	Remove concept con from KB. Removes entire subhierarchy.
`rmchild (con, str)`	bool	Remove child named **`str`** from parent concept **`con`**.
`rmchild (con, num)`	bool	Remove number **`num`** child of parent concept **`con`**.
`rmvals (con, str)`	bool	Remove attributes and values of concept con's attribute named **`str`**.
`rmval (attr, val)`	bool	Remove value **`val`** from attribute **`attr`**.
`rmattrval (con, str1, str2)`	bool	Remove value named **`str2`** from attribute named **`str1`** under concept **`con`**. Also removes the attribute.
`rmattrs (con)`	bool	Remove concept's attributes (except for system internal ones).
`rmattr (con,name)`	bool	Remove the concept's named **`attr`** and values.
`rmchildren (con)`	bool	Remove the concept's children and phrase.
`rmword (str)`	bool	Remove the dictionary concept from the KB.
`prunephrases (hier)`	bool	Remove all phrases from the given subhierarchy.
`replaceval (con, name, str)`	none	Replace named attribute's value(s) with **`str`**.
`replaceval (con, name, num)`	none	Replace named attribute's value(s) with **`num`**.
`replaceval (con, name, con-val)`	none	Replace named attribute's value(s) with concept **`con-val`**
`renameconcept (con, name)`	none	Rename the given concept to name.
`renamechild (con, num, name)`	none	Rename con's numth child concept to name.
`renameattr (con, name, new)`	none	Rename con's named attribute to new.
`movecleft (con)`	none	Move concept before the previous sibling. (Moves concept to the left in its list).
`movecright (con)`	none	Move the concept after the next sibling (Moves concept to the right in its list).
`sortchilds (con)`	none	Sort the concept's immediate children alphabetically.

Function	Type	Description
`sortconsbyattr (arr-c, attr-s, numeric-b, descending-b)`	`arr`	Given an array (multi-valued variable) of KB concepts, sort the concepts by the given attribute. Numeric **`b = 1`** if num, 0. If a string type attribute. Descending **`b = 1`** if descending order, 0 if ascending. E.g., **`G("sorted") = sortconsbyattr(G("cons"),"count",1,0);`** sorts an array of KB concepts by their **`count`** attribute in ascending order, assigning a new sorted array to **`G("sorted")`**. The given array in **`G("cons")`** is left unaltered. New in 1.6
`sorthier (con)`	`none`	Sort the concept's subhierarchy alphabetically.
`attrchange (hier, attr_s, val_s, new_s)`	`bool`	Replace all matching attribute-value pairs in the given hierarchy to have the string value **`new_s`**.

Table appendix B.13: Functions that manage and remove KB objects

KB phrase and node functions

The backbone of the NLP++ KB consists of a hierarchy (or tree) of concepts. In addition to attributes and values, each concept may own a private data structure called a phrase, consisting of one or more nodes in a linear (unbranched) list .These objects are unrelated to parse tree phrases and nodes. A KB node uses the same structure as a KB concept. A concept's phrase may be used to store arbitrary information, as designed by the programmer.

The following table lists the built-in functions for managing KB phrases and nodes:

Function	Type	Description
`findphrase (con)`	`phr`	Fetch the concept's phrase.
`sortphrase (con)`	`none`	Sort the concept's phrase nodes alphabetically.
`phraselength (con)`	`int`	Get the number of nodes in the concept's phrase.
`nodeconcept (node)`	`con`	Fetch the concept that the node is a proxy for (Changed in 1.6).
`nodeowner (node)`	`con`	Fetch the concept that owns the node's phrase (New in 1.6).
`findnode (phrase, name)`	`con`	Find the first named node in the phrase.
`findnode (phrase, num)`	`con`	Find the numth node in the phrase.
`listnode (node)`	`con`	Fetch the first node in the given node's list.
`firstnode (phrase)`	`con`	Fetch the first node in the phrase.
`lastnode (phrase)`	`con`	Fetch the last node in the phrase.

Function	Type	Description
`makephrase (con, name)`	phr	Make a phrase in con by creating a named node.
`addcnode (con, name)`	con	Add a named node at the end of the con's phrase.
`addnode (phrase, name, num)`	con	Add a named node as numth in the phrase.
`rmnode (con)`	none	Remove the node from the concept's phrase.
`rmphrase (phrase)`	none	Remove the phrase from its concept.
`rmcphrase (con)`	none	Remove a concept's phrase.
`renamenode (phrase, name, new)`	none	Rename the phrase's named node to new.
`renamenode (phrase, num, new)`	none	Rename phrase's numth node to new.

***Table appendix B.14**: Functions that manage KB phrases and nodes*

String functions

This is because NLP++ is specifically geared to natural language processing; it requires an extensive set of built-in functions for managing character strings. For example, the **`deaccent()`** function removes accent characters found in languages such as French, in order to enable matching words that differ only in the presence or absence of accent marks.

The following table presents the built-in functions that manage strings:

Function	Type	Description
`deaccent (str)`	str	Replace accented characters in **`str`**.
`dejunk (str)`	str	Replace all but simple **American Standard Code for Information Interchange** (ASCII) chars in **`str`**.
`flt (str)`	float	Convert string or int to float, if possible.
`levenshtein (str1,str2)`	int	**`levenshtein`** edit-distance between two strings.
`num (str)`	int	Convert **`str`** to number, else 0 (Accept **`num arg`**).
`stem (str)`	str	Return noun or verb stem, lowercased.
`strchar (str, num)`	str	Return **`num`**th char of **`str`**, zero-based.
`strchr (str, chstr)`	str	Return a substring of str, starting at the first instance of character **`ch-str`**. Return zero if not found.
`strchrcount (str, chstr)`	int	Count occurrences of character **`chstr`** in **`str`**.
`strclean (str)`	str	Remove extra whitespace in **`str`**.

Function	Type	Description
`strcontains (str1,str2)`	`bool`	True if **str1** is contained in **str2**.
`strcontainsnocase (str1,str2)`	`bool`	True if **str1** is contained in **str2**. Ignore letter case.
`strendswith (str, suffixstr)`	`bool`	True **if str** ends with suffix-**str**.
`strstartswith (str, suffixstr)`	`bool`	True if **str** starts with suffix-**str**.
`strequal (str1,str2)`	`bool`	True if **str1** is identical to **str2**.
`strisalpha (str)`	`bool`	True if str is all-alphabetic.
`strisdigit (str)`	`bool`	True if **str** is all-numeric.
`strnotequal (str1, str2)`	`bool`	True if **str1** differs from **str2**.
`strequalnocase (str1, str2)`	`bool`	True if **str1** is identical to **str2**. Case-insensitive.
`strnotequalnocase (str1,str2)`	`bool`	True if **str1** differs from **str2**. Case-insensitive.
`strlessthan (str1, str2)`	`bool`	True if **str1** lexically precedes **str2**.
`strgreaterthan (str1, str2)`	`bool`	True if **str1** lexically follows **str2**.
`strlength (str)`	`int`	Return the length of **str**.
`strpiece (str, start-num, endnum)`	`str`	Fetch the substring of **str** from index **start-num** to **end-num**. Zero-based.
`struniquechars (str)`	`str`	Return a substring of **str**. Keep only the first instance of each distinct **char**.
`strrchr (str, ch-str)`	`str`	Return the substring headed by the last occurrence of char **ch-str** in **str**.
`strsubst (str, old-str, newstr)`	`str`	Return **str**, substituting **old-str** with **new-str**.
`strtolower (str)`	`str`	Return lowercased **str**.
`strtotitle (str)`	`str`	Return **str** with title capitalization.
`strtoupper (str)`	`str`	Return uppercased **str**.
`strtrim (str)`	`str`	Remove leading and trailing whitespace from **str**.
`strwrap (str, num)`	`str`	Add a newline at every str segment of length **num**.
`str (num)`	`str`	Convert **num** to string (Accept string **arg**).
`strescape (str, charsToEscapeStr, escapeStr)`	`str`	Escape characters in a string.

Function	Type	Description
`strunescape (str, escapedCharsStr, escapeStr)`	`str`	Unescape characters in a string.
`suffix (wordStr, suffixStr)`	`bool`	True if **`suffixStr`** is the suffix of **`wordStr`**.
`xmlstr (str)`	`str`	Convert **`str`** chars to conform to XML.

Table appendix B.15: *Functions that manage strings*

Special functions

VisualText and NLP++ operate within an architecture comprising a pipeline of passes, a KB, and a parse tree. Furthermore, NLP++ endeavors to accommodate multiple natural language processing paradigms, applications, and domains of discourse. As such, NLP++ provides a growing set of built-in functions to support the needs of developers.

Special and miscellaneous NLP++ built-in functions are noted in the following table:

Function	Type	Description
`arraylength (expr)`	`int`	Return the array length of **`expr`**. Warning: **Never returns 0. Array length is 1 or more; check for an empty array separately, if 0 means empty.**
`arraylength(var)`	`int`	Count values in **`var`** (Like call-by-reference). Warning: **Never returns 0.**
`exitpass()`	`none`	Exit immediately from the current pass.
`hitconf(hits,total,fudge)`	`0-100`	Hit confidence, e.g., keyword density in a text. Typical fudge≈3 to 20, adjust as desired.
`inputrange(startn,endn)`	`str`	Fetch input text range with start and end offsets.
`inputrangetofile(startn,endn, outstr)`	`bool`	Print input range to named output stream **`outstr`**.
`permuten(num)`	`int arr`	Randomly permute the integers 0 to num.

Table appendix B.16: *Special NLP++ functions*

Spelling functions

An important concern of natural languages is to ensure the correct spelling of words. NLP++ currently provides built-in spelling functions only for English (primarily American English). As NLP++ is applied to additional languages, built-in spelling functions for those should be implemented as well.

The following table describes the built-in spelling functions for English:

Function	Type	Description
`spellcandidates (word_str)`	`str`	Return a list of possible corrections to **word_str**.
`spellcorrect (word_str)`	`str`	Return the highest-confidence correction to **word_str**.
`spellword (word_str)`	`bool`	[Deprecated] Return 1 if **word_str** is a known word, using the system array of English words. Instead, use **dicttok** or **dicttokz** dictionary-based tokenizer pass.
`strspellcandidate (word_str, list_str)`	`str`	Select the best spell-correct candidate for **word_str**, given **list_str**, list of candidates (e.g., returned by spell candidates).
`strspellcompare (str1, str2)`	`int`	Measure the spelling distance between two given words. The smaller the number, the fewer the corrections to convert **str1** to **str2**.

Table appendix B.17: Functions for English spelling

Math functions

NLP++ currently provides a small number of built-in mathematics functions, as detailed in the following table:

Function	Type	Description
`abs (num)`	`int`	Return the absolute value of **num**.
`random (from_num, to_num)`	`float`	Return a random number in the given range.
`mod (num)`	`int`	Return modulus of **num**.
`log10 (num)`	`float`	Return base 10 log of **num**.)

Table appendix B.18: Built-in math functions

funs.nlp

The tables presented so far have built-in NLP++ functions. Built-in functions have been written and compiled in C++ to promote rapid and efficient processing. As a complete programming language, NLP++ also supports user-defined functions, which are not as fast as built-ins, but can greatly increase the utility and accuracy of text analysis applications. Many applications have been built, and many user-defined functions have been incorporated into function-specific passes of the full English parser.

The following are the function descriptions in the `funs.nlp` file of the full English parser:

- **Word lookup, stemming, and POS tagging:**
    - **lookupalphadicttokz(text, node)**: Looks up a word in the dictionary (`dicttokz` pass), attaches POS and semantic info to a node, sets stem, and handles eventive nouns.
    - **lookupalpha(text, node)**: Looks up a word in the dictionary, attaches POS and semantic info to a node, sets the stem, and handles eventive nouns.
    - **nvstem(txt)**: Computes the stem of a word, using dictionary knowledge for known words and heuristics for unknown words.
    - **nvstemknown(lc)**: Computes the stem for a known word, handling common suffixes and exceptions.
    - **nvstemunk(lc)**: Computes a possible stem for an unknown word (implementation incomplete).
    - **nvsuff(txt)**: Determines the suffix for a noun or verb (e.g., `-s`, `-edn`, `-ing`, `-en`, `inf`).
- **Verb conjugation and agreement:**
    - **vgagree(m, h, b, being, v)**: Checks agreement in verb groups (modals, have, be, being, verb), returns flags for agreement, passive voice, tense, and conjugation.
    - **vconjq(v, need):** Checks if a verb node matches a required conjugation (e.g., `-edn`, `inf`), handling irregular verbs and ambiguous cases.
    - **vconj(v)**: Returns the conjugation of a verb node (`inf`, `-s`, `-ing`, `-edn`, `-ed`, `-en`, or `0`), handling both regular and irregular verbs.
    - **samevconj(v1, v2)**: Checks if two verbs have compatible conjugations, returns the most constrained fit.
    - **vvagree(n1, n2)**: Checks if two verbs or verb groups agree in tense.
    - **vgvgagree(vg1, vg2)**: Checks if two verb groups agree in tense.
    - **verbverbagree(first1, first2)**: Checks if two verbs agree in tense/conjugation.

- **Node and tree utilities:**
    - **nodetext(n)**: Gets the text of a node, using cleaned/corrected text if available.
    - **noderawtext(n)**: Gets the original text for a node from the input buffer, with size limits.
    - **nodetreetext(n)**: Gets the text for a node, using cleaned/corrected text or by prosifying the subtree.
    - **nodestreetext(s, e)**: Gets the text for a range of nodes, concatenating their subtree texts.
    - **phrasetreetext(root)**: Gets the text for a node's top-level phrase.
    - **pnparent(n)**: Fetches the parent of a parse tree node.
    - **getancestor(n, name)**: Traverses up the tree to find an ancestor node with a given name.
    - **findlastnode(n)**: Finds the last node in a list.
    - **pnfindchild(n, name)**: Finds a child node by name.
    - **pnfindattrdown(n, field)**: Finds an attribute starting from the current node, looking down the tree.
    - **setnodevarchain(n, var, val)**: Sets a variable down a chain of nodes.
- **Array and list operations**:
    - **qaddstr(txt, arr)**: Adds a string to an array if it is unique.
    - **qaddvalue(val, arr)**: Adds a value to an array if it is unique.
    - **addvalue(val, arr)**: Adds a value to an array without checking for uniqueness.
    - **push(val, arr)**: Pushes a value onto the front of an array.
    - **rpush(arr, val)**: Pushes a value onto the end of an array.
    - **pushz(val, arr)**: Pushes a value onto the front of an array, treating zero as an array with one value.
    - **rpushz(arr, val)**: Pushes a value onto the end of an array, treating zero as an array with one value.
    - **arraymerge(arr1, arr2)**: Merges two arrays.
    - **arrayreverse(arr)**: Reverses the order of elements in an array.
    - **dedup(arr)**: Removes duplicate values from an array.
    - **unionx(arr1, arr2)**: Returns the union of two arrays, ensuring uniqueness.
    - **intersect(arr1, arr2):** Returns the intersection of two arrays.
    - **intersectcount(a1, a2)**: Counts the number of intersecting values in two arrays.

- **updatearray(arr1, arr2)**: Concatenates two arrays.
- **updatearrayuniq(arr1, arr2)**: Concatenates two arrays, adding only unique values.
- **xferarray(to, field, arr)**: Updates an array from one node to another.
- **xferarrayuniq(to, field, arr)**: Updates an array from one node to another, adding only unique values.
- **valinarray(val, arr)**: Checks if a value is in an array.
- **getposition(ii, arr)**: Gets the position of a value in an array.
- **arrayout(arr, out, sep)**: Prints an array on a line, separated by a character.
- **arrtocommastr(arr)**: Converts an array to a comma-separated string.

- **KB utilities**:
  - **qaddconval(con, key, conval)**: Adds a concept value to a KB concept list if unique.
  - **qaddstrval(con, key, strval)**: Adds a string value to a KB concept list if unique.
  - **convals(con, key)**: Fetches a multi-valued concept attribute from KB as an array.
  - **strvals(con, key)**: Fetches a multi-valued string attribute from KB as an array.
  - **convalsmax(con, key, max)**: Fetches a multi-valued attribute from KB as an array, returns 0 if the number of values exceeds max.
  - **kbchildrentoarray(parent)**: Copies KB children to an array.
  - **wordstodict(words)**: Builds an array of dictionary concepts for an array of words.
  - **wordstoconvals(words, key)**: Builds a unique array of concept values from word lookup.
  - **unioncons(c1, c2)**: Returns the union of two arrays of concepts, ensuring uniqueness.
  - **inhierarchy(con, parent_str)**: Checks if a concept is under another concept by name.
  - **inhier(con, parent_con)**: Checks if a concept is under another concept.
- **String manipulation**:
  - **strdetag(str)**: Removes HTML tags from a string.
  - **strdepunct(str)**: Removes punctuation from a string.
  - **cleantext(str)**: Cleans extra spaces and certain punctuation from a string.

  - **strtokenize(str)**: Tokenizes a string into an array of tokens.
  - **initials(str)**: Gets the initials of each word in a string.
  - **alphachars(str)**: Counts the number of alphabetic characters in a string.
- **Node attribute and feature utilities:**
  - **pnreplaceval(node, var, val)**: Replaces a value in a node's variable.
  - **pnreplacevalrange(var, val, start, end)**: Replaces a value in a range of nodes.
  - **pnaddstr(node, field, str)**: Adds a string to a node's variable.
  - **pnaddval(node, field, val)**: Adds a value to a node's variable.
  - **pnaddvalorig(node, field, ord, val)**: Adds a value to a node's variable at a specific position.
  - **pnaddvalopt(node, field, ord, val)**: Adds a value to a node's variable at a specific position (optional).
  - **pnaddvaluniq(x, field, val)**: Adds a value to a node's variable if unique.
  - **nodearrayadd(node, nm, len, val)**: Adds a value to an array in a node.
  - **nodearrayadduniq(x, field, val)**: Adds a value to an array in a node if unique.
  - **pnrpushuniq(n, key, arr)**: Pushes values onto a node variable, ensuring uniqueness.
  - **pnrmval(n, key, val)**: Removes a value from a node's list.
  - **rmlistval(list, val)**: Removes a value from a list.
  - **rmlistvalcase(list, val)**: Removes a string value from a list, case-insensitive.
  - **nodefeat(n, feat)**: Checks if a node's stem has a feature.
  - **verbfeat(n, feat)**: Checks if a verb's stem has a feature.
  - **rangefeat(start, end, feat, min)**: Checks a range of nodes for occurrences of a feature.
  - **rangefeatcount(start, end, feat)**: Counts occurrences of a feature in a range of nodes.
  - **pnchildsfeatcount(node, feat)**: Counts occurrences of a feature in a node's children.
  - **leftattr(n, attr)**: Gets the value of the leftmost node's attribute in a subtree.
  - **rightattr(n, attr)**: Gets the value of the rightmost node's attribute in a subtree.
- **Clause and phrase analysis**:
  - **clauselastnp(n)**: Checks if a clause ends in a noun phrase.
  - **clauseincomplete(n)**: Checks if a clause is transitive and missing an object.

- **clausecomplete(n)**: Checks if a clause can be standalone.
- **mhbvadv(n x1, n x2, n x3, n x4)**: Looks for adverbials in an `mhbv` phrase.
- **qclausevg(vg, clause)**: Examines a clause's verb group.
- **elliptedpassive(clause)**: Checks if a node is a passive subclause.
- **elliptedactive(clause)**: Checks if a node is an active subclause.
- **phrasalverbq(nverb, nprep)**: Checks if a verb and particle form a phrasal verb.
- **prepositionalverbq(nverb, nprep)**: Checks if a verb and preposition form a prepositional verb.
- **phrprepverbq(nverb, nprep)**: Checks if a verb and particle/preposition form a phrasal/prepositional verb.

- **Math and value functions:**
    - **minimum(a, b)**: Returns the smaller of two numbers.
    - **maximum(a, b)**: Returns the larger of two numbers.
    - **absolute(num)**: Returns the absolute value of a number.
    - **percentrnd(top, bot, n)**: Returns a percentage rounded to n decimal places.
    - **threenorm(str):** Normalizes a numeric string to three or more places.
    - **twonorm(str)**: Normalizes a numeric string to two or more places.
    - **PAD(str, places, ch)**: Pads a string to a given length with a specified character.
- **Date and time utilities**:
    - **monthtonum(text)**: Converts a month name or abbreviation to its numeric value.
    - **monthtonumstr(str)**: Converts a month name or abbreviation to a two-digit string.
    - **getdate(n)**: Computes a date string from node attributes.
- **Language and number utilities:**
    - **languageiso(str)**: Returns the ISO 639-1 code for a language name.
    - **languagefmiso(str)**: Returns the full language name for an ISO 639-1 code.
    - **convertwordnum(str)**: Converts a number word to its integer value.
    - **romantonum(str)**: Converts a roman numeral to its integer value.
- **Alignment and comparison**:
    - **alignNS(node, str)**: Aligns a node's text with a string.
    - **align(str1, str)**: Aligns two strings, returns 1 if aligned with high confidence.

    - **matcharrays(aa1, aa2)**: Traverses arrays until elements do not match, for finding meeting points.
    - **letord(c)**: Returns the order of a letter (1 for a, 2 for b, etc.).
- **Printing and formatting**:
    - **ljust(str, num, out)**: Left-justifies a string in a field.
    - **RJ(item, field)**: Right-justifies a string in a field.
    - **indent(num, out)**: Prints padding spaces.
    - **printch(ch, num, out)**: Prints a given number of characters.
    - **rjx(item, field, ch, out)**: Right-justifies something to print with a leading character.
    - **ctr(item, field, ch, out)**: Pretty-prints centered in a field.
    - **prettystrs(arr, ind, o)**: Pretty-prints an array of strings.
    - **prettypns(arr, ind, o)**: Pretty-prints an array of parse tree nodes.
    - **prettynodes(arr, o)**: Pretty-prints an array of nodes (debugging aid).
    - **pnstrpretty(n)**: Grabs a node's text for pretty printing, with length limits.
    - **pnstrmax(n, MAX)**: Grabs a node's text, delimited by length.
- **Miscellaneous utilities**:
    - **mirror()**: Creates a mirrored output file tree based on the input file path.
    - **mirrordir(outfolder, lastdirflag)**: Creates a mirrored output folder structure.
    - **strtophrase(str, croot)**: Traverses the KB hierarchy to build/get a phrase.
    - **strtodepunctphrase(str, croot, min)**: Traverses KB hierarchy to build/get a phrase, after depunctuating.
    - **lookupinternal(str, croot)**: Looks up a string in a given KB hierarchy.

Utility functions

`UtilityFuncs.nlp` is available when adding a pass to the analyzer sequence, by right-clicking **Library Pass | Utility Functions**. A somewhat different version is also available as the `funs.nlp` pass in the `parse-en-us` example analyzer.

This section organizes the functions of the `UtilityFuncs.nlp` pass into four tables, according to these topics:

1. English grammar
2. Vocabulary
3. Parse tree
4. General function

The following table lists functions related to English language grammar:

Functions	Description
`elliptedactive (clause)`	Check for ellipted active in clause.
`elliptedpassive (clause)`	Check for ellipted passive in clause.
`isnewsentence (node)`	Check if the node starts a new sentence.
`numbersagree (start, end)`	True if the range of nodes agrees on singular/plural.
`samevconj (v1, v2)`	Check if two verbs have the same conjugation.
`verbverbagree (first1, first2)`	Check agreement between two **_verb** nodes.
`vgagree (m, h, b, being, v)`	Check the agreement in the verb group. Return an array with agreement, passive voice, tense, and conjugation.
`vgvgagree (vg1, vg2)`	Check the agreement between two **_vg** nodes.
`vvagree (n1, n2)`	Check agreement between two **_verb** or **_vg** nodes.

Table appendix B.19: *Utility functions for English grammar*

The following table lists functions related to the dictionary and vocabulary:

Functions	Description
`getdate (n)`	Get the date from the node.
`lookupalpha (text, node)`	Look up an alphabetic word. Modifies vars in the given node.
`lookupalphadicttokz (text, node)`	Look up an alphabetic word (with **dicttokz** tokenize pass). Modifies vars in the given node.
`massnoun (n)`	True if given a mass noun.
`monthtonum (text)`	Convert month to number.
`monthtonumstr (str)`	Convert month to number string.
`number (n)`	Check singular/plural/any for noun.
`numberv (n)`	Return singular, plural, or any, for given verb's expectation from its preceding noun.
`nvstem (txt)`	Get stem from noun or verb word.
`nvstemunk (lc)`	Compute possible stem for unknown word. [Unimplemented] [empty]
`nvsuff (txt)`	Get suffix from noun or verb word.
`phrasalverbq (nverb, nprep)`	True if possible phrasal verb + particle.
`phrprepverbq (nverb, nprep)`	True if possible prep/phrasal verb + particle.

Functions	Description
prepositionalverbq (nverb, nprep)	True if possible prepositional verb + particle.
singular (n)	True if noun can be singular.
plural (n)	True if noun can be plural.
vconj (v)	Get verb conjugation. Return conjugation type or 0.
vconjq (v, conj)	Get verb conjugation. Return 1 if found, else 0.
verbfeat (n, feat)	True if verb stem has feature.

Table appendix B.20: Utility functions for the dictionary and vocabulary

The following table lists functions related to the dictionary and vocabulary:

Functions	Description
getrange (max)	Get real **first(A)** and **last(Z)** nodes matching rule, up to max element. Return [**nodeA,nodeZ,ordA,ordZ**].
getrangenodes (ofirst, olast)	Get real **first(A)** and **last(Z)** nodes matching given range of elements. Return [**nodeA,nodeZ,ordA,ordZ**].
literal (n)	True if node is literal.
nonliteral (n)	True if node is nonliteral.
strliteral (nm)	True if string is literal.
strnonliteral (nm)	True if string is nonliteral.
nodefeat (n, feat)	True if node has feature.
nodetext (n)	Same as **nodetreetext()**.
noderawtext (n)	Get node's verbatim text from input buffer.
nodetreetext (n)	Get plain, corrected, or modified text for node.
nodestreetext (s, e)	Get plain or corrected text for a range of nodes.
phrasetreetext (root)	Get plain or corrected text for node's subtree.
pnaddstr (node, attr, str)	Add string value to node's attribute.
pnnameinrange (name, s, e)	Check if name is in node range.
pnparent (n)	Fetch parse tree node's parent. Do not use **pnup()**.
pnreplacevalrange (var, val, start, end)	Replace **var's** value in node range.
prosifysimple (root)	Nonrecursive **prosify** for node's children.
prosify (...)	Prosify (i.e., convert subtree to prose-like string).
prosifyrec (...)	Recursive workhorse for **prosify()**.

Table appendix B.21: Utility functions for the parse tree

The following table lists KB and general utility functions:

Functions	Description
`absolute (num)`	Return the absolute value of **num**.
`addvalue (val, arr)`	Add value to the array, no checking. Return array.
`minimum (a, b)`	Return the minimum of two numbers.
`maximum (a, b)`	Return the maximum of two numbers.
`nameinlist (txt, arr, count)`	See if the name is in the given array and count. Return [1 if present, position].
`subnameinlist (txt, arr, count)`	See if the name is in (or starts) the given array and count. Return [1 if present, position].
`strdetag (str)`	Remove HTML tags from a string.
`qaddconval (con, key, conval)`	Add to kb concept list if unique. Return 1 if unique and added, else 0.
`qaddstrval (con, key, strval)`	Add to kb concept list if unique. Return 1 if unique and added, else 0.
`qaddstr (txt, arr)`	Add a string to an array if it is unique. Return a new array.
`qaddvalue (val, arr)`	Add value to the array if unique. Return a new array.

Table appendix B.22: *KB and general utility functions*

Join our Discord space

Join our Discord workspace for latest updates, offers, tech happenings around the world, new releases, and sessions with the authors:

https://discord.bpbonline.com

APPENDIX C
Miscellaneous Topics

Overview

We discuss various topics tangential to the main presentation of NLP++ and VisualText. This appendix provides overviews rather than detailed documentation. In particular, we address the main differences between the original Windows version and the current VS Code version of VisualText and NLP++. The new version greatly advances the capabilities and usability of the software, but some functionality, such as automated rule generation (RUG) and compiled analyzers, has yet to be made available in the current version.

Original VisualText

The VS Code version of VisualText IDE and the NLP engine runtime system are truly remarkable works, undertaken almost entirely by *David de Hilster*. Here we describe aspects and differences between these and the Original VisualText for Windows (by *TAI*). We note that the original VisualText is still in active use and has various capabilities not yet implemented in the new versions. The download link, for Windows only, is **https://www.textanalysis.com/Products/VisualText/vtpro123987/vtpro123987.html.**

Interconversion of analyzers, NLP++, and KBs

Various differences in the two systems require interconversions:

- **File types**: `.nlp` files vs. `.pat` files
- **Analyzer.seq file**: `nlp` vs. `pat` passes
- **.KB versus .KBB files**: An NLP++ analyzer for conversion in each direction
- **.DICT files**: An NLP++ analyzer for conversion in each direction

The following are the pending tasks:

- Synchronizing analyzers, e.g., tai-parse-en with its original analog, `TAIParse`
- Two-way interconversion of original VisualText analyzers and VS Code versions

Differences between versions

We discuss differences and tradeoffs in using Original versus VS Code.

Note that the Original VisualText IDE has been frozen at version 2.7.1.8, dating back to 2015. The NLP++ runtime system has undergone substantial updates.

Usability and integration

While the original version runs only on the Windows operating system, the current version runs on Windows, Linux, and MacOS. In addition, the current version deploys with software environments such as Python and is tightly integrated with GitHub.

The original version had to be purchased, while the current version is open-source and freeware.

Unicode

An important advantage of the NLP engine is that Unicode is handled very well. While an original VisualText IDE version for Unicode exists, it is not complete, and though the original NLP++ runtime has been updated, its handling of Unicode is not working yet.

Compiled analyzer

An advantage of the original VisualText is that it supports compilation of the NLP++ analyzer code. A compile analyzer button in the **graphical user interface** (**GUI**) generates a C++ code file for each analyzer pass, along with auxiliary files. C++ may be compiled with the Linux **Gnu compiler** (**gcc**) or *Microsoft Visual Studio*. The compiled analyzer code may still be executed in an interpreted or compiled mode.

Compiled KB and dictionary

Original and VS Code versions both embed the dictionary as a subsystem within the KB. Only the original supports compiling the KB (and therefore also the dictionary).

In the original, the interpreted KB is loaded by executing plain-text command files when loading an analyzer. A compiled KB file is generated via the Compile KB button in the VisualText IDE. As with the analyzer code, this generates various C++ files that can then be compiled with Linux gcc or Microsoft Visual Studio. Loading a compiled KB is nearly instantaneous, as compared with an interpreted KB.

There is also a stylistic difference in the way KB and dictionary knowledge are loaded. In the VS Code version, all knowledge is loaded prior to tokenization. If something new is to be added, it is placed directly in the interpreted `KBB` and `DICT` files. However, in analyzers such as parse-en-us, one finds passes that add knowledge in passes after tokenization. This is because a compiled KB (plus dictionary) is assumed to be loaded, which is hard-wired. So, as one develops an analyzer, it is convenient to add knowledge to particular passes, without having to recompile the KB with each addition. Loading knowledge should precede its first use (when desired, that added knowledge can be saved and compiled, creating a new KB version).

User project

Analyzer projects in the original version provide a **USER** folder of C++ files, in which developers may write C++ functions that can be called from NLP++ code, thereby extending the NLP++ language itself.

One example analyzer demonstrated embedding a third-party POS tagger as an NLP++ pass (with appropriate convertors for the tagger input and output).

GRAM tab

In the earliest days of TAI, our target analyzer was a job resume analyzer. Further, we were interested in ways to automate at least some of the NLP++ coding for a text analyzer.

David de Hilster's brainstorm was a GUI interface for highlighting and categorizing input text snippets via a KB hierarchy, dubbed the **grammar** (**GRAM**) subhierarchy. The various categories would have associated stubs, or empty passes, within a skeletal analyzer sequence.

For example, a developer could create a school concept in the GRAM tab hierarchy, then highlight school names in each resume, placing them under the school concept.

At any point, the *Slog* button in the GUI could be clicked, causing appropriate school rules to be embedded in the associated stub or analyzer pass. That process, called RUG, is discussed further in the following section.

In the **analyzer.seq** sequence file, regions of stub passes are delimited as follows:

```
/stub
# Stub passes here…
/end
```

Automated rule generation

While de Hilster conceived the automated construction of a text analyzer (or parts of one) by merely highlighting and categorizing input text snippets in the GRAM tab, it was left to *Meyers* to implement the automatic rule generation (or RUG) algorithms.

This is because an analyzer consists of a sequence, or pipeline, of passes; each stub pass must be *filled with rules* in turn. The RUG algorithm analyzes all the input files containing text snippets for a given stub pass, only up to the point of the current stub pass. Further, the RUG algorithm sees the state of the evolving parse tree at the current stub pass, building rules according to the top-level nodes corresponding to each text snippet.

Thus, the RUG process performs a partial analysis of each input text file many times, once for each stub being filled with rewrite rules.

The example resume analyzer successfully built its stub passes automatically, but the capability was unfortunately not used further (beyond the year 2003 or so).

Graphical user interface and runtime differences

The Original and VS Code GUIs differ dramatically. Beyond that, some behaviors are different as well. Log files, debugging files, and output files may go to different output folders, for example, both systems can execute a subtree of folders and files.

However, the Original loads the KB (and contained dictionary) ONCE and runs all the input files, so that the KB accumulates information across all the files. In contrast, the VS Code version RELOADS THE KBB and `DICT` files for every folder encountered in the subtree. Options to (1) retain the KB and (2) save it at any time would be useful.

NLP++ status and enhancements

In this book, we have noted various enhancements we would like to see in future versions of the NLP++ language, the VisualText IDE, and the NLP engine runtime system. The following are some of those wish list:

- **NLP++ pass file:**
  - **Code region following rule matching**: We have noted that the `@CODE` region operates before any rule matching occurs in a pass file. To execute NLP++ code after rule matching has finished, we need to use the `@CODE` region of a subsequent pass. A more modular and convenient approach would be a code region that operates after rule matching has concluded. It could be named `@POSTCODE`, `@AFTER`, etc.
  - **Pass variables**: Currently, we need to use G-variables (global variables) to pass information across regions of a pass file. Sometimes we use the current `X` context node to store information as well. Both methods have a more global visibility than is needed.

    A more modular approach would use variables whose scope is the current pass file, which could be named P-variables (or pass variables).
  - **Rule variables**: Similarly, we use S-variables (or suggested-node variables) to communicate across the `@CHECK` and `@POST` regions of a rule. However, these permanently reside in the suggested concept of a rewrite rule. An R-variable (or rule variable) could be implemented as a local variable visible only across the `@CHECK` and `@POST` regions associated with the current `@RULE` region.

- **NLP++ names:**
    - **Rule element names**: The names of NLP++ rule elements are restricted to alphabetic for literals, underscore with alphabetic for nonliterals, and special variables (like `_xALPHA`). We would like to see numbers and punctuation marks permitted in naming nonliteral elements.
    - **Function names**: Similarly, we would like to see numbers and punctuation marks permitted in NLP++ function names.

NLP++ actions we have discussed that actions are NLP++ functions that operate within rule contexts, during rule matching (i.e., pattern matching). Even so, actions sometimes overly restrict the type of acceptable arguments. For example, `singler(1,2)` is valid, but `singler(L("start"),L("end"))` is not. Actions are ancient, and we would like to see generalized versions as far as possible. One idea is to distinguish a restricted action name from its more general function counterpart.

Parse tree vs. KB

NLP++ addresses both parse trees and KB hierarchies (essentially trees as well), so it is easy for the programmer to make mistakes, using variables and functions for the wrong tree. Function names that start with `pn` and `kb` can help, and naming variables with these prefixes can help clarify the code base and reduce errors.

KB phrases and nodes

The backbone of the KB (and dictionary) consists of a hierarchy of concepts.

However, the KB also enables each concept to own a single unbranched phrase of nodes, not to be confused with rule phrases, parse tree phrases, and parse tree nodes. A KB node is equivalent to a concept, except that it is not attached to the hierarchy. Rather, the phrase of nodes can be used to store arbitrary, private information for the owning concept.

Join our Discord space

APPENDIX D
Full English Parser Reference

Discussion

The VS Code version of the full English parser is named parse-en-us and is one of the available example analyzers (**https://github.com/VisualText/nlpfix-analyzers**). The original version is called **TAIParse**, as it was developed at *Text Analysis International* (*TAI*), starting around the year 2001. Throughout the years, it has served as a template for various text analyzer applications. General enhancements and fixes have been fed back to the analyzer. Many changes are recorded by date. For example, searching the analyzer sequence for **`02 AM`** yields results like:

```
# CR:      03/20/02 AM.
```

The date that the function **`lookupalpha()`** and others were created by *Amnon Meyers*. Changes to parse-en-us are recorded as late as the year 2020. Note that TAIParse is still actively used, and updates to that have been made at least as late as June 2024 (A pending task is to synchronize these versions).

Analyzer sequence

We break up the analyzer sequence (or pipeline) into blocks of related passes and discuss these in detail in the following sections. The analyzer is bundled with the VS Code NLP++ extension and is available separately in a GitHub repository, at the URL **https://github.com/VisualText/parse-en-us**. The **`spec`** subfolder contains all of the pass files discussed in this appendix.

Function passes

The first block of passes consists of functions for **part of speech** (**POS**), semantics, questions, etc. These are described individually here and collected in the following table (*Table appendix D.1*).

- **dicttokz**: The first pass, as usual, is a rudimentary tokenizer pass. **`dicttokz`** creates a tokenized parse tree that omits all whitespace. This allows faster parsing as well as writing simpler rules lacking whitespace elements. Whitespace information is recorded as attributes on the adjacent parse tree nodes. Also, this tokenizer automatically decorates the parse tree with attributes taken from the KB dictionary, if present. Finally, the multi-pass pipeline architecture enables the analyzer to perform more sophisticated and complete tokenization in subsequent passes (see **`tok10`**, **`tok25`**, **`tok50`**, **`tok100`**, and so on).

- **doc**: A pass consisting entirely of commented lines, used for developer documentation.
- **funs.nlp**: A pass with general-purpose functions, collected and used during many years of analyzer development. [See *Appendix B*, section *funs.nlp*]
- **domfuns.nlp**: Placeholder functions for domain and application-specific semantics.
- **qsemfuns.nlp**: Placeholder for semantics of questions.
- **xmlfns**: Utility functions for outputting XML.

The initial passes of the English parser are summarized in the following table:

Pass	Type	File	Description
1	`dicttokz`	`nil`	Dictionary tokenizer, remove and record whitespace
2	`nlp`	`doc`	Analyzer documentation
3	`nlp`	`funs`	NLP++ utility functions
4	`nlp`	`KBFuncs`	**Knowledge base** (**KB**) functions
5	`nlp`	`posfuns`	POS tagging functions
6	`nlp`	`semfuns`	Semantic analysis functions
7	`nlp`	`qsemfuns`	Question-oriented semantic functions
8	`nlp`	`domfuns`	Domain-specific NLP++ functions
9	`nlp`	`xmlfns`	XML output functions

Table appendix D.1*: Initial passes of the English parser*

Functions in posfuns.nlp

The **`posfuns.nlp`** file contains approximately 50 functions, described in the following, that handle various aspects of POS tagging, verb group analysis, noun phrase processing, and grammatical structure reduction in natural language processing:

- **POS management functions (8 functions)**: Functions that handle the core mechanics of POS tagging, clearing POS assignments, setting POS tags, retrieving POS information from nodes, and managing POS-related node attributes:
    - **clearpos()**: Mark node as not receiving POS
    - **sclearpos()**: Mark suggestion as not receiving POS

  - **chpos()**: Rudimentary POS setting
  - **nodepos()**: Get POS for node
  - **setpos()**: Set POS if possible
  - **setposrange()**: Assign POS to a list of nodes
  - **setposcaps()**: Assign POS to list of caps
  - **forceposrange()**: Force assign POS to node range
- **Performance tracking and scoring functions (4 functions)**: Functions that implement accounting and evaluation systems for tracking rule performance, measuring POS tagging accuracy, and generating statistical reports on parser effectiveness:
  - **posacctini()**: Initialize accounting for rule performance
  - **posacct()**: Track accounting for rule performance
  - **posacctdump()**: Dump POS rule accounting for a pass
  - **scorenodepos()**: Score single POS against key
- **Verb group analysis functions (8 functions)**: Functions specialized in analyzing and processing verb groups, including handling **modal-have-be-verb (MHBV)** patterns, determining voice (active/passive), managing verb conjugations, and resolving ambiguous verb forms:
  - **mhbv()**: Handle verb group in a rule (MHBV)
  - **mhbvfix()**: Fix up a verb group
  - **fixvgattrs()**: Fix up tense and aspect for verb group
  - **fixvg()**: Fix up verb group (with compound support)
  - **fixvgsimple()**: Fix up simple verb group
  - **fixverb()**: Fix up lone verb
  - **vgassigned()**: Check if the verb group has been handled
  - **vgambigedn()**: Check if verb group is ambiguous `wrt -edn`
- **Noun phrase processing functions (6 functions)**: Functions that handle noun phrase construction and analysis, including processing individual nouns and adjectives within noun phrases, managing capitalization effects, and determining proper vs. common noun classifications:
  - **fixnouns()**: Fixup nouns in an NP
  - **fixnoun()**: Fixup individual noun info
  - **fixnounnonhead()**: Fixup nonhead noun in NP
  - **fixnounhead()**: Fixup head noun in NP
  - **fixadjs()**: Fixup adjectives in NP

  - **fixadj()**: Fixup individual adjective
- **Linguistic structure reduction functions (12 functions)**: Functions that convert raw alphabetic tokens into grammatical categories (noun, verb, adjective, adverb) and construct higher-level linguistic structures like noun phrases, verb groups, and adverbial phrases from component parts:
  - **alphatoverb()**: Smart group alpha to verb
  - **alphatovg()**: Smart group alpha to verb group
  - **alphatovgcopy()**: Smart group alpha to verb group, copy from given verb
  - **alphatonoun()**: Smart group alpha to noun
  - **alphatoadj()**: Smart group alpha to adjective
  - **alphatoadv()**: Smart group alpha to adverb
  - **alphaunambig()**: Reduce unambiguous alpha (with POS disregard)
  - **alphaunambigred()**: Reduce unambiguous alpha (old version)
  - **verbtovg()**: Reduce verb to verb group
  - **nountonp()**: Reduce noun to noun phrase
  - **groupone()**: Smart group of one node
  - **groupnp()**: Smart group nodes to noun phrase
- **Phrase construction and grouping functions (8 functions)**: Functions that intelligently combine multiple linguistic elements into coherent phrases, handling **Determiner-Quantifier-Adjective-Noun** (**DQAN**) patterns, prepositional phrases, and compound structures:
  - **prepnptoadvl()**: Reduce prep + NP to adverbial
  - **groupvgprep()**: Join verb and particle/preposition
  - **vgvgcompound()**: Glom two verb groups together
  - **fixnpnonhead()**: Fix adjective, noun, alpha in NP (non-head)
  - **fixnphead()**: Fix the head noun of NP
  - **dqaninfo()**: Setup variables for DQAN analysis
  - **fixaposs()**: Fix up apostrophe-s to verb
  - **vtreebanktopos()**: Convert Treebank to POS notation
- **Morphological analysis functions (4 functions)**: Functions that analyze word forms to determine comparative/superlative degrees for adjectives and adverbs, and handle conjugation patterns for proper POS assignment:
  - **adjconj()**: Get adjective form (comparative/superlative)
  - **advconj()**: Get adverb form (comparative/superlative)

  - **fixadv()**: Fixup adverb morphology
  - **fixvadj()**: Fixup adjective that is also verbal
- **Utility and helper functions (6 functions)**: Supporting functions that provide range-based operations, capitalization handling, copula identification, and various helper operations for the main parsing functions:
  - **sameposrange()**: Intersection of POS for node range
  - **cappos()**: Handle POS for capitalized word
  - **findven()**: Search inside verb group for first verb (must be **-en**)
  - **clausepos()**: Get verb POS for clause
  - **vgpos()**: Get verb POS for verb group
  - **copulaq()**: Check if verbal noun is copula

There are a total of around 50 functions providing a comprehensive toolkit for English grammatical analysis with particular strength in handling morphological ambiguity, complex verb constructions, and sophisticated noun phrase processing.

Functions in semfuns.nlp

There are 41 functions, described in the following, providing a comprehensive semantic analysis framework that builds KB representations of text meaning, handles reference resolution, manages entity relationships, and composes complex semantic structures from parsed linguistic elements. The system is particularly strong in handling discourse-level phenomena like anaphora resolution and cross-clause reference tracking:

- **Semantic infrastructure and initialization functions (3 functions)**: Functions that setup the semantic framework and manage the KB structure for semantic analysis:
  - **seminit()**: Initialize semantics for current parse, setup KB structures
  - **registerpersnames()**: Register person names in the dictionary based on text
  - **findconceptwithparent()**: Lookup semantic concept with given parent name
- **Node semantic extraction functions (3 functions)**: Functions that extract semantic information from parse tree nodes, handling stems, text, and semantic attributes:
  - **nodesem()**: Quick fetch of the *semantic* word for a node
  - **nodestem()**: Fetch stem for a node (lowercased)
  - **semrange()**: Look for semantic content in the range of nodes
- **Registration and KB management functions (7 functions)**: Functions that register various linguistic elements (sentences, clauses, objects, etc.) in the KB for semantic tracking:
  - **sentregister()**: Register a sentence in the KB
  - **clauseregister()**: Register a clause in the KB

- **advlregister()**: Register an adverbial in the KB
- **objectregister()**: Register an actor/object in the KB
- **stateregister()**: Record state in semantics
- **entregister()**: Register an entity reference in the KB
- **newevent()**: Register a new event in semantics

- **Parse tree traversal functions (6 functions)**: Functions that manually traverse different types of clauses and structures in the parse tree to extract semantic information:
    - **clausetraverse()**: Manually traverse a clause in the parse tree
    - **clauseadvltraverse()**: Manually traverse an adverbial in the parse tree
    - **advltraverse()**: Handle a non-clause adverbial
    - **advlshandle()**: Traverse tree of adverbials
    - **advlhandle()**: Handle a clause-independent adverbial
    - **complextraverse()**: Manually traverse a complex clause
- **Reference resolution functions (8 functions)**: Functions that resolve pronouns, objects, events, and entities by matching them with previously encountered elements in the text:
    - **resolveobjects()**: Resolve object reference to objects in text
    - **resolveobject()**: Resolve object reference to objects (exact match)
    - **resolvepro()**: Resolve pronoun reference to objects
    - **resolveevent()**: Resolve eventive NP reference to events
    - **resolveentity()**: Lookup entity reference in entities
    - **clauseresolve()**: Resolve inter-clause references
    - **mergableobjs()**: Check if object reference can be merged with the candidate
    - **anaphoric()**: Traverse events to resolve anaphora
- **Semantic composition functions (7 functions)**: Functions that combine semantic information from multiple sources and compose higher-level semantic representations:
    - **semnpnp()**: Compose semantics for two noun phrases
    - **semnpnouns()**: Get semantics from nouns into NP
    - **semvg()**: Semantics for verb groups
    - **semclause()**: Handle semantics of given clause
    - **semcompose()**: General semantic grouping function
    - **semcomposenp()**: General semantic grouping function for NP
    - **semcomposetwo()**: Compose semantics for two nodes
- **Attribute management functions (3 functions)**: Functions that handle copying and

merging of semantic attributes between different KB concepts:

- **mergeobjectattrs()**: Merge reference attributes into resolved object
- **copyobjectattrs()**: Copy reference attributes into resolved object
- **semactornode()**: Check if semantic content is a good actor

- **Named entity processing functions (2 functions)**: Functions specifically designed to handle named entity recognition and processing within semantic structures:
  - **nenoderange()**: Look for named entities in node range
  - **nechildren()**: Look for named entities in the node's children
- **Utility and navigation functions (2 functions)**: Supporting functions that provide navigation and lookup capabilities within the semantic knowledge structures:
  - **moveback()**: Given a KB clause object, back up one
  - **prevnp()**: Given a sentence node, find its last NP

KB passes

The passes listed in the following table initialize the analyzer and load additional information into the KB:

Pass	Type	File	Description
10	`nlp`	`ini`	Initializations for analyzer.
11	`nlp`	`kbload`	Augment KB dictionary, etc.
12	`nlp`	`kb_geo`	Add geography info to KB.
13	`nlp`	`kb_onto`	Setup an ontology hierarchy in KB.

Table appendix D.2: Initialization and KB passes

Initialization pass

The **`ini.nlp`** pass, described in the following, houses user initializations for the analyzer. Global variables control various aspects of the English parser's behavior, from input/output handling to semantic analysis and performance monitoring:

- **System configuration variables**: Variables that control basic system behavior and platform-specific settings:
  - **G("LINUX")**: Platform flag set to 0 (Windows) or 1 (Linux). Controls file path handling and workarounds for Linux systems. Currently set to 0 for Windows.
  - **G("verbose")**: Controls verbose output generation. Set to 1 to enable detailed logging and debugging information throughout the analysis.
  - **G("error")**: Controls error output generation. Set to 1 to enable error reporting

and diagnostic messages.

- **G("hilite")**: Controls highlighting passes for interactive sessions. Set to 1 to enable syntax highlighting in VisualText IDE sessions.

- **Input processing control variables**: Variables that determine how input text is processed and what format is expected:
  - **G("find html")**: Flag indicating whether to expect and process HTML/XML input. Set to 1 to enable HTML tag detection and processing.
  - **G("allcap")**: Flag for handling all-caps text. Set to 0 by default. When enabled, helps identify and process input text consisting of capital letters.
  - **G("pretagged")**: Flag indicating that input text comprises POS tags (in the style of **Penn Treebank**). Set to 0 for plain text input, 1 for pre-tagged input. Pre-tagged text sets can support automatic testing, scoring, and even automatic generation of analyzer rules and passes.
- **POS tagging configuration variables**: Variables that control the behavior of the POS tagging system:
  - **G("threshold")**: Confidence threshold (0 to 100) for outputting POS tags. Set to 0 to allow *guessing* when the system is unsure. Higher values require more confidence before assigning tags.
  - **G("posacct")**: Flag controlling whether to gather global data on POS tagging rule performance. Set to 0 by default. When enabled, tracks accuracy statistics.
  - **G("bracket")**: Controls noun phrase bracketing in output. Set to 1 to enable bracketing of noun phrases for clearer structural representation.
  - **G("conform treebank")**: Flag to make POS tagging conform to Treebank standards even when disagreeing with those assignments. Set to 0 by default.
- **Output format control variables**: Variables that determine the format and style of analysis output:
  - **G("xml recursive")**: Controls printing of the embedded tagged output file. Set to 0 by default. When enabled, produces XML-formatted output with recursive tagging.
  - **G("xml tags only")**: Controls whether to print only XML tags (excluding embedded text). Set to 0 to include both tags and text content.
  - **G("treebank")**: Flag for printing treebank-style headers in output. Set to 0 by default. When enabled, Treebank-compatible formatting headers are output.
- **Diagnostic and scoring variables**: Variables used for performance monitoring, debugging, and accuracy measurement:
  - **G("scorepos")**: KB concept for managing POS tagging scoring when processing

pre-tagged input. Tracks accuracy metrics.

- **G("mismatch verbose")**: Controls whether to print filenames with mismatch diagnostic output. Set to 1 to enable detailed mismatch reporting.
- **G("mismatch out")**: File handle for collecting single-word POS tagging mismatches when processing pre-tagged input.
- **G("zero out")**: File handle for collecting cases where no POS tag was assigned (zeros) during pre-tagged input processing.
- **G("score date")**: Flag to include date information with scoring output. Set to 1 to timestamp scoring results.

- **Semantic processing variables**: Variables that control semantic analysis and KB operations:
  - **G("semantic processing")**: Master flag controlling whether semantic analysis is performed. Set to 1 to enable semantic processing, including entity resolution and discourse analysis.
- **Development and logging variables**: Variables used for development tracking and usage monitoring:
  - **G("worklog")**: Flag controlling whether to log analyzer runs. Set to 1 in interactive mode to track usage patterns and development activity.
- **Temporary or utility variables**: Local variables used for initialization and setup operations:
  - **L("hello")**: Placeholder variable set to 0, likely used for testing or as a template.
  - **L("fname")**: Local variable for constructing file paths for various output files.
  - **L("file")**: Local variable for file path construction.
  - **L("out")**: Local variable for file handles when opening output files.
- **Special initialization logic**: The file contains several conditional initialization blocks:
  - **Pre-tagged input setup**: When `G("pretagged")` is enabled, the system sets up scoring mechanisms and opens files for collecting mismatch and zero-assignment statistics.
  - **Semantic processing setup**: When `G("semantic processing")` is enabled, calls `seminit()` to initialize the semantic analysis KB.
  - **Worklog setup**: When in interactive mode, sets up logging to track analyzer usage with timestamps and input file information.
  - **Platform-specific file handling**: Uses different file path formats for Windows vs. Linux systems based on the `G("LINUX")` flag.

Dictionary loading system

The **kbload.nlp** file is a comprehensive dictionary loading system that populates a KB with linguistic attributes for thousands of English words. It serves as the lexical foundation for the English parser by defining syntactic, semantic, and morphological properties of words. The following describes the functions and knowledge loaded via the **kbload.nlp** pass:

- **Dictionary management functions**:
    - **dictattr(word, attribute, value)**: The **main** function that adds attributes to dictionary words. It lowercases the word, retrieves or creates the dictionary concept, and assigns the attribute-value pair.
    - **finddictattr(word, attribute)**: Retrieves numeric-valued attributes from dictionary words with error handling.
    - **finddictsattr(word, attribute)**: Retrieves string-valued attributes from dictionary words.
- **Verb classification systems**: This is where verbs are added to the dictionary:
    - **Agent requirements**:
        - **agent-human**: Verbs requiring human-like agents (e.g., announce, say)
    - **Scalar change verbs**:
        - **vscalenum**: Verbs that take numeric values (e.g., rise 10%, fall 20%)
        - **vscalar**: Verbs with directional semantics: plus (enhance, boost), minus (curb, reduce), neutral (maintain)
    - **Complex verb patterns (Based on Longman Grammar codes)**:
        - **that-subjunctive**: Verbs taking subjunctive clauses (demand, insist, order)
        - **copula**: Linking verbs (be, become, appear, seem)
        - **trans/intr**: Transitivity markers
        - **T2, T3, T4, T5**: Various complementation patterns
        - **V2, V3, V4, V8**: Verb + noun + complement patterns
        - **D1**: Ditransitive verbs (give, show, teach)
        - **C1pr**: Verbs taking noun + prepositional complements
- **Phrasal and prepositional verbs**: Extensive catalog of verb-particle combinations with classification:
    - **Value 1**: Phrasal verbs (separable particles): call up, break down
    - **Value 2**: Prepositional verbs (inseparable): account for, apply for
    - **Value 3**: Both patterns are possible

For example, act out, back down, bring up, call off, cut down, etc. (hundreds of entries).

- **Adjective and adverb morphology**:
    - **Exception handling**:
        - **adj-plain**: Adjectives that appear to have comparative/superlative endings but are actually base forms (bitter, clever, proper)
        - **adv-plain**: Similar for adverbs (forever, however, rather)
        - **-er/-est**: Explicit marking of comparative/superlative forms, including irregular ones (better, best, worse, worst)
- **Participial adjectives**: Massive list (1000+ entries) of words marked with `jj-pref` indicating they can function as participial adjectives:
    - **Past participles used as adjectives**: abandoned, accepted, accomplished
    - **Present participles**: amazing, annoying, boring
    - **Un-prefixed forms**: unfinished, unlimited, unprecedented
- **Specialized categories**:
    - **Soft plurals**:
        - **soft-plural**: Plural nouns that can modify other nouns (futures, securities, funds)
    - **Common abbreviations**:
        - **common-cap**: Capitalized forms that act like regular words (PC, PCs)
    - **POS preferences**:
        - **prefer-verb**: Words strongly preferring verb interpretation when ambiguous
        - **prefer-adj**: Words strongly preferring adjective interpretation
- **Linguistic coverage**: The dictionary covers:
    - **Verb subcategorization**: Over 20 different complementation patterns
    - **Semantic classes**: Agent restrictions, scalar semantics, eventive nouns
    - **Morphological variants**: Comparative/superlative, participial forms
    - **Phrasal verbs**: Comprehensive coverage of English particle verbs
    - **Syntactic preferences**: Disambiguation hints for ambiguous words
    - **Integration with parser**: This dictionary provides the lexical foundation that enables:
        - **POS disambiguation**: Preference marking guides ambiguous cases
        - **Syntactic parsing**: Subcategorization frames inform phrase structure
        - **Semantic analysis**: Semantic features support meaning interpretation
        - **Morphological analysis**: Exception lists handle irregular forms

Tagging passes

The passes listed in the following table work on tagging words:

Pass	Type	File	Description
14	`nlp`	`tag50`	Handle (POS) tags in text.
15	`nlp`	`tag100`	Handle POS tags in text.
16	`nlp`	`tags100`	Handle POS tags in text.

Table appendix D.3: POS tagging passes

Summary of HTML/XML tagging files

This three-file system (*Table appendix D.3* above) provides a robust foundation for processing HTML/XML documents within the English parser, allowing text extraction while preserving document structure and semantic markup information. The following describes the tagging actions of the three pass files:

- **tag50.nlp**: HTML comment tag recognition:
  - **Basic HTML comment tag detection**:
    - **Scope**: Minimal focuses only on HTML comments
    - **Conditional execution**: Only runs if `G("find html")` is enabled
  - **Key features are**:
    - **Comment start detection**: Recognizes `<!--` pattern as `_commentTag`
    - **Comment end detection**: Recognizes `-->` pattern as `_EcommentTag`
    - **Simple structure**: Contains only two basic rules for comment boundary detection
  - **Rules are as follows**:
    - **_commentTag**: Matches the literal sequence `<, !, -, -`
    - **_EcommentTag**: Matches the literal sequence `-, -, >`
- **tag100.nlp**: Comprehensive HTML tag processing.

  Full HTML tag recognition and processing system:
  - **Scope**: Comprehensive HTML tag handling with semantic interpretation
  - **Conditional execution**: Only runs if `G("find html")` is enabled

  Key features of HTML header processing are:
  - **Dynamic header mapping**: Converts HTML header tags (`h1` to `h6`) to semantic codes:

        - `h1 | ha, h2 | hb, h3 | hc, h4 | hd, h5 | he, h6 | hf`
        - `Unknown headers | hx`
    - **Start or end tag distinction**: Handles both opening tags (`_ha`) and closing tags (`_Eha`)
    - **Generic tag processing**:
        - **Universal tag recognition**: Handles any HTML tag with pattern `<[/] ALPHA WILD>`
        - **Case normalization**: Converts tag names to lowercase
        - **Dynamic grouping**: Creates semantic groups based on tag names

  The following are the special cases:

    - **Comment integration**: Uses comment tags from `tag50.nlp` to create `_comment` groups
    - **Error recovery**: Handles malformed HTML like `<ALPHA>` patterns
    - **Character entities**: Recognizes HTML character entities and `ALPHA`

  The processing logic is as follows:

    - Extracts the tag name from HTML syntax
    - Determines if it's a closing tag (`/`) or an opening tag
    - Creates appropriate semantic node names
    - Groups the tag structure and assigns semantic labels

- **tags100.nlp**: HTML content zone processing.

  Extract and process content within HTML tags:

    - **Scope**: Content extraction from specific HTML semantic zones
    - **Conditional execution**: Always runs (no conditional guard)

  The following are the key features:

    - **Title processing**:
        - **Global title extraction**: Captures content between `<title>` tags as global title
        - **Text zone grouping**: Groups title content as `_TEXTZONE`
        - **Header flagging**: Marks title content as a header zone
    - **Header content processing**:
        - **Comprehensive header support**: Processes content for all header levels (`ha` through `hf`, plus `hx`)

- **Content extraction**: Extracts text content between opening and closing header tags
- **Zone classification**: Marks all header content as `_TEXTZONE` for further processing

- **Supported header types**:
  - **_title/_Etitle**: HTML title tags
  - **_ha/_Eha through _hf/_Ehf**: HTML `h1` to `h6` headers
  - **_hx/_Ehx**: Catch-all for other header patterns

The system integration is as follows:

- **Processing pipeline**:
  - **tag50.nlp**: Identifies HTML comment boundaries
  - **tag100.nlp**: Recognizes and categorizes all HTML tags, including comments
  - **tags100.nlp**: Extracts semantic content from within the recognized tags
- **Dependencies**:
  - `tag100.nlp` depends on `tag50.nlp` for comment tag definitions
  - `tags100.nlp` depends on `tag100.nlp` for tag structure recognition
  - All three work together to provide complete HTML document processing
- **Configuration**:
  - HTML processing can be disabled globally by setting `G("find html") = 0`
  - The system handles both well-formed and malformed HTML
  - Content extraction focuses on semantically important elements (titles, headers)

This three-file system provides a robust foundation for processing HTML/XML documents within the English parser, allowing text extraction while preserving document structure and semantic markup information.

Zap passes

`zap100` is a preprocessing step that organizes raw text into line-based structures while tracking paragraph boundaries, specifically designed for tokenization workflows that do not rely on whitespace preservation.

Both files serve cleanup and organization roles; `zap100` removes HTML artifacts after content extraction, while `LINES_nosp` (described earlier as working with `dicttokz`) organizes the cleaned text into structured line segments for further processing. Refer to the following table:

Pass	Type	File	Description
17	`nlp`	`zap100`	Zap certain ambiguous POS tags.
18	`nlp`	`LINES_nosp`	Segment lines in a whitespace-free parse tree created by **`dicttokz`** tokenizer.

Table appendix D.4: Cleanup and line-forming passes

The two passes of *Table appendix D.4* are described in more detail here:

- **zap100.nlp**: HTML tag removal:
  - **Purpose**: Clean up HTML tags after content extraction.
  - **Execution**: Only runs if `G("find html")` is enabled.

  Key features are as follows:
  - **Title validation**: Checks if a document title was found during processing:
    - Logs missing titles to `errhtml.txt` if `G("error")` is enabled
    - Logs found titles to `htmltitle.txt` if `G("verbose")` is enabled
  - **Tag removal**: Systematically removes all nodes marked with a `tag` attribute
  - **Clean-up strategy**: Uses `excise(1,1)` to completely remove HTML tag nodes from the parse tree
  - **Function**: Final cleanup pass that removes all HTML markup while preserving the extracted text content for linguistic analysis.
- **LINES_nosp.nlp**: Line segmentation without spaces:
  - **Purpose**: Segment text into lines for dictionary tokenization analyzers.
  - **Execution**: Always runs (no conditional guards) [described earlier, in discussion of `dicttokz`]

  Key features are as follows:
  - **Line grouping**: Creates `_LINE` nodes from any content followed by optional wildcards
  - **Newline tracking**: Uses `varz("NL")` and `var("NL")` to track newline information
  - **Paragraph detection**: Identifies potential paragraphs by counting newlines
    - Increments `X("PARS")` counter for potential paragraphs
    - Sets `S("PAR")` flag when multiple newlines are detected
  - **Flexible boundaries**: Uses `[unsealed]` to allow flexible line boundaries
  - **Single reduction**: Uses `singler(1,2)` to create single line nodes

Pre-tagged text passes

The pre-tagged text series of passes, listed in *Table appendix D.6*, deal with input text sets that use the Penn Treebank Project POS tags (**https://cs.nyu.edu/~grishman/jet/guide/PennPOS.html**), as listed for convenience in the following table:

Num	Tag	Description
1	`CC`	Coordinating conjunction
2	`CD`	Cardinal number
3	`DT`	Determiner
4	`EX`	Existential there (dummy sentence subject)
5	`FW`	Foreign word
6	`IN`	Preposition or subordinating conjunction
7	`JJ`	Adjective
8	`JJR`	Adjective, comparative
9	`JJS`	Adjective, superlative
10	`LS`	List item marker
11	`MD`	Modal
12	`NN`	Noun, singular or mass
13	`NNS`	Noun, plural
14	`NNP`	Proper noun, singular
15	`NNPS`	Proper noun, plural
16	`PDT`	Predeterminer
17	`POS`	Possessive ending
18	`PRP`	Personal pronoun
19	`PRP$`	Possessive pronoun
20	`RB`	Adverb
21	`RBR`	Adverb, comparative
22	`RBS`	Adverb, superlative
23	`RP`	Particle
24	`SYM`	Symbol
25	`TO`	to (English function word)
26	`UH`	Interjection
27	`VB`	Verb, base form (to eat)
28	`VBD`	Verb, past tense (ate, proved)

Num	Tag	Description
29	**VBG**	Verb, gerund or present participle (eating)
30	**VBN**	Verb, past participle (eaten, proven)
31	**VBP**	Verb, non-3rd person singular present (eat)
32	**VBZ**	Verb, 3rd person singular present (eats)
33	**WDT**	Wh-determiner
34	**WP**	Wh-pronoun
35	**WP$**	Possessive wh-pronoun
36	**WRB**	Wh-adverb

***Table appendix D.5**: POS tags used in the Penn Treebank Project*

The following table lists the pre-tagged pass files that handle input texts containing Penn Treebank tags:

Pass	Type	File	Description
19	**nlp**	**pre_100**	Handle pre-tagged text (e.g., Penn Treebank).
20	**nlp**	**pre_200**	Handle pre-tagged text.
21	**nlp**	**pre_300**	Handle pre-tagged text.
22	**nlp**	**pre_400**	Handle pre-tagged text.
23	**nlp**	**pre_500**	Handle pre-tagged text
24	**nlp**	**pre_600**	Handle pre-tagged text
25	**nlp**	**pre_zap**	Zap, splice items in pre-tagged text.
26	**nlp**	**pre_zap1**	Zap, splice items in pre-tagged text.
27	**nlp**	**pre_zap2**	Zap, splice items in pre-tagged text.
28	**nlp**	**pre_badeos**	Handle end-of-sentence in pre-tagged text.
29	**nlp**	**pre_form**	Handle formats in pre-tagged text.

***Table appendix D.6**: Pre-tagged pass files*

All these files are part of a pre-tagged text processing pipeline that only executes when **`G("pretagged")`** is enabled. They handle text that already contains POS tags in a specific format. These passes are for development and testing only, and can be deactivated or removed otherwise. The following describes these pass files in detail:

- **pre_100.nlp**: Special markers:
    - **Purpose**: Identifies special formatting markers in pre-tagged text

- **Functions**:
  - Converts `*x*` patterns to `_COMMENT` nodes
  - Converts lines of `=== (3+ equals)` to `_HRULE` (horizontal rule) nodes

- **pre_200.nlp**: Escape character processing:
  - **Purpose**: Handles escaped characters and special symbols
  - **Functions**:
    - Removes escape sequences (analyzers, `\|`)
    - Processes forward slashes followed by content
    - Removes square brackets `[ and ]`

- **pre_300.nlp**: POS tag structure parsing:
  - **Purpose**: Parses word/POS tag pairs and identifies structure
  - **Functions**:
    - Removes whitespace sequences
    - Creates `_pos` nodes from word/tag patterns
    - Handles malformed tagging with error reporting

- **pre_400.nlp**: POS tag collection:
  - **Purpose**: Extracts and stores POS tag information
  - **Functions**:
    - Collects POS tags ending with $
    - Builds `posarr` arrays of POS possibilities
    - Handles untagged content with the `nopos` flag

- **pre_500.nlp**: Token processing:
  - **Purpose**: Finalizes token processing and assigns POS arrays
  - **Functions**:
    - Assigns collected POS arrays to tokens
    - Handles multi-element texts by creating `_tok` nodes
    - Preserves POS information through tokenization

- **pre_600.nlp**: Dictionary lookup:
  - **Purpose**: Performs dictionary lookups on alphabetic tokens
  - **Functions**:
    - Calls `lookupword()` on alphabetic tokens within multi-token constructs
    - Enriches tokens with dictionary information

- **Pre_zap.nlp**: Comment cleanup:
  - **Purpose**: Removes comments and flattens line structure
  - **Functions**:
    - Removes `_COMMENT` nodes
    - Splices `_LINE` nodes to flatten structure
- **pre_zap1.nlp**: POS node cleanup:
  - **Purpose**: Flattens POS node structure
  - **Functions**: Splices `_pos` nodes to remove intermediate structure
- **pre_zap2.nlp**: Text or slash cleanup:
  - **Purpose**: Final cleanup of parsing artifacts
  - **Functions**:
    - Splices `_text` nodes to remove structure
    - Removes `_slash` nodes entirely
- **pre_badeos.nlp**: Blank line normalization:
  - **Purpose**: Fixes problematic blank lines in pre-tagged text
  - **Functions**:
    - Removes blank lines before alphabetic content
    - Removes trailing blank lines after content
- **pre_form.nlp**: Line formation:
  - **Purpose**: Creates proper line structures for further processing
  - **Functions**: Groups content into `_LINE` nodes, excluding blank lines and horizontal rules

Cycle 0 passes

The files listed in the following table work together to transform raw line-based input into structured text zones ready for linguistic analysis:

Pass	Type	File	Description
30	`nlp`	`CYCLE_0`	Formatting and preprocessing passes.
31	`nlp`	`qline100`	Segment and examine lines of text.
32	`nlp`	`textzone50`	Segment special text zones.
33	`nlp`	`textzone100`	Segment text zones.
34	`nlp`	`zaplines`	Remove line nodes in prose text zones.

Table appendix D.7: Cycle 0 passes creating text zones

The following describes the actions of the Cycle 0 pass files in detail:

- **CYCLE_0.nlp**: Preprocessing documentation stub:
  - **Purpose**: Documentation stub for Cycle 0 processing
  - **Functionality**: Minimal file serving as documentation placeholder for format processing (HTML) and text preprocessing
  - **Key features**:
    - Documents the concept of Cycle 0 as a preprocessing phase
    - Contains only initialization code with no active rules
    - Establishes a foundation for HTML and format processing
- **qline100.nlp**: Numbered line detection:
  - **Purpose**: Line examination and numbered line detection
  - **Functionality**: Identifies and processes numbered lines in text, converting them to text zones
  - **Key features**:
    - Detects numbered line sequences (1, 2, 3...)
    - Converts numbered lines to `_TEXTZONE` nodes
    - Identifies horizontal separator lines (dashes)
    - Tracks line numbering state in global variables
    - Renames qualifying lines for further processing
- **textzone50.nlp**: Text zone merging:
  - **Purpose**: Specialized text zone merging.
  - **Functionality**: Merges adjacent `_TEXTZONE` nodes when numbered lines are detected
  - **Key features**:
    - Conditional execution (exits if no numbered lines found)
    - Merges consecutive `_TEXTZONE` and `_LINE` nodes
    - Consolidates related text regions into unified zones
    - Operates only when `G("num lines")` is set
- **textzone100.nlp**: Text zone creation:
  - **Purpose**: Primary text zone creation from line sequences.
  - **Functionality**: Groups lines into paragraph-like text zones and removes blank lines.
  - **Key features**:

  - Creates **_TEXTZONE** nodes from line sequences
  - Handles first paragraph creation with special logic
  - Uses **paragraph variables** (**PARs**) for grouping decisions
  - Removes blank lines and whitespace through excision
  - Establishes basic document structure

- **zaplines.nlp**: Line node cleanup:
  - **Purpose**: Line node cleanup and statistics
  - **Functionality**: Removes **_LINE** nodes while counting processed lines
  - **Key features**:
    - Operates within **_TEXTZONE** contexts
    - Counts lines processed **(X("line count",2))**
    - Splices out **_LINE** nodes to clean up the parse tree
    - Final cleanup step in the line processing pipeline

Cycle 1 passes

The files listed in the following table represent the core tokenization pipeline, progressively refining tokens from basic cleanup through sophisticated linguistic analysis:

Pass	Type	File	Description
35	**nlp**	**CYCLE_1**	Tokenization, syntax, and initial semantics
36	**nlp**	**tok10**	Tokenize pre-tagged text
37	**nlp**	**tok25**	Reset tokens
38	**nlp**	**tok50**	Tokenize
39	**nlp**	**quotes100**	Flag tokens within quote marks
40	**nlp**	**tok100**	Tokenize
41	**nlp**	**punct100**	Handle punctuation
42	**nlp**	**punct200**	Handle punctuation
43	**nlp**	**dom100**	Domain tokenizer
44	**nlp**	**fnretok**	Multi-token function words
45	**nlp**	**date**	Date recognition and normalization

Table appendix D.8*: Initial Cycle 1 pass files*

- **CYCLE_1.nlp**: High confidence processing documentation:
  - **Purpose**: Documentation stub for Cycle 1 processing, comprising the core of the parser

    - **Functionality**: Placeholder documenting high-confidence standalone processes
    - **Key features**:
        - Documents Cycle 1 as high-confidence processing phase
        - Contains only initialization code with no active rules
        - Establishes framework for confident tokenization and parsing
- **tok10.nlp**: Pre-tagged text artifact handler:
    - **Purpose**: Handles artifacts from pre-tagged text sources
    - **Functionality**: Cleans up double dashes and ellipsis artifacts, groups punctuation sequences
    - **Key features**:
        - Processes double dash sequences (`-- and - -`) into `_dbldash` groups
        - Handles ellipsis patterns (`...`) as `_qEOS` end-of-sentence markers
        - Clears position information and sets `nopos` flags
        - Manages token dissolution and variable copying
- **tok25.nlp**: Token dissolution handler:
    - **Purpose**: Processes dissolved tokens for cleanup
    - **Functionality**: Removes tokens marked for dissolution through splicing
    - **Key features**:
        - Checks for dissolve flag on tokens
        - Splices out dissolved tokens from the parse tree
        - Operates within `_TEXTZONE` contexts
        - Simple cleanup mechanism for tokenization artifacts
- **tok50.nlp**: Advanced token analysis:
    - **Purpose**: Sophisticated token pattern recognition and classification
    - **Functionality**: Handles complex numeric patterns, abbreviations, and proper noun sequences
    - **Key features**:
        - Processes decimal numbers (`num.num`) and fractions (`num/num`)
        - Recognizes ordinal numbers (1st, 2nd, 3rd, 4th)
        - Handles capitalized sequences with connectors (`& /`)
        - Processes negative numbers (`-num`)
        - Identifies US state abbreviations with periods

    - Extensive pattern matching for specialized tokens

- **quotes100.nlp**: Quote context tracking:
    - **Purpose**: Tracks quoted text and applies special processing
    - **Functionality**: Monitors quote state and marks content within quotes
    - **Key features**:
        - Toggles global quote state with double quotes
        - Marks capitalized words in quotes as quoted and cap
        - Tags alphabetic content in quotes as quoted prose
        - Counts quoted capitals and prose statistics
        - Conditional execution (exits if no double-quotes found)
- **tok100.nlp**: Comprehensive retokenization:
    - **Purpose**: Advanced tokenization with idiom recognition and abbreviation handling
    - **Functionality**: Handles complex multi-word tokens, country names, and letter abbreviations
    - **Key features**:
        - Dissolves and splices tokens like `tok25`
        - Recognizes USA patterns (`u.s.a`, `u s a`) as country entities

    Creates letter abbreviations from cap sequences:

        - Handles complex abbreviation patterns with periods and whitespace
        - Sets semantic attributes (country, location, named entity types)
        - Advanced grouping and classification logic
- **punct100.nlp**: Punctuation and abbreviation processing:
    - **Purpose**: Handles periods, abbreviations, and punctuation-based tokenization
    - **Functionality**: Processes company designations, personal titles, and period handling
    - **Key features**:
        - Recognizes company suffixes (inc., co., corp., ltd., llc.)
        - Handles personal titles (mr., mrs., dr., sr., jr.)
        - Creates abbreviation layers for capitalized words with periods
        - Validates against spell-checking and dictionary lookups
        - Complex period disambiguation logic

        - Position and case-sensitive processing
- **punct200.nlp**: Advanced period handling:
    - **Purpose**: Handles unresolved periods and end-of-sentence issues
    - **Functionality**: Error tracking and cleanup for period-related parsing problems
    - **Key features**:
        - Conditional execution (exits if no unhandled periods)
        - Tracks false positives in period processing
        - Generates error logs for unhandled periods
        - Context analysis around problematic periods
        - Rearguard processing for missed punctuation patterns
- **dom100.nlp**: Domain-specific processing:
    - **Purpose**: Handles specialized domain terminology and patterns
    - **Functionality**: Processes business terms, stock symbols, and speech attribution
    - **Key features**:
        - Recognizes stock symbol patterns (`SYMBOL:EXCHANGE`)
        - Handles CEO/CEOs with semantic attributes
        - Processes quoted speech with said attribution
        - Geographic terms and idiomatic expressions
        - Double quote processing and speech tagging
        - Domain-specific semantic classification
- **fnretok.nlp**: Contraction retokenization:
    - **Purpose**: Handles English contractions and merged word forms
    - **Functionality**: Breaks contractions into constituent parts with proper tagging
    - **Key features**:
        - Processes negative contractions (won't, can't, don't, etc.)
        - Handles modal contractions with negation
        - Breaks I'm, you're, we're into subject + verb
        - Sets proper verb tenses and semantic attributes
        - Conditional execution (skips if pre-tagged)
        - Maintains grammatical relationships in contractions
- **date.nlp**: Date and time recognition:

- ○ **Purpose**: Comprehensive date pattern recognition and normalization
- ○ **Functionality**: Identifies various date formats and extracts temporal information
- ○ **Key features**:
  - ▪ Recognize time zones (GMT, PST, MST, CST, EST)
  - ▪ Processes numeric date formats (mm/dd/yyyy)
  - ▪ Handles month names (full and abbreviated)
  - ▪ Extracts day, month, year components
  - ▪ Normalizes two-digit years to four-digit format
  - ▪ Validates date ranges and reasonableness
  - ▪ Sets temporal semantic attributes and reference tracking

Word identification passes

These files, listed in the following table, form the lexical analysis pipeline progressively built from morphological analysis through named entity recognition to comprehensive lexical disambiguation:

Pass	Type	File	Description
46	`nlp`	`feat`	Feature handler.
47	`nlp`	`feat100`	Feature handler.
48	`nlp`	`city`	City name recognition.
49	`nlp`	`country`	Country name recognition.
50	`nlp`	`location100`	Location names.
51	`nlp`	`fnword`	More function-word recognition.
52	`nlp`	`num`	Numeric constructs.
53	`nlp`	`common`	Common words (e.g., irregular verbs).
54	`nlp`	`dictfix`	Dictionary word corrections and enhancements.
55	`nlp`	`lookup_word`	Dictionary word lookup.
56	`nlp`	`lex_unambig`	Unambiguous lexical assignments.

Table appendix D.9: *Word identification pass files*

The following describes the actions of each pass file in detail:

- **feat.nlp**: Morphological feature exceptions:
  - ○ **Purpose**: Handles morphological exceptions for verb forms

- **Functionality**: Identifies words ending in -ed/-ing that are not actually past tense or gerund verbs
- **Key features**:
    - Marks words like *need, feed, seed* as infinitive forms (not past tense)
    - Handles `-ing` exceptions like *bring, ring,* sing (not gerunds)
    - Sets stem attributes for morphological disambiguation
    - Prevents incorrect verb conjugation analysis

- **feat100.nlp**: Mass noun classification:
    - **Purpose**: Identifies and marks mass (non-count) nouns
    - **Functionality**: Comprehensive list of nouns that do not take plural forms
    - **Key features**:
        - Extensive vocabulary of mass nouns (advice, air, bacon, etc.)
        - Sets mass attribute for proper grammar processing
        - Covers abstract concepts, materials, and countless substances
        - Essential for determiner and quantifier agreement
- **city.nlp**: City name recognition:
    - **Purpose**: Automatically generated city name recognition
    - **Functionality**: Recognizes international city names as location entities
    - **Key features**:
        - Multi-word city names (*Alor Setar, Banda Aceh,* etc.)
        - Sets named entity attributes (*location, city, confidence 95%*)
        - Handles whitespace variations in compound city names
        - Extensive list of Asian and international cities
        - Proper noun classification with the singular number
- **country.nlp**: Country name recognition:
    - **Purpose**: Automatically generated country name recognition
    - **Functionality**: Recognizes country names as location entities
    - **Key features**:
        - Single and multi-word country names (*Sri Lanka*)
        - Named entity classification with location semantics

        - Country-specific semantic attributes
        - Confidence scoring (95%) for entity recognition
        - Focus on Asian countries in this implementation

- **location100.nlp**: General location processing:
    - **Purpose**: Advanced location entity recognition and classification
    - **Functionality**: Handles various types of geographic and institutional locations
    - **Key features**:
        - Infrastructure recognition (highways, freeways, trails)
        - Geographic regions (provinces, islands, oceans)
        - Official titles (Secretary of State)
        - Specific locations (*Andaman and Nicobar Islands, Indian Ocean*)
        - Flexible pattern matching for complex location names
- **fnword.nlp**: Function word classification:
    - **Purpose**: Comprehensive function word processing and pronoun handling
    - **Functionality**: Classifies determiners, pronouns, and special word categories
    - **Key features**:
        - Pronoun classification (subject/object: he/him, she/her, etc.)
        - Determiner handling (a, the, these + "us")
        - Indefinite pronouns (anybody, everyone, something)
        - Negative pronouns (nobody, nothing)
        - Verb conjugation requirements for pronouns
        - Semantic person attributes
- **num.nlp**: Numeric pattern recognition:
    - **Purpose**: Advanced numeric pattern processing and formatting
    - **Functionality**: Handles money, percentages, phone numbers, and measurements
    - **Key features**:
        - Percentage recognition (num + %)
        - Money formatting with proper decimal handling
        - Phone number patterns (xxx-xxx-xxxx, (xxx)xxx-xxxx)

        - Currency conversion for cents/pennies
        - Quantity and measurement semantics
        - Modal/determiner cleanup (splicing artifacts)
- **common.nlp**: Common word processing:
    - **Purpose**: High-frequency word disambiguation and correction
    - **Functionality**: Handles common words with multiple POS possibilities
    - **Key features**:
        - Position-sensitive processing (only as adjective vs adverb)
        - POS disambiguation for frequent words (best, data, one, first)
        - Mass noun marking (data)
        - Superlative or comparative handling
        - Treebank conformance for standard POS tags
        - Context-dependent classification
- **dictfix.nlp**: Dictionary correction system:
    - **Purpose**: Corrects and enhances dictionary entries for better parsing
    - **Functionality**: Fixes POS assignments and removes erroneous entries
    - **Key features**:
        - Multi-POS word corrections (affiliate, bar, giant)
        - Removes archaic or rare word senses (even as nouns)
        - Confidence weighting for common usages
        - Stem assignment and semantic attributes
        - Error correction for dictionary inconsistencies
        - Dynamic dictionary modification
- **lookup_word.nlp**: Dictionary lookup engine:
    - **Purpose**: Core dictionary lookup functionality
    - **Functionality**: Looks up words in KB and assigns linguistic attributes
    - **Key features**:
        - Case handling and capitalization detection
        - Unknown word tracking and logging
        - Automatic grouping by POS (prep, det, conj)

- Stem assignment for unknown words
- Dictionary integration with error handling
- Verbose logging for analysis

- **lex_unambig.nlp**: Lexical disambiguation:
  - **Purpose**: Resolves unambiguous POS assignments
  - **Functionality**: Groups words with single POS possibilities and handles high-confidence assignments
  - **Key features**:
    - Unambiguous POS grouping (pos num == 1)
    - High-confidence verb/adverb assignment (>= 90% confidence)
    - Automatic stem generation and semantic assignment
    - Number determination for nouns (singular/plural)
    - Confidence-based classification system
    - Node copying and attribute preservation

Tokenization and entity processing

The files listed in the following table represent advanced tokenization and entity processing, progressively refining from basic tokenization through sophisticated named entity recognition and domain-specific analysis:

Pass	Type	File	Description
57	`nlp`	`tok150`	Multi-word tokens.
58	`nlp`	`dom150`	Idioms and domain-specific tokens.
59	`rec`	`tok175`	Recursive tokenizer pass.
60	`nlp`	`entity100`	Named entity recognition.
61	`nlp`	`tok200`	More tokenization.
62	`nlp`	`lex_unambig2`	Recognize disambiguated tokens.
63	`nlp`	`hilite_alpha`	Highlight unreduced alphabetic tokens.
64	`nlp`	`dom175`	Domain capitalized phrases and others.
65	`nlp`	`caps50`	General capitalized phrases.
66	`nlp`	`incap100`	Process inside capitalized phrases.
67	`nlp`	`dom200`	Domain and idiomatic patterns.

***Table appendix D.10**: Tokenization and entity-processing pass files*

The following describes the actions of the tokenization and entity-processing passes in detail:

- **tok150.nlp**: Advanced tokenization post-processing:
    - **Purpose**: Post-lexical tokenization for multi-token patterns
    - **Functionality**: Handles complex tokenization after individual word analysis, skips pre-tagged text
    - **Key features**:
        - Identifies multi-word capitalized sequences
        - Processes alpha-punct-alpha patterns
        - Removes parenthetical expressions ((), [], {})
        - Marks parenthetical content before excision
        - Conditional execution (exits if pre-tagged)
- **dom150.nlp**: Hyphenated term recognition:
    - **Purpose**: Specialized processing for hyphenated compound terms
    - **Functionality**: Recognizes domain-specific hyphenated adjectives and nouns from pre-tagged text
    - **Key features**:
        - Handles business terms (short-term, pro-forma, buy-out)
        - Statistical POS assignment (77% adjectives for alpha-alpha compounds)
        - Capitalization detection for proper nouns
        - Domain-specific patterns (high-technology, stock-index)
        - Treebank conformance for financial/business terminology
- **tok175.nlp**: Complex hyphenated patterns:
    - **Purpose**: Advanced hyphenated token processing
    - **Functionality**: Handles sophisticated hyphenated constructions and age expressions
    - **Key features**:
        - Age patterns (num-year-old)
        - Numeric sequences (1-for-2, 2-out-of-3)
        - Alpha-conjunction-alpha patterns (alpha-and-alpha)
        - Context-sensitive noun vs. adjective assignment
        - Prevents double-processing with hyphenated flag
        - Statistical defaults for ambiguous patterns

- **entity100.nlp**: Named entity recognition:
    - **Purpose**: Comprehensive named entity identification and classification
    - **Functionality**: Recognizes organizations, locations, and person entities with confidence scoring
    - **Key features**:
        - International organizations (United Nations, UN, EU)
        - Media entities (BBC, NBC, CNN, Reuters)
        - US state abbreviations (n.h. for New Hampshire)
        - Multi-word entity handling with whitespace flexibility
        - Confidence scoring (85 to 95%) for entity types
        - Person name registration for discourse tracking
- **tok200.nlp**: Final tokenization cleanup:
    - **Purpose**: Final tokenization pass with monetary and compound processing
    - **Functionality**: Handles remaining tokens, money expressions, and compound noun patterns
    - **Key features**:
        - Token dissolution and splicing like previous tok files
        - Money recognition (num thousand/million/billion)
        - Specialized financial patterns ($num-a-share)
        - Compound noun processing (noun-noun patterns)
        - End-of-sentence period handling
        - Adjective disambiguation with POS constraints
- **lex_unambig2.nlp**: Secondary lexical disambiguation:
    - **Purpose**: Second pass unambiguous lexical classification
    - **Functionality**: Identical to `lex_unambig.nlp` but for the later processing stage
    - **Key features**:
        - Unambiguous POS assignment (pos num == 1)
        - High-confidence verb/adverb grouping (>= 90%)
        - Automatic stem generation and semantic assignment
        - Node copying and attribute preservation
        - Handles remaining uncharacterized alphabetic tokens

- **hilite_alpha.nlp**: Alpha token highlighting:
    - **Purpose**: Conditional alpha token highlighting for analysis
    - **Functionality**: Simple pass-through highlighting when `hilite` mode is enabled
    - **Key features**:
        - Conditional execution (exits unless `G("hilite")` is set)
        - Matches sequences of alphabetic tokens
        - No-operation processing (highlighting only)
        - Analysis/debugging tool for alpha token patterns
- **dom175.nlp**: Named entity extension:
    - **Purpose**: Extends named entities with additional capitalized terms
    - **Functionality**: Builds on existing named entities by adding adjacent capitalized words
    - **Key features**:
        - Extends person/organization entities with additional names
        - Title capitalization in quotes
        - Conjunction patterns (neither...nor, either...or)
        - Person name registration for tracking
        - Context-sensitive entity type inheritance
        - Complex capitalization pattern handling
- **caps50.nlp**: Capitalization analysis:
    - **Purpose**: Analyzes capitalization patterns for sentence boundaries and proper nouns
    - **Functionality**: Handles mixed-case text regions and sentence-initial capitalization
    - **Key features**:
        - Sentence-initial capitalization detection
        - Quote context handling (quoted vs. prose regions)
        - Inflected verb detection at sentence start
        - Numeric quantifier + adjective patterns
        - Date and acronym recognition
        - Defers capitalization decisions for complex cases

- **incap100.nlp**: Internal caps processing:
    - o **Purpose**: Processes capitalized content within existing caps nodes
    - o **Functionality**: Refines named entity classification within capitalized phrases
    - o **Key features**:
        - ▪ Person title + name pattern recognition
        - ▪ Organization keyword detection (division, department, university)
        - ▪ Entity type propagation to parent nodes
        - ▪ Person name registration and tracking
        - ▪ Confidence scoring refinement (80 to 90%)
        - ▪ Complex nested entity handling
- **dom200.nlp**: Comprehensive domain processing:
    - o **Purpose**: Extensive domain-specific pattern recognition for business and general text
    - o **Functionality**: Large-scale domain pattern processing with company, idiom, and measurement handling
    - o **Key features**:
        - ▪ Company name + designation patterns
        - ▪ Idiomatic verb phrases (look forward to)
        - ▪ Age expressions with number agreement (10-day old vs. days old)
        - ▪ Positional adverb handling (about, around)
        - ▪ Financial terminology and measurements
        - ▪ Complex domain-specific semantic assignment

Sentence passes

The files listed in the following table work in sequence for sentence processing. The pipeline handles dynamic sentence break discovery (**`sent50`**), groups tokens into sentences (**`sent100`**), and cleans up temporary markers (**`sent125`**) to produce clean sentence structures ready for syntactic analysis.

Pass	Type	File	Description
68	**`nlp`**	**`sent50`**	Identify sentence breaks.
69	**`nlp`**	**`sent100`**	Segment sentences.
70	**`nlp`**	**`sent125`**	Remove end-of-sentence tokens.

***Table appendix D.11**: Sentence-processing pass files*

The following describes the actions of the sentence-processing passes in detail:

- **sent50.nlp**: New sentence break processing:
    - **Purpose**: Processes newly discovered sentence breaks
    - **Functionality**: Converts tokens marked with end-of-sentence flags into formal `_EOS` markers
    - **Key features**:
        - Conditional execution (exits unless `G("eos")` is set)
        - Identifies tokens with `eos` attribute
        - Creates `_EOS` nodes from marked tokens
        - Simple transformation for dynamic sentence boundary detection
        - Works with runtime sentence break discovery
- **sent100.nlp**: Primary sentence formation:
    - **Purpose**: Main sentence boundary detection and sentence node creation
    - **Functionality**: Groups tokens into sentence units based on end-of-sentence markers
    - **Key features**:
        - Creates unsealed `_sent` nodes from token sequences
        - Handles multiple `_EOS` types (`_qEOS` for periods, `_EOS` for discovered breaks)
        - Manages quote and bracket contexts (", (, [, <,),], >, etc.)
        - Lookahead processing for period-based sentence endings
        - Fallback sentence creation for remaining ungrouped content
        - Complex punctuation handling around sentence boundaries
- **sent125.nlp**: EOS marker cleanup:
    - **Purpose**: Removes EOS markers after sentence formation
    - **Functionality**: Cleans up temporary EOS nodes within formed sentences
    - **Key features**:
        - Conditional execution (exits unless `G("eos")` is set)
        - Operates within `_sent` contexts
        - Splices out `_EOS` nodes to clean parse tree
        - Final cleanup step in the sentence processing pipeline
        - Maintains sentence structure while removing temporary markers

Syntactic parsing passes

Syntactic parsing is accomplished in multiple passes, performing high-confidence actions first, and using those to increase the confidence of subsequent parsing passes. This constitutes a confidence-first approach to parsing, ideally yielding a single best-first parse tree.

Parsing further consists of reducing POS ambiguities and otherwise gathering information to more accurately perform subsequent parsing actions.

Rather than unconstrained recursive parsing, multiple passes allow explicit control and ordering of parsing, enabling the most accurate best-first results.

The files listed in the following table represent the core syntactic analysis pipeline, progressively building from local high-confidence patterns through comprehensive recursive grammar to final clause-level analysis:

Pass	Type	File	Description
71	`rec`	`pos10`	Recursive parsing pass.
72	`rec`	`inc100`	Recursive incremental left-to-right parser.
73	`nlp`	`inc300`	Incremental left-to-right parsing.
74	`nlp`	`pos25`	Pre-recursive parsing.
75	`rec`	`pos50`	Workhorse recursive parser pass.
76	`nlp`	`study100`	After the recursive parser, study the state of the parse.
77	`nlp`	`pos75`	Continue syntactic parsing.
78	`nlp`	`mhbv100`	Parse verb groups (MHBV).
79	`nlp`	`dqan100`	Parse noun phrases (DQAN).
80	`nlp`	`phr50`	Parse sentence constituent phrases.
81	`nlp`	`pos100`	POS tagging using context.
82	`nlp`	`caps100`	Parse capitalized phrases.
83	`rec`	`pos200`	Additional recursive parser.
84	`nlp`	`dqan200`	Parse noun phrases (DQAN).
85	`nlp`	`pos300`	Additional parsing pass.

***Table appendix D.12**: Syntactic parsing pass files*

The following describes the actions of the syntactic parsing passes in detail:

- **pos10.nlp**: High-confidence local POS tagging:
    - o **Purpose**: Local, high-confidence POS disambiguation within sentences
    - o **Functionality**: Handles determiner-alpha patterns and number agreement for early POS resolution

- **Key features**:
  - Determiner + unknown word patterns (det alpha)
  - Number agreement checking between determiners and nouns
  - Verb conjugation analysis for ambiguous words
  - Unknown word conversion to nouns
  - Position-sensitive POS assignment with confidence thresholds

- **inc100.nlp**: Incremental left-to-right processing:
  - **Purpose**: Incremental analyzer for left-to-right sentence processing
  - **Functionality**: Progressive disambiguation using sentence-initial patterns and context
  - **Key features**:
    - Sentence-initial adverb identification (^ alpha ,)
    - Subject-verb patterns that complement
    - Incremental verb group formation
    - Context-sensitive POS assignment
    - Performance optimization through early disambiguation
- **inc300.nlp**: Incremental processing extension:
  - **Purpose**: Extended incremental processing (currently minimal)
  - **Functionality**: Placeholder for additional incremental processing rules
  - **Key features**:
    - Empty implementation (only header and basic setup)
    - Framework for future incremental analysis
    - Reserved for advanced left-to-right processing
- **pos25.nlp**: Pre-recursive POS processing:
  - **Purpose**: Non-recursive POS tagging before the main recursive parser
  - **Functionality**: Performance enhancement through early pattern recognition
  - **Key features**:
    - Complex DQAN patterns
    - Multi-word noun phrase formation
    - Number agreement verification
    - Sentence-boundary handling
    - Extensive pattern matching for common constructions (3560+ lines)

- **pos50.nlp**: Recursive grammar workhorse:
    - **Purpose**: Main high-confidence recursive grammar processing
    - **Functionality**: Core disambiguation and syntactic analysis engine
    - **Key features**:
        - Massive rule set (17,000+ lines) for comprehensive parsing
        - Recursive pattern matching for complex constructions
        - Determiner and possessive handling
        - Noun phrase formation with agreement checking
        - Central hub for grammatical disambiguation
- **study100.nlp**: Rule generation and analysis:
    - **Purpose**: Study tool for analyzing alpha token clusters and generating rules
    - **Functionality**: Conditional analysis tool for parser development and debugging
    - **Key features**:
        - Conditional execution (only runs in verbose mode)
        - Alpha cluster counting and analysis
        - Rule pattern generation for development
        - Context analysis around token sequences
        - Output logging for parser research
- **pos75.nlp**: Intermediate POS processing:
    - **Purpose**: Intermediate-level POS disambiguation and phrase formation
    - **Functionality**: Handles specific syntactic patterns and phrase construction
    - **Key features**:
        - Verb-to-noun conversions for `-ing` forms
        - Prepositional phrase processing
        - Adjective coordination (adj + conj + adj)
        - Context-sensitive POS assignment
        - Noun phrase formation in specific contexts
- **mhbv100.nlp**: MHBV processing:
    - **Purpose**: Complex verb group formation with auxiliary verbs
    - **Functionality**: Handles MHBV sequences with agreement checking

- **Key features**:
    - MHBV pattern recognition (modal + have + be + verb)
    - Verb agreement validation across auxiliary chains
    - Negation handling within verb groups
    - Voice assignment (active/passive)
    - Complex verb group formation with semantic attributes

- **dqan100.nlp**: DQAN noun phrase formation:
  - **Purpose**: DQAN phrase construction
  - **Functionality**: Forms noun phrases from DQAN sequences with agreement checking
  - **Key features**:
    - Complex DQAN pattern matching
    - Number agreement verification
    - Possessive pronoun handling
    - Noun phrase grouping and attribute assignment
    - Position-sensitive processing (sentence-initial patterns)
- **phr50.nlp**: Phrase-level processing:
  - **Purpose**: Higher-level phrase construction and coordination
  - **Functionality**: Handles verb group coordination and complex phrase patterns
  - **Key features**:
    - Verb group coordination (vg conj vg)
    - Voice agreement in coordinated structures
    - Complex phrase patterns (vg np prep np vg)
    - Noun phrase formation in larger contexts
    - Phrase-level semantic assignment
- **pos100.nlp**: Contextual POS assignment:
  - **Purpose**: Context-driven POS disambiguation
  - **Functionality**: Uses the surrounding context for POS decisions
  - **Key features**:
    - Determiner context for noun assignment
    - Verb group + determiner + alpha patterns

        - Context-sensitive noun vs. adverb disambiguation
        - Voice assignment for verb groups
        - Complex multi-word pattern processing

- **caps100.nlp**: Capitalized phrase processing:
    - **Purpose**: Handles capitalized word sequences and proper noun formation
    - **Functionality**: Groups capitalized words into proper noun phrases
    - **Key features**:
        - Multi-word capitalized sequence processing
        - Named entity formation from caps sequences
        - Unknown capitalized word handling
        - Person name recognition and domain semantics
        - Proper noun classification with confidence scoring
- **pos200.nlp**: Advanced POS processing:
    - **Purpose**: Advanced POS processing with list and coordination handling
    - **Functionality**: Handles noun phrase lists and complex syntactic patterns
    - **Key features**:
        - Noun phrase list formation (noun, noun, conj noun)
        - List extension algorithms
        - Passive voice recognition (`-en` verb forms)
        - Complex coordination patterns
        - Advanced syntactic disambiguation
- **dqan200.nlp**: Extended DQAN processing:
    - **Purpose**: Extended DQAN processing
    - **Functionality**: Handles complex DQAN patterns with particle and verb integration
    - **Key features**:
        - Particle + DQAN patterns
        - Verb group formation from auxiliary sequences
        - Complex number agreement checking
        - MHBV integration
        - Advanced noun phrase construction

- **pos300.nlp**: Final POS processing:
  - **Purpose**: Final-stage POS processing and clause formation
  - **Functionality**: Handles remaining syntactic patterns and clause-level constructions
  - **Key features**:
    - Clausal complement processing (that-clauses)
    - Apposition handling (noun, noun constructions)
    - Final verb group disambiguation
    - Clause-level pattern recognition
    - Voice and tense finalization

Segmentation passes

At this point in the parse, we group non-constituent groups of nodes loosely into segment nodes and then examine within those segments.

The files represent advanced syntactic processing, progressively building from segmentation through conjunction analysis to clause-level processing with sophisticated coordination and voice assignment.

Pass	Type	File	Description
86	`nlp`	`seg100`	Initial segmenter.
87	`nlp`	`qseg100`	Parse inside segments.
88	`nlp`	`sent200`	Parse inside sentences.
89	`nlp`	`qconj100`	Study conjugation.
90	`nlp`	`qseg125`	Parse inside segments.
91	`nlp`	`qconj200`	Study conjugation.
92	`rec`	`qsent50`	Recursive parse in sentences.
93	`rec`	`pos400`	Recursive POS tagging.

Table appendix D.13: Segmentation and recursive parsing pass files

The following describes the actions of the segmentation and recursive parsing passes in detail:

- **seg100.nlp**: Noun phrase segmentation:
  - **Purpose**: Advanced noun phrase formation from alpha token sequences
  - **Functionality**: Handles complex multi-word noun phrases with DQAN patterns
  - **Key features**:
    - DQAN + alpha sequences (det quan adj alpha+)

        - Verb infinitive to noun conversion
        - Number agreement checking and validation
        - Head vs. non-head noun assignment
        - Complex noun phrase construction with multiple alpha tokens
- **qseg100.nlp**: Segment internal processing:
    - **Purpose**: Processes content within identified segments for noun phrase formation
    - **Functionality**: Analyzes segment internals and converts segments to noun phrases
    - **Key features**:
        - Operates within **_seg** nodes to process contents
        - DQAN + alpha-alpha pattern handling
        - Number agreement validation between determiners and head nouns
        - POS assignment for alpha tokens within segments
        - Segment-to-NP conversion with attribute preservation
- **sent200.nlp**: Advanced sentence processing:
    - **Purpose**: Higher-level sentence processing with coordination and voice assignment
    - **Functionality**: Handles complex sentence patterns and passive voice detection
    - **Key features**:
        - NP coordination (np conj np) with verb group integration
        - Passive voice assignment for comma-separated constructions
        - Segment integration with adjective/noun resolution
        - Complex sentential patterns with adverbial modifications
        - Context-sensitive voice assignment (active/passive)
- **qconj100.nlp**: Conjunction analysis:
    - **Purpose**: Analyzes and processes conjunction patterns
    - **Functionality**: Handles coordination of noun phrases and verb groups
    - **Key features**:
        - NP coordination (np conj np) in prepositional contexts
        - Verb group coordination with voice agreement
        - Parallel construction analysis for segment resolution

        - Conjunction binding and semantic composition
        - Context-sensitive coordination processing
- **qseg125.nlp**: Segment resolution:
    - **Purpose**: Resolves segments marked for noun phrase conversion
    - **Functionality**: Converts resolved segments to proper noun phrases
    - **Key features**:
        - Processes segments marked with `resolve = "np"`
        - Alpha-alpha-alpha pattern conversion to noun phrases
        - Head noun assignment and non-head processing
        - Simple segment-to-NP transformation
        - Final segment resolution step
- **qconj200.nlp**: Advanced conjunction processing:
    - **Purpose**: Complex conjunction handling with semantic composition
    - **Functionality**: Advanced coordination patterns and semantic integration
    - **Key features**:
        - Complex NP list coordination (np, np, conj np)
        - Date-sensitive coordination handling
        - NP of NP semantic composition with new text generation
        - Clause formation from coordinated non-verb regions
        - Advanced semantic attribute composition
- **qsent50.nlp**: Sentence-level processing:
    - **Purpose**: Sentence-level pattern recognition and structure assignment
    - **Functionality**: Handles complex sentence patterns and verb group formation
    - **Key features**:
        - Sentence-initial verb recognition with pronoun objects
        - Complex NP coordination (np and np, np of np and np)
        - Prepositional phrase processing with function word recognition
        - Verb group formation with voice assignment
        - Multi-word noun phrase composition
- **pos400.nlp**: Clause context POS processing:
    - **Purpose**: POS processing within clause contexts

- **Functionality**: Handles POS assignment when clauses are present
- **Key features**:
  - NP + alpha-alpha patterns with verb/adjective disambiguation
  - DQAN pattern processing with number agreement
  - Verb group formation with voice assignment (active VBP)
  - Context-sensitive adjective vs. noun assignment
  - Clause-aware noun phrase formation

Clause passes

These are the passes for clauses and sentences. Each sentence may contain one or more clauses.

The files listed in the following table represent advanced clause and sentence analysis, progressively building from clause boundary detection through complex sentence analysis to final POS assignment and discourse-level processing:

Pass	Type	File	Description
94	`rec`	`qclause50`	Recursively identify clauses in sentences.
95	`nlp`	`clause100`	Create clauses within sentences.
96	`nlp`	`clause200`	Splice boundary nodes within clauses.
97	`nlp`	`clause300`	Gather info within clauses.
98	`nlp`	`qseg150`	Parse segment nodes (e.g., within clauses).
99	`nlp`	`sent250`	Merge some clauses within sentences.
100	`nlp`	`clause400`	Parse within clauses.
101	`nlp`	`sent300`	Gather data in sentences.
102	`nlp`	`qsent75`	Study clauses within sentences.
103	`rec`	`phr100`	Recursive parsing within clauses.
104	`nlp`	`qseg200`	Characterize remaining segments within clauses.
105	`nlp`	`qclause200`	Parsing within clauses.
106	`nlp`	`qclause75`	Parsing within clauses.
107	`nlp`	`qclause100`	Parse within clauses, yield well-formed clauses.
108	`nlp`	`sent400`	Study multi-clause patterns within sentences.
109	`nlp`	`qsent100`	Further looks at clauses in sentences.
110	`nlp`	`sent_pos`	POS tagging in sentences (e.g., function words).
111	`nlp`	`clause_pos`	Default POS tagging in clauses.

Table appendix D.14: Clause and sentence processing pass files

The following describes the actions of the clause and sentence processing passes in detail:

- **qclause50.nlp**: Clause boundary detection:
    - **Purpose**: Identifies clause starts and separations within sentences
    - **Functionality**: Detects clause boundaries and assigns passive voice to sentence-initial verb groups
    - **Key features:**
        - Sentence-initial passive voice detection (^ vg with -edn verbs)
        - Clause separator identification (np conj vg, vg conj np)
        - Infinitive clause starts (to vg)
        - Parallel construction handling with elliptical copulas
        - Complex coordination patterns with voice assignment
- **clause100.nlp**: Clause formation:
    - **Purpose**: Groups sentence elements into clause structures
    - **Functionality**: Creates clause nodes from sequences of syntactic elements
    - **Key features:**
        - Groups elements into unsealed clause structures
        - Handles clause separators and boundaries
        - Processes clause starts and optional elements
        - Simple clause grouping with flexible boundaries
        - Foundation for clause-level analysis
- **clause200.nlp**: Clause cleanup:
    - **Purpose**: Removes temporary clause markers and consolidates attributes
    - **Functionality**: Cleans up clause start nodes while preserving attributes
    - **Key features:**
        - Splices out temporary `_clausestart` nodes
        - Copies attributes from start nodes to the clause level
        - Simple cleanup operation within clause contexts
        - Maintains clause structure integrity
- **clause300.nlp**: Clause data collection:
    - **Purpose**: Gathers and records clause-level information and statistics
    - **Functionality**: Analyzes clause contents and assigns pattern attributes

- **Key features**:
  - Verb group counting and tracking within sentences
  - Voice assignment and clause pattern identification
  - First/last element tracking for clauses
  - Sentence-level statistics (first verb clause, clause numbering)
  - Complex attribute management for discourse analysis
- **qseg150.nlp**: Segment processing in clauses:
  - **Purpose**: Processes segments within clause contexts, especially when no verbs are present
  - **Functionality**: Converts segments to noun phrases in verbless clauses
  - **Key features**:
    - DQAN pattern processing in verbless clauses
    - Head noun identification and non-head processing
    - Alpha token disambiguation (noun vs. adjective)
    - Segment-to-NP conversion with proper attribute assignment
    - Context-sensitive processing based on clause verb presence
- **sent250.nlp**: Sentence clause merging:
  - **Purpose**: Handles clause merging and separator cleanup
  - **Functionality**: Merges related clauses and removes clause separators
  - **Key features**:
    - Clause separator splicing and removal
    - *vg to vg* pattern merging for split constructions
    - Voice assignment for merged verb groups
    - Complex clause combination logic
    - Split infinitive construction handling
- **clause400.nlp**: Advanced clause processing
  - **Purpose**: Handles complex clause patterns and verb group combinations
  - **Functionality**: Processes infinitive constructions and clause pattern recognition
  - **Key features**:
    - vg to vg combination with semantic integration
    - Infinitive clause marking and processing

- Voice assignment (active/passive) based on context
- Alpha token disambiguation in clause contexts
- Pattern recognition for clause types (`-ing` patterns)

- **sen\300.nlp**: Sentence statistics and classification:
  - **Purpose**: Counts clauses and assigns sentence level attributes
  - **Functionality**: Provides sentence-level statistics and conditional detection
  - **Key features**:
    - Clause counting and numbering within sentences
    - Conditional sentence detection (^ if patterns)
    - Simple sentence-level attribute assignment
    - Foundation for sentence-level analysis
- **qsent75.nlp**: Complex sentence analysis:
  - **Purpose**: Handles complex multi-clause sentence patterns
  - **Functionality**: Analyzes complex sentence structures with embedded clauses
  - **Key features**:
    - Multi-clause pattern recognition (clause that clause clause)
    - Verb requirement assignment for embedded clauses
    - Voice agreement between related clauses
    - Complex clause coordination with verb position analysis
    - Error handling for clauses without verb groups
- **phr100.nlp**: Phrase formation in clauses:
  - **Purpose**: Forms phrases within clause contexts
  - **Functionality**: Creates noun phrases, prepositional phrases, and handles clause-internal structures
  - **Key features**:
    - To alpha-alpha noun phrase formation
    - Prepositional phrase creation (prep np)
    - Noun + verb group processing
    - Alpha token disambiguation in phrase contexts
    - Clause-internal phrase construction
- **qseg200.nlp**: Advanced segment processing:

- **Purpose**: Processes segments with pronoun and complex DQAN patterns
- **Functionality**: Handles pronouns and complex determiner patterns in segments
- **Key features**:
  - Pronoun + alpha-alpha patterns
  - Complex DQAN processing with verb constraints
  - Adjective vs. noun disambiguation in segments
  - Head noun assignment for complex patterns
  - Context-sensitive segment processing

- **qclause200.nlp**: Clause refinement:
  - **Purpose**: Refines clause structure and handles interrogative patterns
  - **Functionality**: Creates adverbial phrases and handles question transformations
  - **Key features**:
    - Prepositional phrase to adverbial conversion
    - Interrogative pattern transformation to declarative
    - Discontinuous interrogative handling
    - Verb group excision and reclassification
    - Question-to-statement structural conversion
- **qclause75.nlp**: Clause element processing:
  - **Purpose**: Handles specific clause elements and voice assignment
  - **Functionality**: Processes their constructions and assigns default POS tags
  - **Key features**:
    - Existential there processing (there/EX vs. there/RB)
    - Particle processing (up, down, out as adverbs)
    - Passive voice assignment with by-actor phrases
    - Default POS assignment for unassigned elements
    - Context-sensitive element classification
- **qclause100.nlp**: Well-formed clause validation
  - **Purpose**: Validates and assigns patterns to well-formed clauses
  - **Functionality**: Analyzes clause structure and assigns syntactic patterns
  - **Key features**:
    - Clause pattern assignment (nvj, vj, nvp, vp)

        - Subject detection and voice assignment
        - Ellipted copula handling for noun-adjective patterns
        - Complex clause structure validation
        - Voice agreement and verb fixup for ambiguous cases
- **sent400.nlp**: Complex sentence coordination:
    - **Purpose**: Handles complex sentence patterns with multiple clauses
    - **Functionality**: Manages clause coordination and voice agreement across complex sentences
    - **Key features**:
        - Multi-clause coordination with voice agreement
        - Parallel construction analysis and verb agreement
        - Complex clause list processing
        - Voice propagation across coordinated clauses
        - Advanced sentence-level pattern recognition
- **qsent100.nlp**: Sentence clause analysis:
    - **Purpose**: Analyze clause relationships within sentences
    - **Functionality**: Handles clause coordination and "that" clause processing
    - **Key features**:
        - Alpha clause disambiguation and verb group formation
        - Clause coordination with pattern analysis
        - That clause role assignment (IN vs WDT, see *Table appendix D.5*)
        - Complex clause relationship analysis
        - Context-sensitive clause processing
- **sent_pos.nlp**: Sentence-level POS assignment:
    - **Purpose**: Assigns default POS tags at sentence-level
    - **Functionality**: Provides default POS assignments for untagged function words
    - **Key features**:
        - Function word POS assignment (before/IN, except/IN, that/IN)
        - Interrogative pronoun tagging (what/WP, whatever/WP)
        - Determiner assignment (both/DT)
        - Comparative adjective assignment (more/JJR)

    - Default POS tags for common function words

- **clause_pos.nlp**: Clause-level POS assignment:
    - **Purpose**: Assigns default POS tags and handles untagged alphas within clauses
    - **Functionality**: Provides clause-level POS disambiguation with guessing capability
    - **Key features**:
        - Default POS assignment (as/IN, that/IN, more/JJR)
        - Alpha token guessing based on morphological features
        - Threshold-based guessing control
        - Complex verb conjugation analysis (`-ing`, `-en`, `-ed`)
        - Final clause voice assignment for sentence endings

Cycle 2 passes

The files listed in the following table represent the semantic analysis pipeline, transitioning from syntactic parsing to semantic processing with anaphora resolution, KB registration, and entity processing for discourse-level understanding:

Pass	Type	File	Description
112	`nlp`	`CYCLE_2`	Cycle 2: semantic analysis.
113	`nlp`	`qclause300`	Study within clauses.
114	`nlp`	`anaphora100`	Intra-sentential actor/object resolution.
115	`nlp`	`sentsem`	Register sentences in KB.
116	`nlp`	`clausesem`	Register clauses in KB.
117	`nlp`	`inclausesem`	In clauses, register domain actors/objects in the KB.

Table appendix D.15: Cycle 2 passes for semantic analysis

The following describes the actions of the Cycle 2 passes for semantic analysis in detail:

- **CYCLE_2.nlp**: Semantic processing documentation:
    - **Purpose**: Documentation stub for Cycle 2 semantic processing
    - **Functionality**: Placeholder documenting the transition from parsing to semantic analysis
    - **Key features**:
        - Documents Cycle 2 as a lower-confidence semantic processing phase
        - Indicates dependency on evidence from earlier parsing passes

        - Establishes framework for semantic analysis post-parsing
        - Contains only initialization code with no active rules
- **qclause300.nlp**: Clause evidence gathering:
    - **Purpose**: Collects evidence and reasoning information for clause-level analysis
    - **Functionality**: Gathers clause-level semantic information for discourse processing
    - **Key features**:
        - By-actor adverbial identification for passive-to-active transformations
        - Subject detection and assignment at the sentence-level
        - Last noun phrase tracking for anaphora resolution
        - Substitution handling for pronoun resolution
        - Evidence collection for clause-level reasoning
- **anaphora100.nlp**: Intra-sentential anaphora resolution:
    - **Purpose**: Resolves anaphoric references within sentence boundaries
    - **Functionality**: Handles pronoun and relative clause resolution using clause patterns
    - **Key features**:
        - That/which clause resolution with antecedent noun phrases
        - Multi-clause anaphora handling (clause that clause prep clause)
        - Pattern-based resolution (n, v, vg patterns)
        - Remote noun phrase assignment for verb clauses
        - Complex clause coordination with reference distribution
        - Conditional processing based on verb conjugation
- **sentsem.nlp**: Sentence KB registration:
    - **Purpose**: Registers sentences in the KB for semantic processing
    - **Functionality**: Conditional semantic processing that registers sentence structures
    - **Key features**:
        - Conditional execution (only runs if semantic processing is enabled)
        - Sentence registration in KB via the `sentregister()` function
        - Operates at the textzone level to process all sentences
        - Verbose logging for semantic processing tracking

    - Foundation for discourse-level semantic analysis
- **clausesem.nlp**: Clause KB registration:
    - **Purpose**: Registers clauses in the KB for semantic analysis
    - **Functionality**: Clause-level semantic registration with contextual information
    - **Key features**:
        - Conditional execution (requires semantic processing flag)
        - Clause registration via the **`clauseregister()`** function with context
        - Operates within sentence contexts
        - Provides clause and sentence context to the registration function
        - Verbose logging for clause processing tracking
- **inclausesem.nlp**: Intra-clause semantic processing:
    - **Purpose**: Processes semantic elements within clause boundaries
    - **Functionality**: Registers named entities and semantic objects within clauses
    - **Key features**:
        - Named entity and semantic object registration
        - Domain object registration via **`domobjectregister()`** for noun phrases
        - Domain entity registration via **`domentityregister()`** for adverbials
        - Semantic text and value propagation to the clause level
        - Conditional processing based on named entity presence
        - Clause-level semantic attribute management

Highlighting passes

Information highlighting passes for the developers' usage. They are strictly here for debugging purposes and can be disabled when the analyzer is deployed. The **`G("hilite")`** variable turns these passes on and off in the earlier **`ini.nlp`** initialization pass.

The files listed in the following table represent the highlighting and verification pipeline, providing comprehensive visual feedback and verification tools for debugging parser output, analyzing linguistic structures, and gathering discourse-level semantic information:

Pass	Type	File	Description
118	**`nlp`**	**`hilite_undone`**	Highlight unprocessed items in clauses.
119	**`nlp`**	**`hilite_pos`**	Highlight non-constituents in clauses.
120	**`nlp`**	**`hilite_postag`**	Highlight all nodes with POS tags.
121	**`nlp`**	**`hilite_np`**	Highlight noun phrases.

Pass	Type	File	Description
122	`nlp`	`hilite_ne`	Highlight named entities.
123	`nlp`	`hilite_temporal`	Highlight temporal expressions.
124	`nlp`	`hilite_spatial`	Highlight spatial expressions.
125	`nlp`	`hilite_clause`	Highlight all clauses.

***Table appendix D.16**: Highlighting pass files*

The following describes the actions of the highlighting passes in detail:

- **hilite_undone.nlp**: Unprocessed element highlighting:
    - **Purpose**: Highlights unprocessed elements and potential parsing issues within clauses
    - **Functionality**: Identifies unmarked POS instances and problematic constructions for debugging
    - **Key features**:
        - Marks unprocessed alpha tokens, segments, and various POS categories
        - Identifies stray elements not incorporated into larger constituents
        - Highlights problematic constructions (like consecutive verb groups)
        - Sets clause-level flag for elements requiring attention
        - Debugging tool for incomplete parsing
- **hilite_pos.nlp**: Stray POS node highlighting:
    - **Purpose**: Highlights individual POS nodes not incorporated into phrases
    - **Functionality**: Conditional highlighting of unintegrated grammatical elements
    - **Key features**:
        - Conditional execution (only runs if `G("hilite")` is enabled)
        - Highlights standalone noun, verb, and adjective nodes
        - Identifies elements that should be grouped into larger constituents
        - Simple debugging tool for phrase formation issues
        - Operates within clause contexts
- **hilite_postag.nlp**: POS-tagged element highlighting:
    - **Purpose**: Highlights all elements that have received POS tags
    - **Functionality**: Visual indication of successful POS tagging across the parse tree

- **Key features**:
  - Conditional execution based on **hilite** flag
  - Multi-traversal of entire parse tree (**@MULTI _ROOT**)
  - Highlights any node with **mypos** attribute
  - Comprehensive POS tagging verification tool
  - Green highlighting for tagged elements

- **hilite_np.nlp**: Noun phrase highlighting:
  - **Purpose**: Highlights all noun phrase structures in the parse tree
  - **Functionality**: Visual identification of successfully formed noun phrases
  - **Key features**:
    - Conditional execution (skips if **pretagged** or **hilite** disabled)
    - Multi-traversal highlighting for **_np** and **_nps** nodes
    - Verbose logging of noun phrase text to **np.txt**
    - Visual feedback for noun phrase formation success
    - Comprehensive noun phrase coverage verification
- **hilite_ne.nlp**: Named entity highlighting:
  - **Purpose**: Highlights all identified named entities throughout the parse tree
  - **Functionality**: Feature-based matching for named entity visualization
  - **Key features**:
    - Conditional execution with **pretagged** and **hilite** checks
    - Feature-based matching using **ne** attribute
    - Multi-traversal across the entire parse tree
    - Verbose logging with node type and phrase text
    - Comprehensive named entity recognition verification
- **hilite_temporal.nlp**: Temporal expression highlighting:
  - **Purpose**: Highlights temporal expressions and registers them for discourse analysis
  - **Functionality**: Identifies and registers date/time expressions with semantic attributes
  - **Key features**:
    - Multi-condition temporal detection (**sem="date", sem date, date node**)
    - Registration in both clause and sentence contexts

        - Verbose logging of temporal expressions
        - Operates on `advl`, `np`, `fnword`, and `prep` nodes
        - Discourse-level temporal information gathering

- **hilite_spatial.nlp**: Spatial expression highlighting:
    - **Purpose**: Highlights spatial/location expressions and registers them for analysis
    - **Functionality**: Identifies location-based expressions and registers them hierarchically
    - **Key features**:
        - Location semantic checking (`sem="location", sem location`)
        - Registration at clause and sentence-levels via `registerx()`
        - Verbose logging of spatial expressions
        - Operates on `advl` and `np` nodes within clause contexts
        - Hierarchical spatial information tracking
- **hilite_clause.nlp**: Clause structure highlighting:
    - **Purpose**: Highlights clause structures with voice and verb information
    - **Functionality**: Visual representation of clause analysis with voice classification
    - **Key features**:
        - Multi-traversal highlighting of clause nodes
        - Voice classification output (active/passive/novoice/noverb)
        - Verbose logging with voice annotations
        - Clause structure verification and analysis
        - Comprehensive clause processing feedback

Output passes

These 10 NLP++ passes listed in the following table provide the output and debugging infrastructure for the parse-en-us English parser. They include validation tools that score POS tagging accuracy against pre-tagged text and highlight mismatches, export utilities that generate XML output for parse trees and named entities, and development aids that extract grammar rules and provide detailed analysis reports. Together, they form a comprehensive testing framework enabling parser validation, result visualization, and performance measurement across the entire English processing pipeline.

Num	Type	Pass	Description
126	nlp	pos_out	POS tagging output.
127	nlp	pos_out_noscore	POS tagging output without scores.
128	nlp	poserr	POS tagging mismatches (in test texts).
129	nlp	rule_out	Sample pass to output rules for clauses.
130	nlp	trav_dict	Simple dictionary traversal and output.
131	nlp	xmlrecursive	Output parse tree as XML.
132	nlp	ne_out	Named entity output.
133	nlp	ne_xml	Named entity XML output from KB.
134	nlp	fin	Final analyzer processing.
135	nlp	buff_out	Buffered output handler.

Table appendix D.17: Output and final analyzer pass files

The following describes the actions of the output passes and final analyzer passes in detail:

- **pos_out.nlp**: POS tagging scorer:

  Tree traversal, outputting POS tags with scoring, validates pre-tagged text against parser assignments, and identifies mismatches.

- **pos_out_noscore.nlp**: Treebank formatter:

  Tree traversal, outputting POS tags without scoring, creates Penn Treebank-style output with embedded XML tags.

- **poserr.nlp**: POS mismatch highlighter:

  Simple pass highlighting nodes with POS tag mismatches between the pre-tagged input and parser analysis.

- **rule_out.nlp**: Grammar rule generator:

  Analyzes clause structures and outputs pattern matching rules for parser development and testing.

- **trav_dict.nlp**: Dictionary dumper:

  Simple utility traversing dictionary concepts and outputting all entries to a text file for inspection.

- **xmlrecursive.nlp**: XML tree formatter:

  Recursive traversal outputting structured XML tags for noun phrases, verb groups, and clauses with semantic annotations.

- **ne_out.nlp**: Named entity reporter:

  Clause-level traversal outputting detailed named entity information, including semantic attributes and confidence scores.

- **ne_xml.nlp**: XML entity exporter:

  KB traversal generating XML output for resolved named entities with type and confidence metadata.

- **fin.nlp**: Analysis finalizer:

  Cleanup pass handling POS accuracy scoring, file closing operations, and accumulating overall performance statistics.

- **buff_out.nlp**: Tree serializer:

  Complex XML output utility with multiple formatting options for parse tree visualization and analysis.

Display KB

This is one of two passes added by *David de Hilster* to display the KB using the **`DisplayKB`** function. The other pass de Hilster added was pass number 4, which is the **`KBFuncs`** library functions. Refer to the following table:

Pass	Type	File	Description
136	**`nlp`**	**`displayKB`**	Display KB.

Table appendix D.18: *Pass file for displaying the KB*

Index

E

F

G

H

I

K

L

M

N

O

P

R

S

T